LAKE HURON

GEORGIAN BAY

ONTARIO

LAKE ONTARIO

CHIGAN

IANA

DETROIT
Camp Barns

LA

N. YO

OHI

IANAPOLIS
mp Morton

IN

Where

THEY CAME FROM
The IRON BRIGADE
States of the
Old Northwest

1861 - 1865

6TH WIS
2ND WIS
7TH WIS
IRON BRIGADE
2ND WIS
19TH IND
24TH MICH

KENTUCKY

VIRGI

THE IRON BRIGADE

"looking like giants with their tall black hats
. . . and giants they were, in action."

MICHIGAN HERITAGE LIBRARY

THE
IRON BRIGADE
A Military History

ALAN T. NOLAN

With maps by
Wilson K. Hoyt III

973.74/
N787

HISTORICAL SOCIETY OF MICHIGAN
Ann Arbor, Michigan

HARDSCRABBLE BOOKS
Berrien Springs, Michigan

1983

Library of Congress Cataloging in Publication
Data

Nolan, Alan T

The Iron Brigade: a military history

Bibliography: p. 385

1. United States-History-Civil War, 1861 - 1865 -
Regimental histories- Iron Brigade
2. United States. Army. Iron Brigade.
I. Title
E493.5.172N6 1975 973.7'41 75-28242

ISBN 0-915056-16-X (Previously ISBN 0-87020-
157-3)

HENRY A. MORROW, Twenty-fourth Michigan Volunteers.

FOR JANE

Deo gratias

INTRODUCTION TO THE 1983 EDITION

Civil War battles did not consist of an army sweeping forward like an unbroken wave against the battlements of an opponent. Rather, armies fought (as well as marched and camped) in increments of brigades. Composed of three to five regiments, and usually numbering about 3,500 men, a brigade was much like a mini-army. It had its own quartermaster, ordnance, and medical components; artillery batteries and cavalry detachments were sometimes assigned as brigade supports. It is hardly surprising that brigadiers who commanded those units were key figures in battle. They were supposed to be ''fighting generals''--men who led by example-- and if their soldiers were moved to respond in kind, the exalted reputation of brigade and brigadier was assured.

The North had a number of such outstanding units. The Excelsior, Irish, and Sherman brigades come immediately to mind. Yet by far the most famous of them all was the Iron Brigade, the only pure Western brigade in the North's premier Army of the Potomac. The brigade came into being in the autumn of 1861 and consisted of the 2nd, 6th, and 7th Wisconsin plus the 19th Indiana. The 24th Michigan was added later.

The unit was first called the Black Hat Brigade for the conspicuous felt headpieces that the men chose to wear. The brigade earned the right to wear distinctive garb. It suffered a higher proportion of battle fatalities than any comparable unit on the Union side. The heavy losses began with 33 casualties in the brigade's first engagement: an 1862 stand up fight with its Confederate counterpart, the Stonewall Brigade. A couple of weeks later, following marked valor at South Mountain, the unit acquired its more noted nickname. All too quickly the Iron Brigade came to tragedy. It was simply never the same after Gettysburg, where it lost two of every three men who went into battle.

Those Midwestern regiments exhibited combat prowess and a willingness to die that makes their history among the most moving in American military annals. To do the brigade full justice would require an extraordinary effort on the part of any historian. Alan

Nolan made such an accomplishment, which explains why his book (first published in 1961) now enters a third printing.

Nolan was blessed with rich veins of source material; and because he mined them all skillfully, he produced the most informative brigade history of modern times. Coupled with that was his ability to re-create the excitement, drama, and human element of war. In these pages the Iron Brigade lives, knows its glory, and wins its reputation. The movements of the brigade, and the feelings of its soldiers, are beautifully blended so as to produce a human chronicle in an inhuman environment.

Unit histories have long been the most ignored of Civil War studies. That is a keen loss, for in many respects they are the most revealing of military works. Nolan proved that with his history of the Iron Brigade. It is a book that continues to be both a model and an inspiration.

James I. Robertson, Jr.

Virginia Tech

CRITICAL COMMENTS ABOUT THE IRON BRIGADE

"I am immensely impressed . . . This particular Brigade needed a book of its own and now it has one which is definitely first-rate . . . A fine book. . . ''

Bruce Catton

One of the "100 best books ever written on the Civil War."

Civil War Times Illustrated

"Alan Nolan has written a first-rate account of one of the famous fighting outfits of the Army of the Potomac, the Iron Brigade . . . Nolan's book is unit history writing at its best, and it adds much to our knowledge of the larger story of the war . . . "

T. Harry Williams
Louisiana State University

"Mr. Nolan has told the story of the Iron Brigade in expert fashion. Tightly knit, closely written, and carefully documented, The Iron Brigade is military history at its scholarly best . . . "

Thomas H. O'Connor
Boston College

"It combines in a most gratifying manner thorough research, over-flowing knowledge, skillful organization, balanced judgment and good writing . . . This excellent book is a model unit history, and good unit histories are one of the most urgent needs of Civil War literature."

Bell I. Wiley
Emory University

"... stands out from the veritable flood of battle histories, military biographies, and book-length feature stories as an exceptionally able, well-documented, thorough and reliable account. Lacking the rhetorical flourishes which commonly hide ignorance or serve to evade facts, the book has strength and integrity worthy of its subject."

William B. Hesseltine
University of Wisconsin

"Nolan's book is a model military unit history"

David S. Sparks
University of Maryland

"A competent history of the . . . proud regiments that composed the Iron Brigade - the only completely western organization in the Army of the Potomac - has long been needed, and let it be said without equivocation that Mr. Nolan . . . has brought off the job with bright spirit, lively prose and faithful scholarship."

Earl Schenck Miers

"When Alan Nolan's history of the brigade first appeared in 1961, reviews hailed it as 'a model unit history' and 'military history at its scholarly best'. Such evaluations have grown with the years. Nolan's depth of research, grasp of intricate facts, skillful presentation and balanced judgments make this book the best brigade study of the Northern side."

James I. Robertson, Jr.
Virginia Polytechnic Institute and State University

"A painstakingly researched history of a fighting unit from the Old Northwest; no known facts have been omitted."

Civil War Books, A Critical Bibliography
Edited by Allan Nevins, James I. Robertson, Jr. and Bell I. Wiley

AUTHOR'S PREFACE TO THE 1983 EDITION

THE IRON BRIGADE has frequently appeared in books about the Civil War. Even writers of survey accounts have occasion to mention the brigade in passing. These references have established that it was one of the most colorful and distinguished brigades that fought for the Union, but they have been all too brief and have not purported to tell who these soldiers were, where they came from, who their leaders were, or the details of what they did. As a reader I wanted all of these questions answered. I waited for someone else to supply the answers. Finally, I began to look up the answers myself. This book contains the answers to my questions.

This is the third edition of this book. When the second edition was published in 1975 by the State Historical Society of Wisconsin, the late T. Harry Williams kindly provided an Introduction. Asserting that we need more studies of the basic units of Civil War armies, Professor Williams recorded his "conviction that Civil War authors could not understand the operations of the armies, and hence could not explain them to readers, unless they understood how the smallest units, regiments and brigades, were administered and led." He then set forth what this book is all about in words on which I cannot improve:

The Brigade that is the subject of Nolan's book is worthy of study in its own right. Organized near Washington in October, 1861, it consisted of four volunteer regiments, the Second, Sixth, and Seventh Wisconsin and the Nineteenth Indiana, and was the only completely Western brigade in the Army of the Potomac. Later, when the attrition of battle had depleted its numbers, it received the Twenty-fourth Michigan as a reinforcement and thus retained its regional identity. But it merits notice for more than geographical distinction. It was probably the best fighting brigade in the army . . .

. . .

Alan Nolan relates the great story of the brigade, and in doing so he helps us understand how a Civil War army was fought. But he does more. He describes in detail how a volunteer regiment was raised and organized and analyzes the background and motivation of the young men who came forward to serve in the army. He recounts how the officers of the volunteer regiment were chosen, giving needed attention to the political influences that often played on the elections. He records finally how the volunteers were transported to camps and what they did when not fighting and what their reactions were to such issues as emancipation and the future of the black race. In short, in reciting the story of a brigade he also tells the story of a democracy at war, and he thereby demonstrates the the validity of unit history.

I reiterate my thanks to the many persons and institutions that I have previously relied on. To this list I now add those associated with this third edition: John W. and Patricia V. Gillette and Hardscrabble Books; and the Historical Society of Michigan, Thomas L. Jones, Executive Director of the Society, and Mary Steffek Blaske, Programs Administrator of the Society. I am most grateful for their interest and support.

Alan T. Nolan

Indianapolis

CONTENTS

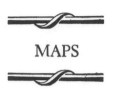

MAPS

Map Note

Several of the maps have been designed for use with the text in more than one place in the book. The reader will especially benefit by referring to the following maps as he reads the following portions of the book:

The Rappahannock-Rapidan Line, p. 48:

The description of the Battle of Fredericksburg in Chapter 9; the Mud March and winter quarters at Belle Plain in Chapter 10; the Battle of Chancellorsville in Chapter 11; and the description of the beginning of Grant's 1864 campaign, which appears in the Epilogue.

Area of the Antietam and Gettysburg Campaigns, page 116:

The description of the march to Pennsylvania which appears in Chapter 11.

The back end paper:

The Frederick's Hall Raid, appearing in Chapter 3; the Coan River-Heathsville Raid, the Westmoreland County Raid and the Port Royal expedition appearing in Chapter 10; the cavalry relief expedition down the Northern Neck, described in Chapter 11; and Grant's 1864-65 campaign appearing in the Epilogue.

ILLUSTRATIONS

October 1, 1861

The war was almost six months old. Bull Run in the East and Wilson's Creek in the West were already history. The ninety-day soldiers, for the most part, had either gone home or had re-enlisted. George B. McClellan was the idol of the Union, although old General Winfield Scott still had thirty days to go before retiring as McClellan's superior. The Seventh Wisconsin Volunteers, having just arrived in Washington, were assigned to the brigade of Brigadier General Rufus King. There the Wisconsin men found two other regiments from Wisconsin—the Second and Sixth Wisconsin Volunteers—and the Nineteenth Indiana Volunteers. Thus began the life of an infantry brigade, which was later to be joined by the Twenty-fourth Michigan Volunteers, and which was to be called the Iron Brigade.

This is the story of the Iron Brigade.

"WE ARE COMING, FATHER ABRAHAM"

"The first proclamation . . . was as potent in bringing warriors to the field as was the whistle of Roderick Dhu in olden times—

'That whistle garrisoned the glen
at once with full five hundred men.'"

From Wisconsin Adjutant General Utley's Report for 1861

PROLOGUE

At 4:30 A.M. on April 12, 1861, a mortar shell burst over Fort Sumter. This was the signal, and in a matter of minutes the massed Confederate batteries were loosed at the symbolic fort. What a distinguished New York senator had called "the irrepressible conflict" had begun. That conflict would determine, in the words of a homespun Western lawyer, whether the "house divided" would stand or fall. Now the Western lawyer and the New York senator sat down as President and Secretary of State to decide what could be done.

Lincoln knew that he could do little himself. He could only lead. If his leadership was to accomplish anything, the people of the North would have to follow him. And whether the people of the North followed him depended on how they felt about the Union. Surely financial gain, an urge to conform, the desire for public acclaim, and like mean motives would influence some people to support the war. But basically, and in the main, Abe Lincoln and the nation itself were dependent on the people's *will for the Union*—on how much blood and money they were willing to pour out to maintain the Republic.

Lincoln had already explained this to the people, in Indianapolis in February on the way to his inauguration. He had said that "not with politicians, not with Presidents, not with office-seekers, but with you, is the question, 'Shall the Union and shall the liberties of this country be preserved . . . ?' " And so, having personally resolved that the Union would not go down without a struggle, the President prepared a proclamation, calling forth the will for the Union. On April 15th 75,000 militia were summoned for ninety days. Having issued

3

the proclamation, Lincoln could only wait and see. On the response to the proclamation, and later summonses for more men, more money, and more sacrifice, Lincoln's resolve and the cause of the Union depended.

THE SECOND WISCONSIN VOLUNTEERS

The people of Wisconsin were among those to whom Lincoln's proclamation was addressed and on whose will the nation depended. Although Wisconsin's quota under the April 15th proclamation included but one regiment of infantry, the response to Governor Alexander W. Randall's call for troops on April 16th was so enthusiastic as to exceed the quota. Among the additional regiments was the Second Wisconsin Volunteers, which assembled at the State Agricultural Society's Fairgrounds in Madison during the first week in May. There it was placed under the command of Colonel S. Park Coon of Milwaukee, who named the camp site Camp Randall, in honor of the governor.

The men of the Second Wisconsin were from widely scattered Wisconsin communities, including Milwaukee, Madison, Racine, Oshkosh, and La Crosse. The Oshkosh company showed a certain pedestrian tendency—not unbecoming to the infantry—when it adopted the name "Oshkosh Volunteers." Not so others of the companies, which arrived in Madison identified as the "La Crosse Light Guards," the "Grant County Grays," and the "Wisconsin Rifles." As these companies assembled in Madison, the term of their enlistment was changed from the announced three months to three years. On May 16th the men were drawn together at Camp Randall and advised of this change. All but one of the ten companies accepted the new term of service, and on June 11th the regiment was mustered into the United States service for three years.[1]

In commissioning Park Coon as colonel, Wisconsin's governor anticipated a technique that President Lincoln was to employ. The war was a sectional rebellion, but within the North and South there were varying degrees of feeling. In the North, attitudes about the issues of the war had tended to coincide with party identification. Accordingly, so as to rally broad support and mitigate the war's partisan identification, Republican executives sought out prominent

Democrats to enlist in the war effort. Colonel Coon, a forty-one-year-old native of New York, was such a man. A graduate of Norwich University in Vermont and a lawyer by profession, Coon had entered Wisconsin Territory in 1843 and had taken a leading role in the constitutional activities resulting in Wisconsin's statehood. He had then been elected attorney general for the state on the Democratic ticket. In 1861 he quickly identified himself as an outspoken Union man. This fact, coupled with his state-wide reputation and his membership in the Democratic party, seemed admirably to qualify him as a leader of Wisconsin's military effort.[2] Although without Coon's public reputation, the regiment's second-in-command, Henry W. Peck of Green County, also had promise. Appointed to West Point from Ohio in 1851, Peck had not graduated from the academy but he had at least some professional training. The regiment's field-officer corps was filled out by the appointment to the majority of Duncan McDonald, a Milwaukee businessman and former colonel of a state militia organization.[3]

As to the enlisted men of the Second Wisconsin, an early view was provided by a letter from one of the recruits, written to his home-town newspaper. Describing the off-duty hours of the men at Camp Randall, the soldier wrote that "our boys stayed quietly in their quarters, read their Testaments, looked at the pictures of their absent loved ones, and tried to keep comfortable."[4] Contemporary news-paper stories do not quite square with this account. Indeed, one Madison daily reported that a group of soldiers had attacked Voigt's Brewery after hours, provoking gunfire from the embattled brewer, which the soldiers countered with stones.[5] Another press release, com-plaining that "the soldiers have not appeared to be under that re-straint which a wholesome discipline would impose," deplored "the roaming of drunken soldiers about the streets at night, howling and smashing things generally."[6] A third recounted that "a few rowdies have been cutting up some rascal pranks—condemned as severely by their comrades as by anyone else—which has necessitated greater strictness with reference to leaving camp. Men are now allowed to leave the camp only in charge of an officer, who is responsible for their good behavior."[7] And apparently unaware of the readers of the Testa-ment, one of the captains of the regiment, English-born and of con-siderable culture, found but a few "very nice fellows" among his new companions. As for the rest, "I am sorry to say that the men on the whole [are] rough, vulgar blackguards . . . not such as I like to associate with. . . ."

That the English gentleman's appraisal of his comrades may be discounted is evidenced by his querulous description of Madison. Conceding that "you might travel 100s of miles and not find a handsomer locality for a city . . . ," he added that ". . . as a town Madison is miserably dull, as a Capitol wretched, no life, no gayety, or scarcely amusement . . . there is scarcely a pretty woman here. . . ."[8] In the final analysis, the newspapers were more charitable than the captain. Acknowledging "the great mass of them . . . to be sterling men," one account suggested simply that there were "some hard cases among them."[9] And another realistically remarked that "among so many it could hardly fail that there should be some of the 'baser sort.' "[10] It might also have been candidly written that Abe Lincoln was in no position to draw lines against "rowdies," "hard characters," or even the "baser sort." The question was whether the men of the Second Wisconsin could become soldiers, and that, despite the unsurprising outbursts of some of them, remained to be seen.

Madison was not long to be troubled by their presence. On June 20th, following what the newspapers called a "collation by the ladies,"[11] the regiment was drawn up before a speaker's stand, erected at Camp Randall, to hear the parting words of the governor. Striking an Old Testament note, and unwittingly prophesying the career of the men to whom he spoke, the chief executive said: "By the shedding of blood atonement has always been made for great sins. This rebellion must be put down in blood, and treason punished by blood." The officers called for "three cheers" for the governor, which, according to witnesses, "were not only given with the heartiest will, but were prolonged into a dozen, with various 'tiger' and 'big Injun' accompaniments."[12] Then, fully equipped by the state except for arms, and clad in new uniforms of plain gray, the Second filed aboard railroad cars for the trip to Washington, by way of Chicago, Toledo, Cleveland, Pittsburgh, and Baltimore. The regiment was composed of ten companies and had a total strength of 1,048 men, including the regimental band of 34 pieces. As in all Wisconsin regiments, the officer corps included three surgeons and a chaplain.

The soldiers' trip to Washington was a series of ceremonies at each railroad stop. In Chicago a military company escort was provided for the men as they marched between trains. In Toledo the townspeople provided a fine breakfast, and the food was served by the pretty girls of the community.[13] At Cleveland, where one recruit reported "hundreds and hundreds of the most beautiful women" along the parade route,[14] "hosts of little girls, dressed in white, with blue and red ribbons in their hair and ornamenting their dresses, came through the depot, and shook hands with the men, and over and over again wished them good bye, and a safe return. . . ." Farther on in Ohio, during a night stop, one soldier witnessed an impressive impromptu welcome. Looking out of the window, "I saw about two hundred ladies on the platform, and about fifty of the regiment engaged in kissing them in such a business-like way, that at first I thought the regiment had got into *active service* in fact. Every man appeared to have taken a contract to kiss every woman in the crowd, and *vice versa*. . . ."[15] Even in Baltimore the soldiers reported that they "were loudly cheered by the crowd as we moved along."[16] Altogether, the Second Wisconsin enjoyed the trip.

Arriving in Washington on June 25th, the regiment went into camp in the suburbs, joining the army of General Irvin McDowell, a West Point professional who commanded the Department of Northeastern Virginia under old General Winfield Scott, the general-in-chief. With the Confederate army at Winchester, near Leesburg and at Manassas, it was commonly believed that Washington itself was about to be assailed. Among the Second Wisconsin's distinctions was that it was the first three-year regiment to arrive in the frantic Capital.

A few days after their arrival in Washington, the Wisconsin men marched across the Georgetown Aqueduct to Fort Corcoran, Virginia, "in the hostile land of treason," as one of the soldiers described it.[17] Just across the Potomac, Fort Corcoran was one of a growing chain of forts that constituted the defenses of the Capital.[18] At the fort the Second Wisconsin was brigaded with the Thirteenth, Sixty-ninth, and Seventy-ninth New York regiments of infantry and a battery of artillery from the regular army, under the command of Colonel W. T. Sherman. Sherman's Brigade was assigned to General Daniel Tyler's Division. The Badgers must have been impressed with their colorful companions in Sherman's Brigade. Cameron's Seventy-ninth New

Yorkers, known as the Highlanders, wore a splendid kilted Scotch dress uniform. Even their fatigue trousers were plaid. The Seventy-ninth behaved colorfully, too, and was to mutiny after Bull Run,[19] but later to redeem itself as one of the fighting regiments of the war. Corcoran's Sixty-ninth New Yorkers were the Irishmen. This, of course, was no novelty to Wisconsinites. Back home in Madison, the Wisconsin adjutant general was carefully and officially classifying the anticipated Wisconsin volunteers as "Americans," "Germans," "Irish," and "Norwegians," and predicting that almost half as many "Irish" would volunteer as "Americans."[20] So it was not simply the Irish origins of the Sixty-ninth New York that distinguished that regiment. But these New York Irishmen were intensely nationalistic. They had come together to fight for the Union, but under a regimental flag of emerald green, emblazoned with the harp of Erin. The Thirteenth New York was no less distinctive than Sherman's other New York regiments. It included a company of firemen from New York City who wore black felt hats and the coats and red shirts of their civilian calling.[21] The Wisconsin soldiers were probably not especially impressed by their brigade commander. Sherman was then simply another officer, and there was no visible promise of either his later eclipse or great fame. The time when a soldier would boast that "I was with Sherman" was years away, but the Second's contact with Sherman was an omen of future association with another fine brigade commander.

On July 16th the first Federal offensive campaign got under way, aimed at the Confederate army at Manassas. As McDowell put his army in motion for Centreville, Tyler's Division led the advance. Two days later, Sherman's Brigade participated in Tyler's "reconnaissance in force" at Blackburn's Ford on Bull Run and witnessed the exchange of artillery and infantry fire on that day. As the day ended, the brigade withdrew from Bull Run, retired to Centreville, and encamped on the Warrenton Turnpike. A few days later, the war began in earnest for the Second Wisconsin as Sherman's Brigade was put in motion down the Warrenton Turnpike as a part of the feinted attack at the Stone Bridge across Bull Run. Arriving opposite the Stone Bridge, Sherman deployed his men, but all was relatively quiet in his front. The Confederates had correctly evaluated the force at the Stone Bridge and moved to their left to meet the main Union assault.

As the Wisconsin men and their New York companions waited, they heard the rising tide of battle to the northwest.

At noon Sherman's Brigade crossed Bull Run north of the Stone Bridge and advanced toward the fighting on the Union right. The Confederates were retreating, and Sherman's Brigade joined in the pursuit of the enemy, across the valley of Young's Branch and toward the Robinson and Henry houses. On the high ground running from the crest of the Henry House Hill to the Warrenton Turnpike at the Robinson house, the Confederate brigades of Stonewall Jackson, Bee, Bartow, and Evans stood intermingled. In front of this position, Sherman's men were put into action in the early afternoon in a series of assaults. Apparently fighting his brigade by regiments, Sherman first sent forward the Second Wisconsin, which advanced steadily up the hill under severe fire which it returned as it advanced. The Second was then repulsed, turned back in some confusion, was rallied, and again fought its way to the brow of the hill, only to be repulsed again. While the Thirteenth New York was similarly engaged on the left of the brigade front, Sherman successively sent forward the Seventy-ninth and Sixty-ninth New York regiments, with similar results.

As the afternoon wore on, the Union withdrawal began, an irresistible movement of men without and against orders. Sherman's men joined in, virtually retracing their steps of earlier that day, across Bull Run and on to Centreville. At 9:00 P.M., McDowell's purpose to stand at Centreville having been abandoned, Sherman undertook his retirement to the Potomac. The Second Wisconsin left behind them the first 23 of their comrades to die, the first 65 to be wounded, and 63 prisoners.[22] The survivors' frame of mind was not recorded, but surely the careless days of May and June must have seemed a long way off in the face of 15 per cent casualties for a short day's fighting.

In the grim hours following the Bull Run disaster, the President summoned a new commander to Washington. General George B. McClellan was thirty-four years old, and destined for a controversial career and a controversial place in history. He looked and acted like a great commander in July of 1861, and he set about at once to reorganize the demoralized Federal troops. The Second Wisconsin was reassembled at Fort Corcoran on July 23rd. There occurred the organizing and drilling of McClellan's early regime and picket duty in the vicinity of Ball's Cross Roads and the Alexandria and Leesburg Railroad.[23] The reshuffling of the army command was also reflected in the regiment. For all of his early appeal to Governor Randall, Colonel Coon was not qualified by either temperament or training for command.[24] Friction with the other officers of the Second had broken out almost as soon as the regiment had reached Washington. Indeed, the officers had waited on the colonel on June 27th and requested his resignation. Although unwilling to accede, Coon had remained in Washington when the regiment marched to Fort Corcoran, and Lieutenant Colonel Peck had been in command in Virginia.[25] But the colonel had rejoined the regiment on the eve of the Bull Run battle, precipitating a command problem that the commander of the brigade resolved to eliminate. As Sherman described the situation years later, Coon was "a good-hearted gentleman, who knew no more of the military art than a child; whereas his lieutenant colonel, Peck, had been to West Point, and knew the drill. Preferring that the latter should remain in command of the regiment, I put Colonel Coon on my personal staff, which reconciled the difficulty." In spite of this opinion, Coon apparently performed well during the battle itself. Writing in his official report, Sherman gave him this credit: "Colonel Coon, of Wisconsin, . . . rendered good service during the day." But the regimental commander resigned on July 30th,[26] thus ending a brief and unhappy career.

Although Lieutenant Colonel Peck and Major McDonald had presumably participated in the efforts to obtain Coon's resignation, they fared no better than the unfortunate colonel. Whatever the facts, their conduct during the battle was criticized in the press and in the published letters of the enlisted men. It was alleged that both men were "among the first to leave the field"; that they were "no where to be seen" during the battle; and that they had "dismounted early in the day and . . . remained back in the wood, so that we had no regimental commander with us." Other members of the regiment came to their defense—it was said that Peck "bore himself bravely and as became an officer"—but the damage to their continued command was done. Although Peck was later to go to war again, in 1863, as a captain of Wisconsin's First Regiment of Heavy Artillery, both he and McDonald resigned from the Second Wisconsin in July and August,[27] leaving the regiment with three vacant field commands to be filled.

The new field officers for the Second, men who were thereafter to be closely identified with the history of the regiment and the Iron Brigade, were Colonel Edgar O'Connor, Lieutenant Colonel Lucius Fairchild, and Major Thomas S. Allen. Like Colonel Coon, O'Connor was a Democrat, but otherwise the two men had little in common. Originally from Cleveland, where Edgar was born in 1833, the O'Connor family had moved to Milwaukee in 1842 and from there to Beloit. In the latter community, Edgar's father was a lawyer and judge, and the boy was appointed to West Point and graduated in 1854. Assigned to the United States Seventh Regiment, the young officer had been sent to the West, to duty at Santa Fe, Pikes Peak, and then for three years at Fort Gibson in the Indian country. In 1857 O'Connor had married the daughter of a prominent slave-owning Arkansas judge. Resigning from the army two years later, he had returned to Beloit and studied for the bar, to which he was admitted in 1861.[28]

Because of his Southern marital ties and the outspoken Democratic partisanship of both himself and his father, it was not surprising that Edgar O'Connor's appointment provoked sharp newspaper questions, questions that persisted although his wife's family was said to be a Union family and apparently had come North after Sumter.[29] Shortly after his commissioning, one newspaper printed an open letter to the colonel, recounting the rumors about his sentiments and questioning his eligibility to command the regiment. The colonel publicly answered:

As you truly say, if the impressions conveyed by the rumors mentioned in your note are correct, I ought not to be at the head of the brave men under my command. . . .

I would be false to myself if I omitted to state that prior to the attack on Fort Sumter, in common with a great majority of my political friends, and associates of the North, I was in favor of compromising the then differences and difficulties, thereby avoiding, if possible the impending civil war. . . .

I have relations, friends and property in the Rebel States. I regret the course they have taken. . . . The separation has been painful, but when traitors take up arms, all personal relations, the ties of consanguinity and property, are to be merged into our higher duty to the Constitution.[30]

Thus did O'Connor respond to his tormentors and, as his directness and candor merited, there the matter rested.

Lieutenant Colonel Lucius Fairchild was thirty years old and also an Ohioan by birth. He had come to Wisconsin with his family in 1846, but at the age of eighteen had set out with a team of oxen, seeking California gold. Returning to Wisconsin in 1855 without a fortune, Fairchild worked for four years in Madison for the Madison and Watertown Railroad. He entered politics in 1859 and was elected Clerk of Dane County. In 1860 he was admitted to the bar and he had also been active in the Governor's Guard, a Madison military company. In response to the initial call for volunteers, Fairchild, as a captain, took the Governor's Guard into the First Wisconsin Volunteers, Wisconsin's three months' regiment. When the term of the First Wisconsin expired, Fairchild obtained a commission as a lieutenant in the regular army, which was quickly followed by commissions as major, and then as lieutenant colonel, of volunteers.[31]

Thirty-six-year-old Major Thomas S. Allen of Mineral Point had also been a member of the Governor's Guard. Born in New York State, Allen had attended Oberlin College in Ohio. Having left school before completing the work for a degree, Allen had entered the printer's trade and had followed it to a Chicago newspaper job. In 1847 he and his family had settled in Dodgeville, Wisconsin, where he had worked as a mine surveyor and schoolteacher, followed by a term as Clerk of the Dodge County Board of Supervisors. The Allens removed to Mineral Point in 1857, where Thomas was elected to the state legislature. The legislative term led to an appointment as Chief Clerk of the United States Land Office at Madison.[32]

With its brand new set of field officers, the Second Wisconsin was transferred on August 27th to the brigade of Brigadier General Rufus King of Wisconsin, joining the Nineteenth Indiana Volunteers and the Fifth and Sixth Wisconsin Volunteers. King's Brigade was camped at Camp Kalorama on Meridian Hill in Washington. On September 3rd, leaving the Sixth Wisconsin in the District of Columbia, King marched his other regiments across the Chain Bridge into Virginia where the Second Wisconsin began construction of the earthworks known as Fort Marcy, part of the defenses of Washington and covering the approaches to the Chain Bridge. On September 25th, four companies from the Second Wisconsin participated in a reconnaissance to Lewinsville, Virginia, of which more will be said in the early life of the Nineteenth Indiana. Except for this activity, the regiment remained at Fort Marcy until October 1st, engaged with pick and shovel.[33]

THE SIXTH WISCONSIN VOLUNTEERS

While Colonel Coon's Second Wisconsin Volunteers were preparing to depart from Camp Randall, the towns and villages of Wisconsin continued to stir. In Baraboo in Sauk County, the organization of a three months' company had begun at a meeting on Saturday evening, April 19th. A few nights later, a second meeting was called for the Sauk County Court House where speeches were made by the leading citizens and the proprietor of the *Baraboo Republic* was so moved that he volunteered to furnish one recruit armed with a Sharps rifle—the recruit, of course, to be one of the employees of the newspaper. As the organizing continued, a captain and first lieutenant were elected by the members of the company and the name Sauk County Riflemen was adopted. Drawn in four-horse wagons and accompanied by Rawley's town band, the Riflemen departed for Reedsburg, where ten more volunteers signed up. Merrimac and Delton were the next communities visited and again recruiting was fruitful. Public subscriptions for support of the soldiers' families amounted to $6,000 during the first week of organization.

By May 4th the organization of the Sauk County company was virtually completed. The men drilled in Baraboo before the "throng," speeches were made, and the women of Baraboo presented each man with a "tasteful and beautiful rosette in the national colors." The soldiers gave three cheers for the ladies, and the company was dismissed, to reassemble a few days later for drill in Reedsburg, where the newly elected captain, Mexican War veteran A. G. Malloy, was presented with a sword by the citizenry. The men then moved on to Delton for a citizens' picnic and then to Prairie du Sac. From there the heroes were conveyed to Sauk City by twenty-four teams of horses belonging to the citizens. When the company returned to Baraboo, 108 men had enrolled, including four of the six sons of a Virginia-born citizen of Excelsior. As the Sauk County men waited in Baraboo for orders to report to Madison, living as guests in the homes of the citizens, word was received that no further three months' companies were needed. The entire company enlisted at once for three years. The mustering officer arrived in Baraboo on June 10th and enrolled the men in impressive ceremonies at which the citizens presented the company with a silk United States flag. At last the day of departure for Camp Randall arrived, an event that attracted the largest crowd in the history of Baraboo. Two thousand people gathered to watch the Baraboo Fire Company escort the soldiers to the train, to hear the choir of the Reverend Thomson, to hear an original poem, and to see the Sauk County Bible Society present each soldier with a pocket Testament.

The Sauk County Riflemen arrived in Madison in mid-June, their uniforms consisting only of gray caps trimmed with green. At Camp Randall the men were issued an all-gray short-jacketed uniform paid for by the state, with a headpiece described by one of the men as "a plug hat with a huge pompon on the front at the top." Assigned to the Sixth Wisconsin Volunteers, then in the process of organization, the Riflemen became Company A of that regiment.[34]

Over in Juneau County, Governor Randall's call was heard by a twenty-two-year-old Ohioan who was visiting in Wisconsin with his father. Rufus R. Dawes knew Wisconsin, having attended the University of Wisconsin at Madison for two years before returning to Marietta, Ohio, to complete his schooling at Marietta College. Dawes also knew something of citizens in arms. His great-grandfather was no less a person than William Dawes, who had ridden south from Boston on the night of April 18th, 1775, as Paul Revere rode north toward Lexington and Concord. Drawing up a pledge for volunteers for an unlimited time, Dawes began recruiting on April 25th. He had posters prepared and, with a sense of his own history, announced, "Enlistments Wanted For The Lemonweir Minute Men!" He was joined in his efforts by John A. Kellogg of Mauston,[35] the Juneau County prosecutor, thirty-three years old, Pennsylvania born, and the grandson of a Revolutionary soldier. Kellogg had entered Wisconsin Territory in 1840 and, although of meager formal education, had successfully read law and been admitted to the bar in Prairie du Sac. At the Madison convention of the new Republican party in 1855, Kellogg had been a member. This experience and his successful campaign for the prosecutor's position had given him a wide acquaintance in the state.[36]

By April 30th Dawes and Kellogg had succeeded in enlisting one hundred men, including many raftsmen from the pineries in the area, rugged men of the outdoors whom Dawes was especially glad to have. At the Mauston meeting at which the company was formally

organized, Dawes and Kellogg were elected captain and first lieutenant without opposition. After a spirited campaign, the remaining
officers were also elected. Then began the efforts to be mustered in.
Influential citizens were dispatched to Madison, and Dawes himself
went to wait upon the governor. Finally, orders having arrived, the
company entrained for Madison on July 6th, assigned to the Sixth
Wisconsin Volunteers. Each of the members of the company boarded
the train armed with a pincushion made by the ladies of Marietta,
Ohio, and forwarded to Dawes, Marietta's native son.

Dawes' company was the last of the ten companies assigned to the
Sixth Wisconsin to arrive at Camp Randall. Undrilled and without
uniforms, the Minute Men were not an imposing sight. Dawes said:
"The men stumbled along in two ranks, kicking each other's heels. . . .
A few wore broadcloth and silk hats, more the red shirts of raftsmen,
several were in country homespun, one had on a calico coat, and
another was looking through a hole in the drooping brim of a straw
hat. . . . The men carried every variety of valise, and every species
of bundle, down to one shirt tied up in a red handkerchief." As the
company approached Camp Randall, they were met by two thousand
men of the Fifth and Sixth Wisconsin Volunteers, drawn up in line
of battle to welcome the newcomers. At the entrance to the camp,
Dawes was greeted by First Lieutenant Frank A. Haskell, the regimental adjutant of the Sixth Wisconsin. Mounted, splendidly uniformed, and already soldierly in his bearing, Haskell directed Dawes
to "form the company in column by platoon" and march to headquarters under the escort of Hibbard's Milwaukee Zouaves of the
Fifth Wisconsin, the best-drilled military company in the state. In
the first of many difficult situations in his military career, Dawes
responded that he would be glad to comply, "but it is simply impossible." Thereupon, accompanied by the Zouaves, the Minute Men
walked at their own gait to headquarters where Colonel Lysander
Cutler of Milwaukee greeted them. Colonel Cutler advised Dawes
that his company was designated as Company K of the regiment, but
unofficially the Minute Men had already been christened by their
Sixth Wisconsin comrades—the name was "Company Q."[37]

As the Juneau County men looked around at Camp Randall, they
learned something of their Sixth Wisconsin comrades. Two of the
companies of the regiment were from Milwaukee, each composed

exclusively of members of one national group. Company D was the Irish company, known as the "Montgomery Guards." Company F, the "Citizens' Corps Milwaukee," was composed of Germans. Both of its lieutenants had European military experience. Another German unit was Company H, the "Buffalo County Rifles." Its captain, J. F. Hauser, had been educated at the military school of Thun in Switzerland, was a veteran of European warfare and had been on Garibaldi's staff.[38] The German officers were not the only veteran soldiers of the regiment. Colonel Lysander Cutler, fifty-three years old but as "rugged as a wolf," according to Captain Dawes, had commanded Maine militia troops during the Aroostook Indian wars of 1838 and 1839. Although born in Worcester County, Massachusetts, Cutler had lived most of his colorful life in Maine. Reared on a farm, he had also learned the clothier's trade, surveyed, and taught school. Having founded his own woollen mill in 1843, Cutler made a fortune within ten years. Then his mill burned down and the fortune disappeared with it. Undaunted, he succeeded in rebuilding the mill and in enlarging his holdings to embrace other factories, tenements, a foundry, a gristmill, and a sawmill. As a leading businessman, Cutler was elected to the Maine senate, college trusteeships and a railroad directorship, but he was financially ruined by the panic of 1856 and moved to Milwaukee to start his career over again.

Cutler's first Wisconsin employment was for a mining company that wanted a man to go west into the Indian country to investigate its claims. Cutler went, although it was a job with clear and present mortal danger, and he remained with the mining company until its operations stalled financially. The coming of the war found Cutler in his own grain and commission business, and with unlikely public employment as the fish inspector for Milwaukee County.[39] Although events were to prove him a successful volunteer officer, he was at first arbitrary and overzealous in his treatment of his junior officers. When the Sixth reached Washington, Cutler instituted a system of examinations for officers who were not acceptable to him. Seven captains and lieutenants were dropped from the regiment almost at once. There was bitter feeling in the regiment, especially where the examinations resulted in the replacement of the officers of the "foreign" companies by men of different national stock.[40] But the replacements were good men, and Cutler could later point to the record of the Sixth as a vindication of his policy.

Julius P. Atwood of Madison, a Vermont-born lawyer and former Madison county judge, was Cutler's second in command. B. F. Sweet, from Chilton, the county seat of Calumet County, was the major. Of unknown New York antecedents, Sweet had arrived in Wisconsin in 1857 and had been admitted to the bar and elected to the state senate. Atwood was to resign because of ill health shortly after the arrival of the regiment in Washington.[41] Sweet then assumed the lieutenant colonelcy, and Edward S. Bragg of Fond du Lac became the major of the Sixth. Destined to be a national political figure after the war, Bragg was a native of New York, where he had been educated at Geneva College and admitted to the bar. Entering Wisconsin in 1850 at the age of twenty-three, Bragg had at once become active in Democratic politics, had been elected prosecuting attorney of Fond du Lac County and a Douglas delegate to the 1860 Democratic Convention at Charleston.[42]

Although never an officer of field grade in the Sixth Wisconsin, regimental adjutant Frank A. Haskell, who had greeted Dawes' company at Camp Randall, was also to be closely identified with the Iron Brigade. A grandson of a New Hampshire captain of the Revolution, the thirty-three-year-old lieutenant was a native of Tunbridge, Vermont. Preceded by his lawyer brother, in 1848 Haskell had left the family's farm and moved to Columbus, Wisconsin, where he was associated with his brother and served as town clerk. In 1850 the youth had traveled to the East to attend Dartmouth College. Graduating in 1854, he returned to Wisconsin, this time to Madison, where he entered the practice of law in the firm of Julius P. Atwood, now one of his superior officers. Like Lucius Fairchild and Thomas S. Allen of the Second Wisconsin, Haskell had been active in the Governor's Guard, and had assisted in the organization of the Anderson Guards, another military company. When the war broke out, Haskell was elected first lieutenant of the Anderson Guards and accompanied them into the Sixth Wisconsin.[43]

The Sixth did not linger long at Camp Randall before proceeding to the seat of war. On July 16th, fully equipped by the state except for arms, the regiment was mustered into Federal service, 1,084 men strong. Leaving for Washington late in July, they encamped on the way at Patterson Park in Baltimore, just two miles from old Fort McHenry. Like their earlier numerical counterparts from Massachusetts, the Sixth contended in Baltimore with the "Plug Uglies," who attacked the regiment's camp at midnight on August 5th. Countering with brickbats—only two companies had as yet been armed—the Wisconsin men successfully held off the attackers with but a single casualty. Wandering through the beleaguered and darkened camp, Lieutenant Kellogg fell into a pit, apparently dug by his comrades for sanitary purposes. The lieutenant was not really hurt, and the regiment quickly discovered that it was not prudent to twit him as the only casualty of the "Battle of Patterson Park."[44] The other result of the fracas was the prompt issue of arms to the rest of the regiment. The weapon available was a Belgian musket, not the soldiers' favorite since, as one of them recorded, "you could most always tell when they were fired by finding yourself on the ground" from the recoil.[45]

After several more days in Baltimore, the Sixth entrained in cattle cars for Washington at midnight and reached the city before daylight on the following morning. The men then slept briefly on the pavement in front of the post office, washed up at the fire hydrants in the streets, and went into camp on Meridian Hill. On August 23rd they were reviewed by Brigadier General Rufus King to whose command the Sixth Wisconsin, Fifth Wisconsin, and Nineteenth Indiana had been assigned. Dawes believed that the regiment had made a poor impression, largely because of "that contemptible brass band of ours," which played so slowly that as the soldiers passed the reviewing stand, "we had to hold one leg in the air and balance on the other while we waited for the music!" The caliber of the regimental band was really not surprising. Whether or not Colonel Cutler was particularly unmusical, it was recorded that whenever a soldier was apprehended for misconduct, his comrades shouted, "Put him in the brass band." On August 26th the men of the Sixth got their first view of General McClellan when he reviewed all of the troops encamped on Meridian Hill. In an example of the strange personal attraction that McClellan possessed, one of the men of the Sixth wrote a letter home that day about how the "boys are all carried away with enthusiasm for McClellan."

The Sixth Wisconsin left their encampment on Meridian Hill on September 2nd and moved to a position near the Chain Bridge. Remaining on the Maryland side of the bridge, they were engaged throughout September on picket duty between the Chain Bridge and

Falling Waters. Here Captain Dawes discovered difficulty in preventing looting by his Minute Men: it "was impossible for me to restrain
men who had been starved on salt-beef and hardtack, when they
were scattered over four miles of territory and sneered at as Yankees
by the people." Indeed, the twenty-two-year-old captain was apparently unusually sensitive to the temptations of his men, because
he went on to say, "The fact is I ate some pig myself."[46]

THE NINETEENTH INDIANA VOLUNTEERS

As in other states, the firing on Sumter found Indiana full of
enthusiasm but little else of the wherewithal for war.[47] Most enthusiastic was Indiana's "fire-eating" chief executive, who was determined
that Indiana's response to Lincoln's proclamation would be spectacular. On April 15th Governor Oliver P. Morton signaled the state's
official reaction with a telegram to the President: "On behalf of the
State of Indiana I tender to you for the defense of the nation and
to uphold the authority of the Government 10,000 men."[48] Then, just
as Governor Randall had done in Wisconsin, Morton sought out a
prominent Democrat to identify with the cause. To the vacant post of
adjutant general, he appointed Lew Wallace of Crawfordsville, widely
known lawyer and Mexican War veteran.

One of Lew Wallace's first duties was to find a site for the encampment of Indiana's soldiers. He selected the State Fairgrounds,
thirty-six acres on the northern outskirts of Indianapolis, and named
the place Camp Morton. The existing frame buildings were quickly
adapted to barracks. The exhibition halls were fitted with bunks for
two thousand men, and the long rows of stalls, one side open to the
weather, were readied for the occupancy of less fortunate recruits, six
men to a stall. Additional wooden sheds and stalls were constructed
and tents were finally resorted to. To Camp Morton had come the
first six three months' regiments numbered "Six" through "Eleven,"
out of respect to the five regiments of Hoosiers who had volunteered
for the Mexican War. In July of 1861, the Nineteenth Indiana Volunteers followed them, but for an enlistment of three years.[49]

Although one company was from Elkhart County, adjoining the
Michigan line near South Bend, the volunteers of the Nineteenth
Indiana were largely from communities in the central portion of the

state, such as Winchester, Muncie, Indianapolis, Franklin, and Spencer.[50] What scenes the new volunteers witnessed at Camp Morton are unrecorded. They probably missed the drill of one company whose captain had been a railroader and who halted his men in an emergency with an urgent "Down brakes!" But the soldiers of the Nineteenth had their own difficulty in adjusting to the strange ways of a military system. Dissatisfied with the food provided at the camp, they rallied to destroy the commissary. The colonel of another regiment ordered out a guard detail and directed the men of the Nineteenth to disperse, an order the soldiers at first refused on the ground that the officer was not "their colonel" and was without any authority to order them about.[51] The man whom the soldiers of the Nineteenth would presumably have obeyed, their "own" colonel, was Solomon Meredith of Wayne County's Cambridge City, a town close to Richmond, Indiana. Later to be closely identified with the Iron Brigade, Meredith was six feet seven inches tall, slender, and, although in his early fifties, as straight as a ramrod. An uneducated and unpropertied North Carolina Quaker who had come to Indiana in 1840, his first Indiana activity was farming. But his real talent was for politics. During the years between his coming into Indiana and the outbreak of the war, Meredith had been twice elected county sheriff, elected to the state legislature, and appointed a United States marshal. At the outbreak of the war, he was again in public office, this time as the Clerk of Wayne County.

Like Governor Morton, Solomon Meredith had left the Democratic party during the 1850's and by 1860 was a leader of the victorious Republicans. At the Republican State Convention of 1860, it was Meredith who moved the nomination of Henry S. Lane for governor, and accepted an amendment to his motion to include Morton for lieutenant governor. On Governor Lane's election to the United States Senate in 1861, Morton had assumed the governorship. He and Solomon Meredith were friends.[52] In Indiana's faction-torn Republican party, this meant that Meredith, like Morton, was the object of the barbs of the factional press, which decried his military ambitions as "brazen impudence and sublime effrontery," and labeled his appointment "a damnable swindle." It was also suggested that "Long Sol" be cut in two, so that "his lower and better half" could be appointed lieutenant colonel of the regiment.[53] But the colonel survived these outcries, and in fact it was said that the Nineteenth Indiana was Governor Morton's pet regiment, because the governor, like Colonel Meredith, was from Wayne County and because Company B of the Nineteenth was composed of Wayne County men.[54]

The Nineteenth's lieutenant colonel was Robert A. Cameron of Valparaiso, Indiana. A native of New York, thirty-three years old, he had come to Porter County, Indiana, in 1843 and had graduated in 1850 from the Indiana Medical College at La Porte. Thereafter, licensed as a physician, his practice had flourished in Valparaiso. Cameron's political background was also typical of the one-time Jacksonian stronghold of Indiana. An ardent Democrat until the Kansas-Nebraska issue, he had then turned to the new Republican party and devoted his considerable talents and energies there. In 1857 he purchased the *Valparaiso Observer*, changed its name to *The Republic*, and published and edited the paper until 1861 when he took his seat in the Indiana House of Representatives, to which he had been elected in 1860. Along with medicine, publishing, and politics, Cameron had long harbored a military interest and had missed the Mexican War only because Indiana's regimental quotas were filled. But in 1861 he went into the Ninth Indiana, a three months' regiment, and obtained a captain's commission. This led to his lieutenant colonelcy in the Nineteenth, where it was soon discovered that two unusually strong and assertive men like Solomon Meredith and Robert A. Cameron were too many. In February of 1862, Cameron was to leave the Nineteenth to become the colonel of the Thirty-fourth Indiana.[55]

Alois O. Bachman was commissioned as major of the Nineteenth and became its lieutenant colonel on Cameron's transfer in February, 1862. Bachman was a native Hoosier, born in Madison, Indiana, in 1839, the child of well-to-do Swiss, who were among the early settlers of Indiana. Entering Hanover College in 1856, Bachman studied there for two years with the announced ambition of practicing law. He was known in the college community for his skills in debating and public speaking. After Hanover, Bachman enrolled at Kentucky Military Institute at Frankfort, and continued there for two and one-half years. During the summers in Madison, he had organized a military company, the "Madison City Greys," and drilled his men regularly. In 1861 Bachman and the Greys enlisted in the Sixth Indiana Volunteers and spent their three months' term of enlistment in the early western Virginia actions. Upon the expiration of this enlistment, Bachman received his commission as major of the Nineteenth.

Bachman's successor as major in February of 1862 was to be Isaac May, a twenty-nine-year-old Virginian who had come to Anderson, Indiana, in 1855 to pursue his trade of cabinetmaking. From cabinetmaking May turned to the legal profession, and the outbreak of the war found him studying law. Although without political identity, the youth had a wide Indiana acquaintance because of his activities in the Independent Order of Odd Fellows. Enlisting as a private, he was at once elected captain of Company A, which put him in contention for the majority when Alois Bachman moved up to the lieutenant colonelcy.[56]

The Nineteenth was mustered in at Camp Morton on July 29th. A week later, in woolen uniforms of "gray doeskin cassimere," and carrying a mixture of Enfield and "Minie Rifles,"[57] the men left for Washington. Their departure was marred by the fact that the bandsmen had to stay behind because their uniforms, which arrived just as the train was ready to start, were pronounced not "fit to be worn by a musician on parade."[58] Later in August, in new uniforms, the band entrained, bearing also the regimental color, the product of the "ladies of Muncie," and formally presented to the regiment by Indiana's representative in Lincoln's cabinet, Interior Secretary Caleb B. Smith.[59]

Arriving in Washington on August 9th with a total roster of 1,046 men, the Nineteenth joined the encampment on Kalorama Heights and was assigned at once to the brigade of Brigadier General Rufus King, along with the Fifth and Sixth Wisconsin regiments. There was widespread sickness in the regiment as the Hoosiers sought to make the adjustment to army food and sanitary facilities. As many as 40 per cent of the men in the command were affected, and it was believed by the doctors and officers that the springs used by the Nineteenth for drinking water had been poisoned. Tests proved the absence of poison, but the sickness continued until in early September the regiment moved across the Chain Bridge into Virginia.

Beyond the Chain Bridge in Virginia, the Nineteenth Indiana participated in the construction of another of the Washington fortifications, Fort Ethan Allen.[60] This activity was interrupted on

September 11th when five of the companies of the Nineteenth participated with the Seventy-ninth New York Highlanders in a reconnaissance toward Lewinsville, Virginia, approximately five miles beyond Fort Ethan Allen. Withdrawing from Lewinsville, the Union force was attacked by Colonel J. E. B. Stuart, and the Nineteenth suffered its first casualties in battle: one killed, one wounded, and three wounded and captured. One of the incidental results of the reconnaissance was the reinstatement in the good graces of the army of the Seventy-ninth New York, which had mutinied after Bull Run and lost its regimental flags as a penalty. Because of the reports of its fine conduct during the Lewinsville affair, General McClellan ordered the return of the flags to the regiment. But the conduct of the Nineteenth Indiana was no less valorous than that of their New York companions. Colonel Meredith reported that his men were under fire for about two hours and that "during the whole of that time behaved with the utmost coolness and gallantry, obeying all orders promptly and with but little confusion. . . ." The novelty of the business of war was apparent from Meredith's report. This was to be the first and last time that his casualties would permit him to name each man and specify his wounds.[61]

Lewinsville was again approached on September 25th when Brigadier General W. F. Smith moved there with a substantial force, including the Nineteenth Indiana and four companies from the Second Wisconsin. A few days later, the Nineteenth advanced again, this time to Falls Church, Virginia. The Hoosiers then recrossed the Potomac to Washington, where they remained until the first days of October.[62]

THE SEVENTH WISCONSIN VOLUNTEERS

Wisconsin had entered the Union in 1848. It was a young state and the last of the full states to be carved out of the old Northwest Territory, the territory which by the Ordinance of 1787 was to permit neither "slavery nor involuntary servitude." Perhaps because of its youth, Wisconsin was anxious for identity, and Governor Randall's plan was to have an all-Wisconsin brigade in the Eastern armies. This brigade was to be commanded by Brigadier General Rufus King. The Second, Fifth, and Sixth Wisconsin, already at the seat of war in Washington, were in the process of assignment to King. In August of 1861—the call had been delayed by the governor until after the harvest—the Seventh Wisconsin Volunteers were to be organized to fill out King's Wisconsin command.[63]

Although not a native of Wisconsin, Rufus King was a distinguished American and an appropriate commander for a Wisconsin brigade. Born in New York City in 1814, he was the grandson of the Rufus King who had been a Massachusetts delegate to the Continental Congress. In 1785 the elder Rufus King had written the resolution proposing that neither "slavery nor involuntary servitude" be permitted in the Northwest Territory. King had also been a delegate to the Constitutional Convention and, as a prominent Federalist, had been appointed by President Washington as minister to Great Britain.

Before entering West Point, Brigadier General King had attended New York's Columbia College, of which institution his father, a militia officer in the War of 1812, was president. Graduating at West Point in 1833, King resigned from the army Corps of Engineers in 1836. From then until 1845, he edited various newspapers in the State of New York, including an Albany daily where he was associated with Thurlow Weed. King had maintained his identity with military affairs in New York and was that state's adjutant general during the administration of Governor William H. Seward.

When King entered the Wisconsin Territory in 1845, he settled in Milwaukee. There he was editor and, for a time, part owner of the *Milwaukee Sentinel and Gazette*. Immediately active in Wisconsin in public affairs, he was in the forefront of the successful fight in 1846 against the proposed Wisconsin constitution and was a member of the 1848 constitutional convention that resulted in the admission of Wisconsin to the Union. King's other interests included public education, and he had been superintendent of schools in Milwaukee and one of the regents of the state university at Madison. In 1861 he was appointed by President Lincoln as Minister to the Papal States. As he prepared to sail to this assignment, Sumter was fired on, and King obtained a leave of absence from his appointment and was at once commissioned a brigadier general of volunteers, charged by Governor Randall with the duty of commanding Wisconsin's regiments in the Washington area. Reporting for duty in Washington on August 5th, King was certainly a promising officer, and combined the qualifications of professional military training and public renown. He was also not in the best of health, and was an occasional victim of attacks of epilepsy, but of this nothing was said in 1861.[64]

The men of the Seventh Wisconsin began to arrive in Madison late in August. Several of the companies were from the same counties from which the Second and Sixth Wisconsin had been recruited, including Grant County, Columbia County, and Rock County. Indeed, Rock County, on the Illinois line and with the communities of Beloit and Janesville, was to have companies in all three of the Wisconsin Iron Brigade regiments. Other companies arriving at Camp Randall for the Seventh were from counties unrepresented in the Second and Sixth regiments. Some of the men in Company A, the "Lodi Guards," were from far-off Chippewa County in the northwestern part of the state.[65]

Regardless of past grievances the townspeople had about the carryings-on of the soldiers, Madison was still preoccupied with military affairs in August of 1861, and the soldiers found that even the assembly chamber of the Capitol had been given over to the "ladies of the city who were making havelocks . . . of coarse white linen."[66] Camp Randall was now a going military establishment. Located near the state university campus just a mile and a half west of the Capitol Square, the camp included thirty acres of ground. The fences around the trotting course and the horse and cattle rings had been removed, and the place no longer bore the appearances of a fairgrounds. In addition to the frame headquarters building, stables, commissary, and hospital, both barracks and tents surrounded the parade area, with "six men to each tent, the captain one tent, the two lieutenants one tent between them." The barracks were composed of long rows of whitewashed buildings, each of which accommodated one hundred men who slept in the three tiers of bunks that lined the walls. Running down the aisleway between the rows of bunks was placed a long, narrow table, with benches on each side. Here the men took their meals, the food coming to the table from a kitchen at one end of the barracks.[67] Here, too, the men said grace, solemnly intoning such blessings as:

> Oh, thou who blessed the loaves and fishes,
> Look down upon these old tin dishes.
> By thy great power those dishes smash.
> Bless each of us and damn this hash.

Another popular prayer at mealtime was a variation of the same theme:

> Now I sit me in my seat
> And pray for something fit to eat.
> If this damn stuff my stomach break,
> I pray that God my soul will take.[68]

The military training of the recruits at Camp Randall had also progressed since the May arrival of the Second Wisconsin. An officer, who incidentally reported that his two uniforms had cost $55.00 and that his sword, sash, and belt required an additional $34.50, gave this description of the routine: "We are called at daylight by the firing of a cannon, then roll call, 1/2 hour to wash and comb hair, then drill at 7 o'clock, then breakfast. We all eat together each company at its own table. After breakfast march to tents to dismiss. At 8 o'clock officers drill, 9:30 drill the company until the drum beats for dinner. At 2:00 sword drill, at 3:00–5:00 drill the men; then supper; after supper dress parade which is over by sunset, from that to 9 o'clock, we study military tactics."[69]

The colonelcy of the Seventh was awarded to Joseph Vandor of Milwaukee, an aristocratic immigrant from Hungary who had been an officer in the Hungarian army. In spite of the logic of the choice, the appointment was not a fortunate one, and Vandor ceased actively to command almost as soon as the regiment arrived in Washington. In January, 1862, he was to resign after having been appointed representative of the United States to the Island of Tahiti.[70] The only statement of the cause of Vandor's difficulties appeared in an anonymous letter in the Wisconsin newspapers. Written by a member of the regiment after his resignation, the account had an authoritative sound, and presumably reflected the truth: "He liked 'his boys,' and the boys liked him. The officers feelings were hurt by his strictures on their military knowledge. They, as well as the men were raw then, and some of them have since regretted their opposition to him. No one seeing him ride his well-trained steed could doubt his courage and training. That voice, though not of the finest English, would wage a charge, and the steed and rider would be expected where the bullets fell thickest. . . . Goodbye, Vandor. . . . Had you adopted a less candid policy in your intercourse with men you would have been with us yet. It is but justice to say, however, that the military examining Boards could find no flaw in your ability, and that you voluntarily resigned. . . ."[71]

Second in command was Lieutenant Colonel W. W. Robinson of Sparta, who was to assume command upon Vandor's resignation. Robinson was a Vermonter, forty-two years old, who claimed Mayflower Pilgrim descent and whose father had been a wounded veteran of the War of 1812. Robinson had attended several schools in Vermont, including the academy at Norwich, and after finishing his own education he had been a teacher in New Jersey and then in Cleveland, Ohio, before heading west for gold. Returning to Ohio in time to be commissioned a lieutenant in the Third Ohio Infantry for the Mexican War, he had ended the war as a captain and had again set out for California and the gold fields in 1852. Employed in California by a Minnesota utility corporation, Robinson returned to Minnesota, founded the town of Wilton, and was commissioned as colonel in the state militia. It was not until 1858 that he moved to Wisconsin, but he had friends there, and his Mexican War experience commended him to Wisconsin's governor.[72]

Charles A. Hamilton of Milwaukee, the first major of the Seventh, was the most well-descended man in the regiment. Alexander Hamilton had been his grandfather, and his father was a prosperous New York City lawyer. Charles had attended schools in New York City and abroad in England and Germany. After admission to the bar in New York, he had come to Milwaukee in 1851 and had developed a highly successful practice there. He was thirty-five years old in 1861, and a leader of the Wisconsin bar. When Hamilton moved up to become lieutenant colonel in the promotions following Vandor's resignation, George Bill, a Mexican War veteran from the town of Lodi and originally a captain in Company A, was promoted to major.[73]

On September 21st, having been mustered in for three years, the ten companies of the Seventh, 1,106 officers and men, entrained for Washington. The receptions by the cities along the way were becoming more and more elaborate. In Chicago, where the regiment stopped to change trains, a formal parade awaited them. Headed by the city officials, the line of march also included the police, bands, the Ellsworth Zouaves and other military companies. Following

Colonel Vandor and Lieutenant Colonel Robinson, both mounted, the Seventh assumed its place in the column. Illuminated by gaslight and a rising moon and to the cheers of the people who crowded the sidewalks along the route, the regiment marched past the Galena Depot, across the Wells Street Bridge, past the Briggs House and the Sherman House, up Clark Street past the offices of the *Tribune*, down Dearborn, and then west past the court house to the Fort Wayne Depot. There the courtly Vandor thanked the escort, especially the band, which, he said, had played an air to which he had marched in Hungary thirteen years ago. The soldiers then entered the cars where hot coffee and rations were distributed, while the officers were feted at the Briggs House as guests of the hotel. It was not until after midnight that the reception was over and the train headed for Washington and the more serious business at hand.[74]

The Seventh arrived in Washington on October 1st. Two days prior to its arrival, orders were issued attaching the new regiment to King's Brigade. But the same order frustrated Governor Randall's plan for an all-Wisconsin brigade. Confronted with the choice of transferring from King either the Nineteenth Indiana or one of his Wisconsin regiments, army headquarters chose the latter, and the Fifth Wisconsin was detached from King's Brigade. There is no record to indicate whether the Washington authorities were purposefully preventing what Wisconsin so much desired. But they were wise to do so, as the South was already learning as it sought to organize a national army in the face of interferences from the states and efforts by the states to keep their regiments together and to control their disposition.

In any event, Rufus King, with his own historical association with the Old Northwest, was to lead a brigade of men from the territory where both slavery and involuntary servitude were prohibited, and it was to be the only distinctively Western brigade in the Army of the Potomac.[75] Bull Run, the first big battle in the East, was over. Only one of King's regiments had been there. But there was a long war ahead before there was to be an answer to Lincoln's question in Indianapolis—Shall the Union and shall the liberties of this country be preserved?—and the Western brigade still had its story to tell.

"RALLY 'ROUND THE FLAG, BOYS"

"We desire a plain flag, but one from which *all the stars* shall shine, and under whose ample folds we can . . . *fight* for the integrity of the Union, and the preservation of the Government."

> *From a Letter of Major William Orr of the Nineteenth Indiana to Indiana's Adjutant General.*

1

A WINTER IN CAMP

"Time is a necessary element in the creation of armies. . . ."
From General McClellan's Report

Brigadier General Rufus King collected his four scattered regiments during the first days of October at the Chain Bridge, east of the Potomac. On October 5th, in the first six of many miles the Wisconsin and Indiana men would travel together, the brigade marched from Washington across the Georgetown Aqueduct to Fort Tillinghast on Arlington Heights, Virginia. Near the home of Robert E. Lee, the brigade went into winter quarters with the army, to remain until March 10, 1862.[1] The soldiers felled trees and constructed their own camp from the ground up, including officers' quarters, cookhouses, and stables. For themselves they erected small log cabins, roofed with canvas, with mud chimneys and sheet-iron stoves.[2] As soon as these facilities were ready, there was time for the men to be trained in the manner of the day, in drill, target practice, and occasional picketing duty. It was also a time to get acquainted.

As of October 15, 1861, the Army of the Potomac was organized into divisions. King's Brigade was part of the division of General Irvin McDowell, the unsuccessful army commander at Bull Run. McDowell's Division also included the brigades of Brigadier Generals Erasmus Keyes and James S. Wadsworth. All of the regiments in Keyes' and Wadsworth's brigades were from New York.[3] There were relatively few Western men in the armies of the East during any period of the war, and during the first year less than twenty Western infantry regiments were located in the Army of the Potomac. Dramatizing this sectional difference in typical fashion, one Westerner wrote home about the "cussed poor country" in the East: "I would

31

not live here if i had the best farm in the country . . . everything is so different from the west." Actually, the men from both sections of the North had more in common than they had differences between them. But the Western men, at least those born in the United States, represented a frontier spirit and pioneer experience and, as a whole, had a rural flavor, unlike the men from the cities of the seaboard states.[4]

Of King's regiments, the Second Wisconsin was the only one that could boast of veteran status. The Nineteenth Indiana had seen some action and had lost five men during the Lewinsville affair, but this was insignificant compared to the concentrated and costly action of the Second Wisconsin at Bull Run. Although one of the Hoosiers in a newspaper letter prematurely claimed for the regiment the title of "Bloody Nineteenth,"[5] Lewinsville did not admit the Nineteenth to the ranks of the veterans. But all four regiments had other things in common. They were largely "country boys," from farms or very small towns, and engaged as civilians in agriculture or in the mechanical skills directly related to the farms. A small majority of the men in the regiments were native-born Americans. But the numbers of foreign born—especially Germans, Irish, and Scandinavians—were substantial enough to prevent anyone's feeling not at home. Although no precise data are available, it may be assumed that the estimates of Wisconsin's adjutant general were substantially accurate. He found that approximately 50 per cent of the Wisconsin volunteers were American born. The Irish and Norwegians—who were almost equal in strength—accounted for approximately 45 per cent of the men. The remainder were largely German, with a few Englishmen, Welshmen, and Canadians. The Nineteenth Indiana included fewer Scandinavians but made up for this with a correspondingly larger group of Germans and Irish. The Indiana regiment also included more Southern-born men, the states of the South having contributed a large share of the mid-nineteenth century Indiana immigration.[6]

Like the men who have fought in other wars, the Civil War soldier did not ordinarily articulate his motives. Attitudes about slavery varied widely, and there was less of the true abolition influence in the West than in the East.[7] Still, although slavery was not wrong in the eyes of some of King's men, to a majority, especially as the war progressed, the question of freedom seemed more and more to be involved, and the friendship of the Negroes came more and more to be appreciated. "May their hopes grow brighter and brighter to the perfect day," wrote one Wisconsin soldier when telling of a Negro woman's saying that the Federal army was "God Almighty come to deliver his children."[8] Another of the Badgers wrote crudely but feelingly of the death of a Negro who "was liked by the boys and treated by them more as a companion than a nigger."[9] And a third man put it this way: "The contrabands are the only people we can depend upon. They tell us where the Secesh are—never lie to us—wish us God speed—and are of great use to us."[10] For the soldiers it was difficult not to sympathize, at least, with an identifiable group of people who were on their side.

But the predominant motive among the soldiers was the maintenance of the national government. The recruitment pledges and slogans for King's regiments spoke entirely in these terms. The South was in rebellion against the "old Flag" and the national government with which the native-born Americans and the immigrants of the Northwest Territory identified themselves. The men enlisted to put down this rebellion. It was as simple as that.[11] Some of the men may have gone beyond this—and beyond the question of slavery—to see a broad difference in cultures in the North and the South, with slavery as one symptom of the Southern culture. The Southern men in King's Brigade had the greatest reason to be aware of this difference. Southerners, like Solomon Meredith and Isaac May of the Nineteenth Indiana, were typically Southern whites who had no stake at all in a system of slave economy and planter politics. Meredith was a poor farmer and Isaac May was a cabinetmaker, competing in the South with slave cabinetmakers. In leaving the South these men presumably acted on the premise that there was nothing there for them. And in leaving the South, they also became *interstate* men, and therefore men with an identification with the *national* government.

Whatever their motives and sectional or national origins, King's men would fight hard enough when given the chance, and the general would have been reassured had he been able to anticipate the spirit that they would display. He should also have been reassured about the leadership the soldiers would receive from their field officers. Although only the youthful Colonel O'Connor of the Second Wisconsin was a professionally trained soldier, the Seventh's Colonel Robinson had been an officer during the Mexican War, and Colonel Cutler of the Sixth had at least some experience as a militia officer. In addition, Lieutenant Colonels Bachman of the Nineteenth and Fairchild of the Second and Major Allen of the Second had an interest in military affairs that predated the war, and some knowledge of military organization and discipline. In an army of wholly untrained civilians, even such slight military background counted for something. And what the field officers lacked in training and experience was certainly mitigated by their personal characteristics. All but two of them were men who had chosen to uproot themselves from their original communities and begin life again on the frontier. Half of them were men who had been elected to public office, an evidence before the days of mass public-relations techniques that they merited the respect of their contemporaries. Few brigades could claim two field officers who had traveled all the way to California and back, like Lieutenant Colonel Fairchild and Colonel Robinson. And there were not too many men like Colonel Cutler who had accepted employment to work alone in the Indian country. All in all, these were men with characters marked by ambition, courage, self-reliance, and a spirit of adventure, men accustomed to civilian occupations of trust, responsibility, and leadership. If General King thought about it at all, he must have known that once schooled in their new calling, such men would perform well in the business of war.

The differences among King's men and the differences between them and their Eastern colleagues were not apparent from the appearance of the troops. All of King's regiments had received the orthodox Federal blue uniforms in September. The Wisconsin soldiers were not pleased with the change, believing that their "good state clothing" was of better quality than the Federal issue. Indeed, some of the Badgers secretly kept their original overcoats, although all of the state-issue garb was supposed to have been sent to Washington. But except for the gray overcoats, gone at least were the days when Confederate gray was worn. And in spite of the preferences of the Wisconsinites, the men were well provided for. In a letter to his sister, Rufus Dawes requested her not to send any clothing to his men, since every man in his company had at least one cloth uniform coat, one overcoat, three pairs of pants, three to five pairs of stockings, two woolen shirts, one undershirt, and two pairs of shoes. According to Dawes, if these were piled onto a man along with two or three blankets, his musket and cartridge box, it was all that the soldier could do to carry the load.[12] In spite of their ample clothing, the men were still poorly armed, and there was no standardization of their weapons. The Nineteenth Indiana had received Springfield rifled muskets, the common shoulder arm of the war, but the Second Wisconsin carried Austrian rifled muskets, the Sixth still had their Belgian rifled muskets, and the Seventh Wisconsin was equipped with a Springfield altered smoothbore. It was not until February, 1862, that the Wisconsin regiments received the new Springfields, a lighter and better gun than the variety of weapons previously available.[13]

During the winter the strength of the four regiments varied from 996 in the Seventh Wisconsin to 821 in the Second Wisconsin. The Sixth Wisconsin claimed 960 and the Nineteenth Indiana 892.[14] The bulk of the Second Wisconsin's loss was accounted for by its Bull Run casualties. The Second's strength report was also complicated by the detachment in December of its Company K, organized into heavy artillery. The replacement company, mustered in on December 20th, joined the regiment in camp in January, 1862, increasing the Dane and Milwaukee county representatives in the regiment.[15] In February, 263 of the 3,669 men in the brigade were reported sick. Although measles and other trivial complaints were often at fault, fatalities were not uncommon, as evidenced by the death of almost sixty of the Hoosiers and an additional seventeen men of the Seventh Wisconsin. The death rate was exceeded only by the rate of discharge for illness. In the Sixth Wisconsin alone, eighty-five enlisted men were mustered out during the winter.[16] Neither the hospitals, located in Washington away from the camp,[17] nor the medical staffs were equal to the great and apparently unexpected task the winter presented. Goaded by the shortage of beds, but with what was surely a misplaced zeal, the surgeon of the Sixth Wisconsin wrote that "we have established a rule that profane words shall at once forfeit a place in the hospital."[18] This professional standard presumably went unnoticed by the Medical Director of the Army of the Potomac, but that officer did demand the discharge of the Nineteenth Indiana's surgeon, citing the "incompetency . . . manifested by the medical officers" of the regiment.[19]

The military condition of the men was apparently superior to their physical condition. At least the state of discipline was satisfactory. General McDowell, with a touch of the age-old professional skepticism, reported to the assistant adjutant general of the army that the brigade was "well disciplined for volunteers." The general went on to say with reference to discipline that "the Nineteenth Indiana [was] the least so," without recording any basis for his qualification.[20]

As the winter passed, the Army of the Potomac remained inactive. Except for Ball's Bluff in late October and Roanoke Island in February of 1862, the Eastern theater of the war was quiet. This was not so in the West where a man named Grant appeared at Belmont, Missouri, in November. The name was heard again in February of 1862, and Forts Henry and Donelson and "Unconditional Surrender" Grant entered the national vocabulary. Activity in the West was to flare up again in March, 1862, at Pea Ridge, Arkansas, and New Madrid in Missouri. But McClellan's men whiled away the winter in camp. "A military life in camp is the most monotonous in the world," wrote Dawes to his sister, in the oldest and newest of soldiers' laments. Of course, there were some interesting goings-on. Secretary Seward visited General King, his adjutant general during Seward's days as governor of New York, and Colonel Meredith, just re-elected as Clerk of Wayne County despite his absence in the field, was visited by Interior Secretary Smith, Meredith's Hoosier Republican colleague. Meredith also had an opportunity to talk with Governor Morton on the latter's winter tour of the Indiana encampments. And the Wisconsin soldiers were cheered by the presence of a party from home, including Governor Randall.[21]

Additional amusement for the soldiers was provided by a controversy in the Seventh Wisconsin where Colonel Robinson had brought his family to Arlington Heights for the winter. In the Robinson household was a daughter, Leonora, who soon became the object of the attention of a lieutenant of the Seventh, twenty-five-year-old Hollon Richardson of Company A. From an objective view, Richardson seemed an eligible suitor. A native of Poland, Ohio, where he had been admitted to the bar in 1857, he was the son of a substantial construction contractor who had moved to Chippewa Falls in 1858. The youth also seemed to have good prospects of his own. In 1860, a comparative newcomer, he had been elected prosecuting attorney of

Chippewa County. As the first man to enlist from that county, his zeal for the war was presumably unquestioned. But none of these things impressed Colonel Robinson, who strenuously objected to Richardson's interest in his daughter, and forbade the two to see each other. Armed with parental authority over his daughter and military jurisdiction over Richardson, the colonel may have felt more secure than most fathers in this age-old situation. But Robinson was defeated when Richardson and the girl eloped to Washington and were married. When the lieutenant returned to his regiment, the soldiers must have waited for the colonel's next move. No further record exists of the event, and there is nothing to show whether Robinson changed his mind or was simply resigned to an accomplished fact. But Lieutenant Richardson remained with the Seventh, and he and Colonel Robinson apparently worked together harmoniously, as their records were later to testify.[22]

More significant than Hollon Richardson's love affair was the return to the brigade of prisoners exchanged during the winter. In January a group of men from the Second, captured at Bull Run, arrived from Richmond, an occasion that provoked a gala reunion. As evidence that the war was young, the returning men were well and "don't look so bad," as one of their comrades phrased it. In April, twenty-three more of the Second put in their appearance, and another celebration took place. Just previously, in March, a lieutenant of the Nineteenth Indiana, captured at Lewinsville, had been exchanged. Released after several months in a tobacco warehouse in Richmond, presumably Libby Prison or one of its predecessors, the poor man's homecoming was marred by the command problem his arrival precipitated. During the officer's absence, his place had been filled, with the result that either the ex-prisoner or his replacement was a supernumerary. The returned hero must have been chagrined when Colonel Meredith, pleading "fairness" to the replacement, solicited the governor to transfer the returnee.[23]

Once their camp was erected, the routine for King's soldiers was not a strenuous one. Reveille sounded at 4.00 A.M. and battalion drill got under way at 4:30, followed by breakfast at seven o'clock. At 8:00 there was company drill for an hour and a half, and after supper at seven, a dress parade followed by tattoo at 9:30 P.M. During the free hours of the late morning and afternoon, the soldiers washed their clothes, maintained their guns and equipment, or were at leisure.[24] In November, at Bailey's Cross Roads, the Army of the Potomac staged a grand review. Seventy thousand men paraded before President Lincoln, the members of the cabinet, General McClellan, and distinguished visitors. Again the band of the Sixth Wisconsin, described now by one of their comrades as "execrable" and "eternally playing the Village Quickstep," was disappointing. The mediocrity of the band was usually offset by the excellence of its drum major, "the finest adornment of the regiment," who "snuffs the air and spurns the ground like a war horse." But even the drum major had an off moment at the review. As the band passed the reviewing stand, General McClellan doffed his hat in salute and the drum major dropped the baton.[25] At a later review, Lord Lyons, the British ambassador, was in attendance, along with a number of officers of the British Brigade of Guards. The British delegation highly complimented the troops. They were "equal to the best of the English army in appearance and drill," which may have been more comforting to the Americans than to the visitors, some of whom were spoiling to embrace the Confederate cause.[26]

In their leisure time, the men engaged in a variety of activities. The Second Wisconsin included several men who had been printers in civilian life. They decided to celebrate Benjamin Franklin's birthday in January. Second Lieutenant George H. Otis, who was to finish the war as Major Otis, and G. M. Woodward, then an enlisted man but later to be adjutant of the Second, were in charge of the dinner. Invitations were mailed to various officers in the brigade, without discrimination against the nonprinters. Although General King responded with a cordial letter of regret, Colonels Cutler and O'Connor were on hand, along with Lieutenant Colonel Fairchild and Major Bragg of the Sixth Wisconsin. The affair was held in a hospital tent, with dinner, speeches, and an original poem read by Toastmaster Woodward.[27]

Other soldiers, men with a commercial bent, found time to make an honest dollar. An enlisted man of the Nineteenth Indiana, a lithographer by trade, forwarded to Governor Morton lithographs of General King and Colonel Meredith, "both of which I have had gotten up, and have control of the original plates." To enlarge his trade, the soldier requested from Morton "a good faithful ambrotype or photographic picture of your patriotic, noble self, for similar purposes." Most of the soldiers occupied themselves in less ingenious ways than the Wisconsin printers and the Hoosier lithographer, by playing whist, and chess, and by boxing. Political discussions were also common. In the Sixth Wisconsin, Abolitionist Dawes, Democrat Bragg, and Republican Kellogg were frequently together, and a three-cornered argument was always available. Others of the men sang, and one company organized a choir. The same company spent $250 on books.[28] Other agreeable pursuits were available at the nearby farms. As one of the Wisconsin soldiers described it, "When we get out from camp we make tolerably free with secesh pigs and hens. . . . Will and Lew and I and three or four more went out and confiscated 7 hens, a pig and a yearling beef."[29] All of these activities were essential to morale. Gambling was officially discouraged and passes to Washington were restricted, not because of any anticipated movement of the army, but because the officers sought to protect their men from the thieves, prostitutes and other bad companions waiting in that city.[30]

The big event of the winter was the association of King's Brigade with Battery B of the Fourth United States Artillery. This story had its beginning in April of 1861, when a pony express rider galloped over the sagebrush plain from Fort Kearny on the Platte River to Camp Floyd in Utah Territory where Battery B was stationed, on the watch against Mormon troubles. As the pony rider neared the post trader's store, he saw on the roof the usual group of soldiers waiting, and as he drew nearer to the camp he could hear over the hoofbeats the soldiers' cry, "Here he comes!" Soon he was reining in, opening the mailbag, and confronting his eager audience with the momentous news that the South had fired on Fort Sumter. Anxious weeks followed as the story unfolded of the fall of Sumter and the call for troops. Some of the men in Battery B were Southerners. Suspicion and mistrust ran through the battery. Several of the Southerners resigned at once and headed for home, while for others from the South there was an agony of soul searching before a decision as to paramount loyalty was reached. But there was neither suspicion nor soul searching on the part of one of the Southerners, Captain John Gibbon, the commander of Battery B. Gibbon was for the Union, and that was that.

Although born in Holmesburg, now a part of Philadelphia, John Gibbon had moved to North Carolina as a child and had been appointed to West Point from that state. He had remained in the army after graduation from the academy in the class of 1847, the class of General Ambrose E. Burnside and Confederate Generals A. P. Hill and Henry Heth of Virginia. Gibbon's military experience included a term as an artillery instructor at West Point, and he had written and published an artillery manual. He had participated in General Winfield Scott's campaign in Mexico and had also seen service in the Seminole Indian War. Gibbon's second in command in Battery B was First Lieutenant Joseph B. Campbell, twenty-five years old and appointed to West Point from New Hampshire. The battery orderly sergeant was James Stewart, who was later to command the battery, and distinguish himself in doing so.

Orders at last came to Camp Floyd directing Battery B to St. Louis for further orders. Packing up their wives, children, and military gear, the soldiers started on foot across the twelve hundred miles to Fort Leavenworth. En route, the party learned of Bull Run from another pony express dispatch. At Leavenworth, John Gibbon heard for the last time from his family in North Carolina. His three brothers were soon to enter the Confederate army, and the family reunion was not to occur until 1865.[31]

Gibbon's Battery did not arrive in Washington until October, 1861. There it was assigned to McDowell's Division. Like all of the regular army batteries, Battery B was short almost half of its authorized complement of 152 men. In November, McClellan authorized the regular batteries to recruit infantry volunteers from the divisions to which the batteries were attached. John Gibbon visited the regiments of McDowell's Division and picked his artillerymen himself. The men were lined up, and volunteers were asked to step forward. Then Gibbon walked down the ranks and made his selections. The same recruiting process was to be repeated, with the result that from November, 1861, until June, 1862, King's regiments and the New York regiments of the division contributed more than fifty of their number to Battery B. Later, more men from King's regiments went into Battery B, and the transfers were to continue throughout the long association of the battery and the regiments of King's Brigade.

Battery B was a fortunate influence for the Wisconsin and Indiana regiments. They found themselves associated with a military company that was honorable and, by American standards, historic. The Fourth United States Artillery was organized in March of 1821. Battery B had participated in the Florida war of 1837. It was at Odgensburg in 1842 and 1843, when Canadian frontier trouble was threatening. In 1845 the battery was in General Taylor's "Army of Observation" at the Rio Grande, and during the Mexican War its guns had performed distinguished service at Buena Vista.[32]

Captain Gibbon and the artillery regulars were also pleased. Gibbon observed that these volunteers were "the finest material for soldiers I ever saw," and that the "first marked feature I noted with these men was their quick intelligence. It was only necessary to explain a thing but once or twice to enable them to catch the idea and then with a little practice they became perfect." The historian of the battery had additional comments about the new artillerymen: "The detached volunteers of 1861 were all young men, fresh from the farms, sawmills and work shops of New York, Wisconsin and Indiana, who had been accustomed to hard work for an honest livelihood, respected themselves, valued their reputations, had honorable ambitions, were keenly solicitous about 'what the folks at home will say about us,' and were ready to fight anything on earth at any time or in any shape!" This, of course, was all to the good. The historian continued: "This was splendid raw material, but it had to be handled 'right side up with care' for the young farmers and lumbermen from Wisconsin, Indiana and New York were 'quick on the trigger' and would not take any nonsense from anybody, with or without shoulder straps." Captain Gibbon was to find himself even more intimately associated with the men from Wisconsin and Indiana a few months later when he assumed command of King's Brigade. But in approaching them as artillerymen, he displayed a fine psychological insight. Gibbon placed small national flags on the battery's six brass guns— twelve-pounder Napoleon smoothbores—and had the flags inscribed with the names of the states from which his new artillerymen had come. Then he told the men: "These guns belong to your states, it is your duty to defend them."[33]

As the winter ended, the Northern high command debated the question of what to do with McClellan's army. These debates and the Confederates' inconsiderate withdrawal from their Manassas line resulted in the Peninsula Campaign of 1862. But of the debates, the common soldier knew nothing. On Washington's birthday King's Brigade drew up in close column before the broad portico of Arlington. Washington's Farewell Address was read to the men. General King then spoke, surrounded by the regimental field officers: Meredith, Bachman, and May of the Nineteenth; O'Connor, Fairchild, and Allen of the Second; Cutler, Sweet, and Bragg of the Sixth; and Robinson, Hamilton, and Bill of the Seventh. After the general's remarks, a salute was fired. Except for target practice, it was the only shooting of the winter for King's Brigade.[34]

FREDERICKSBURG:
A NEW COMMANDER ORDERS BLACK HATS

"Brig. Gen. John Gibbon, U.S. Volunteers, is assigned to the command of the Third Brigade, of King's Division . . ."
Special Orders, No. 46,
Department of the Rappahannock, May 7, 1862

While the Army of the Potomac wintered in the Washington area, the principal enemy forces in the East were concentrated at Manassas, Leesburg, and Centreville, Virginia, with Stonewall Jackson's command holding the Confederate left at Winchester, in the Shenandoah Valley.* All of these troops composed the Confederate Army of Northern Virginia, General Joseph E. Johnston commanding. As the winter drew to an end, Lincoln reluctantly accepted General McClellan's plan to flank this Confederate army and to move toward Richmond by water. But the President was firm on one condition—sufficient troops were to be left in the Washington area to protect that city and, assuming that the Confederates withdrew when McClellan moved, to occupy the important railroad center at Manassas. This condition, and the manner in which McClellan interpreted it, were to play a large part in shaping the career of Rufus King's Wisconsin and Indiana soldiers during the spring and summer of 1862.

On March 8th, anticipating the coming campaign, the President directed the establishment of the corps organization of the Army of the Potomac. McDowell's Division and the divisions of Generals George A. McCall and William B. Franklin formed the First Corps. The command of the corps was assigned to McDowell, and Rufus

* For locations mentioned in this and the immediately following paragraphs, see back end paper and map at page 116.

King was promoted to the vacant post of division commander. King's old brigade was temporarily commanded by Colonel Lysander Cutler of the Sixth Wisconsin, the senior colonel of the brigade. In King's Division, the Wisconsin and Indiana soldiers maintained their distinction as Westerners. The remaining brigades assigned to King, under Brigadier Generals Christopher C. Augur and Marsena R. Patrick, were composed of New York regiments. But Gibbon's Battery B remained as part of the divisional artillery, along with volunteer batteries from Rhode Island, New Hampshire and Pennsylvania.[1]

On the day following the President's order directing the corps organization, word reached Washington of the Confederate withdrawal from northern Virginia to the area of Gordonsville, on the line of the Rappahannock River. General McClellan at once ordered an advance on Centreville, Manassas, and Leesburg, and on March 10th Cutler's Brigade joined the rest of the army in the forward movement. Cutler's men camped the first night just west of Fairfax Court House and reached Centreville the following day. There they unmasked absent and defective fortifications, "Quaker" guns of logs, and the leavings of a much smaller enemy than McClellan had believed to be opposed to him. Although a fanciful Wisconsin soldier wrote home about the Confederate atrocities and grave desecrations that were uncovered, including candlesticks made from the skulls of Federal dead, the only real excitement was provided by great fires started by the Confederates to destroy their abandoned stores of food and material. This excitement was soon over, and the outing ended for Cutler's Brigade on March 15th. On that day the brigade marched in a heavy rain toward Alexandria, and the next day found the men back in their old camp on Arlington Heights.[2]

On March 17th the Army of the Potomac began to embark for Fortress Monroe and McClellan's famous Peninsula Campaign. Cutler's Brigade accompanied the First Corps to Alexandria, where the soldiers encamped for two weeks while the rest of the army was shipped out. But after all of the waiting, McDowell was directed to march his men to Fairfax Seminary, and on April 1st his corps was officially detached from the Army of the Potomac.[3] The President's retention of the thirty thousand men of the First Corps on the line of the Potomac was one of the bitterly debated issues of the war. Whether or not Lincoln was right about the insecurity of the Capital,

his decision deprived Cutler's Brigade of a part in the 1862 campaign before Richmond. The divisions of Franklin and McCall were later to go to the Peninsula. Indeed, General Franklin's division almost immediately rejoined the Army of the Potomac there. But King's Division, after several false starts, was to miss the campaign.

McClellan arrived in front of Yorktown on the Peninsula on April 6th, and promptly employed his superior army in a siege of that poorly defended place. On the same day, a thousand miles away, the Confederate army of General Albert Sydney Johnston struck th encampment of General Grant at Pittsburg Landing in the fir great battle of the West. And later in the same month, New Orlea the South's greatest port, was to fall to Federal arms. For the r little while the principal activities of the war were to center on Peninsula in the East and in northern Mississippi in the West, l complicated and dangerous drama was to be played out in nor Virginia.

McClellan's movement to the Peninsula, and Johnston' drawal to defend Richmond, left other forces of both sides e in Virginia. For the Union, the largest unit was General Frémont's Mountain Department, with headquarters at in western Virginia. A second Federal force was comm General Nathaniel P. Banks, head of the Department of t doah. The remaining command was Irvin McDowell's, ment of the Rappahannock, twenty-thousand men, incl Division and McCall's from the First Corps, stationed in of Washington. Opposing these troops were three sma ate commands, General Edward Johnson's near Sta Richard Ewell's at Gordonsville, and Jackson's, which upper Shenandoah Valley. Altogether, the enemy tro were subject to Jackson's direction, numbered 18 Federal departments were directly under the comr Department, General McClellan having been sho general-in-chief in anticipation of his taking the sula Campaign. That campaign was to be th offensive effort in 1862. A defensive employr primary use of Frémont, Banks, and McDowell, ington area. And if the threat of a Confedera was eliminated, McDowell, at least, was to

Richmond. The Confederates' strategy was precisely the reverse of the Federal. They proposed to defend Richmond against McClellan. The Confederates also intended, with the forces of Jackson and Ewell, to threaten Washington, so as to prevent additional Union troops from going to the Peninsula and increasing the already superior Federal force there. In addition, a measure of Confederate success in northern Virginia could result in the detachment of Union forces from McClellan, thus easing the defensive problems on the Peninsula.

In the Federal plan the soldiers under General McDowell were to defend the northern and eastern areas of Virginia. As soon as his department was created, McDowell undertook to advance his divisions from their Alexandria encampment and toward Fredericksburg on the Rappahannock,* selected as the headquarters of McDowell's department. From there to Richmond was but fifty-five miles, with alternative land and water routes. Cutler's Brigade began its southern advance on April 4th, marching for Fairfax Court House and reaching Bristoe Station, just south of Manassas Junction on the Orange and Alexandria Railroad, on April 6th.[5] Here the Westerners remained until April 13th, bogged down in rain, snow, and Virginia mud. The rain was so intense that the soldiers were confined to their tents for days at a time. The tents were those officially known as "shelter tents," but better known as "pup tents." One of Cutler's soldiers tried to fathom the usefulness of his pup tent, and after noting that it was necessary to crawl into the tent on his knees, he concluded that it was the invention of a preacher who wanted the soldiers occasionally to assume the posture of prayer. It was not enough simply to be confined to the tents while it rained. Rufus Dawes found that after the rains his boots were so wet that he could not get them on, which necessitated more confinement until the boots dried out. But the rains finally abated, and Cutler resumed his march southward to Catlett's Station, where the soldiers were employed for a week in repairs to the Orange and Alexandria Railroad.[6]

While the Wisconsin and Indiana men worked on the railroad, other of the brigades of King's Division, General Augur's New

* The march to Falmouth may be followed by reference to the maps pages 73 and 48.

Officers of the Iron Brigade

RUFUS KING, the first commander.

John Gibbon, second commander of the brigade.

SOLOMON MEREDITH, the third and last commander.

EDGAR O'CONNOR, Second
Wisconsin Vounteers.
Library of Congress

LYSANDER CUTLER, Sixth Wisconsin
Volunteers.
State Historical Society of Wisconsin

THOMAS S. ALLEN, Second
Wisconsin Volunteers.
Library of Congress

ALOIS O. BACHMAN, Nineteenth
Indiana Volunteers.

ALBERT M. EDWARDS, Twenty-
fourth Michigan Volunteers.
Michigan Historical Commission Archives

JOHN M. LINDLEY, Nineteenth
Indiana Volunteers.
Indiana State Library

DENNIS B. DAILEY, Second and
Sixth Wisconsin Volunteers.

HOLLON RICHARDSON, Seventh
Wisconsin Volunteers.
State Historical Society of Wisconsin

RUFUS R. DAWES, Sixth Wisconsin
Volunteers.

JOHN A. KELLOGG, Sixth Wisconsin
Volunteers.
State Historical Society of Wisconsin

JOHN B. CALLIS, Seventh
Wisconsin Volunteers.
State Historical Society of Wisconsin

WILLIAM W. DUDLEY, Nineteenth
Indiana Volunteers.
State Historical Society of Wisconsin

GEORGE H. STEVENS, Second
Wisconsin Volunteers.
State Historical Society of Wisconsin

WILLIAM HUTCHINSON, Twenty-
fourth Michigan Volunteers.
Michigan Archives

MARK FLANIGAN, Twenty-fourth
Michigan Volunteers.
Library of Congress

EDWARD S. BRAGG, Sixth Wisconsin
Volunteers.
State Historical Society of Wisconsin

SAMUEL J. WILLIAMS, Nineteenth
Indiana Volunteers.
Indiana State Library

LUCIUS FAIRCHILD, Second
Wisconsin Volunteers.
State Historical Society of Wisconsin

Yorkers, made a forced march to Falmouth, across the river from Fredericksburg. On the morning of April 18th, Augur pushed into Falmouth and routed the Confederate forces there, but not in time to save either of the bridges, which the Confederates successfully fired with tar and shavings. The Confederates withdrew to a point seven miles south of Fredericksburg, where their commander reported to General Richard Ewell. On the same day a citizen of Fredericksburg described the surrender of that city. A committee representing the mayor and council had met with General Augur with the result, according to the citizen, that "we are in the hands of the Philistines."[7]

On April 23rd the Philistines were reinforced when Cutler's Brigade marched into Falmouth, to find "nearly every white woman . . . crying . . . and all the darkies . . . dancing for joy."[8] The Wisconsin and Indiana soldiers could look across the river to Fredericksburg, a beautiful and historic town and not yet a name associated with heroism and death. Behind the town rose a series of rolling hills, one of which, Marye's Hill, was later to see much of the war. Beyond this high ground was the Wilderness, also a future battleground. The Western soldiers were impressed with the wealth and age of the area, one of them writing that it was "the greatest old foggy place i ever saw, everything has went on from year to year the same . . . the residences of the planters are magnificent and the grounds and walks are all that wealth and taste can make them." But the same soldier was struck with the provincialism of the people, "the most ignorant of any place i have been, they were born and raised here and have never been anywhere else, i have seen old men . . . that told me they were never ten miles from home in their lives, and they know nothing of what is going on, they have never heard of such a state as Wisconsin, and didn't know whether it was a state, county or city."[9]

Having collected his forces at Falmouth, McDowell was now anxious to cross the Rappahannock and occupy Fredericksburg. He understood that there were large quantities of stores there that were daily being shipped south, as well as Union men who sought to be protected from harassment by the secession citizenry and Confederate cavalry. But on April 24th Secretary Stanton advised McDowell against crossing the river. Instead, he was to rebuild the destroyed

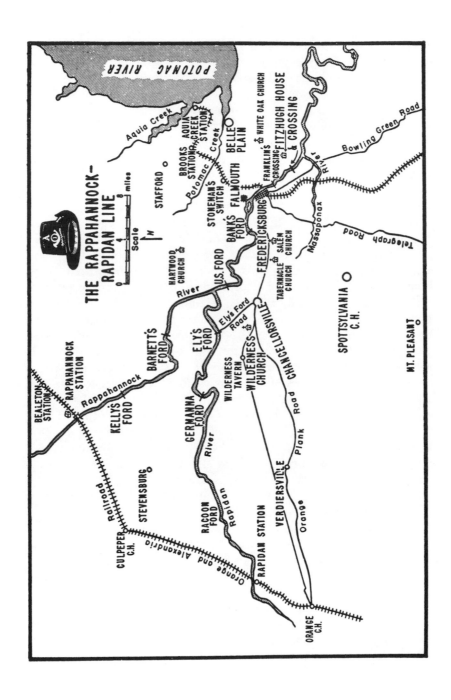

bridges and await further orders. McDowell had more than enough bridgebuilders available, and the Wisconsin and Indiana men built a pole trestle over Potomac Creek and helped with a similar bridge over the Rappahannock.[10] On April 30th, while the bridgebuilding continued, McDowell received authority from Washington to occupy Fredericksburg, although he was expressly prohibited from undertaking any additional forward movement. Two days later General King reported on the completion of the Rappahannock bridge and announced that an infantry company had marched into Fredericksburg. King and General Patrick visited the town, selected posts for sentinels and pickets, and conferred briefly with the mayor.[11]

The first week of May brought an end to the stalemate on the Peninsula. Having successfully stalled McClellan's army while preparing the Richmond defenses, the Confederates evacuated Yorktown, and on May 6th Williamsburg fell to McClellan, and the Confederates retreated farther up the Peninsula. There was also action in Frémont's Mountain Department, where Stonewall Jackson fought an indecisive affair at the town of McDowell, Virginia, on May 8th. But although McDowell was anxious and the Confederate cavalry was active in the area, the common soldier was at rest and apparently free from either arduous duties or the risks of combat. For the Western soldiers, this was becoming the rule and not the exception, and it appeared as if they never were to get into the real war. Indeed, so sheltered were their lives that the march to Falmouth was actually regarded as hard service, one of them writing that it "was the toughest i ever seen, in fact i would not have believed men could stand what we have stood . . . without getting sick and perfectly used up."[12]

In Fredericksburg, McDowell's men took over the town, operating the wagon, blacksmith, and other mechanical shops. Some of Cutler's men took possession of the newspaper plant and briefly published a newspaper of their own, *The Christian Banner*, printed on brown wrapping paper. The town, of course, was extremely hostile to the invaders. The women—"the finest looking women . . . I ever seen,"[13] according to a homesick Wisconsin soldier—preferred walking in the muddy streets to walking under the United States flag hanging over the sidewalks. Cutler's men also went to church in Fredericksburg, or at least the enlisted men were taken to church by their officers.

Dawes reported that a private from his company had escaped from one such detail. Apprehended and permitted to meditate his sins in the guardhouse, the soldier later stated that church was the lesser of two evils. In spite of the Confederate sentiments of the congregations, the soldiers were generous when the plate was passed. But they were not so generous when a minister omitted from the service the usual prayer for the President of the United States. After church a committee of the soldiers waited upon him to advise that his church would be burned down if he failed on the following Sunday to pray for the President. The cleric was a man of discretion, and the prayer was included in the next service; but from the tone of the parson's voice, one of the Westerners stated that he doubted if the prayer "got high enough for the Lord to hear it."

The soldiers also had economic problems in Fredericksburg. Prices were high. A pound of tea sold for seven dollars. In addition, the Confederate storekeepers would not accept United States funds, and the soldiers would not recognize Confederate currency. But Yankee ingenuity was not long daunted, and the soldiers were soon counterfeiting Confederate money in large quantities, thus solving both the difficulties of high prices and exchange. Counterfeit Confederate money was produced in such profusion that it sold for ten cents per thousand dollars, and for a while the Confederate storekeepers were doing a thriving business. But the fraud soon came to the attention of the Union authorities and, in an example of the paradoxical morality of the Civil War, strict orders were issued against counterfeiting.[14]

At Fredericksburg the Western brigade acquired its second permanent commander in the person of artilleryman John Gibbon, now a brigadier general of volunteers. Colonel Cutler returned to the Sixth Wisconsin. Gibbon selected First Lieutenant Frank A. Haskell from the Sixth as his aide and Captain J. P. Wood of the Nineteenth Indiana as brigade adjutant. Gibbon's promotion left a vacancy in the command of Battery B, which was filled by Gibbon's fellow West Pointer, Joseph B. Campbell, formerly second-in-command of the battery.[15]

John Gibbon's promotion had not been easy. With McDowell's endorsement, his nomination for the brigadier's commission had been sent to the United States Senate along with other nominees.

But the artilleryman was passed over by the Senate because of the temporary absence from that politically sensitive body of any senators looking after the interests of deserving North Carolinians. Surely Gibbon had not anticipated this difficulty when he cast his lot with the Union in 1861. In addition to having his family divided against him, it seemed that his career might be halted because of his Southern origin. When he heard the news, Gibbon talked to General James S. Wadsworth, a politically influential New Yorker, and Wadsworth promptly activated his own Senate friends in Gibbon's behalf. Shortly thereafter, the nomination was confirmed, and this impediment to Gibbon's career was not to reappear.[16]

"Bland and genial" had been the adjectives applied to General Rufus King by an officer of the Western brigade.[17] He had been universally liked as brigade commander, "a plain, common man, [who] will listen to the complaint of a private as soon as he will to a colonel."[18] John Gibbon was, to say the least, not "bland," and he certainly made no particular effort to be genial. He was, in short, a thorough soldier. To Gibbon, the men of the brigade were not, of course, entirely unknown quantities. He had already commanded some of their comrades in Battery B. In the first few days of his new command, Gibbon was confirmed in his opinion of these volunteers. If nothing else, they were intelligent and eager, more so than the regulars of Gibbon's experience. The new commander saw his task as simply making first-rate soldiers from first-rate raw material.

At the outset, the Wisconsin and Indiana men had some habits that professional soldier Gibbon would not tolerate. Among their minor vices was the stealing of fences either for fuel or for shelter, or out of pure mischief. This was against the rules, whether or not the victim of the theft was Confederate in his sympathies. Gibbon instituted a simple but effective solution. When a fence was torn down, the regiment camped nearest to it was required to rebuild it. Though the rebuilding of fences infuriated the soldiers, fence stealing was thereafter on the wane. The general took a more affirmative approach in efforts to encourage soldierly bearing and appearance at inspection and drill. He instituted a policy of giving the well-turned-out soldier a twenty-four-hour pass for blackberrying, and discovered that this worked miracles in the appearance of the men. Gibbon also instituted more rigid regulations for sentries. They were thereafter to walk their posts, to "be alive" and to salute all officers. The first offender after the publication of this order was punished by being ordered to sit all day on a barrel in front of the guard tent. The more Gibbon saw, the more he came to believe that, contrary to the tradition of the regular army, a system of awards for achievement, and penalties to hurt their *pride*, were the keys to discipline among his volunteers.[19] Gibbon was also dissatisfied with the standard of drill. After the war, a veteran of the brigade remembered the early days of Gibbon's command. "There were early morning drills, before breakfast, forenoon drills, afternoon drills, evening and night drills, beside guard mounting and dress parades."[20] At first the general did not conduct brigade drill. Then one day he overheard two of his soldiers talking. According to one of them, Gibbon was "only an artillery officer" and didn't know anything about infantry drill. Stung by this remark, Gibbon acquired a manual on brigade drill and was soon proving the soldier wrong.[21]

The new general also had work to do among the officers of the brigade. He formed immediately favorable impressions of Colonel O'Connor of the Second Wisconsin and Colonel Cutler of the Sixth. In O'Connor, Gibbon recognized the West Point training and spirit. Cutler he found to be mature and of soldierly disposition. But the general discovered that none of the officers attended reveille, and an immediate and peremptory order put a stop to this and also assisted in convincing the enlisted men that the new general was not so bad after all. Much more serious was an incident in the Sixth Wisconsin, where Colonel Cutler and Lieutenant Colonel Sweet were in deep disagreement. Sweet had apparently stated openly to his fellow officers that one of Colonel Cutler's written orders contained a falsehood. Cutler had preferred charges against Sweet, and the officers of the regiment and of other regiments in the brigade were beginning to implicate themselves in the dispute. John Gibbon was in a ticklish position. He believed that there was already some dissatisfaction about his appointment to the command. As Gibbon understood it, this dissatisfaction stemmed from the fact that he was neither a Westerner nor a volunteer officer, while his brigade was both Western and volunteer. The general believed that Colonel Meredith was largely responsible for disseminating this feeling, and for this he was, of course, unfavorably disposed toward Meredith.

Now it seemed that he had the makings of a first-class command problem, and would be damned by one or another group of his subordinate officers whichever way he turned.

Gibbon first interviewed Colonel Cutler, and sensed that Cutler, regardless of the merits of the dispute, was motivated by personal feelings and was overly sensitive of his prerogatives as colonel. Gibbon then talked with Lieutenant Colonel Sweet, who openly condemned Cutler for being arbitrary and tryannical, and stated that he would resign and go home before submitting to such an officer. Finally, Gibbon talked to Major Bragg. Although the major disliked Cutler—he had written that he was "gruff and gouty and when roused . . . emitted a grunt, like an enraged porker"—his response to Gibbon was candid and straightforward and won for Bragg the confidence of the general. With the reports before him, Gibbon addressed a carefully worded letter to Colonel Cutler, opening with the statement that the remark attributed to Sweet about Cutler's order was incorrect and that Cutler's order was proper in all respects. The general proceeded to note his observation of "a state of feeling existing among some of the officers of your regiment which is much to be deplored." But, wrote Gibbon, this state of affairs had better be kept from publication and he was not disposed to forward the charges against Sweet for trial because this would require a tedious investigation. Gibbon closed by saying that his action was not to be interpreted as indicating any desire to shield an officer from punishment justly due for an act of disrespect to his commanding officer, and he authorized Cutler to read the communication to the officers of the regiment. As Gibbon had hoped, his letter worked. Cutler, a man of ambition, did not proceed further with the matter, and Lieutenant Colonel Sweet, also ambitious, apparently took steps to avoid his predicament. Approximately a month after the incident, Sweet was to leave the Sixth Wisconsin. But he did not leave in disgrace. Instead, he became the colonel of the Twenty-first Wisconsin Volunteers.[22]

Having solved his command problems, Gibbon turned again to the drill, discipline, and appearance of his brigade. He issued an order requiring the men to procure an entirely new uniform. This was largely that of the regular army, the dark blue single-breasted frock coat with light blue collar trim and reaching almost to the knees, and light blue trousers. The men were also required to obtain white leggings and white cotton gloves, the latter for dress. But most distinctive was the hat. In place of the typical kepi, the men donned the black felt Hardee hat of the regulars, ordinarily worn turned up on the left side and with a great black plume on the right side. Although the Westerners liked the looks of the new uniforms—"they look gay," was the comment of one of the men—there was grumbling because the new outfit depleted their clothing allowance, which, if not expended, was available in cash at the end of the year. But the protests were confined to a youthful prank. One morning the general found his horse equipped with white leggings.[23] Time and fortune were to wear out much of the new clothing of Gibbon's Brigade. But the black hats were to become their trademark.

As the men were drawing their new clothes at Fredericksburg, the Army of the Potomac was slowly moving up the Peninsula toward Richmond. In the West, General Henry W. Halleck's army was inching its way toward Corinth, Mississippi, with U. S. Grant in eclipse as Halleck's deputy commander. With everything quiet in northern Virginia, McDowell was preparing to join McClellan. McCall's and King's divisions of the old First Corps were not so large as they had been earlier in the year. The effects of inadequate physical requirements for enlistments, poor sanitation, and primitive medical knowledge had already taken a heavy toll in sickness and death. The four regiments of Gibbon's Brigade had an original recruitment strength of just over 4,000 men. From this number the Second Wisconsin's Bull Run losses had been deducted. But a consolidated morning report in the middle of 1862, before the brigade had been engaged in combat, showed but 2,800 men present for duty. Of the rest, some were dead, some were on detached service, and the majority had been discharged because of illness.[24]

The experience of Gibbon's Brigade was typical of McDowell's two divisions, which meant that he needed substantial reinforcements if he was to be a strong presence at Richmond. On May 16th a new division was assigned to him, composed of two brigades of infantry and a cavalry brigade under the command of Major General Edward O. Ord. McDowell also acquired two more infantry brigades, one commanded by General Abner Doubleday, the other by General John W. Geary. In addition, the division of General James Shields, detached from General Banks' Department of the Shenandoah, was ordered to move to Fredericksburg. With these reinforcements, Mc-Dowell's present-for-duty strength was increased to 42,000 men.

On May 17th McDowell was advised by Secretary Stanton that he was to move overland to Richmond as soon as he was joined by Shields' Division. Five days later, the advance of Shields' Division pushed into Falmouth. Shields' soldiers were badly used up and in need of shoes, trousers, supplies, and ammunition, and McDowell proceeded at once to outfit them for the march to Richmond.[25] On observing his new companions, one of Gibbon's men recorded that Shields' were "the dirtiest ragamuffins" that he had ever seen. As ragamuffins are wont to do when they associate with the well-dressed, Shields' soldiers christened Gibbon's newly outfitted soldiers the "bandbox brigade." And as the well-dressed do when taunted in this way, Gibbon's Brigade retorted that they would "rather wear leggings than be lousy."[26]

Shields' rear guard pounded into Falmouth on May 23rd. They were not the only arrivals that day. President Lincoln, Secretary Stanton, and their party also arrived. The President reviewed the troops and received the general officers at the Lacy House, a large mansion directly across the river from Fredericksburg, used by McDowell as his headquarters. Here John Gibbon shook the homely President's hand and was asked by him if the general had written *The Decline and Fall of the Roman Empire*. Lincoln made another obvious joke or two which didn't much impress General Gibbon, but which, so the general later recalled, somehow broke the ice and put everyone at ease.[27] With Lincoln's blessing, it was decided that McDowell's movement to Richmond would commence at once and that King's Division was to lead the advance. The order convinced Gibbon's soldiers that, having seen them, the President knew that they were the ones who could capture Richmond.[28] But McDowell's march to Richmond was precisely what the Confederate command proposed to prevent. Stonewall Jackson had lingered in the upper Shenandoah Valley after the engagement at McDowell, Virginia. Now he was reinforced by parts of Ewell's force. He knew, too, that Banks was without Shields' Division. On May 23rd, even as McDowell and the President were discussing the move to Richmond, Jackson struck Front Royal, overwhelmed Banks' small garrison, and seized the Federals' supplies and stores accumulated there. Banks' main body, at Strasburg, at once undertook a retreat down the valley, closely pursued by Jackson and skirmishing with him all the way, to Winchester and then to Martinsburg. On May 26th Banks crossed the Potomac at Williamsport, and escaped annihilation.*

Jackson's movement immediately had its desired effect. On May 24th the President ordered McDowell to "lay aside for the present" the march to Richmond and to send twenty thousand men at once to the Shenandoah Valley. Eight miles south of Fredericksburg, Gibbon's men learned of McDowell's bewildering order to halt, and on the 29th the division was ordered to return to Fredericksburg and to march northward with all speed to Catlett's Station. That night, Gibbon's soldiers set down their sixty pounds of weapons and equipment six miles north of Fredericksburg, after a fourteen-mile march in the broiling sun.[29]

The northward march of King's Division was but a small part of McDowell's complicated disposition of his troops in the desperate attempt to trap Stonewall Jackson. On May 30th, en route to Catlett's, King was ordered to march to Front Royal. McDowell closed his order with this flourish: "If I have my old division we will whip them. The whole country is looking with anxiety and hope." Then he added a tidbit of pure good news—Corinth, Mississippi, had been evacuated to Halleck, and the Union was continuing its advance in the West.[30]

McDowell's heroic sense was not wasted on the grandson of Rufus King of the Continental Congress. He advised McDowell that his infantry soldiers would reach Catlett's by the morning of the 31st, and he added that McDowell's "news will stir them up."[31] King then proceeded to do a little stirring up of his own. Gibbon's Brigade took the road at 8:30 A.M. on the 30th, to pursue their most grueling march to date. It was one of those humid days with intermittent rainstorms which ruined the roads but did not mitigate the heat. The soldiers had not gone far before they began to shed their excess equipment, "issuing overcoats to the rebel cavalry," they called it, but even with their lightened burden many men simply could not make it. In the Sixth Wisconsin 150 men fell by the roadside, later to revive and

* For locations mentioned in connection with Jackson's movements, see back end paper and maps at pages 73 and 116.

catch up with the column as it went into camp. The signs of comradeship that combat soldiers begin to feel for one another cropped out on the march. Abe Fletcher, one of the big and rugged pinery men from the Sixth's Company K, carried his own knapsack. But he also carried two more, belonging to less favored of his companions. Hugh Talty, the smallest man in the Sixth, also carried an extra knapsack as he slogged along in his too big uniform, keeping up a steady stream of insolent and humorous remarks. Talty and Mickey Sullivan were the Irish wits of the regiment, and Talty was having one of his better days. A high light of the march was the sight of a real live Confederate soldier, a deserter from Jackson's forces. The Federals could only agree with the deserter's comparison of the competing armies: "You uns is pack mules, we uns is race horses." Indeed, a Wisconsin soldier had already written, "For God's sake kill us off in battle and don't do us to death as pack mules." King finally halted his suffering column six miles from Catlett's Station. The men had marched a hard twenty miles in one day, which was not bad for garrison soldiers.[32]

When King's infantry arrived at Catlett's on May 31st, new orders were received from McDowell. The division was to entrain for Piedmont, just five miles from Front Royal. McDowell warned King that he would be fired on between Catlett's and Thoroughfare and that beyond Thoroughfare the railroad grades were so steep that the men would have to leave the train while it ascended. King at once directed the loading of Augur's and Patrick's brigades, at the same time informing McDowell that the first brigades were loading and that Gibbon's men would bring up the rear. There were sufficient cars for Augur's men and two of Patrick's regiments, and these troops shipped out under Augur's command while King, Gibbon, and Patrick and the remaining regiments waited for more rolling stock. On the following morning, still waiting for the expected railroad cars for his infantry, King dispatched his cavalry, artillery, and trains on foot to Haymarket and Thoroughfare Gap, there to await further orders.[33]

While King was striving to reach the scene of action, Stonewall Jackson, assisted by torrential rains and Federal errors, was effecting his escape. On June 1st the Confederates moved through Strasburg, slipped between the jaws of the Federal forces, and passed on up the

valley. Still waiting for rolling stock at Catlett's, King learned the
bad news when McDowell, instructing him to halt his movement,
wired that "the enemy has flown."[34] At about the same time King
probably also learned of an action that had begun on the Peninsula
on May 31st, the Battle of Fair Oaks, in which General Joseph E.
Johnston had attacked McClellan. The affair was renewed on a
smaller scale on June 1st, but the results of both days' fighting were
indecisive, except that Johnston was severely wounded and was soon
replaced by General Robert E. Lee as commander of the Army of
Northern Virginia. Pursued by Frémont, Shields, and Banks, Jackson
may also have learned of Fair Oaks and Johnston's wound, as he
moved up the valley to perfect his escape, on June 8th and 9th, with
the engagements at Cross Keys and Port Republic.

With his command divided—part at Front Royal and part waiting
at Catlett's—King had been completely left out of the movement
against Jackson after the June 1st escape at Strasburg. Now he got his
command together and, after some uncertainty, received orders for
his division to move back to the Rappahannock.[35] Gibbon's Brigade
arrived at Falmouth in time to witness the departure for the Peninsula of the last regiments of McCall's Division.[36] Lieutenant Colonel
Sweet was now transferred to command of the Twenty-first Wisconsin, and Major Bragg moved up to replace him as lieutenant colonel.
The filling of the major's place was not so simple. Rufus Dawes had
the best paper claim, because he was the senior captain. But his
seniority was only technical because the relative seniority of the captains had been settled by the drawing of lots. Colonel Cutler also
had a candidate. He wanted Captain Frank A. Haskell as his major
and he sought to mitigate Dawes' seniority claim by assembling and
polling the officers. Much politicking preceded the officers' caucus.
When the votes were counted, Dawes was the winner, by fourteen
votes to thirteen. The political maneuvering for the commission was
not confined to Falmouth. In Madison, the partisans of Dawes and
Haskell besieged the governor, urging one or another of the men for
advancement. Finally, the governor decided, and Rufus Dawes became the major of the regiment.[37]

The political fireworks that had surrounded the promotion of
Rufus Dawes was not by any means an unusual phenomenon. In
Gibbon's regiments, and presumably throughout the army, the pre-

occupation with advancement, even at the noncommissioned level, was a principal pastime. Everyone—friends, relatives, army comrades —participated, and no military situation was so critical that it postponed hostilities over who was to receive what rank. For the soldier in the field, seeking advancement, a common technique was to activate the prominent civilians from his community. These men in turn waited on the governor, often bombarding him with politically coercive messages. Typical was the work of a Kendallville, Indiana, banker, a party stalwart to whom the governor was doubtless indebted politically. In interceding for a captain in the Nineteenth Indiana, the banker put the governor on the defensive with a note which stated that "he is from my district and [you] cannot deal falsely with him."[38] Another accepted method required the aspiring officer to insist that the vacant post be filled by a vote of the other officers, but only, of course, if a poll indicated that this technique assured victory. A third point of view—respected by senior officers and decried by the juniors—demanded that seniority should govern promotions, and this method, though often violated, was widely observed. But because there were always rivals for each vacancy, a combination of all techniques was invoked in each dispute, with the result that there was neither a consistent nor a logical pattern, even within a particular regiment. The good will of the regimental commander was, of course, a valuable asset to an ambitious lieutenant or captain. By definition, the colonel was already influential with the state administration, as his own commission testified. Moreover, a bewildered governor, harried on all sides by conflicting claims, was often willing to fall back on the colonel for advice as to whom he should promote. In the case of Rufus Dawes, Governor Randall passed over Lysander Cutler's wishes, but a strong stand by a strong colonel often carried the question.[39]

When the politicking in the Sixth Wisconsin subsided, Gibbon's men had a chance to think over their recent experiences. The abortive movement to catch Stonewall Jackson was looked back on in anger. For reasons that they themselves probably could not have explained, Gibbon's soldiers held McDowell responsible for the failure. They argued that he was at least incompetent. Some even believed that he was disloyal.[40] John Gibbon did not share these views, but he had his own critical ideas of the situation. He reasoned that the Federals' failure was the result of bungling by the Washington administration, which had made the strategic decisions and directed the troop movements. These decisions and directions had not only been erroneous; Gibbon also questioned whether the Washington administration should have had the jurisdiction to decide and direct at all. In this opinion, and in similar opinions of other events of the war, Gibbon evidenced a point of view common to many of the professional soldiers of the day. They believed that the war should have been in the hands of the military, free and clear of the political objectives and necessities of the war and uninhibited by civilian control. This view would have seen some nonexistent line drawn between diplomacy and war and between the government and the military forces of the government. George B. McClellan was the most famous exponent of this extraconstitutional concept. Although of a vastly different character and psychology than McClellan, and with a different strategical and tactical sense, John Gibbon shared his military philosophy in this respect.[41]

And so the month of June drew toward its end. Gibbon's Brigade, still untried in battle but hardened by the recent marches, was back again in the now familiar Falmouth surroundings. Again it looked as if the Western men were going to join the army on the Peninsula, where, it was still expected, the war was soon to be won.

3

JOHN POPE'S ARMY:
AN END TO FILE CLOSING

"Our boys are growing enthusiastic in the prospect of a general who has a little life."

From Rufus Dawes' Journal

On June 26, 1862, President Lincoln moved to bring some order out of the confused situation in the Federal command in Virginia. On that day he created the Army of Virginia, composed of the hitherto independent forces of Frémont, Banks, and McDowell, and certain detached commands, including the troops in Washington. To command of this army Lincoln appointed Major General John Pope, a graduate of West Point and a breveted veteran of the Mexican War, who had recently come to prominence as a result of his capture of Island No. 10 in the Mississippi River. Pope brought to the East a reputation for bold and aggressive leadership. Although this favorable reputation was soon damaged by a series of bombastic orders which he issued as Commander of the Army of Virginia, he set about organizing his command with commendable energy.

In addition to the Washington troops, Pope's army was composed of three corps. Frémont's Mountain Department became the First Corps, with Frémont in command. Banks commanded the Second Corps, composed of the troops that had been known as the Department of the Shenandoah. McDowell's corps was the Third Corps. The corps command arrangement was altered at once with respect to Frémont's Corps. That general protested his being superseded by Pope, a junior officer, and Secretary Stanton at once accepted Frémont's request to be relieved. Stanton's order relieving Frémont also appointed General Rufus King in his place as commander of the First Corps, but King declined the command, and General Franz Sigel became Frémont's successor.[1] On paper, Pope's army included 77,779 officers and men present for duty, of which 56,093 were in the three corps that comprised the field force proper. Although he no longer had the divisions of McCall and Shields, McDowell's Corps numbered 25,607 officers and men and was the largest of the three. It included King's Division, Ord's, now under the command of James B. Ricketts, the detached brigades of Doubleday and Carroll, and Bayard's cavalry brigade. Leaving King's Division at Fredericksburg, to maintain the line of communications north of the Rappahannock and to preserve the railroad from Aquia, Pope moved to concentrate his widely scattered force along the line of the Rappahannock.[2]

While all of this was happening in Pope's command, events on the Peninsula were reaching a climax. On June 26th, the day that Pope's army was created, Lee undertook an offensive to drive the Federals from the gates of Richmond. The first battle was at Mechanicsville, north and west of Richmond, which was followed by McClellan's retreat across the Peninsula to the James River, fighting all the way. Although not defeated in battle, McClellan's campaign had clearly suffered a setback. His army was now based on Harrison's Landing on the James, south and east of Richmond, and Lee was now between him and Pope's army. This meant that Rufus King at Fredericksburg had things to do, to find out what the enemy planned from its new and better position at Richmond. On July 3rd, from Warrenton,* McDowell ordered King to ascertain whether any Confederate forces were coming north from Richmond to Gordonsville, south of the Rapidan on the Virginia Central Railroad. On the following day, King advised that his cavalry was patrolling the roads in front of Fredericksburg and that he would keep a sharp eye to the fords of the Rappahannock. There was no news from his scouting parties, but slaves reported Ewell at Gordonsville with a small Confederate force. Throughout July, King's cavalry was to be engaged in acquiring information and in railroad and communication raids.[3]

While the cavalry was busy on the roads between Fredericksburg and Richmond, Gibbon's Wisconsin and Indiana infantrymen de-

* For locations involved in King's reconnaissance efforts, see back end paper.

voted themselves to better things. On the Fourth of July, the brigade celebrated with games, horse races, foot races, and a sack race. Officers and men participated indiscriminately, with regiment competing against regiment, and everybody pitching in to try to catch a greased pig. But after this diversion, the soldiers again began to chafe under the routine of camp life. "Of course we feel eager to be something more than ornamental filecloser," wrote Major Dawes in his journal.[4] Fortunately, General Gibbon also assumed that this was not the destiny of his Westerners, and he resumed his efforts to perfect the discipline of his brigade. Learning of the way that the men had thrown away equipment on their recent marches, Gibbon set up internal controls according to the regulations, designed to prevent such waste. Regimental officers were made responsible for the quartermaster's reports, and the soldiers were to be charged with equipment they threw away. The brigade's camp, on a plain near the Lacy House, was organized as if it were in the presence of the enemy. A chain of sentinels was placed round the camp, and officers of the day and officers of the guard were detailed and instructed. The entire brigade was also ordered to turn out under arms at reveille. As soon as the drums ceased beating, the companies were to move out at double quick and form on the colors. Gibbon then mounted, galloped through the camp, inspected each regiment, and dismissed it. Although the men may have at first believed that this was much ado about nothing, they cooperated, and the companies even began to vie with one another in getting into line. As fate was to arrange it, the brigade's first big fight, now less than sixty days away, was to be one in which they were taken wholly unawares by overwhelming numbers. At that time, not only stout hearts but conditioned reflexes were to make the difference between performing well and performing badly. John Gibbon was determined to develop these reflexes.[5]

Gibbon's command was not the only one trying for a more perfect organization. On July 23rd there arrived in Washington a new general-in-chief, Henry Wager Halleck, U. S. Grant's commander from the West. Halleck was a West Pointer, a man of high intellectual powers, who was credited with the general management of the successful Union campaigns in the West. He succeeded lawyers Lincoln and Stanton, who had acted together as generals-in-chief after McClellan had been removed from over-all command at the time of his taking the field in April. General Halleck's first major decision was as difficult a one as he was ever to face: What to do with McClellan's army, again inactive, and facing Lee in front of Harrison's Landing.

While Halleck and the administration weighed the question of McClellan's disposition, King continued his reconnaissance activities south of the Rappahannock, supplementing the findings of his cavalry with data supplied by slaves and spies. On July 24th King received Pope's congratulations for his diligence and a series of new intelligence missions. The commanding general was still anxious about the possibility of a Confederate build-up in the Gordonsville area, and King decided on a reconnaissance in stronger force than he had previously undertaken. He ordered Gibbon to take a mixed column of cavalry, infantry, and artillery toward Orange Court House, north of Gordonsville on the Orange and Alexandria Railroad. With Second and Sixth Wisconsin as part of his infantry, Gibbon proceeded on the 24th down the Orange Plank Road, passing through Chancellorsville and skirmishing lightly with the Confederate cavalry to within a mile and a half of Orange Court House. He then withdrew in the face of increasing opposition, without casualties but with the desired information. Apparently concerned at King's previous threats against the railroad, the Confederates had sent Jackson from Richmond to Gordonsville. Gibbon probably overestimated Stonewall's numbers when he reported that he had 30,000 men, but this was a detail. Returning to Falmouth on the 27th, Gibbon wrote his report and took the trouble to congratulate the Second Wisconsin on its conduct during the march.[6]

A few days following Gibbon's Orange Court House raid, Halleck advised Pope that he was free to move King's Division from Fredericksburg as soon as Burnside's troops arrived there from Fortress Monroe.[7] Then on August 3rd Halleck's really significant order was issued. McClellan was directed to evacuate the Peninsula, a decision creating an urgent mission for Pope's army—to prevent a concentration against McClellan during the evacuation. This meant that Pope had to intensify his threats against the Confederate communications and their Gordonsville build-up. On August 5th the Frederick's Hall Raid opened, the most extensive of the communication raids up to that time. The objective was the interruption of the Virginia Central Railroad at Frederick's Hall Station, south of the North Anna River.

The force included an entire infantry brigade, Gibbon's Brigade, supported by cavalry and artillery. Whether or not the Wisconsin and Indiana soldiers realized the significance of August 5th at the time, the Frederick's Hall Raid marked the first *action* of the brigade as a whole, and signaled a new phase in its career.*

The raid got underway at 2:00 A.M. as the men moved out of their Falmouth camps in the darkness, crossed the river, and passed through Fredericksburg. Gibbon then divided his force. Colonel Cutler and the Sixth Wisconsin, together with a squadron of cavalry and an artillery section moved along the familiar Orange Plank Road toward Chancellorsville. Gibbon and the other three regiments, accompanied by the Third Indiana Cavalry and a Rhode Island battery, took the Telegraph Road. General Hatch, who now commanded the brigade previously commanded by Augur,[8] and elements of his brigade followed Gibbon. Once again the weather was insufferably hot and was to play its part in the fortunes of the operation.

Fifteen miles south of Fredericksburg, at the town of Thornburg, Gibbon was met by a Confederate cavalry force. He dispatched a rider to Cutler, advising him of this opposition and telling him to move "early and cautiously." Although the Confederates opposing Gibbon withdrew when fired on, Gibbon's column was effectively halted for the day by the heat, which had prostrated many of his men. But on the following morning Gibbon moved forward again, leaving seventy casualties from the heat with Hatch, who had by this time come up to Thornburg. After proceeding seven miles, Gibbon's cavalry reported that Jeb Stuart, with a large force, was moving north on the Bowling Green Road toward the rear of the column. Fearing that Stuart would get behind him, and knowing that surprise was no longer his ally, Gibbon decided to retreat. He reached Hatch's Thornburg camp during the afternoon of the 6th, by which time Hatch and Stuart had become engaged. Although harassed severely by Stuart's assaults on their outposts and stragglers, Gibbon and Hatch remained at Thornburg through the night of the 6th, returning the fire of Stuart's horsemen. On the following morning, still skirmishing with Stuart, Gibbon moved the entire force to the Orange Plank Road to protect Cutler's retreat.

Cutler's force had left the Orange Plank Road on the morning of

* The Frederick's Hall Raid is mapped on the back end paper. See also map at page 48.

the 5th and had marched over country roads to Spottsylvania Court House, nineteen miles from Fredericksburg, arriving there at 11:00 A.M. After a halt to rest his column, Cutler moved on another eight miles to Mount Pleasant, where he bivouacked for the night of August 5th. But at 11:00 P.M., Cutler received Gibbon's dispatch from Thornburg. Cutler called a midnight council of the field officers of his column, with Lieutenant Colonel Bragg and Major Dawes representing the infantry. Among the other officers, the most prominent was cavalryman Judson Kilpatrick, later to be a colorful and controversial figure. While the tired troopers and infantrymen slept, Cutler outlined the facts to his officers. They were isolated from Gibbon's supporting column and it had already met the enemy. Ahead of them was the North Anna River, which could not be forded and south of which they could be trapped if the few wooden bridges were burned. Frederick's Hall Station, their destination, was seven miles beyond the river. Cutler proposed going on, but said that if they were to go on it would have to be at once. Bragg, Dawes, and Kilpatrick unhesitatingly approved Cutler's proposal. The council having supported him, Cutler sent his column forward at 2:00 A.M. Because of a guide's mistake, the men marched an extra ten miles and did not reach Carl's Bridge on the North Anna until 8:00 A.M. There 155 exhausted men and a company of cavalry were left under Captain Philip Plummer of the Sixth Wisconsin, charged with protecting the bridge for the retreat.

Having filled their canteens and laid aside all excess equipment, the remainder of the force crossed the 150-foot bridge span, forty feet above the water level. Two miles from Frederick's Hall Station, Cutler sent forward the cavalry, who swooped into the village, cut the telegraph wires, picketed the roads, and began destruction of the railroad. The infantry and artillery moved in at 4:30 P.M. Posting the guns so as to command the village, and with the greater portion of the infantry disposed so as to defend against attack, the remainder joined the cavalry in destroying the railroad and burning whisky and corn belonging to the Confederate army. By 6:00 P.M. two miles of railroad had been destroyed and the work was done. The column immediately undertook its retreat, reaching the river without mishap at 9:00 P.M. After the raiders had crossed, the bridge was destroyed and the exhausted column, having marched thirty miles since 2:00 A.M., staggered two more miles into camp.

At 11:00 P.M., just twenty-four hours from the receipt of the earlier dispatch, Cutler heard again from Gibbon. This time the news was of Jeb Stuart's force and the peril to the whole enterprise. Regardless of the need, there was no time for further rest, and at 4:30 A.M. Cutler's column again set out, heading for Spottsylvania Court House, where Gibbon's force was to be waiting. Two miles beyond Spottsylvania, Cutler's men met Gibbon's, and the exhausted men of the Sixth rejoined their Wisconsin and Indiana brethren. The reunited column then camped for the night and returned to Fredericksburg at 1:00 P.M. an August 8th. Cutler's contingent had marched ninety miles in blistering heat in three and a half days. But all of the results were not so satisfactory. Gibbon had to report the loss of fifty-nine men from his brigade, the exhausted men from the Second and Seventh Wisconsin and the Nineteenth Indiana who had straggled on the 6th and 7th and who were captured by Stuart.

So ended the first engagement of Gibbon's Brigade. Fifty-nine men had been lost, which was not to be discounted. But perhaps the others had learned a lesson—to straggle was to be lost. Except for the Sixth Wisconsin the entire brigade had now seen the enemy, fired at him, and received his fire. As for the Sixth, the Frederick's Hall Raid could now replace the "Battle of Patterson Park" with the Baltimore Plug Uglies as its martial baptism. And there were other fruits of the action. Colonel Cutler had shown that he had not only a soldierly bearing. He had commanded a mixed force of infantry, cavalry, and artillery and had acted with judgment, daring, and dispatch, when all of these were needed. Cutler, indeed, had graduated from the class of the militia officers fighting against the Aroostook Indians, and his junior officers had also performed well. In his report, the colonel who had sought to frustrate Dawes' promotion singled him out for high praise.[9]

While Gibbon's Brigade was engaged in the Frederick's Hall Raid, Pope began the advance of his army across the Rappahannock to Culpeper Court House, directly north of Gordonsville on the Orange and Alexandria Railroad.[10] From this point, a massive threat to the Confederate concentration at Gordonsville would be unmistakable. On the 8th, Burnside's troops having arrived at Fredericksburg, King's Division and Doubleday's Brigade were ordered to make the forty-five mile march to Culpeper, an order that came at a bad time for General King. Whether or not his epilepsy was involved, the general was sick and had been for several days, beset by pain, debilitation, and great weakness. But he was still able to exercise command and he set about at once preparing his division for the march.[11]

While King was preparing to move, General Banks, having advanced beyond Culpeper, was renewing acquaintances with Stonewall Jackson, who had concentrated his three divisions at Gordonsville. Believing that he might be able to fall on a portion of Pope's army before it was reinforced, Jackson had advanced from Gordonsville on August 7th. On the 9th Stonewall came up to Cedar Mountain and found Banks' Corps drawn up behind Cedar Run.* Banks had 8,000 men and Jackson had 24,000, but, misinterpreting an ambiguous verbal order from Pope, the Federal commander attacked Jackson, and the bloody Battle of Cedar Mountain ensued. The Federals fought well and handled Jackson very roughly, only to be overpowered by sheer force of numbers. At darkness, Banks fell back to his earlier position behind Cedar Run where Sigel's Corps and Ricketts' Division were now posted.

In the meantime, King had begun his march. Two brigades and a battery crossed the Rappahannock at Fredericksburg, marched out the Orange Plank Road through Chancellorsville, and crossed the Rapidan at Ely's Ford. The remainder of the division, and Doubleday's Brigade, marched north of the Rappahannock, intending to cross the Rappahannock at Kelly's or Barnett's Ford, directly east of Culpeper.[12] The march started well enough, with the soldiers singing songs and hymns, but the day was miserably hot and the road was dusty. Gradually the singing subsided, and then the straggling began as some of the men found themselves unable to keep up the pace. At 1:00 P.M. there was a halt at a stream, and the stragglers caught up with their comrades. Then the march was resumed in a rainstorm that worsened the road. Still the men pressed on, covering twenty-one miles on August 10th. If they had any idea that they would be congratulated for their effort they were to be disappointed. General Pope reported that the enemy was in great force and that "we are now engaged." King was to leave his wagons and to "push forward day and night until you join us." King issued the appropriate orders, and his soldiers started out, apparently at last on their way to battle.[13]

* For the march to Cedar Mountain and the withdrawal to the Rappahannock, see back end paper and map at page 48.

After the war, some of the Wisconsin veterans of Gibbon's Brigade remembered this as their toughest march—weather hot, roads poorly surfaced and muddy, no rest periods, streams to wade, and with the cooks so exhausted that each man drew his rations and cooked for himself. The troops hurried on and reached Stevensburg, six miles from Culpeper, on the night of the 11th. But that same night saw another frustration of their expectations as Jackson withdrew from Cedar Mountain and recrossed the Rapidan.[14]

When Gibbon's men came on the scene of the Battle of Cedar Mountain, they had their first view of the horrible aftermath of combat. The Union dead had been buried, but in shallow graves which neither dignified nor concealed their deaths. The Confederate dead and the horses of both sides had not been disposed of, and Gibbon's men were put to work cremating the carcasses of the horses. As they went about their task they learned another of the bits of miscellaneous information which soldiers later try to forget: the scent of corrupting animal flesh is not so offensive as that of corrupting human flesh.[15]

King's Division was left in the Cedar Mountain area and was to remain there for a week, but other elements of Pope's army followed Jackson on August 12th, occupying the bank of the Rapidan from Raccoon Ford to the base of the Blue Ridge. Thus far Pope had been successful in his mission of diverting the Confederates from McClellan. But now Lee became convinced of McClellan's imminent departure from the Peninsula, and he decided to concentrate against Pope in his exposed position on the Rapidan, before McClellan could reinforce him. The tables had been neatly turned on Pope. Now his army became the quarry instead of McClellan's. On August 13th, even before McClellan had actually begun his withdrawal, Longstreet's Corps and Stuart's cavalry were ordered to the Rapidan to join Jackson, increasing Lee's force to almost 55,000 men against Pope's 46,000, including the divisions of Reno and Stevens that had come to him from Burnside's command at Falmouth. Pope's new task, and Halleck set it forth for him, was simply to avoid being overwhelmed until McClellan could reinforce him. For the next little while, the war in Virginia was to be a race between Lee and McClellan, with the defeat or safety of Pope's army as the prize.

On the day following Lee's order to Longstreet to proceed to the Rapidan, McClellan got his forces into the race as General Porter's

Fifth Corps struck out for Williamsburg. But Lee had the head start, as well as a better route, which made it clear that Pope could not maintain his present exposed position. On the 18th, having learned of the Confederates' advance from his cavalry and a captured dispatch, Pope undertook his retreat from the Rapidan to the line of the Rappahannock. Gibbon's Brigade was ordered to march at 10:00 P.M. The general was apprehensive of the move, knowing that to "green troops," as he called his soldiers, a retreat was a severer test of discipline than an advance. In a retreat in the presence of the enemy, as was true on August 18th, inexperienced soldiers tended to develop an "escape" psychology and to become disorderly and disorganized. Actually, the Western soldiers behaved well, but the army's movement as a whole was confused. There was poor synchronization between the wagon trains and the troops, the roads were jammed, and the timetables became more and more useless as the night progressed. Gibbon's men were unable to move until 10:00 A.M. on the 19th, twelve hours after the designated hour, and during these twelve hours they had been standing by, under arms and without sleep. When the march finally began it was hot, dusty, and interrupted by the wagon trains. Well after dark on the 19th, the brigade was halted on the road for the night, still five miles south of the Rappahannock. But Captain Kellogg and Company I of the Sixth Wisconsin, detailed with others in the division to build a bridge to overcome the bottleneck at the passages of the river, were not permitted even this respite. The bridgebuilders had to work all night, and morning saw the fruit of their labors in a second span available to their comrades. Gibbon's Brigade crossed on the morning of the 20th on the Orange and Alexandria Railroad bridge and went into camp a mile beyond. The rest of the army followed, and by the afternoon of the same day all of Pope's army was safely across. It was none too soon. Lee's army, the two corps of Jackson and Longstreet now together, was already crossing the Rapidan and pressing for the Rappahannock.[16]

Ordered to hold the Rappahannock line until aid from McClellan arrived, Pope concentrated his army between Sulphur Springs and Kelly's Ford. Occupying the center, near Rappahannock Station, was McDowell's Corps, in which General Abner Doubleday's brigade was no longer a detached command. His three regiments—the Seventy-sixth and Ninety-fifth New York and the Fifty-sixth Pennsylvania—were now assigned to King's Division, joining the brigades of Gibbon, Hatch, and Patrick. Altogether King had 10,000 effectives, including artillery and a regiment of New York cavalry.[17] The soldiers of King's Division had seen the Confederate cavalry across the river from Rappahannock Station on August 20th. On the following morning there was more excitement as the Confederate batteries began to throw shells across the river. The Federal artillerists responded, and the Western soldiers, except for the Second Wisconsin, which had seen and heard plenty of artillery at Bull Run, had their first experience of hostile cannon fire. It was plain to see that this was their first experience, as they marched behind the Federal batteries, toward the right flank of the division. With the projectiles falling all about them, the men marched stoically on, until an officer in a nearby regiment was hit and killed. Thereafter, the art of taking cover was discovered, and it seemed both wise and soldierly to avoid a collision with an artillery shell. Despite appearances, the Confederate gunners were simply probing the Federal line looking for a place of minimum opposition at which to cross the river. Some cavalry in King's front crossed during the afternoon, and the Sixth Wisconsin skirmished with them long enough to resent the fact that the Confederate horsemen had donned Federal blue coats for the occasion. More excitement was provided when Cutler and Dawes were deprived of a cup of coffee by a Confederate artillerist who sent the coffeepot into the sky with a perfect shot. But the day closed with Lee still on the south side of the Rappahannock and with Pope's army safe from harm.[18]

During the next three days, events along the Rappahannock moved rapidly to a climax as strong reinforcements from McClellan began to arrive. The first to come was John F. Reynolds' Division from Porter's Corps, which was assigned to McDowell's Corps. Also available were Porter's other divisions, Morell's and Sykes', and the divisions of Hooker and Kearny from Heintzelman's Corps. Altogether, these five divisions from the Army of the Potomac numbered 30,000 effectives, which meant that Pope's danger had passed. But while Pope turned to thoughts of an offensive, Lee continued to maneuver for a river crossing. On the 22nd he got a small infantry force over, which was almost trapped when rains swelled the river, and Stuart's horsemen crossed and struck the Federal train at Catlett's Station, capturing prisoners and burning stores, baggage and dispatches. Significantly, because Gibbon's headquarters guard and sick bravely defended the Westerners' twenty-one wagons, Gibbon's train was among the few saved from destruction.[19]

At last, on August 25th, tired of jockeying with the Federals along the river, Lee dispatched Jackson's Corps to the Confederate left to get behind Pope. With his usual vigor, Jackson set out along the Confederate side of the Rappahannock, following the northwesterly course of the river. Although Pope was at once aware of the movement, he did not know Jackson's destination, and guessed that the most likely goal was the Shenandoah Valley. To determine the Confederates' purpose, Pope employed McDowell's Corps in a reconnaissance to Sulphur Springs on August 26th, which only confirmed the absence of Jackson's force and also incidentally disclosed the continuing and deepening illness of General King, who was temporarily forced to hand over command of his division to General Reynolds.[20] Thus while Pope tarried at the Rappahannock, Stonewall Jackson and 25,000 men marched through Amissville, Orlean, Salem, and Thoroughfare Gap, bound for Manassas. Arriving there and at Bristoe on the night of August 26th, the Confederates had a field day. The small garrisons were quickly overwhelmed, and into Jackson's hands fell the enormous stores of Pope's army. Having eaten their fill, the lean Southerners loaded up what they could carry and set fire to the rest, sending millions of dollars up in smoke.

Pope knew nothing of Jackson's blow at Manassas until he was advised on the night of the 26th that the enemy's cavalry had broken the railroad there. Although he initially misjudged the significance of the event—and ordered General Heintzelman to send only a regiment to the rescue—by midnight he had begun to suspect that Jackson was at Manassas in force. Belatedly, he decided to move his army northward, to cope with Jackson, wherever he was. On the morning of the 27th, leaving Banks' Corps to cover the movement of the trains from Warrenton Junction to Manassas, Pope ordered the bulk of his army to concentrate near Gainesville on the Warrenton Turnpike, seventeen miles east of Warrenton. McDowell's Corps, just west of Warrenton, and Sigel's Corps were to follow the turnpike and were to reach Gainesville by the night of the 27th.

Sigel's men led off for Gainesville on the 27th, followed, in order,

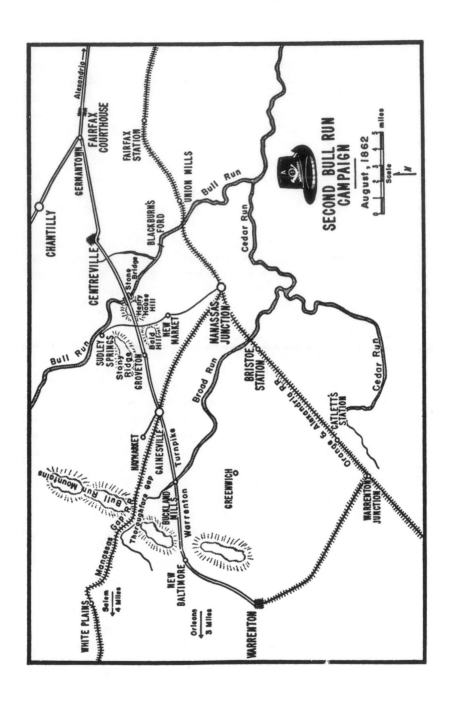

SECOND BULL RUN
CAMPAIGN

August, 1862

Scale

miles

by the divisions of Reynolds, King, and Ricketts. McDowell's marching order to King had sounded brisk: "Have the column closed up, leaving no stragglers, and have the whole appear creditable." Perhaps McDowell knew of the temptations the soldiers would encounter at Warrenton. Temptations there were, indeed. As Gibbon's soldiers marched into the town they saw burning wagonloads of hardtack and pork, a tragic picture to hungry soldiers whose haversacks were empty. The column passed through Warrenton and proceeded east, Sigel's Corps reaching Buckland Mills in time to save the bridge on Broad Run which the Confederate cavalry had sought to burn. Sigel pushed forward to Gainesville as the day closed, and behind him, along the turnpike, marched McDowell's divisions.[21]

On the night of the 27th, while McDowell's soldiers busied themselves with eating and preparing for a night's rest, the general was otherwise engaged. He was now receiving the reports of his cavalry, and he was learning a great deal. In his march to Manassas, Jackson had come through Thoroughfare Gap. More important, the rest of Lee's army was following the same route and would be coming through the gap soon. Recognizing at once the importance of closing the gap, McDowell, as senior corps commander, ordered the whole of Sigel's Corps to Gainesville and Haymarket. The latter village was between Thoroughfare Gap and Gainesville. Reynolds' Division was directed to remain at Buckland Mills where it would be on the flank of any force emerging from the gap. Unaffected by these new plans, Gibbon's soldiers were bedding themselves down amid the stones on the turnpike. It was a clear summer night, and seemed to the Western men like many other nights since they had volunteered a year previously. There was no apparent reason to savor the air especially or to reflect about life. Tomorrow would be another day, and tomorrow night would be another night, as uneventful as had been August 27th. Certainly the Wisconsin and Indiana soldiers would have been surprised at the suggestion that this would be the last night on earth for many of their number. Unlike their comrades from the Army of the Potomac, who had been at or near combat areas for weeks at a time, death had not yet become a constant companion to them. If and when their time for dying came, Gibbon's men expected advance notice and plenty of time to prepare for it.

Although August 27th had been uneventful for the men on the

Warrenton Turnpike, others of Pope's soldiers had found more excitement to the east, near Manassas. There Jackson had been positively found and identified, first by Heintzelman's regiment sent out on the night of the 26th and then by Hooker's Division, which had attacked Ewell's Division at Bristoe and had driven the enemy to Broad Run. With Jackson located, a great opportunity now confronted Pope, the chance to overwhelm Jackson, isolated from the rest of Lee's army. Accordingly, except for Banks' Corps, ordered to Warrenton Junction, Pope directed his eastern divisions—Morell, Sykes, and Kearny—to converge on Manassas, joining Hooker there. In addition, instead of leaving a part of his force to the west, between Jackson and Thoroughfare Gap, Pope instructed McDowell and Sigel, and the divisions of Reno and Stevens from Greenwich, to march on Manassas on August 28th. Thus, the door between Jackson and Lee was opened, and McDowell's arrangements, interposing a force between the enemy wings, were set aside.[22]

For the movement to Manassas it was Pope's intention that the troops of McDowell and Sigel would march *en echelon*, their right resting on the Manassas Gap Railroad and their left sweeping northward, through the country between the railroad and the Warrenton Turnpike. Since it was believed that Jackson was below the turnpike and about to be engaged at Manassas, this meant that McDowell and Sigel were expected to come in on Stonewall's right and block his escape. In preparing for the march, McDowell departed from instructions in one respect. Because of his knowledge of Lee's route, he detached Ricketts' Division to Thoroughfare Gap, where it was to arrive at 3:00 P.M. and engage Longstreet, delaying the Confederates until the night of the 28th. With the remaining three divisions of his corps and Sigel's Corps, McDowell set out for Manassas on the morning of August 28th.[23]

Sigel's Corps led the march. Sigel was suposed to follow the line of the Manassas Gap Railroad, which pursued a direct southeasterly course between Gainesville and Manassas. Reynolds' and King's divisions marched on Sigel's left, which meant that they continued along the Warrenton Turnpike toward Gainesville. Just beyond that point, they were to leave the pike and veer toward Manassas. As Gibbon's soldiers moved out along the pike they had a glimpse of their division commander. Haggard and obviously ill, Rufus King stood by a log fire at the roadside. This was an uninspiring picture, but it is doubtful if the men anticipated that illness would create any special hazard for their welfare. Their spirits were in any case depressed by the tedium of the march. Contrary to orders, Sigel had carried his wagons with him, and they crowded the roads and forced the troops to halt and fall out from time to time while the road was cleared. Additional delays were caused by Sigel's mistaking his route. The men used the frequent halts to whatever advantage they could, to make coffee, to sleep or at least lie down. During one of these periods, when Gibbon's men were just beyond Buckland Mills, they witnessed the movement to the rear of several hundred Confederate prisoners. The Southerners looked ragged and defeated, which must have been reassuring, and their presence at least indicated that the march was for a good purpose and that the enemy was ahead.[24]

After Sigel's Corps had finally cleared the turnpike, Reynolds, next in the line of columns, was able to cross the railroad at Gainesville. At midday, just beyond Gainesville, the head of Reynolds' column was fired on by artillery as it prepared to leave the turnpike and move southward toward Manassas. The artillery fire came from a hill near Groveton, farther east on the pike. Reynolds' artillery responded to the Confederate guns and a skirmish line was sent forward, but the Confederate pieces withdrew and, supposing that the enemy was simply a small detached element or a cavalry party, Reynolds' Division continued its interrupted movement.[25]

Gibbon's men were halted in the road while Reynolds and the Confederates exchanged artillery fire ahead of them. After resting at ease while the situation cleared, they resumed their spasmodic forward movement, passing slowly through Gainesville and halting again on the pike while the cavalry of General John Buford rode by in the direction of Thoroughfare Gap. After the cavalry had passed, the brigade was again ordered forward, marching two or three miles and finally turning off the turnpike down a country road toward Manassas. But the column had not proceeded more than two miles through the wooded countryside when another halt was ordered. There was brief excitement when the brigade was ordered to form a line of battle, but the order was at once countermanded and the column was again directed to be at ease. Waiting impatiently, John

Gibbon rode ahead and joined McDowell and other officers on a hill that afforded a good view of the countryside, but he did not learn the reason for the delay—or how long it was expected to last—and at length he returned to his brigade. There he found a growing interest in food developing among the men, and the regimental officers suggested that a beef ration be issued. In spite of misgivings because of uncertainty about the duration of the delay, Gibbon gave his consent.[26]

While King's Division rested in the woods near Gainesville, events at Manassas had taken an unexpected and disturbing turn. Jackson's Corps—all 25,000 Confederates—had vanished. Pope had reached Manassas, but the enemy was not there. The divisions of Kearny, Reno, and Stevens had moved on to Bull Run and had crossed the run. Though the Federals had gone all the way to Centreville, the enemy was nowhere to be seen. As the afternoon progressed, the pursuit of Jackson ground to a standstill. But it was at least established that he was not at Manassas, and this meant that McDowell's movement had to be reconsidered. Accordingly, during the halt of King's Division in the woods along the country road leading from the Warrenton Turnpike, McDowell received three orders from Pope. The first of these, written about 1:00 P.M. and reflecting Pope's belief that Jackson was fleeing for Aldie Gap, directed McDowell to move on Gum Spring, north and west of Centreville and opposite the gap. The Gum Spring order was countermanded almost at once by a second order, which told McDowell to halt the movement to Manassas, requested his views, and described several alternative possibilities. The third order, received by McDowell after 4:00 P.M., announced that Jackson had been found, east of Manassas Junction and near Centreville. McDowell was ordered to march at once on Centreville, ten miles east of Gainesville on the Warrenton Turnpike, and Sigel—who had now reported personally to Pope—and Kearny, Reno, Stevens, and Hooker received similar directions.[27]

Upon receipt of the third order, McDowell directed King to return to the turnpike and to follow it to Centreville. Then the corps commander rode to Reynolds, who was now three miles from Manassas, and directed him to march on Centreville by the road through New Market. Then McDowell left his command and rode for Manassas, in order to report personally to Pope. But he did not find the army commander at Manassas, and while riding from Manassas with his staff he became lost and was separated from his divisions for the night, a night on which his soldiers were sorely to need their able and zealous but hapless corps commander.[28]

Immediately after McDowell's departure, King turned his division northward for the turnpike. It was now late afternoon, approximately 5:00 P.M., and the sun was beginning to set.[29] The division was isolated from the rest of McDowell's Corps, and from their other comrades in Pope's army. The soldiers would have to march more miles, but this was their only military accomplishment to date and they had a good road and the Confederates were many miles away. *Or were they?* The fact was that they were not. At the precise moment that King's isolated column reappeared on the turnpike, Stonewall Jackson's nearly 25,000 men were massed approximately two miles away.

Having enjoyed the massive bonfires at Manassas Junction on the night of the 26th, and after Ewell's engagement at Bristoe with Hooker on the afternoon of the 27th, Jackson had turned his attention to extricating himself from his dangerous position. He knew that he was blocked on the west by the troops of McDowell and Sigel in the Gainesville area. Facing him at Bristoe were the divisions from the corps of Heintzelman, Porter, and Banks, too many men for Stonewall to handle. To the northeast was Centreville, but this would remove him from Lee's route of march and force a retirement through Aldie Gap. There were other, equally unattractive possibilities. But nearby was the battlefield of Bull Run, containing good defensive ground immediate to Thoroughfare Gap. Accordingly, Jackson's divisions, by noon on the 28th, had reached the battleground where their commander had earned his name. Protected and informed by Jeb Stuart's cavalry, Jackson determined to hide until Lee was within supporting distance.[30]

Jackson's hiding place was on wooded Stony Ridge, north of and roughly parallel to the Warrenton Turnpike. There the Confederates were "packed like herring in a barrel," according to one of them, their line extending from Groveton on the right to Bull Run at Sudley Springs on the left. In addition to the natural advantages of the ridge, a railroad embankment had been constructed along its crest. The position was well described by Colonel W. W. Blackford, Stuart's engineer officer:

The position was a wonderfully strong one along the line of an old rail-road where there were successive cuts and fills of from eight to fifteen feet, making most formidable breastworks for infantry both in the cuts and behind the banks, while the elevated ground in rear gave position for artillery to fire over their head.

The left flank was covered by Bull Run and the right rested on the crest of a ridge which could be crowned with batteries to enfilade the whole front. The high ground was wooded, and in these woods Jackson massed his corps, hiding them completely, while Stuart surrounded them by a curtain of cavalry. . . .

In the late morning of the 28th, Jackson had ridden over to his right and had personally observed the movements of Sigel and Mc-Dowell. He had directed the artillery fire on Reynolds' Division, just before it had turned off the pike for Manassas. He had also observed King's Division disappear from the pike in the afternoon, as it pursued its original march. Believing that the Federal army was in retreat for Alexandria, Jackson much regretted the apparently vanishing opportunity to strike the Federals on the turnpike. But as the afternoon progressed, and while King's Division was resting in the woods along the country road, Jackson at last heard from Lee. Longstreet was at Thoroughfare Gap, was expected to force it in spite of Ricketts' opposition, and was within supporting distance.[31] Jackson's passive role was ended. He was no longer under any necessity to hide, and could unleash his naturally aggressive instincts and talents. It was at this point in history that King's Division of 10,000[32] men, alone and unsuspecting, suddenly reappeared on the turnpike, bound for Centreville.

And so the stage was set. Gibbon's Western soldiers had been together for almost a year and had never been seriously engaged. Now, without the slightest anticipation of anything of the sort, Gibbon's Brigade—2,100[33] soldiers in their distinctive regulation uniforms and black-plumed hats—were marching into the waiting arms of Stonewall Jackson's Corps.

4

THE BATTLE AT BRAWNER FARM[1]

"the little hill whereon they stood was a roaring hell of fire."
From a Wisconsin soldier's letter to his brother

Hatch's Brigade was in the lead as King's Division returned to the turnpike for the march to Centreville. Behind Hatch came Gibbon's, followed in order by Doubleday's and Patrick's brigades. As he rode back onto the pike, General Gibbon found the ailing General King seated by the roadside with his staff, eating supper. Gibbon spoke briefly with the division commander and was instructed to follow Hatch's column eastward on the pike. Gibbon's Brigade then waited while Hatch's command moved out.[2]

The march to Centreville promised an unusual opportunity to the soldiers of the Second Wisconsin, the only battle-tried veterans of Gibbon's Brigade. Two and a half miles to the east of Gibbon's column was the crossroads village of Groveton. A mile and a quarter farther on was the Henry House Hill, scene of the Second Wisconsin's action at the Battle of Bull Run. The turnpike passed over the northern face of the hill. After almost a year of *telling* their Wisconsin and Indiana comrades of the heroic deeds of 1861,[3] the men of the Second were now to have the chance of *showing* the hallowed ground to their still untried comrades. Perhaps the men of the Second hoped to terminate their reminiscences at the Henry House Hill and avoid any discussion of the scene of their retreat. But this was unlikely because the route of march continued for approximately another mile and crossed Bull Run at the Stone Bridge.

There were other landmarks in the irregular and rolling Virginia countryside which Gibbon's men would pass before they reached the site of the Battle of Bull Run. Approximately a quarter of a mile to the north, running almost parallel to the turnpike, was a gentle and irregular ridge. The crest of the ridge was one hundred feet above the level of the turnpike, but the incline was gradual and the ridge did not appear to be formidable. North of the crest of this ridge the ground dipped slightly. Then, a quarter of a mile from the first crest, the ground again rose to the line of a second ridge, and became densely wooded. Just inside the wooded area was the abandoned railroad embankment, following its southwesterly course toward Gainesville. The second ridge, wooded and fortified by the railroad embankment, was Stony Ridge, bivouac of Stonewall Jackson's men.

Ahead of Gibbon's column, the first road running north from the turnpike was Page Land Lane, an undistinguished country road a half-mile east of the point at which Gibbon had re-entered the turnpike. This road followed the lay of the land, running due north up the gradual ridge and then, another quarter of a mile farther on, crossing the wooded railroad embankment. After passing Page Land Lane, another half a mile of marching would bring Gibbon's men opposite the farmhouse and barn of the Brawner family, located a quarter of a mile north of the turnpike on the crest of the gentle ridge. There was a farm lane leading from the turnpike to the Brawner house, and in the yard of the house and extending to the east was an orchard. Except for the orchard, and a small grove of trees at the house and barn, the ground around the farm buildings was cleared from Page Land Lane to beyond the farm lane. Both the fields in front and to the north of the farmhouse were open. But Brawner's open fields were bordered on the east by a rectangular wood that lay south and east of the farm buildings. From west to east, the wood was approximately a fifth of a mile long. Its northern edge—which was enclosed by a zigzag rail fence—began seventy-five yards south of the crest of the ridge on which the farm buildings were situated, and extended down to and south of the turnpike. Inside the rectangular wood the ground was rugged and irregular and dipped down to the level of the turnpike at the eastern edge of the wood, where another open field extended to the north from the turnpike.

Although all of this typical geography, identified by one onlooker as simply "a farm-house, an orchard, a few stacks of hay, and a rotten 'worm' fence,"[4] lay ahead of Gibbon's marchers, it had no possible interest to them as they approached it. But it was very soon to be a

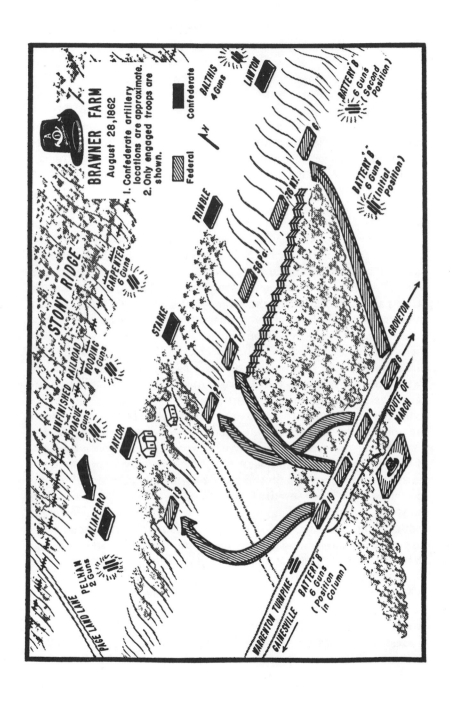

battlefield, their own battlefield, bounded on the south by the turnpike; on the north by the woods at the railroad embankment, a half-mile from the turnpike; on the west by Page Land Lane and on the east by the eastern outskirts of the rectangular wood, a mile from Page Land Lane. Almost in the middle of this area were the Brawner farmhouse, barn, and orchard. Running through the area east and west was the crest line of the ridge on which the farm buildings and orchard were located. The entire expanse was open except for the orchard and the rectangular wood, the latter occupying the southeast corner of the whole.[5]

General Hatch's Brigade reconnoitered the Brawner farm area before Gibbon's men moved out on the turnpike. Hatch sent forward the red-legged Fourteenth Brooklyn Zouaves as skirmishers north of the pike, and his batteries shelled the wooded hills to the north and east of the route of march. Hatch's skirmishers turned up several mounted Confederates toward Groveton, but these withdrew when fired on and no alarm was felt by the Federal column.[6] After Hatch's Brigade had passed out of sight over the hills to the east of the Brawner farm, Gibbon put his own column in motion. Since there was no anticipation of combat, Gibbon was not closed up on Hatch, and behind Gibbon, Doubleday's and Patrick's brigades permitted convenient marching intervals to develop.[7] Gibbon's men marched in column of fours, the Sixth Wisconsin in the lead, followed, respectively, by the Second and Seventh Wisconsin and the Nineteenth Indiana. Battery B brought up the rear. The soldiers marched with arms at will, with no thought of battle. Rufus Dawes remembered that the brigade marched along "as unsuspectingly as if changing camp."[8] The head of the column passed Page Land Lane and moved on to the Brawner farm lane. It was sunset, the "hour was very delightful, and my horse and I were just wide awake enough to keep in the beaten road," recalled an officer.[9] Some of the Western soldiers must have glanced to their left across the open fields and seen the Brawner farmhouse and orchard outlined against the rays of the setting sun. Although the ground looked unprepossessing to a prairie farmer's eye, the stillness and peace of the scene were reminiscent of home.

As Gibbon's soldiers proceeded on their way through the peaceful countryside, their decidedly unpeaceful adversaries behind the railroad embankment on wooded Stony Ridge were preparing to strike. General William B. Taliaferro's Stonewall Division was ordered to deploy. Baylor's Stonewall Brigade, almost 700 strong, was on the right. Next to Baylor's was Starke's Brigade of 1,200 officers and men, which was to form directly north of the Brawner farmhouse and orchard. Johnson's Brigade, also 1,200 strong, and the division's remaining brigade, commanded by the general's brother, Colonel A. G. Taliaferro, and including another 1,200 officers and men, were to be in reserve behind Baylor's and Starke's. To the left of the Stonewall Division were the brigades of Ewell's Division. Trimble's 1,200 men were to form on the left of Starke's, directly north of the rectangular wood. Lawton's Brigade, still further to the left and 2,100 men strong, comprised the left flank of the Confederate front line and extended to the east of the eastern edge of the rectangular wood. Early's and Hays' brigades, 3,900[10] more officers and men and assigned by Ewell to Early's command, were behind Lawton's and within supporting distance.[11] Although not immediately available, the six brigades of A. P. Hill's Division were in support, resting to the left and rear of Ewell's brigades.[12]

The Confederate infantry was to be well supported by artillery. From the Stonewall Division, Wooding's four-gun battery and the batteries of Poague and Carpenter were to be placed in front of Starke's Brigade in an extended line running east and west of the Brawner house, so as to fire over the heads of the Confederate infantry.[13] Farther to the left, Balthis' four-gun battery from Ewell's artillery was directed to take post along the line of the railroad embankment.[14] The remaining corps artillery and the twenty guns of Major John Pelham of Jeb Stuart's cavalry division, whose troopers were to protect Jackson's right flank during the fight, were also ordered up, although Jackson was not to delay the assault until their arrival.[15]

Jackson had poised a mighty blow. His front line of 5,200 officers and men included four infantry brigades, two from the Stonewall Division and two from Ewell's Division, with the remaining four brigades from these divisions, 6,300 officers and men, in immediate reserve and with Hill's brigades also available. The infantry was to be supported at the outset by the artillery batteries of Wooding, Poague, Carpenter, and Balthis. Pelham's horse artillery guns and the remaining corps artillery were en route to the field, and the cavalry itself was on the right flank, assigned to detect and defend against any Federal turning movement there.

It remained simply for Jackson to signal the assault. Even as Hatch's skirmishers had passed by, he had ridden out from the woods and examined the unsuspecting Federal column from the crest of the ridge near the Brawner farm buildings.[16] Hatch had passed on, and then came Gibbon's men. Colonel Blackford has described the dramatic scene that Stonewall Jackson's lieutenants now observed:

Sometimes he would halt, then trot on rapidly, halt again, wheel his horse and pass again along the front of the marching column, or rather along its flank. About a quarter of a mile off, troops were now opposite us. All felt sure Jackson could never resist the temptation, and that the order to attack would come soon. . . .

Presently General Jackson pulled up suddenly, wheeled and galloped towards us. "Here he comes, by God," said several, and Jackson rode up to the assembled group as calm as a May morning and, touching his hat in military salute, said in as soft a voice as if he had been talking to a friend in ordinary conversation, "Bring out your men, gentlemen!" Every officer whirled around and scurried back to the woods at full gallop. . . .

As the officers entered the woods, sharp, quick orders to fall in rang from the rank to rank, followed by the din of clashing arms and accoutrements as the troops rapidly got under arms, and in an incredibly short time long columns of glittering brigades, like huge serpents, glided out upon the open field, to be as quickly deployed into lines of battle. Then all advanced in as perfect order as if they had been on parade, their bayonets sparkling in the light of the setting sun and their red battle flags dancing gayly in the breeze. Then came trotting out the rumbling artillery . . . they quickly unlimbered and prepared for action.[17]

This stirring picture of the Confederate advance was not visible to Gibbon or his men. Riding at the head of his troops, the general was passing along the pike behind the rectangular wood. Behind him, and also secluded by the wood, was the Sixth Wisconsin. The remaining regiments and Battery B were stretched out along the pike in front of the open Brawner fields, but they, too, were unaware of their danger, for although the Confederates had now left their wooded lair, they were still unseen as they traversed the dip in the ground behind the Brawner ridge.[18] But Gibbon finally received a split-second warning. As the general and the head of his brigade emerged from the eastern edge of the rectangular wood, they came to the open field extending away to the north. Gibbon jogged ahead of the leading regiment and mounted a gentle rise a few yards north of the pike where he paused to look around. Hatch's Brigade was already out of sight. But Gibbon's attention was at once attracted by the sight of a number of horses coming out of the timber approximately a mile north and slightly to the east of Gibbon's position, the area which Hatch's skirmishers had recently reconnoitered. The horses belonged to Balthis' battery, which was vying with the other Confederate guns for the honor of the first shot.[19] Gibbon scarcely had time to consider whether the horses were those of friend or foe, or to notice that the horses were pulling field pieces, when they presented their flanks. Then recognition dawned on artilleryman Gibbon: guns were coming into battery and were preparing to fire on his column.

The general now reacted quickly. He dispatched a staff officer to the rear to bring up Battery B. In another instant the first of Balthis' shells came screaming in and, according to the historian of the Sixth Wisconsin's leading company, the soldiers made "so polite a bow" as the shells passed over the heads of the column.[20] The fire from Balthis' battery was at once duplicated by Wooding's guns firing from behind the Brawner farmhouse into Doubleday's and Patrick's brigades.[21] While the Sixth Wisconsin took cover behind a slight embankment at the roadside, a result of the road's having been cut through an irregularity in the ground, Battery B came up the pike at a gallop. Eager hands tore down the turnpike fence and the guns passed into the field and were placed on the knoll from which Gibbon had first seen Balthis' guns. With shells bursting all about, Captain Campbell put his guns to work responding to Balthis, while Gibbon rode into the edge of the rectangular wood to the left and front of Battery B to observe the effect of its fire.[22]

Concluding at once that his old artillery command would master Balthis' guns, the general quickly turned his attention to Wooding's battery, which, along with Balthis', he assumed, because of Hatch's prior reconnaissance, to be horse artillery unsupported by infantry. To silence Wooding, Gibbon turned to the Second Wisconsin, veterans of battle and led by West Pointer O'Connor.[23] The Second was directed to leave the pike and advance up the Brawner ridge to take Wooding in the flank. Because of its position in the column just behind the Sixth Wisconsin, the Second had to march to the rear to approach its quarry. Colonel O'Connor directed the soldiers into the rectangular wood, through which they marched obliquely to the rear. Gibbon, who had ridden toward the fire of Wooding's battery, met the troops in the wood and rode with O'Connor and the Second into the open field in front of the Brawner farmhouse. In the field, and to the tune of the fire from the artillery, the Second was formed in line of battle, with skirmishers out, and silently moved up the gentle slope toward the farmhouse. Ahead of the Second Wisconsin were the apparently isolated Confederate guns. Directly behind them on the turnpike were their comrades of the Seventh Wisconsin, and the Hoosiers of the Nineteenth, now the rear of Gibbon's force.[24]

At the crest of the Brawner ridge skirmishers from Starke's Brigade, firing from close range from the yard of the farmhouse and from the orchard, suddenly opened on the right of the unsuspecting Wisconsinites. But in spite of their profound surprise, the Badgers did not falter. The regiment wheeled to its right to face the flank attack, and the skirmishers pressed forward and drove in Starke's skirmishers as Wooding's battery unlimbered and withdrew.[25] At once Baylor's Confederates, advancing toward the farmhouse, opened fire from the Second's left flank.[26] To meet the fire from Baylor, Gibbon ordered the Nineteenth Indiana to form on the left of the Second, and the Hoosiers promptly moved up the slope toward the farm buildings and opened a hot fire on Baylor. But the Confederate fire immediately spread up and down their overlapping line and, realizing now the force of the Confederate assault, Gibbon dispatched requests for assistance to General King and to Doubleday and Patrick, ordered up the Seventh Wisconsin from the pike to the right of the Second, and directed the Sixth to take position still farther to the right.[27]

Because of the intervening wood, the Sixth had heard but not seen the rising crash of musketry as the Second and the Nineteenth Indiana had become engaged. But then an officer brought the Sixth's order to advance, and Colonel Cutler commanded, "Forward, guide center." With flying colors advanced, the Sixth scrambled up the roadside embankment, pulled down what remained of the turnpike fence, and crossed the open field east of the rectangular wood in line of battle. Making a half-wheel to the left at the northern edge of the wood, the Sixth opened fire. Arriving in line at the same time, the combined fire of the Sixth and Seventh regiments temporarily blunted the force of the Southern onslaught, and the Confederates fell back from the orchard and the edge of the wood. But Trimble's and Lawton's men now added their rifles on the Confederate left, and Jackson's line again advanced and stood firm.[28]

The battle was now joined. Gibbon's line was just south of the crest of the Brawner ridge. It followed along the ridge line, passed just north of the edge of the wood and stopped at its northeast corner. The Nineteenth Indiana held the left flank at the Brawner farmhouse. Then came the Second and Seventh Wisconsin, in order, facing the farmyard and orchard, with the Seventh fighting with its back to the wood. Next to the Seventh was a gap in Gibbon's line of several hundred yards along the edge of the wood, before the Sixth Wisconsin's post on the right flank at the northeast corner of the wood. There the ground was considerably lower than that occupied by the rest of the Federals, so that the men of the Sixth, with Battery B firing over their heads, looked up and to their left across the intervening unoccupied ground to observe the efforts of their comrades. Although Battery B, which had by now driven off Balthis' battery, continued to fire away at the Confederate line from its position to the right and rear of the Sixth,[29] both of Gibbon's flanks were in the air and his 2,100 infantry faced 5,200 Southerners in the four Confederate brigades initially engaged. The longer Confederate front line overlapped both Federal flanks even before any Confederate reserves entered the fray. Gibbon's one battery was no match numerically for the Southern guns, but General Taliaferro later recalled the terrible effectiveness of Battery B. "The Federal artillery was admirably served, and at one time the annihilation of our batteries seemed inevitable, so destructive was the fire." Poague's, Wooding's, and Carpenter's batteries, outmatched and in trouble, were moved to the overlapping Confederate right to enfilade the Federal infantry. To these guns Major Pelham added two rifled cannons which fired into the Federals at a range of sixty yards. But the close proximity of the contending lines of riflemen now sharply limited the usefulness of the Confederate guns.[30]

The terrible odds facing Gibbon's men at the onset of the battle did not impress Stonewall Jackson. Shortly after the action commenced, doubtless expecting Gibbon to be supported, Jackson put in Colonel Taliaferro's brigade to the right of Baylor's, extending the Confederates' right flank and increasing their infantry engaged to 6,400 men. Two of Early's regiments were also directed to the Confederate right while the balance of Early's two brigades, his own and Hays', were ordered forward. But here the railroad embankment, previously Jackson's ally, turned to the Union's benefit. Unable to pass over the embankment in their immediate front, Early's men moved to their right and were forced to break ranks and file through a narrow cut in the embankment. While the Confederates sought to re-form south of the embankment, Battery B, which had now advanced from its original position, found their range and poured on them what Early described as "a galling fire of shells and canister," killing and wounding thirty-four of Early's officers and men. Early was finally to succeed in forming his men to the left and rear of Trimble's Brigade, but the battle did not wait for these reinforcements, and they arrived too late to become engaged.[31] A similar fate befell the men of A. P. Hill's Division. Archer's and Branch's brigades were ordered up behind Ewell's Division, where they withstood Battery B's cannonade without casualties and were withheld from the battle until too late. Branch's Eighteenth North Carolina and all of Gregg's Brigade were finally sent for late in the engagement, but arrived in line only after the firing had ceased.[32]

Gibbon found himself without available reserves to match the increasing Confederate threat. His repeated calls for help to King and Patrick were fruitless, the latter's brigade moving up the pike to the field too late to participate. But as a result of the direct appeal from Gibbon, and without an order from King, Doubleday did pitch in to the fray.[33] Shortly after the action commenced, the Fifty-sixth Pennsylvania and Seventy-sixth New York marched along the pike under the fire of the guns of Wooding, Poague, and Carpenter, and reached the rear of Gibbon's line at the Brawner farm. They then advanced through the Brawner fields and the rectangular wood between the Seventh and Sixth Wisconsin and went into action, filling the gap in Gibbon's line along the edge of the wood[34] and increasing Gibbon's infantry force to 2,900 officers and men.[35] Later in the action, and too late to become engaged, Doubleday also sent forward his remaining regiment, the Ninety-fifth New York, which proceeded up the pike, passed the wood, and took position in support of Battery B.[36]

From the first infantry fire until the last, the battle continued unabated for more than two hours.[37] It was a stand-up fight at a maximum range of seventy-five yards, with no respite and with neither side entrenched or covered. Trimble's men for a time advanced a few yards to the zigzag fence at the wood, and forced Doubleday's regiments back. On the Federal right the Sixth Wisconsin also slowly pressed forward and forced Lawton's men back twenty yards before the Confederates again powered their way to their original line. Colonel Taliaferro's Brigade on the Confederate right drove in in time to check and then drive back an advance of the Nineteenth Indiana to the farmhouse. But except for these movements, neither side advanced or retreated, the Confederates holding the farmhouse and the northern edge of the orchard and the Federals clinging to the farmyard, the southern edge of the orchard, and their line along the northern face of the wood.[38] The fiercest action took place on the Union left, in and around the farm buildings and orchard. Gibbon never left this part of his line, and there the feverish and bloody action reached its climax amidst the roar of the weapons and the shouts and cheers of the soldiers.[39] Gibbon, who was to be in many battles, later said it was "the most terrific musketry fire I . . . ever listened to." General Taliaferro reported the fight as "one of the most terrific conflicts that can be conceived of." Another Confederate participant wrote that in the gathering darkness "everything around was lighted up by the blaze of musketry and explosion of balls like a continuous bright flash of lightning."[40] The power of Gibbon's fire is attested by the Confederate reports. General Taliaferro referred to Gibbon's numbers as "greatly superior" to those of the Confederates. The Southerners also were frankly admiring of the resistance they met. Jackson reported that the Federals "maintained their ground with obstinate determination," and General Taliaferro said that the enemy "withstood with great determination the terrible fire which our lines poured upon them."[41]

What a participant called the "sheet of fire"[42] that extended from each line to the other had its devastating effect on both sides. In their exposed and stationary positions officers and men were cut down in terrifying numbers. The casualties in the ranks of the officers were unusually startling. Shortly after placing his regiment in line, the Second's Colonel O'Connor went down mortally wounded, to die that night. Major Allen of the same regiment was hit twice but managed to stay on the field until the fighting ceased.[43] On the Union right, while directing the fire of the Sixth from his front and center position, Colonel Cutler was struck in the leg and carried from the field by his horse. On the other flank of the Federal line the Nineteenth Indiana's youthful Virginian, Major May, also fell in the yard of the Brawner house, fatally wounded.[44] The Seventh Wisconsin, fighting at the orchard, saw Colonel Robinson, Lieutenant Colonel Hamilton, and Major Bill wounded, although the grandson of Alexander Hamilton kept the field until the firing ceased. To the right of the Seventh, the colonel of the Fifty-sixth Pennsylvania fell wounded as he led his regiment into the gap in Gibbon's line, and five captains of the Seventy-sixth New York were also killed and wounded.[45] For the Confederates the losses among the officers were even more appalling. The Federal rifles accounted for the commanders of both of the Confederate divisions engaged. General Taliaferro was shot in the foot, neck, and arm, and gave up command of the Stonewall Division after the engagement. Ewell's leg wound was more serious, and required amputation. His services were lost to the South until the Gettysburg campaign.[46] The casualties among brigade and regimental officers were just as imposing. Brigadier General Starke was wounded and out of action briefly, and the Stonewall Brigade lost two regimental commanders killed and another wounded.[47]

Darkness and the tacit consent of the opposing commanders at last broke off the engagement. As the firing slackened, Gibbon ordered the Nineteenth Indiana to fall back obliquely from the Brawner farmyard to protect the badly overlapped Federal left. The Hoosiers ceased firing as they withdrew, and the Confederates threw men forward into, but not beyond, the farmyard, before again withdrawing. The Nineteenth then formed its line with its left at the turnpike and extending almost directly north along the western edge of the wood. On the right flank, commanding in place of the wounded

Cutler, Lieutenant Colonel Bragg directed the Sixth to move by a backward step, keeping up its fire and maintaining its alignment with the slowly withdrawing Federal center. The Sixth then recessed its right toward the turnpike and took position along the eastern edge of the wood,[48] as the Second and Seventh Wisconsin and Doubleday's two regiments fell back into the wood itself.[49] Although the Federal line had given "three good Union cheers, the claim of victory," the Southerners did not pursue and were satisfied to hold the ground occupied by them as the action broke off.[50]

Shortly after 9:00 P.M.,[51] satisfied that the battle was over, Gibbon set out from his left flank to find and report to his division commander. He found General King sitting with his staff and with Generals Hatch and Doubleday in the field just east of the wood, near the point at which the first Confederate artillery fire had been directed. There the officers were soon joined by General Patrick whose brigade King now ordered up. According to Doubleday's aide, "The officers of the respective staffs were seated a little outside the inner circle, orderlies held the horses ready for instant use in the road close by, and the firelight shone upon the anxious faces of men conscious of a grave responsibility." Flushed with the excitement of battle, Gibbon freely expressed his anger at the meager assistance his command had received. He learned that Hatch, although not summoned by either Gibbon or King, had turned back with his command at the sound of the battle, but had arrived too late to become engaged.[52] The inaction of King and Patrick was apparently not explained then and is inexplicable today. But the engagement was over, and the significant question at the moment was what King's Division was to do. While the wounded were collected, the generals turned to this issue.

The last order issued to the division was McDowell's direction to march on Centreville, which reflected Pope's belief that Jackson was there. But although King seemed to Gibbon to be still disposed to carry out the Centreville order, the day's combat and reports from Gibbon's prisoners established that the division was in the presence of Jackson's whole force, which deprived the Centreville order of its logic. An alternative was for the division to maintain its position, but it was isolated, heavily outnumbered, and with two of its brigades already badly mauled. In addition, Longstreet was believed to be nearby, and the two Confederate corps could surely crush King. McDowell was absent and unavailable. King was without authority to order a Federal concentration, and even had he had the power, he was without intelligence as to Pope's orders at the corps' command level and he did not know where the parts of the Federal army were or were supposed to be. The remaining alternative and the one pressed by Gibbon, was to move elsewhere to find support, and the most likely place for this was Manassas Junction, the prior point of concentration of Pope's forces and the last known headquarters of Pope himself. After some discussion, and in the face of indecision and reluctance on the part of the others to propose any resolution of the issue, Gibbon, although the junior general officer, took a piece of paper and by the light of a candle wrote out his proposal for a move on Manassas. Gibbon passed his proposal to Hatch, Patrick, and Doubleday and then handed it to General King. All agreed it was the best thing to do under the circumstances, and General King then prepared a dispatch to McDowell so advising the corps commander. This dispatch was handed to one of McDowell's staff officers, an attendant at the council, who volunteered to carry it to McDowell, although he confessed that he did not know where Mc-Dowell was.

Thus it was decided that King's Division would march away from Stonewall Jackson's Corps, for which the Federal army had been vainly searching for two days. Because of the Federal withdrawal, the final collision between the two armies was to be further postponed. And King's movement not only gave Lee time to join Longstreet's Corps to Jackson's, it also removed the one Federal force interposing between the two Confederate corps.[53] Since King was the commanding officer, he was responsible for the decision, one of several Federal moves that fatefully affected what happened during the next two days. For his part in influencing the decision, John Gibbon, on May 7, 1863, sent a manful letter to King, which he authorized King to publish. In the letter, Gibbon admitted his part in the decision, acknowledged that later knowledge proved that he was wrong, and stated simply that the movement seemed the best thing to do at the time.[54] But neither at the officers' council on August 28th nor when he wrote this letter did Gibbon know of King's curious activities prior to the assembling of the officers' council. As Gibbon's action was drawing to a close, and while Gibbon was tending to the withdrawal of his left flank, General Reynolds and one of his staff officers had arrived on the field and had met with King. King and Reynolds had then agreed that King would maintain his position and that Reynolds would bring up his division for the following morning. King then sent a dispatch to Ricketts suggesting that Ricketts join his force to King's and stating that he would stay where he was until he heard from Ricketts. King and Reynolds had even gone so far as to dispatch another of McDowell's aides, who, like the one later sent by King, did not find McDowell, to tell their corps commander this and the fact that King would not move without instructions from McDowell. After his meeting with King, Reynolds only incidentally learned of King's subsequent and unilateral abandonment of the plan to stand firm, which forced Reynolds to give up the idea of joining King in front of Jackson.[55]

King's decision to march away eliminated, at the least, the chance to assemble King's, Reynolds', and Ricketts' divisions, the last named having withdrawn from Thoroughfare Gap to Gainesville and then marching for Bristoe because King's movement on Manassas left it isolated. To these three divisions Sigel's Corps could probably have been added, and Jackson could have been assailed at dawn on August 29th as the rest of the Federal army approached the field and before Longstreet was up. As a matter of fact, General Pope had learned of Gibbon's battle with Jackson on the night of the 28th; because of it, and before learning of King's unexpected withdrawal, Pope sought to move the army toward Groveton so as to strike Jackson before Longstreet arrived. This plan Pope abandoned on learning later of King's withdrawal and of the consequent movements of Ricketts and Reynolds.[56] Had Gibbon known of Reynolds' meeting with King, and the possibilities Reynolds' availability offered, he would probably not have been so generous in his later letter. In any event, conceding that the McDowell Court of Inquiry was correct when it found that McDowell's absence on the night of August 28th was a primary cause for the acts that night of King and the others, it was a bad night for King. Having in mind that he had thus far shown promise, it is fair to say that his illness, which finally forced him to give up his command on the following day,[57] was his excuse for the poor reconnaissance of the division, the failure to support

Gibbon, and his ambivalence and final error in deciding to move away from Jackson after Gibbon's battle.

With the decision to march to Manassas made, Gibbon's command looked to their casualties in preparation for the march. In the darkness, the surviving Wisconsin and Indiana soldiers scoured the battlefield for fallen men in blue, often looking into the dead faces of friends, not only of the days of the brigade but also from childhood in Madison, Oshkosh, Baraboo, or Indianapolis. Like all recent battlefields, this one was a horror. Most of the dead and wounded of both sides lay precisely as they had fallen, in rows seventy-five yards apart with their heels in line. Other dead and maimed men had staggered or dragged themselves backward after they were hit, so that the rectangular wood was strewn with bodies and rang with the groans and cries of the wounded. Gibbon's men left their dead unburied, time not permitting this amenity, and collected the wounded together in several stations in the wood where the surgeons went to work.[58] From the reports of his officers, Gibbon now totaled his losses. Battery B, which had never closed with the Confederate infantry, had escaped with but a few wounded men.[59] But the infantry returns were staggering! Gibbon counted 133 dead, 539 wounded, and 79 missing, for total casualties in excess of 33 per cent, including seven of the twelve field officers of the brigade. The losses were unequally distributed over the four regiments. The Sixth Wisconsin, protected by the low ground it occupied and away from the blazing activity at the farmhouse and orchard on the Union left, lost only 72 in killed, wounded, and missing. But the survivors of the Second Wisconsin had surely earned their right to reminisce, 298 of approximately 500 men having fallen in that regiment. The Nineteenth Indiana and Seventh Wisconsin equally shared the remaining losses for a casualty rate of almost 40 per cent in each regiment. To these losses the Union added those in Doubleday's actively engaged regiments. The Fifty-sixth Pennsylvania had lost 61 of its 300 men, including, in addition to its colonel, four captains. Losses among the New Yorkers of the Seventy-sixth regiment amounted to approximately 100 officers and men.[60] All of this meant that the six Federal regiments engaged had lost 912 of 2,900 men, for an aggregate average loss of almost 33 per cent. Almost incredibly, all of this had happened in just over two hours of fighting! The Wisconsin and Indiana men were finally in the war—of that there could be no doubt. And Rufus Dawes recorded their reaction when he wrote that the Brawner Farm engagement "eradicated our yearning for a fight." After that, he said, the soldiers were "ready but never again anxious" for combat.[61]

The "black-hatted fellows," as the Confederate prisoners in the woods that night called Gibbon's men,[62] had also taken a heavy toll of their adversaries. Douglas Southall Freeman found the battle one of Jackson's costliest in casualties for the numbers engaged.[63] In addition to the thirty-four men in Early's Brigade killed and wounded by the guns of Battery B,[64] almost 2,200 of the 6,400 men in the five Confederate brigades in the infantry combat were killed or wounded. Percentage losses were the heaviest in Trimble's Brigade. Fighting at the eastern end of the orchard and along the zigzag fence in front of the rectangular wood, Trimble lost 759 of his 1,200 officers and men to the rifles of the Seventh Wisconsin and the two regiments sent in by Doubleday. On the Confederate right, near the farm buildings, one of every three officers and men fell in the Stonewall Brigade, Starke's and Taliaferro's. And the Sixth Wisconsin, which lost only 15 per cent of its 504 officers and men, inflicted 20 per cent casualties on Lawton's 2,100-man brigade on the Confederate left, stronger medicine than the badly outnumbered Badgers received.[65] No returns are available for the other supporting but unengaged brigades, or for the artillery or cavalry, but Stonewall Jackson's men surely had cause to remember their new-found Western opponents, who stood and fired away no matter how few of them there were and no matter how many of them were killed.

It was after midnight when Gibbon's soldiers were ordered from their lines to the turnpike for the march to Manassas. There some of the wounded men who could be moved were loaded into ambulances, and those who could not find places in the ambulances prepared to make it on foot. A line of march was finally established, and the exhausted soldiers, having muffled their tin cups and other noisy accoutrements, set out at 1:00 A.M. for Gainesville, through which they had previously passed just prior to Jackson's attack. At Gainesville, King proposed to turn south eastward on the Manassas-Gainesville Road, the same road Sigel and Reynolds had previously followed en route to Manassas.[66] As the Wisconsin and Indiana soldiers marched away from the battlefield, anxiety over their wounded comrades left behind was added to the fatigue and sorrow for the dead. Some of the abandoned wounded were attended by Jackson's surgeons, and others had their cries for water answered by Jeb Stuart's cavalry after King's column moved out. On the following day the wounded came within the lines of Sigel's Corps when it reached Gibbon's battlefield. And again on August 30th various of Sigel's commands on the Union left found Gibbon's hospitals in the woods and rendered further treatment and succor.[67]

For the survivors, the march itself was a nightmare, with wounded men who should not have been moved at all struggling to keep up on foot and avoid capture. Some of these men were virtually dragged along by their comrades. Rufus Dawes gave his horse to a wounded captain of the Sixth Wisconsin. As the horse walked along it picked up additional passengers, each stirrup strap and finally the horse's tail becoming the rod by which a wounded and weary man was able to keep going. But Private Hugh Lewis of the Second Wisconsin was not one of those clinging to Dawes' horse. Yet he somehow made the march, although the wound in his arm required its amputation at Manassas. Another private from the Second, E. S. Williams, also hobbled and crawled along on a shattered leg which the surgeons removed on his arrival at Manassas. Finally, as day was breaking, the troops approached the Junction and a halt was called. The marchers pitched headlong to the ground and fell asleep beside the road while the officers at once requisitioned rations and ammunition for the new day.[68]

The brigade's first battle was over. Years later, General Taliaferro was briefly to sum up what the men of both sides had done: "Out in the sunlight, in the dying daylight, and under the stars, they stood, and although they could not advance, they would not retire. There was some discipline in this, but there was much more of true valor." The Confederate general did not even claim victory, and called Brawner Farm a drawn battle.[69] Another commentator, this time an Englishman with a Confederate point of view, later agreed with General Taliaferro about the valor of both sides: "The men who faced each other that August evening fought with a gallantry that has seldom been surpassed," he said. But he also went further: "The Federals, surprised and unsupported, bore away the honours. The

Western Brigade, commanded by General Gibbon, displayed a coolness and a steadfastness worthy of the soldiers of Albuera."[70]

But the judgments of history were unknown in 1862 to the "Black Hat Brigade," as Gibbon's men, borrowing the Confederates' terminology, were now to call themselves. Of more concern to them was what John Gibbon thought about the day. And Gibbon would never again patronize his volunteers. As of ten days previously, he had referred to them as "green troops." But just after August 28th he spoke of them as the brigade "I have the honor to command."[71] *

*Alan D. Gaff's 1985 book, *Brave Men's Tears: The Iron Brigade at Brawner Farm*, significantly enlarges on the description of this battle.

5

SECOND BULL RUN

The brigade "behaved here with its usual gallantry. . . ."
From General Gibbon's Report

John Gibbon was too excited to sleep in the early hours of August 29th. In the deteriorated state of command, with his corps commander missing and General King at least physically incompetent, the restless Gibbon decided to establish direct contact with Pope, the army commander. After ordering the establishment of a camp for the survivors of his hard-fighting brigade, Gibbon remounted and rode for army headquarters. Passing through Manassas Junction, he viewed the desolate rubble left by Jackson's raid on the night of August 26th. After making several inquiries, he finally found Pope quartered in a house in Centreville. He reported his engagement and remained while the commanding general considered the troop dispositions necessitated by the unexpected movements of King's and Ricketts' divisions during the night.[1]

Believing that Longstreet's Corps was still west of Thoroughfare, Pope had again turned his attention to his original plan of overwhelming Jackson. That general's whereabouts were now definitely known. Sigel's Corps, together with Reynolds' Division from McDowell's Corps, was already in position in Jackson's front near the Warrenton Turnpike at the Henry House Hill.* The rest of the army was distributed from Bristoe Station on the west, where Ricketts' Division of McDowell's Corps and the two corps of Porter and Banks were located, to Centreville on the east, where Reno's two divisions and Heintzelman's Corps had spent the night of August 28th. Between these two forces, resting near Manassas Junction, were the

* For locations described in this chapter, see map at page 73.

99

brigades of Gibbon, Doubleday, Patrick, and Hatch from King's Division. King's Division was now temporarily commanded by General Hatch, and Colonel Timothy Sullivan had succeeded to command of Hatch's Brigade of New Yorkers.[2]

To concentrate against Jackson, Pope now directed Heintzelman and Reno to join Sigel and Reynolds by marching from Centreville to Gainesville. Pope's left was to be composed of King's and Ricketts' divisions and Porter's Corps. At 5:00 A.M. Pope dictated an order to Porter, directing him to take his corps and King's Division to Gainesville. This order the commander gave to Gibbon with instructions to transmit it to Porter at Manassas.[3]

After procuring a fresh horse, Gibbon rode back to Manassas and delivered Pope's order to Porter. While the two officers talked, McDowell, having at last found his way, joined them, and he, too, read the order. Gibbon heard McDowell request Porter to place King's Division on the right of the column so that the divisions of McDowell's Corps would be closer together. Then Gibbon conducted Porter's leading division, Morell's, to the Manassas-Gainesville Road and rode with it as far as his own camp. Pope's 5:00 A.M. order to Porter was supplemented at 6:30 A.M. by a joint order to McDowell and Porter, directing both of their commands to march for Gainesville. This order detailed Pope's plan for the next two days. Although he did not forbid an attack on Jackson on the 29th, it was the commanding general's idea that the two wings of his army were first to establish communications along the Warrenton Turnpike and then to halt while supply arrangements were made. Then, on the 30th, the whole command was to fall on the supposedly isolated Jackson. In his order to McDowell and Porter, Pope disclosed his misunderstanding of Longstreet's progress: he did not expect the latter to arrive before the night of August 30th or on the 31st.[4]

Even as Pope was issuing his orders for August 29th, Sigel's skirmishers were exchanging fire with Jackson's along the Warrenton Turnpike a mile or two east of Groveton. Reynolds' Division, on Sigel's left, joined in, and soon a heavy engagement was in progress. Heintzelman's Corps and Reno's divisions heard the firing as they marched down the turnpike to join Sigel. In their camp along the railroad track near Manassas, Gibbon's soldiers and their comrades of King's Division also heard the sounds of battle as they cooked a fresh beef ration and prepared coffee. Porter's Corps was passing Gibbon's Brigade as the latter breakfasted, and the battered Westerners ruefully scrutinized the fresh and hearty men from the Army of the Potomac. Jeers and friendly insults were exchanged, and Porter's men, displaying in jest an attitude their corps commander and General McClellan harbored in earnest, shouted their disparagement of "Pope's army." "We are going up to show you 'straw feet' how to fight," said the veterans of Malvern Hill. Their eyes falling on one of Porter's Zouave regiments, the veterans of Brawner Farm yelled back: "You'll get the slack taken out of your pantaloons and the swell out of your heads."[5]

As Gibbon's soldiers prepared to fall in behind Porter's Corps on the Manassas-Gainesville Road, Sigel and Reynolds, now joined by Heintzelman and Reno, withstood Jackson's midmorning counterattack above Groveton. The Federals then launched repeated but uncoordinated assaults on the Confederate line, extending behind the railroad embankment from Sudley Springs to Groveton. In the afternoon, and while the assaults on Jackson continued, Longstreet's Corps arrived on Jackson's right, extending the Confederate line to the south, across the turnpike, and toward the Manassas Gap Railroad.

As the Wisconsin and Indiana soldiers fell in behind Porter's Corps, they might have remarked on the differences twenty-four hours had wrought in their brigade. In numbers they were reduced to 1,250 officers and men,[6] not many more than the original recruitment strength of each of the four regiments. In addition to the empty places in the ranks of the brigade, the field officer corps had suffered fearful losses. From the Nineteenth Indiana Colonel Meredith and Lieutenant Colonel Bachman remained, but Major May was dead. Colonel Cutler of the Sixth Wisconsin was gone, en route to a Washington hospital with his leg wound. This left Lieutenant Colonel Bragg and Major Dawes, with Bragg in command. But among the field officers of the Second and Seventh Wisconsin, only Lieutenant Colonel Fairchild of the Second had passed unscathed through the fire at Brawner Farm. Gibbon had consolidated the two regiments, whose survivors did not exceed 600 men, under Fairchild.[7]

At the head of the advancing Federal column, Generals Porter and McDowell rode along until the rear of Porter's Corps had passed the junction of the Manassas-Gainesville and Manassas-Sudley roads. At this point the two generals decided to separate their forces, Porter's Corps continuing on the road to Gainesville and McDowell leading the divisions of King and Ricketts up the Manassas-Sudley road. As for Porter, who later received an order from Pope to attack Jackson's right, an order which Porter did not and could not obey, the road to Gainesville took him out of the battle and led, instead, to his court-martial and one of the celebrated controversies of the war. But McDowell's command marched on to reach the Warrenton Turnpike and the left of the Federal line facing Jackson.[8]

It was late afternoon when Gibbon's men reached the scene of action. As on the evening before, at Brawner Farm, no one was enjoying the sunset. At first the division was formed in line of battle beside the turnpike. McDowell then received orders to pursue the Confederates, who were said to be falling back, and he ordered the brigades of Hatch, Doubleday, and Patrick to follow them westward on the turnpike toward Gainesville. Gibbon's Brigade was detached and ordered north, up the Manassas-Sudley road. As they marched, on their left, out of sight behind the woods, the troops of Sigel and Reynolds fought on. The air was rent with musketry, cannon and cheers. It seemed inevitable that Gibbon's men would soon join the battle. But after marching for a mile and a half, a staff officer directed the brigade to support the reserve artillery batteries posted on a hillock by the road. There they remained out of action, while the other three brigades of the division, having marched for a mile west on the turnpike, battled for an hour with the supposedly retreating Confederates. The advent of darkness finally terminated the fighting all along the line. General Hatch withdrew his three brigades along the turnpike,[9] and Gibbon's men slept on the ground in line of battle, tossing uncomfortably in their battle equipment.[10] It had been a strange and harrowing day for the Wisconsin and Indiana regiments, although certainly an improvement over the day before. Around them had raged a great but indecisive battle, estimated by General Pope to have cost the Federal army 8,000 casualties. The two armies now nursed their wounds and waited in close proximity for the new day and the climax of the struggle.

The morning of August 30th dawned clear and sunny. Porter's Corps had now rejoined the army and was posted north of the turnpike on the Federal left, facing to the northwest toward Jackson's position on Stony Ridge. As the morning wore on with nothing more than skirmishing and an exchange of artillery fire,[11] Gibbon left his men to visit Pope's headquarters, located directly behind Gibbon's line. Unlike General McClellan, John Pope was not a "fuss 'n' feathers" commander, and Gibbon found the command post in the open air, equipped with cracker boxes for seats. Here Gibbon heard Pope's open complaints about Porter's activity of the previous day, presaging the later and formal summoning of a court-martial. Gibbon remained at headquarters while intelligence reports of the enemy were brought in, among them those of Generals Heintzelman and McDowell, reporting the disappearance of the enemy from the positions where his flanks had been at the close of the day before. To the sanguine Pope, and in spite of the contrary opinion of Porter, these reports meant only one thing: The Confederates were retreating to the west. Accordingly, at noon, Pope issued an order for a pursuit under McDowell's command. Porter's Corps, followed by the divisions of King and Reynolds, was to lead the Federal pursuit on the Warrenton Turnpike. Ricketts' Division, followed by Heintzelman's Corps, was to push forward on Porter's right, on the parallel line of the Sudley Springs-Haymarket road. Sigel's Corps and Reno's divisions were to form the army's reserve.[12]

There was only one defect in Pope's plan, but it was a fundamental one: the Confederates were by no means in retreat. Jackson had adjusted his line, as disclosed by the Federal reconnaissance, but he had not retired. He was massed where he had now been for two days, behind the railroad embankment. And where Jackson's right ended above Groveton, Longstreet's line joined Jackson's and extended in a southeasterly direction across the turnpike and beyond. Longstreet's men did not have the benefit of the railroad embankment, but the ground they held followed the line of a gentle ridge and was protected by a wood. In anticipation of Pope's assault, the Confederates were ready to make the best use of their advantageous ground. Jackson had posted his artillery in the center of his line on the high ground behind the railroad embankment. There the guns could fire over the heads of the Confederate infantry into the ranks of any attacking force. To Jackson's guns were added those of Longstreet's Corps, also posted on high ground and positioned so as to enfilade any force attacking Jackson's front.[13]

As the moment approached for the Federal advance, ominous intelligence forced adjustments in McDowell's dispositions. Reynolds, who had discovered the presence of Longstreet's men, reported that a large Confederate force was massed south of the turnpike, overlapping the Federal left. Recognizing this threat to his left flank, McDowell withdrew Reynolds' Division from Porter and posted it on Bald Hill, a commanding eminence south of the turnpike. McDowell also brought to the left two infantry brigades and two batteries from Ricketts' Division, weakening Heintzelman's column, which was organizing on Porter's right. The withdrawal of Reynolds altered the role of King's Division in the projected pursuit. Instead of supporting Porter's Corps, Hatch was now ordered to post the division on Porter's right and to advance to the attack with Porter. This extended the front of the Federal advance over a line a mile and a quarter long, with King's Division on the right and opposing the center of Jackson's line, and Porter's divisions on the left, overlapped by Longstreet's Corps. In this disastrous alignment, the Federals were to move out over irregular ground and through patches of woods which would break their lines, and, because Jackson's line was bent back toward the west, the Federal left had farther to go before striking the Confederate line than did the men of King's Division on the right. This meant that if the Federals were to attack simultaneously, Porter's Corps would have to change front and wheel to its right while advancing toward the Confederates. Perhaps all of these disadvantages could have been overcome had the Confederates been retreating. But they were fatal conditions for an advance against strongly defended works, with massive artillery available and an ideal field of plunging fire for both the Confederate rifles and guns.[14]

At 4:00 P.M., amidst a rising skirmish firing, the long blue lines started forward over the mile-and-a-quarter front. On the Federal left, Porter's men, cheering as they struggled through the wood that separated them by six hundred yards from Jackson's line, fell immediately under the direct fire of Jackson's artillery and the enfilading fire from Jackson's right. As they broke through the wood, already disorganized, they were met by a withering rifle fire from the Confederate infantry, who were themselves protected in their sheltered positions from the Federals' fire. But Porter's men continued to advance, and the Federal commanders saw their lines torn to pieces as the railroad embankment was approached.[15]

Despite the apparently foregone conclusion of Porter's attack on the left, Stonewall Jackson did not view it in any sense as a forlorn hope. Jackson saw that "as one line was repulsed another took its place and pressed forward as if determined by force of numbers and fury of assault to drive us from our positions." Fearing that the "impetuous and well sustained onsets" would break his line, Jackson called for reinforcements. Lee turned to Longstreet. But that general's enfilading artillery was now at its maximum effectiveness. To Longstreet it was evident that the attack against Jackson "could not be continued ten minutes under the fire of his batteries," and he made no movement with his infantry.[16] Porter's survivors reached the railroad, and in the hand-to-hand combat there, Confederate General Johnson saw "a Federal flag hold its position for half an hour within 10 yards of a flag of one of the [Confederate] regiments . . . and go down six or eight times. . . ."[17] But at the end of this half-hour, the Federals, beaten and in confusion, withdrew across the artillery-swept open ground to the wood. A second attempt to advance was made, and then the tragedy on the left closed as the troops drifted slowly to the rear.

To the right of Porter, advancing in line with Porter's men, General Hatch first sent forward the Second United States Sharpshooters as skirmishers. Clad in their unusual green uniforms, the Sharpshooters were followed by Hatch's old brigade and then Patrick's. Behind Patrick's were Gibbon's men. They moved into a single line of battle as they advanced, the Nineteenth Indiana in the center, the consolidated Second and Seventh Wisconsin on the left, and the Sixth Wisconsin on the right. Doubleday's Brigade formed the rear rank of the division's line.[18] As the division entered the wood in its front—a wood so heavy and overgrown that the officers had to dismount to lead the troops—the furious, enfilading Confederate artillery fire was loosed from the left. But the men worked their way forward, prey to an enemy that they could not even see. In the wood, the unmounted officers soon lost contact with their men, and the regiments became separated. Still the advance continued in spite of the bloody work of the Confederate cannon, each line rushing forward when the line in its front moved, and taking cover between the forward movements.[19]

Ahead and out of sight of Gibbon's men, Hatch's Brigade finally reached the far edge of the wood. Through the increasing smoke and fire, the New Yorkers could now see their objective. Directly in front of them was a rail fence. Beyond the fence was an open field and beyond that the railroad embankment, a wall of earth twelve to fifteen feet high. Crowning the embankment were the musket barrels and slouch wool hats of Ewell's Division, Gibbon's adversaries of two days before, and now occupying the center of Jackson's line. On the higher ground in the rear of the infantry were the Confederate guns, still firing and ready to murder the Federals as soon as they entered the open field of fire. Hatch's Brigade paused but a moment, just long enough to see what was ahead of them and to glimpse Porter's men already moving over the open ground to their left. Then the New Yorkers pushed over the rail fence and, with a shout, rushed into the withering fire, which at once included Longstreet's guns firing almost directly into the left flank of the charge. The odds were too great. General Hatch himself was struck down and again the division was without a commander. A few valiant spirits reached the embankment, there to be battered by stones thrown by the Confederates and fired into by their Federal comrades from behind. The others were slaughtered as they advanced or were driven back, pursued by a heavy line of Confederates.[20]

As the disorganized New Yorkers fell back into the wood, they rushed in confusion into Patrick's lines. Amidst the storm of artillery, to which the infantry fire of Confederate skirmishers was now added, Patrick's men began to disintegrate and join Hatch's fugitives in retreat. In their retrograde movement, the two disordered brigades ran into Gibbon's line, and the Wisconsin and Indiana soldiers heard a strange new command from their general. "Stop these stragglers. . . . Shoot them if they don't!" said Gibbon, with revolver drawn. In response to the bayonets of Gibbon's Brigade and the feverish activity of their own officers, the broken brigades rallied behind Gibbon's, which now formed the front line on the Federal right, and the Sixth Wisconsin's Company K was sent forward as skirmishers, opposing the Confederate line which had pursued the retreating Federals into the wood.[21]

Although the disorder on the right was checked, the Federal attack was now broken all along the line and a general withdrawal was in progress. The brigades of Hatch, Patrick, and Doubleday were ordered back to the higher ground to the rear. Separated from Gibbon and the Sixth Wisconsin, the Nineteenth Indiana and Fairchild's consolidated Wisconsin regiment went back with the rest of the division, leaving Gibbon and the Sixth Wisconsin alone in the wood. Unaware of the withdrawal, and receiving no order to retreat, Gibbon held the Sixth to its work. The lonely regiment hugged the ground, already scattered with the division's casualties, and exchanged fire with the probing Confederate skirmishers. Although there was a lull in the battle, the wood was still a place of death, and Rufus Dawes remembered how a "bullet would strike a man who would writhe, groan and die. . . ." Finally, realizing the isolation of his one remaining regiment, Gibbon prepared to withdraw. Leaving a line to cover the movement, the remainder retreated to the edge of the wood. There the men faced by the rear rank and, before the eyes of virtually the entire Federal army, proceeded at the double quick over the open field to the Federal line, three-quarters of a mile away.[22] As the Badgers approached the Union position, John Gibbon, pleased with the perfection of their movement, and no longer a martinet so far as his fighting Westerners were concerned, doffed his hat in salute. Then the men of the Sixth rejoined their division on a hill behind the Dogan House, near the Groveton crossroads. King's Division, heavily supported by six batteries of artillery, was faced to the northwest toward Jackson's line, from which they were separated by the wood from which they had so recently withdrawn.[23]

Now it was the Confederates' turn. Before the Federals could recover from their bloody repulse, which also included the defeat of Heintzelman and Ricketts on the extreme Federal right, the entire Confederate line moved forward, led by Longstreet's Corps on the right and extending to A. P. Hill's Division on Jackson's left flank. Because of Pope's concentration north of the turnpike, Longstreet's divisions were initially unopposed as they pressed forward, pivoting toward their left and the Henry House Hill, south of the Warrenton Turnpike and key to the possession of that highway. Looking to their left and rear, Gibbon's Brigade watched Longstreet's deployment as his corps advanced steadily in column by division. It was a breathtaking sight, and the threat posed to Pope's army was equally breathtaking. The Warrenton Turnpike was Pope's line of retreat. If the Confederates overran the turnpike, they could roll up Pope's left or get into his rear. Either of these events would rout Pope and leave Lee at large but a hard day's march from Washington.

As Longstreet's column approached Bald Hill, southwest of the Henry House Hill, it ran into Warren's Brigade. Warren was swept away, and Longstreet rolled on to strike the men of Sigel's Corps and Ricketts' and Reynolds' divisions, who had been rushed to Bald Hill in a desperate effort to protect the turnpike and save the Union left. Sigel and Ricketts momentarily threw back Longstreet's advance, only to be driven from the hill by the seemingly invincible Confederate power. Longstreet moved on to the Henry House Hill, the last barrier to the turnpike and the smashing of Pope's left. There the Confederates were met by a mixed force of infantry and artillery as the climactic moment on the left arrived.[24]

While the battle raged on their left, Gibbon's soldiers hugged the ground, harassed by a galling artillery fire and watching Battery B and the other Federal batteries near the Dogan House fire to their left into Longstreet's Corps.[25] But this passive role ended as Jackson's line[26] at last emerged from the wood in Gibbon's front. At the first appearance of Stonewall's men, Gibbon mistook them for Federals retreating from the wood where he had so recently been engaged. He rode among the Union batteries and told them not to fire. The tension among Gibbon's men was momentarily relieved when a German captain of a New York battery, apparently undeceived by the situation, responded to Gibbon's order with a lusty: "Gott im Himmel, General . . . by Jesus Christus why you say no shoot?" Almost immediately, the oncoming line was recognized, and the Federal infantry and artillery opened up. The first round from the thirty-six Federal cannon tore great gaps in the Confederate line. "Set them up on t'other alley," shouted an Irishman in the Sixth Wisconsin,[27] as the brigade fired and the Confederates faltered and fell back. A second Confederate thrust developed to Gibbon's immediate left, directed at the flanking of the batteries there. Changing front, the Second and Seventh Wisconsin advanced on this column and drove Jackson's men back as the firing continued up and down the line on the Federal right.[28]

Although King's Division continued to hold firm, the position of the Federal right depended on the halting of Longstreet's advance south of the turnpike. When Longstreet's Corps overran Bald Hill, the Federal right was flanked, and as the gray tide spread to the north and west around the base of the Henry House Hill, it threatened the rear of the blue line north of the turnpike. While the struggle for the Henry House Hill continued, orders were given for King's Division and the remaining Federals north of the pike to withdraw. Moving by the right of companies, and accompanied by the artillery, Gibbon's Brigade undertook its retreat, followed closely by Jackson's men.[29] The Confederates did not fire at their retreating foe, and contented themselves with shouts of "Get, you sons of bitches, get!" And Gibbon's men "got," as one of them later remembered the manner of their withdrawal,[30] to the southeast toward the rear of the Henry House Hill.[31] Even as the Federal right withdrew in the approaching dusk, the Confederate assault, described by one expert as "the most superb manifestation of the power and glory of the short-lived Confederacy," was grinding to a stop all along the line. That the Union army had been beaten could not be denied. But despite heavy straggling, the Confederates had not broken Pope's line or taken the Henry House Hill, around which the horseshoe-shaped line of the Union still held firm.[32]

Pope now undertook his retreat. Gibbon's Brigade was assigned to cover the movement, and the Western men established their line beside the Warrenton Turnpike on the northern face of the Henry House Hill. Their inseparable comrades of Battery B unlimbered for action in support of the infantry. The sun was now disappearing in an atmosphere heavily clouded from the smoke of battle. Although the enemy was unseen, the Confederates were close enough to permit the Wisconsin and Indiana soldiers to hear the officers' commands to their men, while cannon fire sounded in the distance to the right and to the left. In the deepening darkness, these final sounds of battle died away and quiet settled over the field. On Gibbon's right there remained only the division of General Kearny of Heintzelman's Corps, which finally moved through Gibbon's position and passed to the rear. From Reno's Division on Gibbon's left, no word had been received, although it was to precede Gibbon's Brigade from the field. Gibbon at last rode over and guided the last of Reno's brigades and artillery to the Warrenton Turnpike.[33]

At approximately 10:00 P.M.,[34] having built campfires to deceive the enemy, Gibbon's Brigade and Battery B fell in for the march to the rear. At the Stone Bridge over Bull Run, the usual signs of an army's retreat appeared. From the overturned wagons, the Wisconsin and Indiana soldiers were permitted to supply themselves with bread. Crossing the bridge, Gibbon found the road blocked by a slowly moving mass of stragglers, wagons, artillery, ambulances, and wounded, some of whom were borne by their comrades in hand litters. The brigade followed along the pike until it reached Cub Run, two miles beyond the Stone Bridge.[35] There Gibbon directed his staff to put the brigade into camp and, following what was becoming his habit, rode off for army headquarters in Centreville, where he found McDowell and accepted an invitation from Pope to spend the night. The field officers could now survey the casualties of the brigade. Although the Westerners had been on the periphery of the titanic struggle of the last two days, 15 more men were dead, 87 more wounded, and 41 more missing, most of whom had fallen in the wood in Jackson's front.[36] Including the losses at Brawner Farm, in their first three days of fighting almost 900 of Gibbon's men were casualties.

The Federal army awakened on August 31st to find rain falling on the scene of defeat. To those who were already comparing yesterday's defeat with the 1861 Bull Run Battle, the rain must have seemed an appropriate symbol. Gibbon's Brigade crossed Cub Run in the morning and marched for Centreville. There the army, strengthened by the arrival of Franklin's and Sumner's corps, went into camp and proceeded to straighten itself out. Scattered units were pulled together, rations were issued, and patrols sent out to discover Lee's intentions. Gibbon's men, together with the rest of McDowell's Corps, encamped for the night on the eastern outskirts of the town.[37] Major Dawes established a picket line in the wood near the bivouac of the Sixth Wisconsin. One of the pickets, tense and exhausted from the events of the preceding days, placed himself facing the regimental camp, and, when approached by a relief detachment, fired and killed one of his comrades. Here was another casualty to be duly accounted for in the next day's field return for the brigade: 1,427 officers and men present for duty.[38]

Although the rain continued on the following day, the Confederate army was now marching to its left, an ominous development, since it meant that Lee was headed still farther *north*. A movement by Jack-

son on Fairfax Court House, directly in Pope's rear, caused Mc-
Dowell's Corps to be dispatched toward the place, four miles east
on the Warrenton Turnpike. Reaching Germantown, junction of the
road to Chantilly, Gibbon's Brigade established a line of battle and
listened to the sounds of fighting at Chantilly, five miles to the northwest. The Westerners were not sent into the fray, but the day had
not been without its accomplishments. En route to Germantown, the
column had passed a Federal wagon train bound for Centreville and
loaded with fresh bread. Bayonets fixed, Gibbon's ranks had parted,
permitting the wagons to pass between the lines of hungry men.
Having speared the bread, the Westerners proceeded on their way,
comforted in having assisted the quartermaster in feeding the Federal
army.[39]

While Gibbon's Brigade rested at Germantown, General Halleck
and the administration were weighing the desperate question of what
to do about Pope's army. Pope himself had already suggested a withdrawal to the defenses of Washington. On September 2nd, suspect-
ing that Lee proposed to invade Maryland, Pope again proposed the
Washington move to Halleck. This time Halleck agreed, and ordered
the retreat. Gibbon's Brigade marched by way of Falls Church to
Upton's Hill, twelve miles from Germantown and very near their
Washington camp of the previous winter.[40] As they approached their
camp sites, the Wisconsin and Indiana soldiers learned of the administration's second decision. McClellan was assigned to the command
of the Washington fortifications and the troops for the defense of
the city. Thus did Lincoln choose between Pope, in whom the army
and the people had lost confidence, and the general who still inspired
their confidence. The President, of course, knew the agonies of this
choice. There was little cause for reliance on McClellan. But the
public still relied on him, and this was the paramount requirement
of the moment. On hearing the news, General Hatch, who had returned to his command, swung his sword and called for three cheers.
Throwing their black hats in the air, Gibbon's Brigade enthusi-
astically joined in the celebration.[41]

The brigade was to remain at Upton's Hill until September 6th,
while the army was reorganized. During the first two days, rations
were scarce, and one of the Wisconsin companies now found occasion to use the cash fund it had accumulated from the sale of excess

rations during the previous winter. The soldiers feasted on canned turkey and similar delicacies, all the more exciting because many of them had never seen "canned goods" before.[42] Additional diversion was provided by political news involving Lieutenant Colonel Bragg. Solicited by mail to run for Congress on the Democratic ticket, Bragg responded: "Say . . . that I shall not decline a nomination on the platform, the Government must be sustained, but my services can not be taken from the field. I command the regiment, and can not leave in times like these." Colonel Cutler also provided the brigade with something to talk about. Having purchased a new uniform, the wounded colonel, leaning on two canes, went to pay his respects to Secretary Stanton. As Cutler approached him, the irascible Stanton, with a glance at the new coat and bright brass buttons, blustered: "What in the hell and damnation are you doing in Washington? Why don't you go to your regiment, where you are needed?" The erstwhile Indian fighter, adventurer, and millionaire responded: "If I had not been shot and a fool, I would never have come here. Good day, Mr. Secretary."[43]

These events did not obscure the significance of the army's state of affairs. Behind and in plain sight of Gibbon's camp was the Capitol building. Looking the other way, the soldiers could see the flags of Lee's army, or at least one of them thought he could.[44] "Well here we are," wrote one of them, "just where we were a year ago." And another candidly reported that "instead of dating this letter, as we had hoped, from the Rebel Capitol, it is dated from our own."[45]

6

SOUTH MOUNTAIN:
THE IRON BRIGADE IS NAMED

"The Western men had met . . . men as brave as themselves and far more advantageously posted."
From Confederate General D. H. Hill's account in Battles and Leaders

War Secretary Stanton could speak unjustly to wounded colonels from Wisconsin. He could also write eloquently about his feeling for the Federal Union. "I believe that God Almighty founded this Government," he wrote in 1862. Yet in the autumn of 1862, the death of the Union seemed to be at hand. In the West, where an unbroken string of victories had thus far marked the Federal effort, the tables had suddenly turned. A Confederate invasion was sweeping into Kentucky, and a Federal defeat at Richmond, Kentucky, on August 30th, threatened Louisville and even Cincinnati. In the East, the victorious Confederates were also marching northward. On September 5th Lee's army crossed the Potomac into Maryland and marched for Frederick. In addition the congressional election was approaching. Democratic candidates who did not stand on Lieutenant Colonel Bragg's platform were talking about peace to the discouraged Northern people. Lincoln summed it all up in words Gibbon's Western soldiers could understand: "The bottom is out of the tub," said the President.

To sustain the war, the task of the Union in the East was the defeat of Lee. This was the responsibility of McClellan's Army of the Potomac, comprising seven corps, including the corps from Pope's Army of Virginia, now merged into the Army of the Potomac. In

113

the Army of the Potomac, McDowell's Corps again assumed its original numerical designation as the First Corps. But the commander of the First Corps was no longer McDowell. He was relieved, at his own request, to face groundless charges of disloyalty and drunkenness, of which he was soon to be acquitted by a court of inquiry. In his place, command was assigned to Major General Joseph Hooker. Hooker's First Corps and Reno's Ninth Corps were constituted as the right wing of the army, with General Ambrose Burnside as right-wing commander.

King's Division was the First Division in Hooker's First Corps, with Ricketts and General George G. Meade commanding the Second and Third divisions, respectively. King having been relieved, General Hatch was formally assigned to his command. As before, it included four brigades: the First, formerly Hatch's New York brigade, now under Colonel Walter Phelps, Jr.; the Second, Doubleday's Brigade; the Third, Patrick's New Yorkers; and the Fourth, John Gibbon's Westerners in their black hats. The division's artillery still included Battery B with its Indiana and Wisconsin volunteers. And the Wisconsin and Indiana soldiers were no longer the only Western infantry in the corps. Doubleday's Brigade of three New York and Pennsylvania regiments had been reinforced by the addition of the Seventh Indiana Volunteers, veterans of Cedar Mountain and Jackson's Valley Campaign.[1]

In Gibbon's Brigade, the reorganization of the army was reflected in the rise to prominence of three new officers in place of those who had fallen at Brawner Farm. In the Nineteenth Indiana, Captain William W. Dudley of Company B was appointed acting major, replacing Isaac May. Dudley was nineteen years old, a native of Vermont and grandson of a Massachusetts colonel of the Revolution. After attending preparatory schools in Vermont and in New Haven, Connecticut, a shortage of funds had frustrated the youthful captain's ambition to enter Yale College. Dudley left school in 1858 and emigrated to Richmond, Indiana, in 1860. There he was engaged in the grain milling business at the outbreak of the war, when he was elected captain of Wayne County's Company B.[2]

The other new faces in regimental command were George H. Stevens of the Second Wisconsin and John Benton Callis of the Seventh Wisconsin. Stevens, twenty-seven years old, was the son of a wealthy New York shipping merchant. Born in New York City, he had attended private schools there before coming to Wisconsin and entering the retail grocery business. He owed his majority to the promotion of Lucius Fairchild to colonel on September 8th, in place of Edgar O'Connor, and Thomas S. Allen's advance on the same day to the lieutenant colonelcy.[3] Captain John B. Callis of the Seventh Wisconsin was assigned to the command of that regiment, in the absence of Colonel Robinson, Lieutenant Colonel Hamilton, and Major Bill, all convalescing from wounds. Like Gibbon and Colonel Meredith of the Nineteenth Indiana, the thirty-four-year-old Callis was a North Carolinian. Born in Fayetteville in 1840, his family had moved to Lancaster, Wisconsin. In 1848, an uneducated pioneer youth of twenty, Callis left home and traveled to St. Paul, Minnesota, where he was employed by the United States in the construction of Fort Gaines. Among the builders of the fort was a young army captain named Todd whose sister was married to an undistinguished Illinois lawyer, Abraham Lincoln. Following his Minnesota sojourn, Callis, like Colonels Fairchild and Robinson, had tried the gold fields of California. From California he ventured to Central America before returning to Lancaster in 1853, where he settled, married, and engaged in trade until he undertook the raising of Company F of the Seventh Wisconsin.[4]

Its reorganization completed, the Army of the Potomac set out on September 6th to meet the Confederates. Gibbon's Brigade was turned out that night, packed its gear, and marched at 11:00 P.M. for Maryland. In the hot and sultry night, the soldiers crossed the Long Bridge into Washington and swung along until they reached the White House. While the head of the column was clearing the streets beyond, a halt was called in Gibbon's ranks and the soldiers rested in the street in front of the Executive Mansion. There the Western men saw a strange but inspiring picture. The yard of the White House was liberally strewn with reclining soldiers, resting up for the continuing march. Moving among them with pail and dipper in hand was the shirt-sleeved Abraham Lincoln, his tall form stooping occasionally to give water to a soldier.[5] To the unself-conscious President, this must have seemed a natural thing to do. Surely at this moment in history he could have repeated to the soldiers what he had said in Indianapolis, "Not with Presidents . . . but with you, is the question: 'Shall the Union . . . be preserved?' "

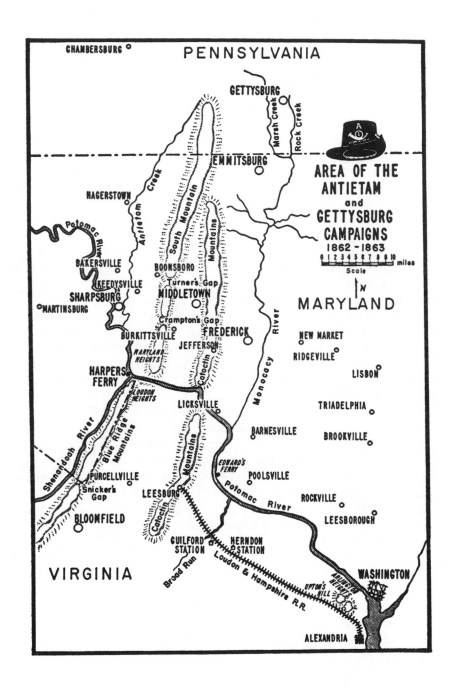

AREA OF THE
ANTIETAM
and
GETTYSBURG
CAMPAIGNS
1862 - 1863

0 1 2 3 4 5 6 7 8 9 10 miles
Scale

N

PENNSYLVANIA

CHAMBERSBURG

GETTYSBURG

Marsh Creek

Rock Creek

EMMITSBURG

MARYLAND

HAGERSTOWN

Antietam Creek

South Mountain

Catoctin Mountains

Potomac River

BAKERSVILLE

BOONSBORO

Turner's Gap

KEEDYSVILLE

MIDDLETOWN

SHARPSBURG

MARTINSBURG

Crampton's Gap

FREDERICK

Monocacy River

NEW MARKET

BURKITTSVILLE

JEFFERSON

RIDGEVILLE

MARYLAND
HEIGHTS

LISBON

HARPERS
FERRY

LOUDON
HEIGHTS

LICKSVILLE

TRIADELPHIA

BARNESVILLE

BROOKVILLE

Shenandoah River

Blue Ridge Mountains

Catoctin Mountains

EDWARD'S
FERRY

POOLSVILLE

PURCELLVILLE

Snicker's
Gap

Potomac River

ROCKVILLE

LEESBURG

LEESBOROUGH

BLOOMFIELD

Catoctin

GUILFORD
STATION

HERNDON
STATION

WASHINGTON

VIRGINIA

Broad Run

Loudon & Hampshire R.R.

UPTON'S
HILL

ARLINGTON
HEIGHTS

ALEXANDRIA

On the next afternoon the army reached Leesborough, Maryland, where a halt was called while the many stragglers from the all-night march caught up with their units. Then on to Rockville and camp for the night, twenty-seven miles from Upton's Hill. As one Hoosier private noted in his diary, the day had offered "nothing to remind us . . . of the holy Sabbath, nothing but long lines of soldiers, weary and faint traveling along through heat and dust. . . ." On the succeeding days, as the march proceeded through the rolling countryside to Brookville, Triadelphia, Lisbon, and New Market, the scene was described again by the Indiana private: "Thousands upon thousands of infantry, lines of cavalry sweeping by, the heavy artillery wagons with their grim death-dealing loads lumbering along, the long trains of government wagons . . . as we see them from each hill-top." On the 13th the column reached Frederick, Maryland, McClellan's point of concentration, and now evacuated by Lee as the Confederates moved west.[6]

At Frederick, Hooker's Corps camped two miles southeast of the city, in the valley of the Monocacy River.[7] Striking an unwarlike note, Rufus Dawes wrote that "there are few fairer landscapes in our country than this valley affords." But he quickly returned to the point: "From right to left along the valley below us, were stretched the swarming camps of the blue coats, and every soldier felt his courage rise at the sight." While Dawes waxed enthusiastic over the scene, John Gibbon rode to army headquarters on the outskirts of the city and visited his friend McClellan. Watching McClellan at work and in consultation with his aides, Gibbon was impressed. "Like a skillful driver, he seemed to have his team well in hand and to be able to judge at once whether reports made to him were correct or not," wrote John Gibbon. But the visit was more productive than this. From the commander himself Gibbon learned of McClellan's possession of a Confederate order that told of the plans and locations of the Confederate army. Equipped with a table of his adversary's movements, the Federal commander told Gibbon that if the army would "do two good, hard days' marching," Lee would be defeated. Always ready to champion his brigade, Gibbon assured McClellan that his command would do its part. He also added that it was much reduced in strength; he should like to have another regiment assigned to him, as soon as a new one was available. And Gibbon was particular about the type of regiment he wanted. He did not want just any regiment; the new regiment must be a *Western* regiment. To this McClellan responded with a promise: the next Western regiment to reach the army would go to Gibbon.[8]

The phenomenal find that McClellan disclosed to Gibbon was Lee's Special Order No. 191, issued on September 9th and setting forth his army's operation for the ensuing week. It was a bold operation. The principal force of Longstreet's Corps, approximately half of his army of 50,000 men, was dispatched by Lee to Boonsborough and Hagerstown, west of South Mountain, with D. H. Hill's Division, recently arrived from Richmond, as its rear guard. The other half of Lee's army was divided into three parts, each with a particular objective. The first part, Jackson's Corps, was to move on the Union garrison at Martinsburg, Virginia, south of the Potomac, and to cooperate in an attack on Harpers Ferry, where another small Union force was stationed. The second part, composed of McLaws' Division, also a recent accession to Lee's army, and the division of R. H. Anderson from Longstreet's Corps, was to move, under McLaws' command, directly against Harpers Ferry and to occupy Maryland Heights, north of the Potomac and commanding Harpers Ferry. The remaining Confederate detachment was Walker's Division, the last of Lee's newly acquired divisions. It was to occupy Loudon Heights, south of the Potomac and overlooking Harpers Ferry. When their objectives had been accomplished, the three commands were directed to rejoin Lee and Longstreet at Boonsborough and Hagerstown, where McLaws and Walker were to be assigned to Longstreet's Corps and D. H. Hill to Jackson's.[9]

Lee's scattering of his army offered McClellan the chance to strike Lee in the Boonsborough-Hagerstown location before his detached forces could rejoin him. To do so, the Federals would have to march westward. The principal route from Frederick was the National Road, which ran in an east-west direction over the twenty-four miles to Hagerstown, where what was left of Lee's army was encamped. The National Road first crossed the Catoctin Mountains, a ridgelike eminence four miles west of Frederick. Beyond the Catoctins was Middletown. Beyond Middletown, and approximately halfway from Frederick to Hagerstown, the National Road crossed South Mountain, a part of the Blue Ridge, rising precipitously almost a thousand feet above the surrounding countryside and extending all the way to the Potomac, fifteen miles away, where the ridge culminated in Maryland Heights. Two of the principal gaps in South Mountain were McClellan's avenues of approach over this natural barrier between his army and Lee's. The first of these was Turner's Gap, through which the National Road itself passed. Approximately five miles below Turner's, near the town of Burkittsville, was Crampton's Gap.[10]

Unaware of their army commander's great find, Gibbon's soldiers awakened on the bright morning of September 14th to the sound of the church bells of Frederick. The bells rang not only because it was Sunday but also to celebrate the arrival of the Federal army, the city's "host for deliverance" from the Confederates, as Rufus Dawes recorded it. It was now sixteen hours since Lee's plan had been discovered. Lee had already learned of McClellan's find and had immediately reinforced the South Mountain defenses in McClellan's path. Sixteen hours had been lost, but at last the Federal army started to move. While Franklin's Sixth Corps headed for Crampton's Gap, Reno's Corps and Hooker's Corps stepped off at daylight to take the National Road toward Turner's Gap.[11] Entering Frederick, a tumultuous welcome overwhelmed the blue-coated columns, the loyal Marylanders cheering and waving as the long lines of Ninth Corps and First Corps veterans passed along the flag-draped streets. This was a welcome contrast to the stony hostility of the Virginia towns, especially when to the cheers were added the more tangible tributes of pies and cakes and ice water. While Gibbon's men were in the city, General McClellan rode in, passing along the flank of the marching column. The people pressed about the Federal commander, and the marching men, many of whom had already straggled badly, had to stop and wait for the route to clear. During one of the halts, gathering his men about him, General Gibbon addressed them. They should know, he said, what McClellan had told him of the importance of the march the army was now embarked upon. Applying the approach that had thus far worked so well, he expressed his confidence that they could be depended upon not to straggle. McClellan had promised the brigade the next *Western* regiment to join the army. Amid excited cheering, Gibbon concluded, "General McClellan made this promise because he knows of no better place where a new regiment can learn how to fight!"[12]

Following the general's speech, Gibbon's Brigade resumed its march through Frederick. Beyond the town, stragglers from other commands began to appear. In response to Gibbon's suggestion, the brigade jeered at the stragglers. All of the drummers in the brigade, moved by Gibbon to the head of the column, beat out "The Rogue's March," and a concerted verbal barrage was visited on the erring soldiers, forcing them forward to their commands. Although pleased at the disappearance of the stragglers, Gibbon was more concerned at the effect of the event on his own command. By taking up the anti-straggling cause, Gibbon's soldiers developed their own solution for straggling. During the rest of the long march, as the general put it, "It became an honorable ambition to remain in the ranks, instead of constantly inventing pretexts to fall out."[13]

In the late morning the column reached the summit of the Catoctin Mountains, where the fences and trees bore the signs of a cavalry skirmish of the preceding day. From the summit, the soldiers looked ahead to Middletown and, in the distance beyond the town, South Mountain. Sounds of battle emanated from the direction of South Mountain where, in an effort to turn the right of the Confederate defenders at Turner's Gap, Federal cavalry and two of Reno's Ninth Corps divisions, Cox's and Willcox's, were already engaged on the Sharpsburg Road which ascended the mountain to the left of the National Road.[14] Quickening its pace, Gibbon's column entered Middletown to another rousing welcome from the citizens, whose excitement was increased by the nearby fighting and the appearance in the streets of wounded men returning from the mountain battle. Beyond Middletown, but still two miles from the base of South Mountain, the division halted for coffee in a field beside the road. It was now midafternoon and, battle or no battle, the soldiers felt that it was time for refreshment. But before the men could build their fires, they were ordered to fall in and move forward. Up and down the line came the news: The First Corps was to carry the crest of South Mountain that night.[15]

Ahead of Hooker's Corps, right-wing commander Burnside ordered the remaining divisions of Reno's Corps, Sturgis' and Rodman's, to the support of Cox and Willcox in the assault up the Sharpsburg Road. Arriving at the base of the mountain at 3:30 P.M., Sturgis and Rodman deployed their men on either side of the road and became engaged. While Reno's reinforcements were deploying,

Meade's Division, leading Hooker's Corps, advanced on the National Road to the mountain's base, then marched toward the Old Hagerstown Road which ascended the mountain to the right of the National Road. Behind Meade, and arriving as Reno's reinforcements started their ascent up the Sharpsburg Road, came Hatch's and Ricketts' divisions of Hooker's Corps, who were deployed at once and followed Meade's men.[16] Gibbon's Brigade marched with Hatch's Division over the broken and rocky ground at the base of the mountain. But before the Westerners reached the Old Hagerstown Road, John Gibbon received a direct order from General Burnside, recalling his brigade and Battery B to the National Road. The Western soldiers and their artillery left Hatch's column, countermarched to the National Road, and again advanced toward the mountain.[17]

The Federal plan had now matured. Reno's Corps, attacking up the Sharpsburg Road, was to strike the Confederate right flank. Hooker's Corps, moving up the Old Hagerstown Road, was simultaneously to launch its assault on the defenders' left flank. As soon as the flank attacks had developed, Gibbon's Brigade alone, supported by Battery B, was to ascend the National Road and hit the center of the Confederate line. Thus Gibbon's Brigade, as at Brawner Farm, was to be fighting its own fight. But unlike their engagement on the night of August 28th, what the Western soldiers did at South Mountain would be observed by others of their comrades. Their corps commander would know about it, and so would General Burnside, whose headquarters were on high ground a mile behind Gibbon's line. With Burnside at his headquarters was George B. McClellan.[18] Thus, the commanding general would also have a front-row seat to watch the action of Gibbon's Brigade.

The Confederate forces awaiting the assault of Burnside's wing had been steadily reinforced after the morning action with Reno's leading divisions. Now confronting the Federals was a collection of units under the command of General D. H. Hill. John Gibbon and his Confederate brother Lardner had been groomsmen in D. H. Hill's wedding years before, but this was all by the way at the moment, and Hill was girding for the defense of the mountain. His command included the brigades from his own division and from the divisions of J. R. Jones and John B. Hood of Longstreet's Corps. Also on hand were artillery batteries from his own division and from the Confederate army's artillery reserve, and the dismounted cavalry of Rosser's regiment and the horse artillery guns of Pelham. As the Federal attack developed, General Longstreet arrived, to take over command as senior officer on the field.[19]

At the center of the Confederate line, in the gorge of Turner's Gap at the mountain summit, was the 1,100 man brigade of Colonel A. H. Colquitt, five Alabama and Georgia regiments from D. H. Hill's Division. At this point, the gap was reduced to a narrow defile through which the National Road passed. Rising sharply on both sides of the road were wooded hills. To the natural advantages of the pass was added a stone wall which ran north at right angles from the road to the wooded high ground beyond. In front of the gorge with its stone wall barrier, running downhill to the east whence the Federals would come, were other stone fences, woods, ravines, and farm buildings on both sides of the road, providing ideal cover for pickets opposing any force ascending the mountain to the gorge.[20]

Under the personal direction of D. H. Hill, Colquitt's regiments were placed so as to take full advantage of their admirable defensive ground. North of the road, the Twenty-third and Twenty-eighth Georgia were placed behind the stone wall, from where the sloping ground in their front provided an ideal field of fire on the narrow pass. To the south of the road, on the wooded hillside that also commanded the pass, were the Thirteenth Alabama and the Sixth and Twenty-seventh Georgia. In front of this main line, Colquitt distributed several companies of pickets in the hiding places afforded. Thus, with his flanks anchored by the wooded hillsides on either side of the pass and with the narrow gut of the pass defended by the stone wall, Colquitt waited for any move up the National Road.[21]

Gibbon's Brigade, now halted in a field off the road, awaited the order to advance. Directly ahead, two miles up the National Road, Colquitt's Brigade lay in wait. Two miles to the right of Gibbon's men, Rufus Dawes could see his First Corps comrades on the Old Hagerstown Road, "long lines and heavy columns of dark blue infantry . . . pressing up the green slopes of the mountain, their bayonets flashing like silver in the rays of the setting sun, and their banners waving in beautiful relief against the background of green." About the same distance to the left were Reno's men on the Sharpsburg Road. Gibbon's men could not see the Ninth Corps, but one of

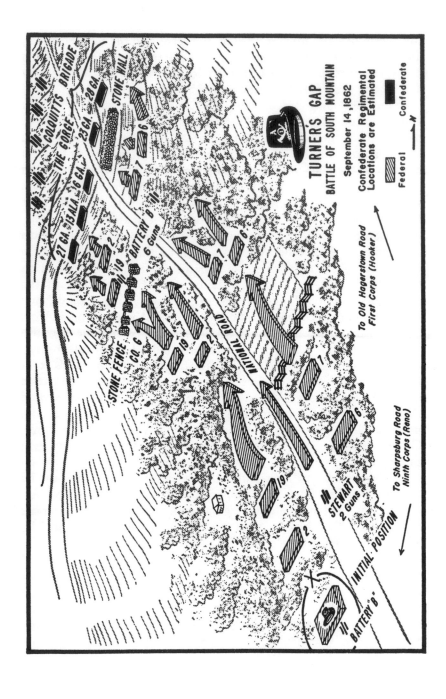

TURNER'S GAP
BATTLE OF SOUTH MOUNTAIN

September 14, 1862

Confederate Regimental
Locations are Estimated

Federal   Confederate

the Westerners recorded "a crash of musketry, and the roll of cannon, and a white cloud of battle smoke . . . above the trees" to the left. As the Western soldiers waited, they could also see shells bursting over and among the Federals advancing to the right and left.[22]

In the developing flank assaults, the Confederates opposing Hooker and Reno fought with great determination, taking advantage of the natural cover their high ground afforded. But the Federals ground slowly ahead, up the rugged mountainside, impeded but never checked by the plunging fire of their adversaries. At last, after an hour of waiting, and just as the sun began to sink behind the mountain summit, a rider from Burnside raced to Gibbon with the order: the troops on both flanks were making good progress; attack at once.[23]

Gibbon first deployed his skirmishers, one company from the Sixth and one from the Second Wisconsin. Behind the skirmishers, marching by the right of companies, the Nineteenth Indiana moved out on the left side and the Seventh Wisconsin on the right side of the road. Following the leading regiments by two hundred yards, and formed in double columns, came the Second Wisconsin behind the Nineteenth Indiana, and the Sixth Wisconsin behind the Seventh. The right section of Battery B, two guns under Lieutenant Stewart, was placed on the road itself, a little in the rear of the brigade's front line. Thus quickly formed, with a cheer the men stepped off, passed quickly through a slight dip in the ground in their front and started their ascent into the mountain gorge. Mounted on his horse, and riding on high ground from which he could view his whole force, Gibbon accompanied the front line, exhorting the Westerners with the repeated command of "Forward! Forward! Forward!"[24]

As the men began their climb they were at once opened on by Colquitt's pickets firing from behind logs, fences, rocks, and bushes. Assisted by Lieutenant Stewart's guns, which unlimbered at intervals to fire into the thickets from which the enemy fire came, the Western soldiers returned the fire, and moved on. Now the Confederate artillery joined the engagement. Posted on the high ground to the right and rear of the Confederate main line, the guns overshot the Seventh and Sixth Wisconsin on the right of the road. But on the left, behind the Nineteenth Indiana, a shell fell among the men of the Second Wisconsin, killing and wounding seven of the Badger soldiers.[25] Still the blue ranks moved steadily up the steep mountainside, apparently ignoring their occasional casualties and returning the Confederate picket fire. A half-mile from their starting point, the Seventh Wisconsin came to a fence, beyond which was an open field skirted by woods at its upper edge. From the woods a heavy Confederate fire swept the open field. Checked only momentarily, the Seventh climbed the fence, crossed the field, and drove the enemy from the woods. In line with the Seventh, advancing with flankers out, the Nineteenth Indiana was slowed by heavy fire coming from within and around a farmhouse to the left. Meredith called for Stewart's guns, which, coming forward on the road, unlimbered and threw several shells into the house, clearing this obstruction from the Nineteenth's way.[26]

Cheering now in the face of increasing rifle fire and heavier casualties, the brigade steadily advanced for another three-quarters of a mile, driving the Confederate outposts into the narrowing gorge.[27] A quarter of a mile from the main line, the Federals struck the principal Confederate advance force.[28] In front of the Nineteenth Indiana the Hoosiers uncovered a stone fence running south at right angles to the road. From behind it the Confederates poured a hot fire into the Indiana line and, firing to their left, enfiladed the Seventh Wisconsin advancing north of the road. At Solomon Meredith's order, the Nineteenth's Company G wheeled to its left and moved to flank the fence. At the same time Captain Callis, commanding the Seventh Wisconsin, changed front so as to throw the right of his regiment forward and to the left, toward the fence. In an instant, a wood to the right of the Seventh exploded with a deadly fire into the backs of the wheeling Wisconsin men. For a few minutes there was grim execution in the Seventh, its color disappearing and reappearing as one color-bearer after another was shot down.[29] But Gibbon moved the Second Wisconsin into the front line, in between the Nineteenth and Seventh, and ordered the Sixth Wisconsin to the right of the Seventh to meet the assault from the wood. Amidst the crash of rifle fire, Lieutenant Colonel Bragg commanded: "Deploy column! By the right and left flanks, double quick, march!" and the right wing of the Sixth swept into the field beside the cheering Seventh and fired into the deadly wood. Unable in the close quarters of the pass to move his left wing into the front line, Bragg now ordered his right wing to lie down and sent the left wing leaping over them to fire at the unseen Confederates. Repeating this unique maneuver, the Sixth delivered four volleys by wing and drove the gray marksmen from the wood.[30] At the same time, on the Federal left, the Nineteenth's Company G succeeded in flanking the stone fence in its front. Confronted with a direct flank fire and by heavy fire from the front, the remaining Confederates behind the fence were broken, retreating or surrendering to their Indiana foes.[31]

Now the Westerners reached the defenders' main line at the apex of the pass. Although exhausted from the climb and the ceaseless fighting, the massed Federals rushed forward, shouting wildly from throats burning and bitter with powder and smoke.[32] As they came into view of the Confederates on the rising ground forty yards away, a thousand rifles poured down from the stone wall and the hills on both sides, lighting up the gathering darkness and halting the Federal advance. Rallying in the darkness under cover of the uneven ground, Gibbon's men aimed and fired at the flashes of the Confederate guns as the battle roared toward its climax amidst the shouts and expletives of the soldiers of both sides.[33] The Seventh Wisconsin faced the murderous fire directly in front of the stone wall. To their right was the Sixth Wisconsin. But to the left of the Seventh, where the narrowness of the pass afforded insufficient room for a regimental front, the Second Wisconsin's right wing occupied the ground alone. When its ammunition was gone, the left wing of the Second and right and left wings of the Nineteenth Indiana took turns on the Union left, fighting until their ammunition was also expended. So furious was the Federal fire in front of the stone wall that to Colquitt it seemed that the two Georgia regiments there faced "at least five, perhaps ten, times their numbers." Battery B now joined the tempest. Captain Campbell had arrived with the battery's remaining guns, and over the heads of the Federal infantry, the six guns fired into the darkened hillsides from which flashed the Confederate rifle fire.[34]

Aware of the terrible casualties in the pitched battle at the stone wall, Gibbon now directed the Sixth Wisconsin to move around the flank of the defenders' line. Bragg ordered Major Dawes to continue firing with the Sixth's right wing, and led the left wing up the steep and wooded hillside toward the Confederate left and rear. Although opposed by a heavy fire from behind rocks and trees, Bragg's command labored up the hill, dislodged the enemy and, reaching higher ground, opened fire. Despite the hail of bullets provoked by Bragg's position, Dawes now moved the Sixth's other wing to the right so as to join Bragg's wing in a semicircle around the Confederate left. But this advantage was promptly neutralized as an ammunition shortage, already felt by the Nineteenth Indiana and Second Wisconsin on the Federal left, spread up and down the Sixth Wisconsin's line. Just as crippling, the rifles of the Sixth were now too hot for loading and too full of carbon for safe use.[35] In front of the stone wall, the Seventh Wisconsin, too, was by this time virtually out of ammunition, and had already emptied the cartridge boxes of the dead and wounded. At this critical moment, locked in the dark with a powerful enemy, it appeared that the brigade, for all of its hard fighting and heavy losses, would forfeit the battle. Gibbon's order to the men was grim: Hold your ground with the bayonet.[36]

The crisis occasioned by the ammunition shortage lasted only briefly. Gibbon, to whom word had been brought of the success of both Hooker and Reno, sent word to his regiments to cease firing, that the battle was won.[37] But the Western soldiers were not through yet. The Confederates in front of the Sixth and Seventh Wisconsin, apparently thinking that the slackening Federal fire meant withdrawal, commenced an advance. While Bragg's men opened a sharp fire in the woods on the Federal right, Callis ordered the Seventh to its feet and, with fixed bayonets charged the advancing Confederates. Firing at close range, the Seventh broke the gray line and the Confederates retired in confusion to their stone barricade. There the defenders, also suffering for want of ammunition, gradually ceased firing, and at 9:00 P.M.,[38] with both sides resting in close proximity, the bloody work at Turner's Gap drew to a close.

A worried Lee now met behind the Confederate line with Longstreet and D. H. Hill. Lee's army was still scattered, and would remain so until Harpers Ferry fell. To hold the Federals at South Mountain was therefore still crucial to the Confederate plan. But this was no longer possible, and Lee knew it. Franklin's Sixth Corps had succeeded in forcing Crampton's Gap to the south. At Turner's Gap the Federals had also won the day and were in possession of the mountain crest. McClellan's leisurely advance and the defense of the gaps had purchased a valuable day for Lee, but both Hill and Longstreet discouraged the prospect of renewing the fight on the next day. Accordingly, although retreat virtually abandoned the divisions of McLaws on Maryland Heights, Lee ordered an immediate Confederate withdrawal to Sharpsburg. There he hoped to reunite his army before McClellan attacked him in force.[39]

Lieutenant Colonel Bragg was among the first to suspect that Colquitt's men were withdrawing. Shortly after the final flare-up in front of the Sixth and Seventh, Bragg told Dawes that he heard the enemy moving away. Up and down the battered Federal line the word was passed. Hoping to provoke a response, the Sixth Wisconsin rent the smoky darkness with three cheers for the "Badger State," followed by more cheers from the other Wisconsin and Indiana soldiers. In the eerie silence that followed, volunteer skirmishers felt the enemy positions, still without discovering any signs of the foe. Then, wary of surprise and advised by Gibbon that they would shortly be relieved, the Western soldiers settled down to wait on the ground they had won.[40]

With the enemy's departure came an opportunity for Gibbon's men to learn of the day's events elsewhere along the Federal line. General Reno's death was reported, but Gibbon's soldiers, many of them Southern born, were spared D. H. Hill's official statement: "General Reno, a renegade Virginian, . . . was killed by a happy shot from the Twenty-third North Carolina."[41] General Hatch was also a casualty, severely wounded, and General Abner Doubleday now assumed permanent command of the First Division.[42] But of more concern to Gibbon's soldiers were their own wounded and dying, scattered up and down the mountainside and now sought out by their comrades. Rufus Dawes was engaged in this dolorous task, and his description of it cannot be improved upon: "Several dying men were pleading piteously for water, of which there was not a drop . . . nor was there any liquor. Captain Kellogg and I searched in vain for a swallow for one noble fellow who was dying in great agony from a wound in his bowels. He recognized us and appreciated our efforts, but was unable to speak. The dread reality of war was before us in this frightful death, upon the cold hard stones. The mortal suffering, the fruitless struggle to send a parting message to a far-off home, and the final release in death, all enacted in the darkness. . . ." Finally, the stretcher-bearers reached the field and carried the surviving wounded back to the houses and barns near Middletown.[43]

At midnight, elements of Sumner's Second Corps arrived to relieve Gibbon's Brigade. Three of the weary Western regiments—sixteen hours had passed since they had heard the Sunday-morning church bells in Frederick—retraced their steps along the National Road to camp.[44] But not the Sixth Wisconsin. Off in the wooded hills above and to the right of the rest of the brigade, Bragg's exhausted soldiers continued to wait. The Sixth's regimental adjutant was dispatched to the commander of the newcomers and was advised that he would not order his men into the woods at night. So the Sixth held its ground until morning and was privileged to see beyond the stone wall the same hideous sights Dawes had seen in his search for the Federal wounded. The Confederate dead and wounded were there, including one young Georgia boy who had lain on the ground all night, his face a gore of blood, and who staggered crazily to his feet and fled as the Wisconsin soldiers approached him. When at last relieved, Lieutenant Colonel Bragg's official comment was appropriately caustic: "Soon after daylight my regiment was relieved by the Second New York . . . who had been lying in the field, under cover of a stone wall, at a safe distance in the rear, refreshing themselves with a good night's sleep, after a long and fatiguing march of some ten miles."[45]

During the night, and while his survivors did what they could to be ready for the morrow, Gibbon counted his losses: 37 killed, 251 wounded, and 30 missing, a total of 318 officers and men, approximately 25 per cent of the brigade. The Seventh Wisconsin, which had fronted on the deadly stone wall, was the heaviest loser, 147 from that regiment having gone down. Ninety-two were casualties in the Sixth, the next highest contributor, largely victims of the flanking movement up the hillside to the right of the stone wall. Of the remaining two regiments, the Nineteenth Indiana suffered 53 casualties and the Second Wisconsin 26.[46] The brigade had suffered far more severely than its well-protected adversary. Colquitt's losses were never officially reported, but D. H. Hill, remarking on the Confederate brigade's superb defensive location, later set its casualties at approximately 100 men.[47] On the Federal side, comparative casualties were startling. Gibbon's Brigade had sustained greater losses than any other Federal brigade engaged. In the First Corps its casualties were twice those of any other brigade.[48] These proud statistics were a doubtful distinction. Well might the soldiers from the

Old Northwest have questioned the fate that had caused them to leave their corps and press alone up the National Road. But the manner in which Gibbon's losses had occurred had not gone unnoticed. McClellan and Burnside and a number of other officers had seen it all, the initial advance up the mountainside, the unflinching progress as the enemy's fire increased, and the dogged movement, always forward, into the darkness, marked toward the end by the flashes from the opposing lines of rifles.[49] To Burnside, it was "a most brilliant engagement." McClellan officially reported that "General Gibbon, in this delicate movement, handled his brigade with as much precision and coolness as if upon parade, and the bravery of his troops could not be excelled." The commanding general also later reported that in talking that night with Corps Commander Hooker, the word "iron" was used to describe the performance and that Hooker had referred to Gibbon's as his "iron brigade."[50] The Western soldiers immediately seized on this as their title, and the reputation of the brigade and its new name were soon broadcast around the Federal campfires.[51]

On the rocky sides of South Mountain at Turner's Gap, Gibbon's soldiers acquired a reputation, a reputation they would have to sustain with further bravery, and which would somehow make them brave, as brave as an "Iron Brigade."

7

ANTIETAM

"Gainesville, Bull Run, South Mountain . . . , in the intensity and energy of the fight and the roar of firearms, . . . were but skirmishes in comparison to this of Sharpsburg."

From a letter of Gibbon's aide, Frank A. Haskell,
Sixth Wisconsin Volunteers

The dawn of September 15th found the Army of the Potomac preparing to move out in pursuit of Lee. In the Iron Brigade, the new day also disclosed two more casualties, temporary in character but organizationally important. Although well enough to continue in the field, Colonel Fairchild and Colonel Meredith were unable to exercise command as a result of complete physical exhaustion, complicated in Meredith's case by the aftereffects of a fall from his horse in the whirlwind at Brawner Farm. In the Second Wisconsin, Lieutenant Colonel Allen assumed command. Lieutenant Colonel Alois O. Bachman relieved Meredith in the Indiana regiment.[1] For the rest of the brigade, the night's sleep had provided at least a partial restoration, and the men began to cook breakfast, their first food in twenty-four hours. Fires were lighted, haversacks were opened, and the soldiers' beloved coffee brought forth. But even as the breakfast preparations were in progress the order to move was received, and the hungry men fell in for the march to Boonsborough.[2]

John Gibbon led his Iron Brigade up the National Road behind the Second Corps. During a brief halt while the column was organized, the brigade was ordered to pass through the Second Corps and rejoin its own First Corps, leading the advance. Marching through the ranks of the Second Corps lining each side of the road, the Westerners set off for the summit of South Mountain. After passing the grisly stone wall and the scenes of their battle, the brigade came to the Mountain House, a landmark on the summit and now temporarily occupied by General Sumner, commander of the Second Corps. Sumner had witnessed the Iron Brigade's attack of the night before, and his adjutant now told Gibbon that the general had just instructed his corps to cheer the Iron Brigade as it passed through. Gibbon was disappointed that his quick movement had anticipated the greeting from the Second Corps. But his personal satisfaction at Sumner's intention was real because that general was known to be ordinarily opposed to such demonstrations as destructive of discipline.[3]

Unaware of what they had missed on top of South Mountain, Gibbon's soldiers continued the march down the western slope. Soon they were met by inspiration of a different sort as loyal inhabitants of the area gathered along the route of march. One aged man, deeply agitated by the Confederate invasion and the recent battle, spoke to Rufus Dawes: "We have watched for you, Sir, and we have prayed for you and now thank God you have come," said the Union man. Then he mounted a bank by the roadside and shouted his joy to the soldiers, who cheered lustily in return. At Boonsborough, only recently evacuated by the Confederates, the people thronged about the soldiers, shouting and waving the "old flag." Beyond the town, the Federal column turned left, to follow a road to the southwest, toward Sharpsburg. At midday the Iron Brigade came to Keedysville, two miles from Antietam Creek and three miles from Sharpsburg. Emerging from Keedysville, the Federals were greeted by artillery fire from cannon posted on the outskirts of Sharpsburg. As the Federal artillery unlimbered to respond, the First Corps left the road and entered a ravine affording protection from Confederate shell fragments. There the infantry was at ease and, making quick work of the nearby fences, the soldiers of the Iron Brigade at last enjoyed their coffee. Later in the afternoon, as the Federal army gathered along the eastern bank of the Antietam, the Western soldiers proceeded up the creek out of artillery range and bivouacked for the night. Although the march for the day had covered only fourteen miles, Gibbon's survivors of the South Mountain fight were still much the worse for wear. In the Second Wisconsin alone, forty-one men had been compelled to leave the ranks and remain behind during the day. Now the rest of the brigade, 800 effectives, fell into an exhausted sleep.[4]

By the early morning of September 16th all six of McClellan's corps, 75,000 ready for duty, had assembled along Antietam Creek. Opposing them were but 18,000 Southern soldiers, Lee's detached commands having not yet rejoined his army. But McClellan did not attack, and Lee's force rapidly increased as the day progressed. During the morning, Jackson's Corps arrived, except for the division of A. P. Hill. Harpers Ferry had surrendered on the previous day, and Hill had been left behind to parole prisoners and secure the captured property. As the day dragged on with nothing but artillery and picket firing, Walker's Division came up from Loudon Heights. On the morning of the 17th McLaws' divisions were to reach Sharpsburg, bringing the Confederate army to full strength except for A. P. Hill's Division. Even with Hill, Lee could muster only 50,000 men to face 75,000 Federals, and McClellan's delay on September 16th gave Lee the opportunity to concentrate most of his outnumbered force.[5]

The 16th of September also saw McClellan's ultimate resolution to attack the Confederates. Their line, facing east and running in a north-south direction on a slight ridge or divide between Antietam Creek and the Potomac, extended over a front of approximately three and a half miles. The left flank curved west to the Potomac. The right flank was anchored on Antietam Creek, approximately a mile from the Potomac. Bisecting this line on the Confederate left, at the point at which it curved to the west, and running south along the ridge line into Sharpsburg, was the Hagerstown Turnpike. McClellan's army was distributed opposite Lee's line, east of Antietam Creek. The Federal commander's plan was an orthodox one: to assault the enemy's left, then his right and, as soon as one or both of the flank movements was successful, to attack the center with the Federal reserve. In the attack on the left, the First Corps was to lead off, supported by the Second, Twelfth and, if necessary, the Sixth Corps. Accordingly, at 4:00 P.M. on the 16th, the First Corps divisions of Meade, Ricketts, and Doubleday, between 12,000 and 13,000 men, crossed the Antietam opposite Keedysville at the fords and a bridge near Pry's Mill.[6]

With Meade's Division leading, the Federal soldiers marched westward toward the extreme left of the Confederate line, two miles away at the Hagerstown Turnpike. The Federal route passed through open fields, gardens, and orchards, and the soldiers of the Iron Brigade filled their haversacks with apples as they advanced. Toward dusk, ahead of the Iron Brigade, Meade's skirmishers came in contact with the enemy, but the advance slowly moved forward in the face of mounting resistance. Finally, at 9:00 P.M., the Federal column was halted for the night. Doubleday's Division bivouacked along the east side of the Hagerstown Turnpike on a slight east-west rise of ground on the Poffenberger farm. To Doubleday's left were the camps of Ricketts' Division. Meade's skirmishers picketed the area in front of Doubleday and Ricketts, but Meade's main force encamped behind these two, constituting the reserve for the corps. Muskets loaded and formed in close column, the soldiers of the Iron Brigade lay upon the ground amidst their comrades of Doubleday's Division. There was a drizzling rain and, with the certain prospect of battle in the morning, the night was dismal. As one of Westerners re-membered it, "Nothing can be more solemn than a period of silent waiting for the summons to battle, known to be impending."[7]

Facing to the south toward the east-west extension of the Con-federate line, the First Corps was now astride the slight ridge over which Lee had distributed his force. If the Federals could pierce the Southern defense and reach the high ground there that com-manded the Confederate line, Lee's army could be dealt a decisive defeat. This was Hooker's purpose, to move down the ridge to the Confederate rear. South of the buildings and woodlot of the Poffen-berger farm was the farm of D. R. Miller, a half-mile away. The Miller house, situated east of the turnpike, was surrounded by an orchard, garden, and the usual outbuildings. Across the pike, op-posite the house, were the Miller barn and stack yard. A half-mile beyond the Miller farm was a more distinctive structure, a small brick church, painted white. This church stood just west of the pike and belonged to the Dunker sect. It rested on the highest ground along the ridge, and thus marked the key to domination of this part of the battlefield.

In addition to the farm buildings and Dunker Church, there were other landmarks in the area. On the Federal left—a quarter of a mile east of the turnpike—was a woods, to be known historically as the "East Woods." West of the turnpike, opposite the East Woods, was another woods, the "West Woods," which grew larger as it extended to the south where it surrounded the Dunker Church. Between these two woods, and lying halfway between the Miller farm on the north and the church on the south, was open ground. On the east side of the pike this ground was occupied by a large cornfield in which the corn stood higher than a man's head. Across the pike from the cornfield was a narrow strip of pasture ground, skirted on its south and west sides by the irregular West Woods. The sleeping Western soldiers could not, of course, see any of this small, gently rolling square of ground. But they would see it soon and they would never forget it, bounded on the north by the Miller farm, on the south, a half-mile away, by the little church, on the east by the East Woods, and on the west, a half-mile away, by the West Woods. The square was crossed north and south by the turnpike and east and west by the cornfield and pasture between the two woods. Within the square, movement in any direction was obstructed by numerous farm fences and by the high post-and-rail fences that were erected along both sides of the turnpike.[8]

Since the Federal activity late on the 16th had advertised the impending assault on the left, the Southerners had readied the defense of this position. To this sector Lee had assigned Stonewall Jackson with the Iron Brigade's old foes from Brawner Farm, Jackson's Division, now commanded by J. R. Jones, and Ewell's Division, now under General Lawton. Directly to the right of the Federals, at the extreme left of the Confederate line, and positioned so as to enfilade an attack down the pike, were Stuart's cavalry and a heavy concentration of artillery, with Early's Brigade from Ewell's Division in support. Next to this force and facing north were Jones' Brigade and the Stonewall Brigade from Jackson's Division, formed in the West Woods in front of the Dunker Church, their right resting on the turnpike. In the rear of these brigades in the woods behind the church were A. G. Taliaferro's and Starke's brigades, also from Jackson's Division. Jackson's artillery was placed among his brigades, including the batteries of Poague and Wooding that had signaled the beginning of the fight at Brawner Farm.[9]

Across the turnpike from Jackson's Division were the men of Ewell's Division, also heavily supported by artillery. Lawton's Brigade, with Hays' behind it, rested with its left on the turnpike and facing

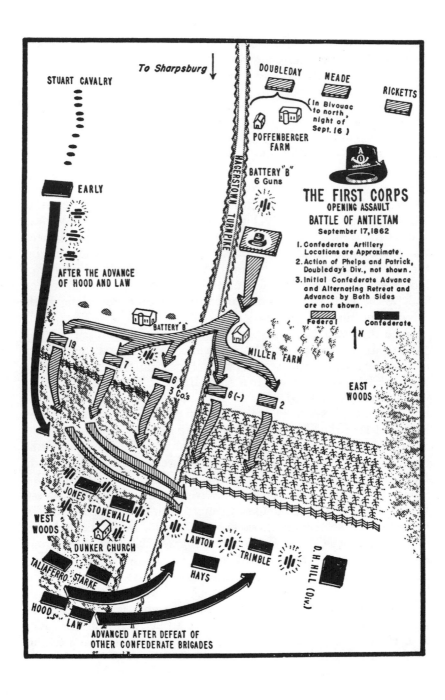

To Sharpsburg

STUART CAVALRY

DOUBLEDAY

MEADE
(In Bivouac
to north,
night of
Sept. 16)

RICKETTS

POFFENBERGER
FARM

EARLY

HAGERSTOWN TURNPIKE

BATTERY "B"
6 Guns

THE FIRST CORPS
OPENING ASSAULT
BATTLE OF ANTIETAM
September 17, 1862

1. Confederate Artillery
   Locations are Approximate.
2. Action of Phelps and Patrick,
   Doubleday's Div., not shown.
3. Initial Confederate Advance
   and Alternating Retreat and
   Advance by Both Sides
   are not shown.

AFTER THE ADVANCE
OF HOOD AND LAW

Federal   Confederate

N

BATTERY "B"

MILLER FARM

EAST
WOODS

19

7

6
3 Co.'s

6 (-)

2

JONES
STONEWALL

WEST
WOODS

DUNKER CHURCH

LAWTON

TRIMBLE

TALIAFERRO
STARKE

HAYS

D. H. HILL (Div.)

HOOD
LAW

ADVANCED AFTER DEFEAT OF
OTHER CONFEDERATE BRIGADES

toward the cornfield. To the right of Lawton was Trimble's Brigade, also facing the cornfield and extending toward the East Woods where its flank met the left of D. H. Hill's Division. Hill's line ran north and south and formed a right angle with Trimble's.[10] Skirmishers from all of the infantry commands were already forward, around the Miller farm buildings and in the cornfield. And in the woods behind the church were the reserves for this sector of the Confederate line, the brigades of Hood and Evander M. Law from Hood's Division of Longstreet's Corps. These two brigades had already engaged Meade's skirmishers and were now encamped in the West Woods cooking rations. But they were available for the defense of the Confederate left and, including D. H. Hill's Division, gave Stonewall Jackson in excess of 9,000 infantry opposed to the First Corps.[11]

At the earliest dawn on the 17th, the Iron Brigade was awakened by the long roll and by the beginning of a Confederate cannonade. The soldiers moved into line to the accompaniment of shells screaming overhead and skirmish firing to the left and front of their position.[12] As soon as the men were formed, and having detached Doubleday's old brigade, now under Lieutenant Colonel J. William Hofmann, to observe Stuart's artillery concentration to the right, Hooker put his corps in motion. Behind Meade's skirmishers, the Iron Brigade, followed by Phelps and Patrick, led Doubleday's Division down the left side of the turnpike. To Doubleday's left was Ricketts, advancing toward the East Woods in line with Doubleday. Following Doubleday and Ricketts was the main body of Meade's Division. As Battery B opened a heavy fire over their heads, the Iron Brigade moved out in column by division, its front line composed of the Sixth Wisconsin on the right and the Second on the left, followed by the Nineteenth Indiana and the Seventh Wisconsin.[13] No Confederate infantry was in sight, but the artillery fire was severe. The column had just begun to advance when a shell exploded on the ground in the midst of the Sixth Wisconsin, tearing both arms from one of the soldiers, severing Captain David K. Noyes' foot, and killing or wounding eleven of the Badgers. Knowing that such a calamity was the severest test of the discipline of the men, Gibbon long remembered how the casualties were promptly removed from the column and how the men moved forward quickly at the word of Lieutenant Colonel Bragg.[14]

Now the brigade passed around the Poffenberger farm buildings and into the farm woodlot. As the shot and shell whistled through the trees, severing branches which fell among his soldiers, Gibbon organized for battle. Two companies of the Sixth Wisconsin were assigned to Captain Kellogg as skirmishers. Behind them the brigade was deployed in two lines of battle and advanced to the edge of the woodlot.[15] Across an intervening field, the Confederate pickets opened fire from the Miller farmhouse, yard, and orchard. But Kellogg and his skirmishers raced over the field and drove the Southerners from the house and yard, followed by the brigade, which maneuvered rapidly around the buildings and fences in spite of a rising musketry fire from the orchard. Men were falling now, and here and there gaps appeared in the lines of the brigade. As the Sixth Wisconsin negotiated the obstacles in the farmyard, Major Dawes watched Captain Edward A. Brown shout a command to his company and fall dead as a bullet entered his open mouth. After the farmyard the orchard was reached, as the Confederate skirmishers continued their backward movement. Beyond the orchard was another field, and then came the cornfield where the Confederates from Ewell's Division, having advanced from their original line, were heavily concentrated.[16] Hooker saw them "from the sun's rays falling on their bayonets projecting above the corn," and so did John Gibbon and the Iron Brigade. Glancing to his right across the pike and beyond the narrow field there, Gibbon also saw something else—Confederates from Jackson's Division were advancing through the West Woods to Gibbon's right and threatening to take him in the flank.[17]

To meet the enemy in the West Woods, Gibbon ordered the Seventh Wisconsin and the Nineteenth Indiana to the right. Marching by the flank, these regiments swept across the turnpike through the Miller barnyard, deploying in the narrow field opposite the Sixth and Second Wisconsin, the Nineteenth on the right and extending its flank into the northern extension of the West Woods. With horses straining to the whip, Stewart's artillery section also careened across the pike and through the barnyard, unlimbering thirty yards beyond the pike in front of the barn and straw stacks to the left of the Seventh Wisconsin.[18] The three right companies of the Sixth Wisconsin, Captain Kellogg commanding, followed, taking a position beside the post-and-rail fence to the right of the pike. All of this took but a minute, and then, as Ricketts' Division entered the East Woods to their left, the Second and Sixth Wisconsin leaped over the orchard fence and raced for the cornfield as the Nineteenth Indiana and Seventh Wisconsin climbed a pasture fence in their front and advanced into the West Woods, toward the church. In between the two wings Stewart's guns opened as Kellogg's companies, at the pike, advanced in line with their comrades.[19]

At once the Confederate line, infantry and artillery, exploded, and what Confederate General Early would later call "a terrible carnage"[20] began. To the right of the turnpike, the Nineteenth and Seventh, greatly assisted by the guns of Battery B, ground slowly forward through the West Woods, the men of Jackson's Division falling back or retreating across the turnpike to the cover of the cornfield.[21] From the cornfield a cruel fire was directed against Stewart's guns. Fourteen of Stewart's men fell in the first ten minutes of action before Captain Campbell brought up the remaining guns of the battery and occupied the barnyard and the pike to Stewart's left.[22] The hottest inferno was in the cornfield, a "bloody, dismal battlefield," according to General Hooker, a casualty himself.[23] There, where the Sixth and Second wrestled with the brigades of Lawton, Trimble, and Hays, Major Dawes led the Sixth's left wing against the blinding fire. As the blue line slowly advanced, Bragg, commanding the Sixth's right wing at the turnpike fence, went down. To the left of the Sixth the same grim promotion process was operating in the Second Wisconsin as Lieutenant Colonel Allen fell among the battered and bloody cornstalks, leaving Major Stevens in command.[24] Still the Iron Brigade and Battery B, firing into the cornfield, poured forth what Stonewall Jackson called a "terrific storm of shell, canister and musketry," and at last the Confederates were driven back. The line of the Sixth and Second, now joined by Phelps' Brigade and followed by men from Meade's Division, surged after them, through the corn and to a rail fence that skirted the southern edge of the field.[25]

From the cornfield fence it was but a thousand yards[26] across open ground to the objective, the Dunker Church, its white walls backed by the green of the West Woods behind and to the right of the church. And driving through the West Woods were the Nineteenth Indiana and Seventh Wisconsin, now reinforced by the men of

Patrick's Brigade. Over the cornfield fence went the Sixth and Second, racing for the church. But the men of Ewell's Division, although greatly reduced in number, rallied at the woods and again blasted the Federal ranks, driving the blue advance back behind the fence. The Federals leaped the fence and again rushed forward, "loading and firing with demonical fury and shouting and laughing hysterically," as Dawes remembered it, and the thinned Confederate line broke and retreated into the woods. Some tried to climb the turnpike fence, there to be shot and die in grotesque array as the Federals pressed on.[27] The church was two hundred yards away from the Iron Brigade, closing in on both sides of the turnpike. Both Confederate division commanders were wounded, and General Starke, Jones' successor in command of Jackson's Division, was dead. General Early marked the losses for the three brigades from Ewell's Division that had met the whirlwind in the cornfield: "Colonel Douglass, commanding Lawton's brigade, had been killed, and the brigade had sustained a loss of 554 killed and wounded out of 1,150, losing 5 regimental commanders out of 6; Hays' brigade had sustained a loss of 323 out of 550, including every regimental commander and all of his staff; and Colonel Walker and 1 of his staff had been disabled, and the brigade he was commanding [Trimble's] had sustained a loss of 228 out of less than 700 present, including 3 out of 4 regimental commanders." Similar catastrophe had befallen Jackson's Division in the West Woods. In Stonewall's words, "thinned in their ranks and exhausted of their ammunition, Jackson's division and the brigades of Lawton, Hays, and Trimble retired to the rear. . . ."[28] For the Federals the day was almost won.

But it was not won. In the midst of the shattered Confederates there suddenly appeared a long and steady line of gray, sweeping from the woods behind the church. These were the brigades of Law and Hood, yelling and firing as they came! Law's Brigade, driving east, crossed the turnpike in front of the church and spread to the north and east toward the left flank of the Sixth and Second Wisconsin. Hood's Brigade, behind Law's, rushed directly into the Sixth and Second in front of the cornfield. To the Federals, physically exhausted and with guns too dirty to fire effectively, the Confederate fire was "like a scythe running through our line." The Federal line faltered and retreated, back to the cornfield, back through the cornfield, stumbling over the bodies of the dead and wounded of both sides, pursued by the new Confederate power.[29]

At the northern edge of the cornfield, with every color-bearer and member of the color guard killed or wounded, Dawes seized the colors of the Sixth Wisconsin and, above the roar, rallied the Wisconsin men. To his right was John Gibbon, dismounted and grimed and black with powder and smoke. Captain Campbell was a casualty, with multiple wounds in the neck, shoulder, and side, and Battery B was crippled by the loss of men and horses. But John Gibbon did not propose to lose his guns, now threatened with capture. The general ran to Dawes and commanded him to bring the surviving infantry to the battery. Waving the regimental flag, Dawes led the soldiers to the guns as they opened with canister on the Confederates at close range.[30] And suddenly other assistance was available to the embattled survivors of the cornfield. Looking to their left, the Seventh Wisconsin and Nineteenth Indiana had seen the flank of the Confederate juggernaut that was shredding their comrades' line. Wheeling to the left, the Seventh and Nineteenth, followed by Patrick's Brigade, crossed the turnpike and pitched in to the Confederate flank. Now it was the Confederates' turn to flee as the enfilading fire cut them down. Swinging to the south, the Seventh and Nineteenth followed the Confederates through the cornfield and into the open field opposite the church. There, as Lieutenant Colonel Bachman fell, mortally wounded, leaving nineteen-year-old Captain Dudley in command of the Indiana regiment, the Confederate line rallied and again advanced, driving the Federals once more into the cornfield and against the turnpike fence.[31]

The finale of the First Corps was at hand at the cornfield, a hideous and disorganized mass of fire and cross fire. John Bell Hood called it "the most terrible clash of arms, by far, that has occurred during the war." To Gibbon's aide, the Sixth Wisconsin's Frank A. Haskell, it was like "a great tumbling together of all heaven and earth."[32] Gibbon himself labored at the guns of Battery B, trying desperately to save them in the wild tumult that surged about. The surviving cannoneers worked in a frenzy, firing so fast that a gunner was crushed beneath one gun as it recoiled. Seeing that the elevating screw of another gun had run down so that it was firing over the enemy, Gibbon leaped into the battery himself, ran up the screw, and took over the gun. "Give 'em hell, boys!" roared the old artilleryman as the battery blazed away into the cornfield.[33] For several minutes the fateful struggle continued, neither side able to obtain an advantage. But new Confederate blood was forthcoming, Early's Brigade and Jeb Stuart's guns, which now moved to the battle vortex from their position on the extreme Confederate left. Marching unseen through the West Woods north of the church, Early picked up the survivors of Jackson's Division and advanced toward the right and rear of the Seventh Wisconsin and Nineteenth Indiana, located east of the turnpike and facing toward the cornfield. The Nineteenth and Seventh and Patrick's Brigade, hotly contending with Hood's and Law's brigades in their front, were suddenly enfiladed from a range of one hundred yards by Early's men. To meet the new assault, the Federals faced right and fell back across the turnpike, toward their original battle position at the Miller barnyard. There the Confederate artillery found them, pouring a heavy fire of grape and canister into their right flank. At the same time, relieved of the pressure from the Nineteenth and Seventh, the enemy in the cornfield redoubled his effort, and the gray-clad soldiers advanced to within fifteen yards of Battery B and the Sixth and Second Wisconsin. Supported by their Iron Brigade kinsmen and double-shotted with canister, the guns continued the fight, whole ranks of the enemy going down in the effort to seize the battery.[34] But the Confederates could not quite reach the guns, and Gibbon, aware that his men were almost without ammunition, prepared to extricate his exhausted force.

Of the 800 officers and men who had marched out that morning in the Iron Brigade, 343 were killed and wounded. An additional five were missing for total casualties of 42 per cent. The Sixth Wisconsin, rallied now at the guns of Battery B, had suffered most severely, 152 of its 314 officers and men having gone down. The cornfield also accounted for the next highest casualties in the brigade, in the Second Wisconsin, where 86 were killed and wounded. Among all the brigades in the First Corps, only in George Hartsuff's Brigade of Meade's Division, which had also been engaged on the previous day, did losses surpass those of the Iron Brigade, the shock troops of the First Corps.[35]

Taking advantage of an interval between assaults, Battery B

Men of the Iron Brigade

MAIR POINTON of Baraboo, Wisconsin, was a member of Company A of the Sixth Wisconsin, the Sauk County Riflemen.

WILLIAM YOUNG, a student from Detroit, enlisted in the Twenty-fourth Michigan on August 15, 1862, at the age of 13. Despite the gun carried in this photo, he was a drummer in Company G. He served throughout the war. Here he wears the Iron Brigade's frock coat, but not the black hat. According to the regiment's historian, the hats were not received by the Twenty-fourth until March 27, 1863.

Ray Russell

HENRY W. RANDALL of Company D, Twenty-fourth Michigan, native of
New York state, a farmer in Birmingham, Michigan, when he enlisted.
Wounded at Gettysburg, he is pictured in a hospital uniform holding in
his left hand a battered Iron Brigade hat with the light blue infantry hat
cord and tassel. His right hand shows his wound.

Ray Russell

CHARLES A. KEELER of St. Joseph, Michigan, enlisted in Company B of the Sixth Wisconsin. Here he wears the uniform prescribed by General Gibbon shortly after he assumed command on May 7, 1862. Keeler was grievously wounded in both legs at Gettysburg.

Alan T. Nolan

CORNELIUS WHEELER of Dodgeville was a member of Company
I of the Second Wisconsin.

JOHN VOLLENWEIDER, Company C of the Seventh Wisconsin, was from Harrison. Enlisting as a musician on August 3, 1861, he was promoted to Principal Musician on July 1, 1863—the first day of Gettysburg. The circle appearing on the hat below the regimental numeral is the First Corps insignia.

PETER LARSEN of Franklin, Wisconsin, and of Company D,
Seventh Wisconsin. The photograph is dated 1864, suggesting
that the frock coat, as well as the Hardee hat, was reissued from
time to time.

HEADQUARTERS of the Twenty-fourth Michigan at Camp Iabella, Belle Plain, Va., during the winter of 1862-3 sketched by H.J. Brown of the Twenty-fourth Michigan.

TWENTY-FOURTH MICHIGAN in bivouac sketched by H.J. Brown of the regiment.

limbered up to withdraw when Gibbon's order finally came. Although it had suffered heavy casualties and had lost 33 horses killed and wounded, the guns moved quickly up the turnpike to the ridge in the rear of the Poffenberger farmhouse where the Iron Brigade had bivouacked the night before. Behind them the gunners left a mass of dead Confederates, piled on top of one another in front of the gun positions. But—and this is the pride of an artilleryman—although some of the guns had but two remaining horses, not a single gun or caisson was left behind![36] The Iron Brigade followed the battery as the First Corps withdrew all along the line.[37] By mid-morning the battered Westerners were out of action, posted along the east side of the turnpike in the wood on the Poffenberger farm, supporting Battery B and a heavy artillery force there. The battery was again to go forward briefly,[38] but not the Iron Brigade. It had some activity when Sedgwick's Division of the Second Corps broke while fighting west of the Dunker Church and retreated to the north toward the Iron Brigade's line. Intending to stop Sedgwick's fugitives, Gibbon ordered his brigade to attention and sought to draw his sword, only to find that the hilt had been shot away. But even without this dramatic gesture by their commander, the Iron Brigade assisted in blocking the way, and Sedgwick's men were re-formed. Late in the day the Confederates opened a heavy artillery cannonade in the Iron Brigade's front. The Federal guns responded, and a furious duel raged for half an hour and then died away.[39] Except for these events, the Iron Brigade remained inactive during the titanic corps-by-corps Federal assaults to the south, culminating as the day drew to a close with Burnside's final attack on the Confederate right. The Ninth Corps crossed the Antietam and drove into Sharpsburg, only to be checked by the arrival of A. P. Hill's Division from Harpers Ferry. Perhaps in no other battle did a great army come so close to destruction as did Lee's at Antietam. But McClellan would not take the ultimate risk, and the planned attack by the Federal reserve never took place, the day closing with the Fifth Corps and most of the Sixth idle and uncommitted.

As quiet finally settled over the bloody field—scene of the most sanguinary single day of the war—the Western soldiers, having succeeded in getting something to eat, went into bivouac where they had rested during the day.[40] Nearby were the survivors of Battery B, whose losses for the first time matched those of their Iron Brigade comrades. The battery had taken one hundred officers and men into action and had lost forty of them to death and wounds! Except for occasions when a battery was overrun and captured, this set a casualty record for a single engagement. As it developed, the wounded Captain Campbell was never to return to the battery, and Lieutenant James Stewart, who had enlisted in 1851 as a private, now took command. Stewart was a superb soldier, much beloved by his men. As one of the cannoneers phrased it, "No man as brave as Stewart could possibly have been mean or cruel." The battery historian remembered that Stewart, known to the men as "Old Jock" because of his Scottish birth, "always showed an especial affection for the boys who had stood by him in that awful carnage" at Antietam. And it was also recorded in the history of the battery that "the recruits of 1863, even with Gettysburg on their records, always took off their caps to the old Antietam boys whenever there was a campfire debate about prowess, and cordially yielded the palm to the iron veterans who had braved the butchery of that fatal Cornfield on the Sharpsburg Pike."[41]

On the 18th, Robert E. Lee, whose army of 50,000 had suffered casualties of almost 14,000 men, defiantly stood his ground. But McClellan did not attack, and the day was spent in tending to wounded and burying some of the dead. From their position beside the turnpike, the Iron Brigade watched wagonloads of legs and arms pass en route from the field hospitals to burial.[42] That night, apparently satisfied that McClellan would let him escape, Lee quietly led his beaten army across the Potomac. McClellan contented himself with a token pursuit, and the Maryland campaign was over. The Confederates' departure permitted the Iron Brigade a chance to view the scene of their great struggle. To Rufus Dawes, the scene was "indescribably horrible," with "great numbers of dead, swollen and black under the hot sun," scattered over the field. The cornfield was leveled by bullets and crowded with the corpses of the blue and the gray, the dead of the Iron Brigade lying beside their battered black hats. The dead were also piled up along the Hagerstown Turnpike. Dawes remembered how his horse, "as I rode through the narrow lane made by piling the bodies along beside the turnpike fences, trembled in every limb with fright and was wet with perspiration."

Later, making a grim comparison, Dawes believed that the Fredericksburg stone wall, Spottsylvania's Bloody Angle, and Cold Harbor
were all surpassed by the Antietam turnpike "in manifest evidence
of slaughter." Probably the most grotesque sight was provided by one
of the horses left in the Miller barnyard by Battery B. Two days
after the battle the beast was still there, "apparently in the act of
rising from the ground. Its head was held proudly aloft, and its fore
legs set firmly forward. Nothing could be more vigorous or lifelike
than the pose of this animal. But like all surrounding it on that
horrid aceldama, the horse was dead."[43]

Lee's retreat from Antietam also afforded President Lincoln an
opportunity to issue the Emancipation Proclamation. Perhaps some
of the Iron Brigade soldiers, mirroring diverse opinions throughout
the North, disapproved of this act, but one of the men of the Seventh
Wisconsin recorded his reaction in a letter home. In words that
showed that the Antietam slaughter had not moderated his iron
spirit, and expressing an understanding presumably common to many
of the soldiers, the soldier said: "I don't no what effect the President's proclamation will have on the South, but there is one thing
certain it is just what was wanted, and if they don't lay down their
arms we will have to annihilate them, niggers, cotton and all, it will
make hard times for a while but it will forever settle the everlasting
slavery question. . . ."[44] A few days after the proclamation, the
President traveled to Sharpsburg to visit McClellan and review the
army, drawn up in line in front of Sharpsburg where Lee's men had
so recently been. On the following day, harking back to May at
Fredericksburg, one of the veterans of the Seventh Wisconsin
penned a letter home: "I tell you it was quite a contrast between
yesterday and the last time he reviewed us, it was at Fredericksburg
last summer, we were then out with 700 men, while yesterday the
Reg. had out only 190 men, it looked small i tell you, our whole
brigade is not as large now as our regiment was then. . . ."[45] A soldier
of the Sixth Wisconsin also wrote a letter describing the scene: "We
had about two hundred and fifty men in our ranks. . . . Our battle
flags were tattered, our clothing worn, and our appearance that of
men who had been through the most trying service. . . . Mr. Lincoln
was manifestly touched at the worn appearance of our men, and he,
himself looked serious and careworn. He bowed low in response to

the salute of our tattered flags."[46] And another soldier of the Iron Brigade, a private of the Nineteenth Indiana writing in his diary, commented on "Father Abe's" appearance: "His beard unshaven gave him a rough camp look, altogether he is the man to suit the soldiers."[47]

As the encampment at Sharpsburg continued, Lieutenant Colonel Bragg, still convalescing from his wound, returned for a visit before traveling to Wisconsin on leave. The "little colonel," as the men called Bragg,[48] was always welcome, and especially now when his activities provided the Iron Brigade with the principal topics of camp conversation. Bragg had been nominated for Congress as an independent "War" candidate with the support of one faction of the Democratic party. Now word was received that the Republican Union Congressional Convention, meeting in Fond du Lac, had seconded his nomination. The Republican resolution rejected partisan "subdivisions of the National friends" and called for Bragg's election "notwithstanding upon questions of civil administration, he sustains a creed different from ours." In the political backwash of Second Bull Run and the Confederate invasion of Kentucky, Bragg was to be defeated.[49] But his nomination was a matter of deep pride to the Iron Brigade. Bragg's other distinction resulted from a tragically erroneous telegram dispatched the day after Antietam to his wife at Fond du Lac. Confusing the wounded Bragg with the Sixth's dead Captain Brown, and mincing no words, the telegram stated: "Your husband was shot yesterday. I will send him home by express."[50] The mistake was not corrected until after official and family mourning was underway in Fond du Lac. Then the town turned its sympathy to Mrs. Brown, also of that community.[51] Bragg hastened to reassure his wife, writing a long letter about his wound and its aftermath. After describing the bullet's impact, the letter continued: ". . . I felt faint and was back a few rods, where I met the Gen'l who gave me some whiskey (the first I have tasted since I have been in service) and I revived again and felt as well as ever. . . ." Apparently it was necessary even in these circumstances for the dutiful husband to keep the record straight about his personal habits! And to cap the incident, and perhaps to mitigate his own offense at leading her husband into evil ways, John Gibbon wrote a note to Mrs. Bragg, closing with the admonition: ". . . the best advice I can give you is that given my own wife, never believe your husband is dead until he himself writes you it is so."[52]

As October came, the Army of the Potomac prolonged its Sharpsburg stay, reorganizing, and receiving reinforcements. Although it was not clear at the time, the great crisis of the Union was passing because of Lee's defeat at Antietam and because of solid Federal victories in the West, at Corinth, Mississippi, and Perryville, Kentucky. General Gibbon continued to marvel at his volunteers. Just after the battle another sign of their distinction appeared. As in any battle, there were many stragglers at Antietam, men who had left the battlefield and gone to the rear. Army headquarters had called for a return on the 18th and 22nd of September, and a comparison of the two showed that the First Corps had nearly doubled during the four days. Part of the increase could be accounted for innocently, but some of it represented simply the return of the stragglers. But not in the Iron Brigade! Gibbon traced his discrepancy, and proudly noted that "my Brigade had increased about 80 men and *everyone* of these were men who had returned from detached service and hospitals so that I had *no* stragglers."[53] On October 7th the proud general issued orders to the Iron Brigade, taking official notice of what General McClellan had recently written about them to the governors of Wisconsin and Indiana. The soldiers in the black hats were drawn up on dress parade to hear these words written by McClellan to Wisconsin's chief executive: "I add . . . the expression of my great admiration of the three Wisconsin regiments in Gen. Gibbon's Brigade. I have seen them under fire, acting in a manner that reflects the greatest possible credit and honor upon themselves and their state. They are equal to the best troops in any army in the world." And to Oliver P. Morton of Indiana a similar message had been sent, including this statement about the Nineteenth Indiana: "I am glad to say that there is no better regiment in this or any other army."[54]

Surely the backs of the Iron Brigade soldiers must have stiffened at the eloquent tributes from the commanding general, to be appearing soon, as they must have realized, in their home-town newspapers. Unfortunately hundreds of their surviving comrades, lying in crude hospitals from Frederick to Sharpsburg, missed the dress parade and the words of General McClellan. And one of these, a soldier of the Sixth Wisconsin writing in his diary, was much more eloquent than George B. McClellan. The soldier wrote: It "was a painful day to me. All day I sat up and looked upon a scene of suffering. Sergeant Whaley was lying by my side in agony. He was one of my first and kindest friends from the beginning. We tented together from the first. We went on all the hard marches, and finally met a sad fate upon the same tainted field. We had suffered everything together that would make one soldier love another, and now we lay near each other; he was wholly unable to help himself and I was but little better. I had a prospect of soon having the chance to avenge the wound but his was dark forever. We were in a large church but no comforts of account could be bought, borrowed or stolen." On the following day, the soldier, who was expected to recover, was moved from the church. But his friend, who was known to be dying, was left behind to die. The diarist told of leaving his beloved friend "with scarcely a parting word. I did not like to leave him this way but this was by far the best way to do it. I merely informed him that I was going. He started to rise up in haste but again sank back and wished to know if I wanted my tin cup and I told him no, that I would try to get another."[55]

8

REORGANIZATION

"HEADQUARTERS FIRST ARMY CORPS,
"Camp near Sharpsburg, October 8, 1862

"Special Orders,)
No. 24   )

. . .

"II. The following new regiments now en route for this corps are assigned as follows: First Division (Gibbon's brigade), Twenty-fourth Michigan Volunteers . . ."

. . . .

"HEADQUARTERS FIRST ARMY CORPS,
"Camp near Purcellville, November 4, 1862.

"Special Orders,)
No. 44   )

. . .

"III. Brig. Gen. John Gibbon, . . . will assume command of the Second Division of this corps . . ."

John Gibbon had requested a new *Western* regiment for his brigade. In the Old Northwest, at Detroit in Wayne County, Michigan, the new regiment had its beginnings, while Gibbon's Brigade camped at Falmouth and before it had distinguished itself in battle in Virginia.[1]

On July 12, 1862, Michigan's Governor Austin Blair issued a call for six new regiments of volunteers. To stimulate enlistments, Detroit's Mayor William C. Duncan summoned a war meeting, to assemble on July 15th on the Campus Martius, marked today by

Michigan's Soldiers' and Sailors' Monument at the intersection of Michigan and Woodward avenues. At the appointed hour in the late afternoon, the officers of the meeting, led by the mayor, filed onto the flag-draped wooden grandstand erected for the occasion. Among them was Lewis Cass, Michigan's most prominent elder citizen. Born in 1782, Cass had been a general officer in the War of 1812, governor of the Michigan Territory, Jackson's Secretary of War, minister to France, United States senator, Democratic presidential nominee, and Buchanan's Secretary of State. Never a critic of slavery or the South, Cass was nevertheless a Union man. A prominent actor in the turbulent beginnings of the new nation—he and his force had been surrendered to the British against their will when Detroit was surrendered during the War of 1812—Cass mounted the platform in 1862 to support the new generation in the new crisis.

The meeting began auspiciously enough with a patriotic speech by Mayor Duncan, followed by remarks from other distinguished townsmen. It was not until the third speaker had finished that the crowd showed any unruly spirit. Then the atmosphere rapidly deteriorated and jeering and shouting prevented the beginning of the fourth speech. From the confused babble of the crowd it was learned that the purpose of the meeting had been misrepresented or misunderstood. The audience believed the meeting had been called to propose a draft. As soon as this was understood in the grandstand, Henry A. Morrow, Judge of the Recorder's Court of Wayne County, stepped forward to explain that the purpose of the meeting was simply to induce volunteers. One of the listeners shouted to Morrow, "Will you go?" and the judge answered: "I have already said I would. The government has done as much for me as for you and I am ready to assist in upholding it!" In the midst of the mixture of cheers and taunts that met this exchange, the meeting suddenly erupted in violence. A cluster of men rushed the stage, menacing the speakers. From the shouts of the leaders of the mob, Eber B. Ward and Duncan Stewart, prominent businessmen and Union leaders in Detroit, seemed to be the quarry. Wayne County Sheriff Mark Flanigan briefly checked the onslaught, while the platform emptied. Then the mass of angry men reached the platform, smashing the grandstand and shredding the patriotic bunting. Surging into the street, the attackers swept on to the Russell House Hotel, located at the corner of Woodward Avenue and the Campus Martius, where Ward and Stewart had taken refuge. But, revolvers drawn, Sheriff Flanigan and his deputy mounted the hotel steps and held the mob at bay until the people dispersed as darkness fell. Although it was commonly believed that Confederates who had crossed from Windsor, Canada, had triggered the outburst, the incident left the city of Detroit under a dark stain of disloyalty. As Detroit's *Advertiser and Tribune* put it, the event was "one of the most melancholy spectacles it was ever our lot to witness."

In the shock that followed the riot of July 15th, the Union element of Detroit at once decided to repair their city's humiliation. The night after the riot, public officials and civic leaders met at the Michigan Exchange, a hotel on Jefferson Avenue, to plan for a new war meeting. They also decided upon a more material demonstration of the loyalty of Wayne County. A regiment of volunteers would be raised, in addition to the quota of six regiments recently solicited from the state. Thus would Detroit and Wayne County be vindicated and the July 15th riot avenged. Since the raising of a regiment separate from the state's quota required the governor's approval, representatives were hastily dispatched to Lansing, where consent was obtained, allegedly only after the chief executive's wife had intervened in behalf of the idea. On July 19th, in terms defiant of the dissenters, the sponsors issued the call for the new meeting:

Men of Detroit! The fair fame of your city is at stake. Come forth in your might and prove your patriotism. . . . Shall a few pestilent sympathizers with treason neutralize your patriotic effort? . . . rebuke the traitors and vindicate the patriotism of the city. All who favor an energetic prosecution of the war are requested to meet on the Campus Martius on Tuesday afternoon at 3 o'clock, July 22, 1862.

The sponsors were not to be disappointed. A crowd assembled on the 22nd, including organized companies of employees from the foundries, machine shops, and shipyards, and scores of other Union sympathizers, many of them armed with clubs. Again Mayor Duncan presided, surrounded by other notables, among them Lewis Cass, Episcopal Bishop Samuel A. McCoskry, and Father Paul Lefevre of St. Peter and Paul's Catholic Cathedral. Sheriff Flanigan announced that he and Judge Morrow were going to raise a regiment. Then

Duncan Stewart came forward to talk in concrete terms of what he would do to stimulate enlistments. From his own funds, he committed himself to the following: five dollars to each man in the first company to enlist; four dollars a month during the war to twenty-five soldiers' families of four children; and two dollars a month to twenty soldiers' families of three children. Warming to the applause, Stewart turned his wrath on the city aldermen. Alleging that they were withholding relief assistance from the wives of soldiers on the ground that their husbands, as civilians, had spent their money on whisky, Stewart concluded with this epigram: "I have more respect for a drunken patriot than an unpatriotic alderman."

The principal address was given by Judge Morrow. With frequent references to his own Virginia origin, the judge pictured the country "as contemptible as Mexico or Morocco" unless the rebellion was subdued. At length the speaker closed:

One word for myself. I am going to the field. I invite you to go with me. I will look after you in health and in sickness. My influence will be exerted to procure for you the comforts of life, and lead you where you will see the enemy. Your fare shall by my fare, your quarters my quarters. We shall together share the triumph, or together mingle our dust upon the common field. We are needed on the James River. Our friends and brothers are there. Let us not linger behind. . . .

Unmarred by any sympathy with secession, the meeting adjourned, and recruiting was instituted at other, smaller meetings throughout the county. Morrow, whose commission as colonel was officially dated August 15th, and Sheriff Flanigan, commissioned lieutenant colonel on the same day, led the recruiters, supported by the business and clerical sponsors of July 22nd and by Governor Blair, United States Senator Jacob M. Howard, and the state's lieutenant governor. In Detroit, the Perkins Hotel on Grand River Avenue, the Biddle House at Jefferson Avenue and Randolph Street, and Degendre's Hall resounded with the call to arms. From these meetings the recruitment rallies spread to other towns and townships, to the Congregational Church at Wayne, to Livonia Center and to Redford Center, where, following a mortgage foreclosure, the Methodist Church had been sold back to the congregation for the notes of the members. The owner of the notes agreed to forgive the debt of any man who enlisted, and nearly every note was canceled on the spot. Grosse Point, Plymouth, and Dearborn also conducted rallies, and the family physician of Dearborn canceled the bills of all who enlisted, and pledged his services, free of charge, to their families. Flat Rock was the scene of the meeting for the southern townships, Brownstown, Huron, and Sumpter. There a sword and belt were presented to Lieutenant Walter H. Wallace who had lost an eye with the Second Michigan Volunteers at Fair Oaks and who was now recruiting Company K of the new regiment. Impelled by the stigma of the first meeting, recruiting continued at a record pace, accompanied by voluntary contributions that afforded the volunteers from the City of Detroit gratuities varying from $10 to $30 each, in addition to the Federal bounty of $100 for each man in the regiment.[2] On August 11th, at a meeting at Wyandotte, the regimental quota, ten companies totaling 1,030 officers and men, was filled.

Unlike the Wisconsin and Indiana regiments that had at the outset reported to a central military camp, early Michigan regiments had gathered at various places through the state, including Ann Arbor, Grand Rapids, Adrian, and Detroit's Fort Wayne.[3] Morrow's regiment, numbered the Twenty-fourth Michigan Volunteers, was allotted the State Fairground on Detroit's Woodward Avenue, also known as the "Detroit Riding Park." On July 29th the early companies assembled, and gave the place the new name of Camp Barns, in honor of Henry Barns, editor of the *Advertiser and Tribune*. On August 13th and 15th the Federal mustering officer arrived, and the Michigan men were enrolled in the service of the United States for three years. Within a matter of days the new regiment was equipped, the uniform consisting of the typical kepi and short, dark-blue blouse with light-blue trousers.[4] Drill began immediately, although frequently interrupted by numerous formal presentations of swords and other military trappings, as the Detroit Bar Association, the First Methodist Episcopal Church of Detroit, the Molders' Association, and other organizations honored their members in the regiment.

The Campus Martius was the scene of an elaborate presentation ceremony. There the regiment paraded on August 26th to receive its color, the national flag inscribed with the name "24th Michigan Infantry." A spokesman for the donors, Messrs. F. Buhl, Newland & Co. of Detroit, manufacturer and dealer in hats, furs, gloves, and

buffalo robes, delivered the flag to Colonel Morrow with this orator-
ical flourish: "In the smoke and din of battle, may its beautiful folds
ever be seen till victory shall bring peace to our distracted country."
The colonel, who had previously been given a horse by his friends,
"to bear you triumphantly against our country's foes," was now the
recipient of a sword, to "gleam at the head of your columns until
there is no longer an enemy to meet them." Equal to the occasion,
Colonel Morrow responded with the promise of the battle cry
"Detroit and Victory!" The ceremony completed, the regiment returned to Camp Barns, where preparations were in progress for
imminent departure for the war.

Colonel Morrow, so graceful in ceremonial circumstances, was
later to show substantial military gifts. Born in Warrenton, Virginia,
in 1829, he had attended the Rittenhouse Academy in Washington,
D.C., and as a youth had been a page in the United States Senate,
where Senator Cass had befriended him. The Virginian had early
shown his martial interest, enlisting at seventeen with a Maryland
and District of Columbia regiment in the Mexican War. For a year
the youth soldiered, participating in the battle of Monterey and the
campaign against Tampico. In 1853, through Senator Cass's advice,
Morrow had come to the Old Northwest, to settle in Detroit, to
study law and be admitted to the bar in 1854. After two elected
terms as city recorder, Morrow, a Democrat, had been elected judge
of the Recorder's Court, a trial court of limited civil and criminal
jurisdiction.

Morrow's second in command, Lieutenant Colonel Mark Flanigan
of Detroit, was thirty-seven years old and a native of Ireland. Prior
to his election as county sheriff in 1860, Flanigan had been employed
as a butcher. The sheriff measured an imposing six feet four inches
in height and had a reputation for physical courage, but these were
his only apparent qualifications for military office. Aware of the need
for an experienced field officer, Morrow and Flanigan discouraged
the immediate appointment of a major for the regiment. On arriving
in Washington, the majority was awarded to Henry W. Nall, captain
of the Seventh Michigan and a veteran of the Peninsula battles and
Antietam. Nall, who had been a clerk in civil life, was English-born,
thirty-one years old and, like Morrow and Flanigan, from Detroit.

In addition to Morrow and Flanigan, four of the original officers were to become noteworthy during the regiment's career: Edwin B. Wight, William W. Wight, Albert M. Edwards, and William Hutchinson. The first of these, Edwin B. Wight, twenty-four-year-old native of Detroit, was to succeed Nall as major upon the latter's discharge in 1863. A graduate of the University of Michigan, Wight had studied for the bar but had abandoned his legal studies to go into the lumber business. William W. Wight, Edwin's older brother, the first captain of Company K, was to finish his career as lieutenant colonel of the regiment. William was born in New York, and at the age of forty-five was engaged in 1862 as a farmer at Livonia, Michigan. Captain Albert M. Edwards of Company F, also to achieve the rank of lieutenant colonel, was twenty-six years old, a native of Maine, and had attended the University of Michigan prior to his employment in Detroit as a newspaperman. A sergeant in the First Michigan Volunteers, a three months' regiment, Edwards had been captured at First Bull Run and imprisoned at Castle Pinkney and the Charleston jail until exchanged. In spite of his unfortunate military experience—he had drawn lots with fellow prisoners in Charleston to see who would be hanged in retribution for the threatened Federal execution of Confederate privateers—Edwards had come forward for the Twenty-fourth, although only released from prison on May 20, 1862. Canadian-born William Hutchinson of Company G, twenty-two years old and, like Lieutenant Colonel Flanigan, employed as a butcher in Detroit, was later to reach the rank of major. Originally commissioned a first lieutenant, Hutchinson had enlisted with his employer, also a butcher, who commanded Company G. Others of the officers were also men of promise—one of the lieutenants was the son of United States Senator Howard—but Edwin and William Wight, Albert Edwards, and William Hutchinson were the men who were to achieve field-grade status in the Twenty-fourth Michigan Volunteers.

The regiment was overwhelmingly from Wayne County, scene of the disgrace of July 15th. Of the officers and men, 428 were from Detroit itself and 479 were from other townships of the county. The remaining 123 volunteers were from neighboring Monroe, Washtenaw, Oakland, and Clinton counties and had crossed over into Wayne County to join. The organization was also distinctive as a "family regiment." There were 135 pairs of brothers in its ranks. In two of the companies, there were no less than ten pairs of brothers, and Company H included not only the brothers Daniel and John Steele, but also their father, forty-three-year-old Samuel Steele. Other statistical data are available, carefully assembled by the regimental historian. Thus, although the average age was between twenty-five and twenty-six, the regiment contained fifty men between the ages of forty and fifty. The oldest volunteer was James Nowlin, seventy years old, and the youngest, the drummer boy, thirteen-year-old Willie Young, who was to serve throughout the war. As in other Iron Brigade regiments, the Western character of the soldiers was largely newly acquired. Three hundred and twenty-five of the recruits were foreign born, Germany and Ireland accounting for 100 and 85 of these, respectively. Of the approximately 700 native-born Americans, Michigan was counted as the birthplace of just less than half, New York State accounted for 250, and a very few were born in Southern states. Following the pattern of the Iron Brigade, the Twenty-fourth had a distinctly rural flavor, listing 412 farmers as compared to 88 factory laborers. Scattered through the regiment were ten students, six lawyers, five physicians, five teachers, three ministers and, as was not unusual for a regiment from a maritime state, thirty-four sailors, men whose background was particularly ill suited to the life of a Civil War infantry soldier.

Their organization and preliminary training completed, the Michigan men departed from Detroit on Friday, August 29th, the day following the Iron Brigade's baptism at Brawner Farm. Surrounded by cheering crowds, the soldiers marched out of Camp Barns at 5:00 P.M. and filed down Woodward to Jefferson Avenue, where the column met the party of General Orlando B. Willcox, former colonel of the First Michigan Volunteers, who had been wounded and taken prisoner at First Bull Run, exchanged on August 17, 1862, and was soon to return to the Army of the Potomac to command a division of the Ninth Corps at South Mountain. Escorted by General Willcox's party, the Twenty-fourth proceeded to the Michigan Central Wharf, at the foot of Shelby Street on the Detroit River. There the soldiers were drawn up for a typical departure ceremony, including the inevitable execrable poem, "and return them to our firesides, crowned with liberty and peace," this time the effort of a patriotic lady from Redford.

At last the soldiers boarded the *May Queen* and the *Cleveland*, the ships were cast off, and the journey to the front began, across Lake Erie to Cleveland and then by train to Pittsburgh, Harrisburg, and Baltimore, where the regiment waited a day in the rain while five other new regiments were entrained for the Capital. Cattle cars were finally available, and at 3:00 A.M., the men started, arriving in Washington at noon on September 1st.

In the atmosphere of disaster that followed Second Bull Run, the new soldiers were served their first Federal meal in temporary barracks in the city. As if to mark the unseen barrier between peace and war, one of the enlisted men remembered that the fare was "food that would insult a hog" and that "a single company could have eaten the whole spread had the quality of the food admitted . . ." After this unsatisfactory repast, the men crossed the Long Bridge on their way to Fort Lyon, Virginia, and saw further evidence of the barrier they had crossed as ambulances rolled by crowded with the wounded from the recent battles. This—and not the food—"caused the first emphatic impression of the work we had enlisted to engage in," wrote one of the men. On September 3rd, at Fort Lyon, where the new soldiers spent their first night in the open in the midst of a cold rainstorm, they saw the "jaded, foot-sore and dusty fragments of the once magnificent Army of the Potomac," as Pope's soldiers passed by to their Washington camps.

Despite their own high expectations, the Western recruits were not immediately permitted to join the embattled Eastern army. While their future comrades of the Iron Brigade fought the Confederates in Maryland, the Twenty-fourth Michigan remained in or near Fort Lyon and later at Fort Baker, across Anacostia Creek. There the soldiers settled into camp routine, broken occasionally by visits from friends or relatives from home—"anybody, or even a dog, from Wayne County was welcome in camp," wrote a homesick private—and by a formal review by General Woodbury on September 21st. The general pronounced the regiment "as fine a body of men as he ever saw," but "he probably made the same remark to every regiment," wrote the disillusioned regimental historian. Following the review, a sham battle was staged before Governor Blair, in which one man was disabled with a leg wound, another by powder burns, and a third by a ramrod shot from a comrade's gun. Despite these untoward events, the soldiers remembered their Fort Baker days as ". . . three of the happiest weeks of army life . . . gladdened with daily mails, a good place to sleep, and ample and wholesome food; our evenings gleeful with music, dancing, and song, while the prayer meetings were well attended by such as found interest therein."

Finally the day came for the regiment to join the army in the field. On the early morning of September 30th, the men of the Twenty-fourth marched into Washington to entrain for Frederick. Because transportation was unavailable, the regiment bivouacked in the East Park of the Capitol grounds, next to the Capitol itself, temporarily a hospital for the wounded from Antietam. Boarding the cars during the night, the regiment started on the morning of the 1st of October. From the slow-moving train, the soldiers, like their predecessors, were greeted by the Marylanders, including "one old man, with snow-white head, and grandchildren by his side, [who] waved the old flag at us with an energy that would have borne him to the field had his years permitted." The same soldier who recorded this scene also noted a few "motionless hands and silent lips. . . . No more the slave will do their waiting—the true secret of their grumpy sullenness and soured mien." At the Monocacy River the men left the train and camped until October 6th in the fields beside the railroad track. While they were there the President's train passed by as he returned to Washington from reviewing the army at Antietam. Head uncovered, the chief executive "stood at the rear of his train, bowing to us as it slowly moved by," wrote one of the Michigan soldiers. Like the Wisconsin and Indiana soldiers whom Lincoln had just reviewed, the Michigan recruits recorded that the President "looked careworn from the weighty matters upon his mind," and they responded to his greeting with lusty "Michigan cheers." Resuming their journey on the 6th, the Twenty-fourth marched through Frederick, still full of the wounded from Antietam, over the Catoctin Mountains and into the valley at Middletown. On the 7th the march was resumed, through Turner's Gap, Boonsborough, Keedysville, across the Antietam on Burnside's Bridge and, on the night of October 8th, to camp a mile southeast of Sharpsburg. Although their camp site was not a fortunate choice, located as it was next to a large pile of amputated limbs and surrounded by farm buildings that housed Confederate wounded under the care of Federal surgeons,

the Twenty-fourth had at last reached the army. Already reduced by
illness from 1,030 to 898[5] officers and men, the Michigan soldiers
bedded down for the night, anxious to discover to what command
they were to be assigned.

Despite McClellan's promise to Gibbon, the route of the Twenty-
fourth Michigan to the Iron Brigade was neither direct nor assured.
On September 6th, while the regiment lingered in the environs of
Washington, army headquarters had ordered it to the Twelfth
Corps.[6] On September 30th this order was countermanded, and the
Twenty-fourth was assigned to the First Corps, but not to Gibbon's
Brigade. The 121st Pennsylvania had been selected as Gibbon's reinforcement.[7] Although there is no record of any action taken by Gibbon to remind McClellan of his promise, such efforts were probably
made. With ready access to McClellan, the commander surely must
have stirred himself to maintain the Western integrity of his now
distinguished brigade. At the eleventh hour, on October 8th, the day
of the regiment's arrival at Sharpsburg, the final assignment was
made. On October 8th the Michigan men were directed to Gibbon's
Brigade, and McClellan's promise was redeemed.[8]

John Gibbon inspected his new regiment on October 9th. To the
newcomers it seemed that the stern commander "received us with
considerable reluctance." The regimental historian well described
what followed: "Our regimental inspection over, we were drawn up
in front of the rest of the brigade, whom we almost outnumbered.
Our suits were new; their's were army-worn. Our Colonel extolled our
qualities, but the brigade was silent. Not a cheer. A pretty cool reception, we thought. We had come out to reinforce them, and supposed they would be glad to see us." Anxious to explain this apparent
hostility, the historian cast about for a reason. "The brigade was a
good one. It had already won envious fame . . . , won the title of the
'Iron Brigade,' and had a right to know before accepting our full
fellowship if we, too, had the mettle to sustain the honor of the
brigade."

In believing that their new comrades were hostile or reluctant to
receive them, the Michigan soldiers had misunderstood. The point
was that the Iron Brigade veterans *were* veterans. For them all of
the initial luster had been rubbed off the war, just as it had been
rubbed off their uniforms. Their regular army coats had largely worn

out and they were outfitted in a mixture of blue coats of various lengths and styles. As one of them wrote at the time, "The feathers in our hats were drooping and the white leggings, which, as protection to the feet and ankles, were now more useful than ornamental, had become badly soiled."[9] Drawn up before the Twenty-fourth Michigan, virtually a troop of civilians, with bounties in their pockets, fresh faces and new equipment, and *without* black hats, it was too much to expect the veterans to demonstrate. But although the "old soldiers" were to make typical fun of the Michigan men, and for the moment to withhold full comradeship from them,[10] the private comments of the veterans were in sharp contrast to their outward appearances. In a letter dated October 9th, the day of his first inspection of the regiment, the brigade commander wrote of being "very much pleased with its appearance. From its bearing I have no doubt it will not be long before it will be a worthy member of the 'Black Hats.' "[11] Rufus Dawes also recorded the arrival in friendly terms. "A fine new regiment has been added to our brigade. They are a splendid looking body of men, entirely new to the service. . . . Their ranks are full now, and they are, as we were, crazy to fight."[12] Another Wisconsin soldier, an officer of the Seventh regiment, wrote of his reaction, ". . . if they fight as well as they look, our Brigade will give the Rebs a warm reception when we meet them."[13] That, of course, was really the key. To be accepted, all that the Michigan men would have to do was to fight well, to fight "as well as they looked."

That the Westerners were pleased with their new comrades is readily understood. The Twenty-fourth Michigan represented manpower, an item sorely needed by the brigade. Although varying widely from time to time, its strength had steadily diminished from 4,000 men to less than the strength of one of the original regiments. Illness, wounds, and death, from battle and disease, were the principal causes. To these were added the detachment in December, 1861, of the Second Wisconsin's Company K, now a heavy artillery unit, and the occasional detailing of men to Battery B. The latter process, again invoked after Antietam, had just cost the depleted brigade twenty more Wisconsin and Indiana veterans. Twenty of the Michigan newcomers were also turned over to the battery on October 11th.[14] Besides these losses, in August of 1862 the regimental bands had been mustered out. This act, pursuant to the army's general order of July, cost the Iron Brigade regiments their musicians and, despite the need for men, a strict view of the status of the bandsmen was adopted. It was felt that musicians, having enlisted as such, could not be simply converted to riflemen. The men were therefore ordered to be mustered out. Like other brigade commanders, John Gibbon softened the blow by organizing a brigade band, which retained at least a few bandsmen from each regiment. Besides these, other bandsmen doubtless re-enlisted as riflemen, although without the privilege of returning to their original regiments. Although no precise statistics are available, as many as eighty men were lost to the brigade as a result of the destruction of the regimental bands.[15]

On the credit side, the Twenty-fourth Michigan was not the only addition to the brigade. In January of 1862, the Second Wisconsin had obtained a new Company K to replace the detached heavy artillery company.[16] There was also a steady stream of men returning to their regiments from hospitalization following illness and wounds. In the Sixth Wisconsin, for example, a return in late October showed 313 effectives as compared to the 250 just after the bloodletting in front of Sharpsburg.[17] Later in the war, wounded and invalided Iron Brigade soldiers were placed in the Veteran Reserve Corps, there to engage in garrison and other limited service until again fit for the field, when the men were transferred back to their regiments.[18] The remaining additions were draftees, who were not to begin to arrive until 1864,[19] and the volunteer recruits who reached the regiments from time to time.

For the Nineteenth Indiana, volunteer recruits were available as early as September, 1861, when a civilian from Winchester wrote to Governor Morton about transportation for ten volunteers, "good healthy young men," whom he had rounded up at the request of the captain of Company C. Since the Nineteenth did not receive its first recruits until November, 1861,[20] the men were apparently enrolled in a new regiment organizing at the time. The governor also received letters directly from would-be recruits for the Nineteenth, including one in May of 1862 from a Madison County youth, with two brothers in the regiment, who offered the services of "me and a neighbor boy."[21] Even in the early months of the war, officers of all of the Iron Brigade regiments were occasionally sent home to sign up such prospects and to keep them from the newly organizing regiments.[22] The conflict between filling up the old regiments and raising the new ones was poignantly illustrated by the plight of a citizen of Yorktown, Indiana. Intent on raising a company to support his captaincy in a new regiment, the citizen wrote a heated letter to the adjutant general, complaining that five of his men had been mustered as recruits into the Nineteenth, and lamenting, "Had I known that I have no power to hold them I certainly would not have devoted the past month to recruiting them."[23]

The experience of the captain from Yorktown was not, unfortunately, a typical one. In spite of logic and the urgings of the military authorities, the states concentrated throughout the war in raising new regiments in preference to filling up their old and depleted organizations. Indiana and Michigan, like the others, made halfhearted efforts to maintain the strength of their existing regiments, and Wisconsin was reputedly more successful than most in this respect. But the number of volunteer recruits was never enough to keep the veteran regiments at anything like full strength, and new regiments continued to be organized without regard to the needs of the regiments in the field.[24] Throughout its history, the Nineteenth Indiana received a total of only 219 recruits. All of these were volunteers, although some of them may have volunteered as an alternative to an immediate draft. Added to the original volunteers, these recruits gave the Nineteenth a total membership for the war of 1,273 officers and men. Among the Wisconsin regiments in the Iron Brigade, the Second, which received neither draftees nor substitutes throughout its service, had a total roll of 1,288 officers and men, including 137 recruits and its new Company K acquired in January, 1862. The Sixth claimed a total of 1,906 officers and men, of whom 247 were vounteer recruits and 551 were draftees and substitutes. Four hundred and twenty-nine volunteers and 256 draftees and substitutes were recruited for the Seventh, giving that regiment a total of 1,714. For the Twenty-fourth Michigan, 216 volunteers were recruited for the field, of whom all but seventeen, recruited in April and December, 1863, enrolled during 1864. The Michigan regiment thus claimed a total enrollment of 1,246 officers and men.[25]

In October, 1862, the Iron Brigade also had a new corps commander, General John F. Reynolds of Pennsylvania. A career soldier,

Reynolds became the third commander of the First Corps, following McDowell and Hooker. No record exists of the soldiers' reaction to Reynolds' appointment. After all, a corps commander was a relatively remote figure to a private soldier, and it may be assumed that the Iron Brigade was more concerned about its own field officers, much affected by the recent fighting. In the Second Wisconsin, Colonel Fairchild, Lieutenant Colonel Allen, and Major Stevens were on hand, and Stevens now had the experience of having handled the brigade at Antietam during Fairchild's absence and after Allen's wounding.[26] Major Rufus Dawes commanded the Sixth Wisconsin, pending the return of Lieutenant Colonel Bragg or Colonel Cutler, the latter of whom had not yet recovered from his Brawner Farm wound. Colonel Robinson and Lieutenant Colonel Hamilton, also victims of Brawner Farm, would shortly rejoin the Seventh Wisconsin, but Major George Bill was still missing from the Seventh, and Captain Callis, the South Mountain and Antietam commander, continued to act as major. Major Bill was never to recover sufficiently to return to the field and was to resign in January, 1863. Callis then received his majority, confirming a command he had in fact held for four months.[27]

But it was in the Nineteenth Indiana, from which Colonel Meredith was only temporarily absent[28] as a result of his fall and fatigue, that the real task of reorganization was to be undertaken. Lieutenant Colonel Alois O. Bachman and Major Isaac May were dead and their places had to be filled. Following a familiar pattern, the appointments provoked much wrangling and political infighting. Besides Captain Dudley, the Antietam commander after Bachman's fall, Captain Samuel J. Williams of Company K and Captain John M. Lindley of Company F were the principal contenders for the vacant posts. Williams, a native of Montgomery County, Virginia, had moved to Indiana in childhood. His family had settled on a farm near Selma in Delaware County, where Samuel was brought up and educated in the common schools. Moving into Selma in 1855, Williams had engaged in warehousing and stock shipping and had participated in politics, first as a Democrat and then in the emerging Republican party. It was Williams who had raised Company K, a Delaware County company.[29]

Considerably less is known of Williams' rival, Captain John M.

Lindley of Indianapolis. The son of Jacob Lindley, an importer of China and glassware whose store was located at 16 West Washington Street in Indianapolis, John worked for his father and was the original captain of Marion County's Company F.[30] In the struggle for preferment, General Gibbon passed over Samuel J. Williams, recommending to Governor Morton the appointment of Lindley and Dudley as lieutenant colonel and major. Colonel Meredith, the governor's friend, disagreed. He preferred Williams for the lieutenant colonelcy, and Dudley, who was willing to waive his claim for the higher office, for the majority. The matter was ultimately settled as the colonel wished, and Lieutenant Colonel Samuel J. Williams and Major William W. Dudley were appointed, their commissions dating back to September 18, 1862. The vanquished Captain Lindley, who was not disposed to be gracious about the matter, grumbled briefly about resigning. But the crisis passed, aided by a soothing letter to Lindley from Dudley, "your affectionate brother in arms."[31]

At last refitted and reorganized, and after what the Washington administration considered another undue delay, the Army of the Potomac moved out as October closed, headed for "a big fight or a foot race," as one of the Iron Brigade phrased it. Gibbon's men marched with the First Corps from their camps at Bakersville,* Maryland.[32] The route of march passed the Antietam battlefield and then retraced the Antietam preliminaries, to Keedysville, over South Mountain at Crampton's Gap and to Berlin. On October 30th, to the appropriate strains of "Yankee Doodle," the soldiers crossed the pontoons into Virginia, described by one of the Michigan newcomers as the land of "saucy secessionists, the young ladies singing secession songs." The column then marched over the Blue Ridge at Snicker's Gap, where the advance of the army skirmished with the Confederates as the march continued. On November 4th the Federals marched into Bloomfield, destined to be the scene of the end of an epoch for the Iron Brigade.[33]

As he entered Bloomfield at the head of his dusty line of iron men, General John Gibbon was directed to report to the corps commander. Arriving in Reynolds' presence, Gibbon was offered the command of the Second Division of the First Corps, in place of General Ricketts. As the surprised brigadier later described it, "My first feeling was one

* Locations on the march to Virginia appear on the map at page 116.

of regret at the idea of being separated from my gallant brigade," a re-action so apparent that General Reynolds had already said "Well, if you don't want it I will offer it to . . ." before Gibbon recovered him-self and accepted the advancement. The necessary orders were at once prepared and Gibbon was promoted.[34] With him was to go Lieutenant Frank A. Haskell of the Sixth Wisconsin, the general's aide, who "was better qualified to command an army corps than many who enjoyed that honor," according to Gibbon.[35] Haskell was to continue to distinguish himself, to write a famous letter about Gettysburg, and to die at Cold Harbor as colonel of the Thirty-sixth Wisconsin Volunteers.

When Rufus King, the Western brigade's first commander, left the field on the day following Brawner Farm, his military career was on the wane. Indeed, his military reputation was irrevocably stigma-tized by his curious conduct during and immediately after that en-gagement. His health only temporarily restored, King later performed garrison duty at Fortress Monroe, sat on Fitz-John Porter's court-martial, and served as military governor of Norfolk. In October, 1863, again a civilian, he assumed the post of Minister to the Papal States, the appointment the outbreak of the war had postponed.[36] John Gib-bon's departure from the brigade was of an entirely different order. His career was on the rise. He was to be wounded at Fredericksburg as commander of the Second Division of the First Corps, to com-mand a division of the Second Corps at Chancellorsville and Gettys-burg, where he was again wounded, and finally to achieve corps command as the Federal lines choked Lee to death in Virginia.[37] That the Iron Brigade was John Gibbon's creation is an inevitable conclusion. Assuming command in May, 1862, Gibbon had found the Westerners wanting in many soldierly qualities. Vigorously, but never brutally, he had pursued their drill and discipline, relying on modest incentives instead of harsh penalties. Anxious to develop *esprit de corps* in the indifferent volunteers, he had perceived their unique Western character and had used it as his foundation. Know-ing that *pride* is a basis for discipline, Gibbon had adopted the regu-lar army uniform, distinguishing the appearance of his soldiers and causing them to distinguish themselves. And after months of file closing, battle had come to the brigade on August 28th, suddenly, unexpectedly, and viciously, in circumstances most likely to stampede soldiers unaccustomed to battle. Inspired by the personal bravery of their commander, they had not wavered then or thereafter, and when their character had become known they had acquired a reputation and a proud name. All of this was Gibbon's work, as was the sensible decision, when reinforcements came, to maintain the Western character upon which he had built the spirit of the brigade.

Years later Gibbon remembered his sadness at Bloomfield on November 4th, waiting for the moment of parting, "not only from my gallant little brigade but from my own battery which usually accompanied the brigade into battle. In the two united, I had the most implicit confidence, always knowing I could depend upon them." Gibbon's regret was aggravated by the command situation. Of the four colonels of the Wisconsin and Indiana regiments, only Colonel Fairchild of the Second was in the field, and his commission was junior to that of Colonel Morrow who had reached the bridgade less than a month previously. As Gibbon recorded it, "feeling as averse as if trusting a cherished child in the hands of a strange and inexperienced nurse," he sought Morrow's waiver in favor of Fairchild. But, again in the general's words, "although a young soldier I found him disposed to cling as tenaciously as an old one to the rights of his rank, and he declined to yield." Gibbon carried his troubles to the division commander, but Abner Doubleday declined to act. His efforts having gone for naught, Gibbon sat his horse by the roadside on the morning of November 5th and watched his Westerners, his Iron Brigade, move out.[38]

A brigade on the move is in no position to commemorate the loss of its commander, however important he is in its eyes. So it was with the Iron Brigade. Surely there were heartfelt leave-takings that night at Bloomfield, marred, perhaps, by the general's concern with the question of his successor, a preoccupation that was almost unsoldierly, and testifies to his emotional involvement with the brigade. Like any other commander, Gibbon had his detractors, including one Wisconsin soldier who anonymously described him in a Wisconsin newspaper as "arbitrary, severe and exacting . . . distant, formal and reserved . . ." and "a manufactured artistocrat, who owes all his importance to the circumstances that created him."[39] Reflecting on the recent incredibly hard fighting, another Wisconsin soldier conjured up this conclusion in a letter to his father: "It has come to light Gen.

Gibbon used us harder than was necessary by throwing his Brigade clear in the advance, and then refusing support when offered by other Generals. . . ."[40] But these were minority reports. A Hoosier private recorded this impression in his diary: "He has a keen eye, and is as bold as a lion, is respected by his men, who have great confidence in his abilities as a leader." Another soldier, remembering Brawner Farm, wrote: "How completely that little battle removed all dislike for the strict disciplinarian, and how great became the admiration and love for him, only those who have witnessed similar changes can appreciate. . . ." A third described him as "a most excellent officer . . . beloved and respected by his whole command."[41] It was left to Rufus Dawes to spell out Gibbon's character and what he had meant to the Iron Brigade: "Thoroughly educated in the military profession, he had also high personal qualifications to exercise command. He was anxious that his brigade should excel in every possible way, and while he was an exacting disciplinarian he had the good sense to recognize merit where it existed. His administration of the command left a lasting impression for good upon the character and military tone of the brigade, and his splendid personal bravery upon the field of battle was an inspiration." Summing it all up, the North Carolinian, "brave and true," was, in short, a "jewel."[42]

As for John Gibbon's ultimate feelings about the Iron Brigade, these appeared after the war in his answer to an invitation to a reunion of all honorably discharged soldiers from Wisconsin. Still in the army, and in words which he would surely have also applied to *all* of the soldiers of the Iron Brigade, the general stated: "I was not a Wisconsin soldier, and have not been honorably discharged, but at the judgment day I want to be with Wisconsin soldiers."[43]

9

RETURN TO FREDERICKSBURG:
THE TWENTY-FOURTH MICHIGAN EARNS THE
BLACK HAT

"Terrible as it was to some, to us it was really almost nothing compared with Antietam."

From a letter of Rufus Dawes

Led by Colonel Henry A. Morrow, their untried temporary commander, the Iron Brigade pursued the First Corps' line of march to Piedmont and then to Warrenton, Virginia. There the brigade arrived on November 7th, the weather closed in, and camp was established. To the Wisconsin and Indiana veterans, this was familiar country. It was even more familiar to Colonel Morrow. Riding into Warrenton at the head of the brigade from the West, the erstwhile Virginian passed the house in which he had been born and, but a few yards away, the cemetery in which his mother lay buried.[1]

At Warrenton the Western soldiers soon discovered that the bad weather was not the only cause for the army's hesitation. A critical shortage of commissary supplies prevailed, and the army was not to resume its travels until its stomach could be filled. The Iron Brigade was entirely without food for two days, provoking one of the soldiers from Michigan to record that "the soldier's ration is more than he can ordinarily eat when he gets it, but for one reason and another, he scarcely ever gets it." But despite the tone of the comment, the men of the Twenty-fourth were not disposed to be philosophical, and one of their Wisconsin comrades noted that the soldiers of the "new regiment . . . have been shouting: 'Bread! Bread!' at the top of their voices all day."[2]

The same army headquarters that had failed to supply the men with food had issued strict orders against foraging, but some of the Iron Brigade veterans preferred disobeying orders to joining in the fruitless protests of their Michigan comrades. Even so, the prospects for foraging were not bright. "This part of Old Virginia is perfectly used up, all rails burned, pigs and chickens killed, horses and cattle gone, most of the houses deserted . . . ," wrote a Wisconsin soldier.[3] But this was apparently an overstatement. A Hoosier diarist and his friend found a pig and "about one gallon [of] beans . . . so [we] are living on beans and meat,"[4] and a private of the Sixth Wisconsin, having eluded the headquarters cavalry patrol, succeeded in bringing in a sheep. Had the regimental officers enforced the foraging prohibition, the cavalry patrol would have been unnecessary, and foraging would have been effectively stopped at the regimental level, or at least reduced to an absolute minimum. But this was an area in which the Civil War command system broke down, because the officers, at least the volunteers, simply would not cooperate. Some of the officers closed their eyes to the violations; others, often acting out an elaborate charade, actively connived with the enlisted men. On the march to Fredericksburg, Lieutenant Colonel Bragg, who had rejoined the Sixth Wisconsin after his Antietam wound, pointed out a group of farmhouses to his hungry soldiers, told them he was going to take a nap, and that he did not want to "see or hear of your foraging on this march." Joining his men an hour later for a feast of ham and eggs, Bragg inquired where the food had come from, and listened with a straight face to their statement that the kindly Southern farmers had insisted that they take it. When the soldiers finished their account, the lieutenant colonel sighed with relief, remarking, "That's all right; I was afraid you had stolen them."[5]

The Warrenton famine was, of course, of brief duration. A nearby gristmill was seized and put into operation, supplies from Washington reached the camp, and the soldiers returned to their usual menu, described by one of the Michigan men as "Breakfast—Coffee, Hardtack, Pork. Dinner—Hardtack, Pork, Coffee. Supper—Pork, Coffee, Hardtack." And in spite of the Twenty-fourth Michigan's cries for bread, when it did arrive the regimental historian described it in less than enthusiastic terms: "Our bread is of cracker shape and thickness, about four inches square, and very hard—hence the name 'hardtack.' The boxes containing it frequently were marked 'B.C.' evidently the manufacturer's initials, but the soldiers insisted that it stood for 'Before Christ,' when the stuff must have been made. To make it palatable it is soaked a few minutes in cold water, which leavens it to a pulp, and we then fry it on our tin plates, with a slice of pork. Hot water has no effect on the hardtack except to make it tough like leather." The historian then expanded his theme: "Sometimes the pork is fried in tin plates, sometimes . . . a slice is stuck on the end of a ramrod and held over the campfire, a hardtack being usually held under in order not to lose any of the grease that melts out of it."[6]

While the Iron Brigade was encamped at Warrenton, there occurred a major upheaval in the army's high command. In another of the controversial events surrounding his career, George B. McClellan was dismissed. It is often asserted that the soldiers' reaction to the removal of their favorite was violent to the point of mutiny and that McClellan was widely solicited to retain power by force. Whatever the feeling in the army generally, there was nothing mutinous about the Iron Brigade's response to the news. According to Major Dawes: "There was considerable expression of feeling. No acts of insubordination occurred." Colonel Cutler had at last returned to duty and, with seniority over Morrow, was in command of the brigade. Referring to the talk of resignations in other organizations, Dawes reported that "in our brigade, the sturdy faithfulness of Colonel Lysander Cutler, then commanding, and his known determination of character, had an excellent restraining influence. He declared that he would recommend for dismissal, for tendering a resignation while in the presence of the enemy, any officer who offered to resign for such a reason. There were no resignations sent to his headquarters."[7] And despite his previous intrigues about the command and his own preferment, McClellan seemed to share Cutler's view of the military thing to do. The army was quietly turned over to his appointed successor, General Ambrose Burnside, and after a final farewell tour of the troops McClellan left the war. A few days later, as the public argument about McClellan's removal continued, a Wisconsin man in the Iron Brigade wrote a letter home. Impartially condemning "your traitor Dem. papers [which] raised the howl that it was done for political purposes" as well as "the damned infernal lies, in our republican papers . . . [which] are becoming a corrupt lying and party loving power," the soldier had this to say about the question of command:

The Army stands by the old flag . . . the American soldier is true to his country, true to his oath, and resolved to fight the rebellion to the bitter end no difference who commands. . . . i am not a McClellan man, a Burnside man, a Hooker man, i am for the man that leads us to fight the Rebs on any terms he can get. . . .[8]

As long as this attitude prevailed among the men who had to fight the war, the "old flag" was likely to continue to wave.

Without changing the corps structure, General Burnside organized the Army of the Potomac into three "grand divisions," the right, the left, and the center, each made up of two corps. Sumner was assigned to command the Right Grand Division, Hooker the center, and William B. Franklin the left. Franklin's force included the Sixth Corps and Reynolds' First Corps, composed, as before, of the divisions of Meade, Gibbon, and Doubleday. In addition to the Iron Brigade and Phelps' Brigade, Doubleday's Division included Rogers' Brigade—formerly Patrick's—and Doubleday's old brigade, now commanded by Colonel James Gavin. Battery B was still attached to the division, along with Gerrish's New Hampshire and Reynolds' New York batteries.[9]

The Army of the Potomac was not the only unit listing a new commander in November of 1862. After repeated efforts, the Nineteenth Indiana's Solomon Meredith had in October been commissioned a brigadier general of volunteers. Still not entirely well, Long Sol had returned to Indiana with the announced plan of obtaining an Indiana brigade, to include the Nineteenth and Seventh Indiana, both distinguished veteran organizations, together with new regiments which the new general proposed to recruit.[10] While he was in Indiana, John Gibbon was promoted to division command, and the chance of obtaining the Iron Brigade was suddenly presented to Meredith. Doubtless employing standard political techniques, the details of which are unrecorded, the Hoosier general succeeded in securing Burnside's recommendation[11] and, having returned to the army, was able to announce in a letter to Governor Morton that "I have been assigned to this glorious old 'Iron Brigade' . . . which I consider the highest honor . . . [and] a very high compliment." Thus did the Western brigade acquire the third of its commanders, two of whom, Gibbon and Meredith, were men of North Carolina origin.[12]

The rising career of Solomon Meredith had not gone unnoticed by General John Gibbon. After Antietam, Gibbon had recommended Colonel Lysander Cutler for brigadier,[13] and he also had a high opinion of the Second's Colonel Fairchild, in whose behalf Gibbon sought Colonel Morrow's waiver when the command of the brigade was temporarily vacated at Bloomfield on November 4th. But Gibbon had a low opinion of Meredith's military ability, and later wrote of his feeling of "outrage" at Meredith's "by purely political influence . . . getting himself appointed a Brig. General of Volunteers, a position he was in no way fitted to fill." When he subsequently learned that Meredith's brigadier generalship had led to the command of his old brigade, Gibbon's response was furious: ". . . to relieve a competent colonel [Cutler] and put that fine body of men in charge of an incompetent Brig. General was a step which excited not only my indignation but my apprehensions." Although he had been promoted to the command of a division which did not include the Iron Brigade, and was no longer in any way responsible for it, John Gibbon could not resist intervening against Meredith. Learning from General Franklin that Burnside himself had requested Meredith's assignment to the brigade, and unwilling to intrigue at the level of the army command, Gibbon resorted to more devious tactics. Having discovered that Hooker had recommended Long Sol for the brigadier generalship in the first place, Gibbon sought him out and, in his own words: "I laid the case before him, frankly telling him why I did not want this Brig. General to have command of my old brigade, the character of the troops composing which he well knew, and ended by requesting him to apply for the officer for duty in his Grand Division where he could assign him to a position where he could, at least, do as little harm as possible." Although by Gibbon's account Hooker admitted that his original recommendation of Meredith for the general's commission was prompted by the solicitations of Meredith's "many strong friends," Hooker rejected Gibbon's plea and Meredith's appointment was undisturbed.[14] *

It is impossible at this late date to determine whether Gibbon was correct in his harsh appraisal of Solomon Meredith. In Meredith's be-

---

*Recent research discloses that Meredith sought by political pressure to have the Nineteenth transferred from Gibbon's brigade in the summer of 1862 because Gibbon had criticized that regiments's discipline.

half, it is apparent that Gibbon harbored a grudge, beginning with his belief that the tall Hoosier had spoken against Gibbon's appointment to command of the brigade in May. John Gibbon would have been more than human if this belief had not at least unconsciously colored his opinion of Meredith as a soldier. There was also something to be said in response to Gibbon's denunciation of Meredith's use of political influence to further his career. Despite the evils of the method, it was almost universally observed throughout the army. The Americans of the day were a crudely political people, and had not abandoned their habits because of the war. It is almost a certainty that the other colonels of the Iron Brigade had also sought the command through political friends, just as they had resorted to such contacts for regimental commands. Indeed, Gibbon, himself, when he believed his cause just, had worked through the politically influential General Wadsworth to obtain his own confirmation as a brigadier. Thus there was something unreal, and therefore unjust, in his singling out of Meredith for criticism in this respect. Whatever Meredith's faults, Gibbon alone left a record unfavorable to him. No other officer of the brigade wrote critically, and the available expressions of the common soldier were decidedly friendly. A Wisconsin veteran, heralding Meredith's appointment to command, said that "he always was a favourite,"[15] and an Indiana diarist, writing just before the promotion, spoke of a personal characteristic of the man. "I again testify to the kindness of our worthy Colonel Meredith,"[16] wrote the soldier. Surely kindness counted for something. Finally, granting that Meredith was not in Gibbon's class as a soldier, the later career of the brigade certainly did not justify Gibbon's apprehensions. As the brigade commander, Meredith was shortly to be involved in an ambiguous incident at Fredericksburg, which may or may not constitute a black mark on his record. But if he may be judged on the basis of the conduct of his soldiers, a practical test, Meredith was one of many men who found themselves, without training or experience, commanding soldiers in wartime. Extroverted and ambitious by nature, accustomed to asserting themselves, these men did the best that they could, for themselves and their responsibilities, and they somehow sufficed.

Meredith's promotion to command of the brigade left the Nineteenth Indiana with a vacant field command and occasioned the usual unseemly contention among the officers. Although Lieutenant Colonel Williams and Major Dudley might logically have expected to be advanced, the political struggle assumed that the colonelcy was wide open. Whatever their advantages, Williams and Dudley were taking no chances, and a caucus of all the officers was promptly assembled. As reported to Governor Morton in a letter that described the dissenters as "sore heads," all but Captain Lindley and three others voted for the advancement of Williams and Dudley. The same caucus gave Muncie's Captain Alonzo J. Makepeace of Company A an eleven-to-five margin over Lindley for the major's commission, with a few scattered votes for other captains. The officers' poll was followed by a vote of the enlisted men, and the governor received a long petition apparently signed by all of them, including four who signed with "X, his mark," urging the advancement of Williams. In addition to the persistent John M. Lindley, a vigorous claim for the colonelcy came from Captain Luther B. Wilson of Company E, also a Muncie, Indiana, man. So strong was Wilson's case that General Meredith, still behind Williams and Dudley, intervened in their behalf with a letter to his friend the governor. The general disclosed that Wilson, who had recently returned from leave, was openly claiming that Governor Morton had promised him the command. This, said Meredith, would constitute a "manifest injustice to the service," since the regiment was "all for Williams" and "has been a unit since Lt. Col. Cameron was transferred" the previous February. Referring to Wilson's political backer in Indiana, also a party friend of Meredith, Long Sol acknowledged that he would like "to accommodate my friend . . . but I say to you that it will not do to appoint Capt. Wilson colonel of the 19th. . . ."

Despite Meredith's forceful position, Wilson did not give up easily. Several enlisted men who had signed the petition for Williams now wrote the harried governor, claiming that they had done so under a misunderstanding and really preferred Wilson. One of these waverers, a sergeant, signed his name "for the company," presumably in an effort to falsify the numbers of the Wilson group. The issue raged throughout December and into January when Williams and Dudley at length moved up to colonel and lieutenant colonel.[17] Wilson fell entirely by the wayside, leaving Captain Lindley and Captain William Orr of Company K, a new contender, to fight it out for the majority.

The twenty-four-year-old Captain Orr was a native of Delaware County, Indiana, and the son of a Virginia family that had emigrated to the Hoosier state and settled in the town of Selma. A graduate of the Indianapolis Law School, and a lawyer by profession, Orr had also been a schoolteacher and was widely known as a public speaker. Since Colonel Williams was also a Selma man, one suspects that Orr was not without an ally in the contest with Captain Lindley. As the senior of the two, Lindley was to serve as acting major while the issue was pending. But it was not until May of 1863 that he finally prevailed over Orr and was formally awarded the majority.[18]

While the Nineteenth Indiana wrangled about who was to be its new commander, the First Corps was moving south from Warrenton toward the Rappahannock, over roads made extremely difficult by the bitter winter rain and snow. Burnside's plan, which the army was now in the process of executing, was to "make a rapid move of the whole force to Fredericksburg, with a view to a movement upon Richmond from that point." Evacuated by the Federals in September, Fredericksburg was but lightly held by the Confederates, and Lee's army, reorganized and reinforced with conscripts, was principally located at Culpeper and in the Shenandoah Valley. Vital to the Federal plan was speed of movement, so that the river could be crossed before the Confederates concentrated to dispute the passage. Pontoons had been ordered for bridging the river, and were to be available at Fredericksburg upon the arrival of the army.[19]

Despite the weather, the new campaign had begun well enough. On November 17th the head of Sumner's Grand Division reached the Rappahannock at Falmouth and placed its artillery so as to command Fredericksburg.* Two days later, Franklin's Grand Division reached Stafford, eight miles northeast of Falmouth, and Hooker's force was even closer, opposite United States Ford, on the river northwest of Fredericksburg. The whole movement had been marked by rapid, orderly marching, in contrast to what Lincoln had called McClellan's "slows," and the Federal army was now based on Aquia Creek and the Rappahannock, a more convenient and secure line than the Manassas Gap and Orange and Alexandria railroads. Even more promising, Lee was uncertain as to the Federals' real purpose and was

* Preliminaries of the Fredericksburg campaign may be followed by reference to map at page 48.

not ready to defend the Rappahannock line. There was, however, one critical fault in the Union plan. The bridging materials were not yet available and (an issue which is still debated) the river was declared unfordable. As the November days rolled by, the weather worsened and the river rose. Still the pontoons did not arrive, and on the 25th, at last aware of the situation, Lee undertook his concentration. Thus, the great chance of Burnside's campaign was lost at the river's edge and the stage was set for one of the great tragedies of the war for the Union.

While the situation was developing in front of Fredericksburg, the soldiers of the Iron Brigade and their First Corps comrades were assembling near Aquia Creek. On November 25th the brigade reached Brooks Station on the railroad between Aquia Creek and Fredericksburg. Not knowing of the plan of the campaign, the soldiers proceeded hopefully to prepare their huts for the winter. There was some slight cause for optimism. "We have a rumor in camp, that a cessation of hostilities have been agreed upon between the two armies for thirty days," reported a soldier of the Nineteenth Indiana.[20] But even as the winter quarters were erected, the men were skeptical of the permanency of their situation and caustically apprehensive of the future. "There is an aspect of winter quarters for the Army, but no one expects that our Commanding General will publish orders to that effect. O, no, 'Richmond must fall,' 'Lee's army must be bagged.' There must be another bloody battle. Nothing less will appease our valiant 'stay-at-home rangers,' " wrote a Wisconsin soldier. As the Western soldiers awaited developments, the routine of army life went on. Rufus Dawes found himself assigned to conduct the regimental courts-martial, a chore he described as follows: "A full record of proceedings and evidence in each case tried has to be made *pro forma*, which involves much labor. My standard of fines for misdemeanors ranges from three dollars to thirteen dollars, the maximum allowed by law. As for example, 'for killing a rabbit,' ('rabbits' are covered with wool in this country)—about four dollars; 'for a knock down,' eight dollars, and for getting drunk and kicking up a row generally, thirteen dollars."[21] While Dawes was so employed, the men of the Twenty-fourth Michigan were detailed to guard the railroad from Aquia to Fredericksburg. Scattered by companies over several miles of track, and exposed to the freezing winter rains, the regiment suffered heavily from illness and disease. Often bedded down in simple hospital tents, the sick had little chance to recover from such maladies as pneumonia, and nine men died in the course of a few days. Not unnaturally, among the first was James Nowlin, the seventy-year-old volunteer. For the new regiment, in the words of its historian, "that row of graves on yonder knoll told the sad story of . . . hardship" at Brooks Station.[22]

Just after midnight on December 9th, the First Corps marched away from Brooks Station, heading for the Rappahannock. Each soldier carried sixty rounds of ammunition, which effectively disposed of the illusion of a peaceful winter. After a brief march over what one of the Iron Brigade soldiers described as "the roughest roads I ever saw," the column halted five miles from the river. On the following day the march was resumed, but the traffic was heavy as the huge Federal army completed its concentration, and the Iron Brigade again encamped after having moved only two miles closer to the river.[23] Ahead of the brigade, in the early morning of December 11th, the laying of the pontoon bridges began at last. Two were to be put down directly in front of Fredericksburg, another, the "middle bridge," three-quarters of a mile down the river, and two more, placed side by side, were to be located a mile east of the middle bridge. These last two, known historically as Franklin's Crossing, were the destination of the Iron Brigade and their comrades of the First Corps and Franklin's Grand Division.[24]

The First Corps began to move at 5:00 A.M. on the 11th, marching to the sounds of distant artillery and musketry fire. Separated from the river's edge by heavy woods, the soldiers of the Iron Brigade could not see the river drama, but heavy clouds of smoke were visible to them, rising above Fredericksburg, which had been set afire by Federal artillery seeking to drive out the Confederate sharpshooters on the opposite bank. After repeated halts, the brigade reached the river, but although the bridges were completed the main body of the army was withheld while skirmishers secured bridgeheads on the south side. Amidst a growing atmosphere of pessimism, the Iron Brigade bivouacked in the woods, ready to cross the next day.[25]

A heavy fog hung over the Rappahannock as the soldiers awakened on the morning of December 12th. Although the fog obscured many of the sights—and was thus a blessing for the Federals—it did little to reduce the sounds of the army's preparations. The soldiers hastily formed ranks in the midst of a tumult of drum and bugle calls, to which the shrieking of Confederate long-range artillery projectiles was soon added.[26] Despite the noise and confusion, Colonel Morrow chose the occasion to make a short speech to his regiment, reminding them on the threshold of their first battle that "Wayne County expected every man to do his duty."[27] Then the Sixth Corps led Franklin's Grand Division over the river, turning to its right, toward Fredericksburg, when it reached the south side. At 1:30 P.M. the First Corps followed, with Gibbon's Division in the advance, followed by Meade and Doubleday. Doubleday's men were well closed up, and three of his brigades crossed on the upper bridge while the Iron Brigade and the division's artillery crossed by the lower. Gibbon and Meade deployed their divisions at once, Gibbon to the right joining the Sixth Corps' line and Meade to the left, extending his left flank to Smithfield, a plantation on the riverbank approximately a mile beyond the crossing. Advancing his artillery to the front to answer the heavy Confederate cannonade, Doubleday massed his infantry at the crossing as the reserve for Gibbon and Meade. When these divisions advanced, Doubleday's columns faced left and, led by the Iron Brigade, marched down the river behind Meade's lines. At the Bernard house, a fine stone mansion on the riverbank three-quarters of a mile from the crossing, the brigade was halted at 5:00 P.M. Supported by Battery B, the brigade went into camp in the yard of the Bernard house as the day closed.[28] The night was bitterly cold, and the soldiers slept on the ground without fires, scraping together piles of leaves for bedding. In the camp of the Sixth Wisconsin, Colonel Cutler, fifty-five years old and still badly crippled from his Brawner Farm wound, shared a bed of leaves with Rufus Dawes for the long, uncomfortable night.[29] The river crossing had been successful and, despite the Confederate artillery fire, the Iron Brigade counted but one casualty, a soldier of the Seventh Wisconsin who had been killed by an artillery shell as the brigade moved down the river.[30]

Elsewhere along the river, Sumner's Grand Division had crossed at the upper bridges and spread to the right and left, connecting its line with that of the Sixth Corps. Hooker's Grand Division was held on the north side of the river, and crossed over the following day behind Sumner, except for the divisions of Sickles and Birney which

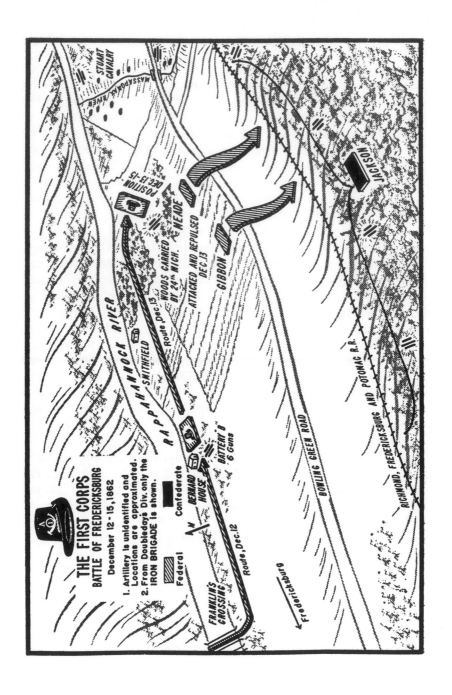

THE FIRST CORPS
BATTLE OF FREDERICKSBURG
December 12 - 15, 1862

1. Artillery is unidentified and Locations are approximated.
2. From Doubleday's Div. only the IRON BRIGADE is shown.

Federal

Confederate

FRANKLIN'S CROSSING

Route, Dec.12

BERNARD HOUSE

N

Fredericksburg

BATTERY "B" 6 Guns

RAPPAHANNOCK RIVER

SMITHFIELD

Route, Dec.13

WOODS CARRIED BY 24th MICH.

POSITION DEC. 13-15

MEADE

ATTACKED AND REPULSED DEC.13

GIBBON

BOWLING GREEN ROAD

RICHMOND, FREDERICKSBURG AND POTOMAC R.R.

JACKSON

STUART CAVALRY

MASSAPONAX RIVER

were to come in behind Franklin's men. Facing the Federals' 116,000 effectives were Lee's 72,000 men occupying the wooded heights located approximately a mile from the river and looking down on the plain into which the Federal army had debouched. In front of Franklin's Grand Division, the plain was enclosed on the east by the Massaponax River, which ran northward into the Rappahannock three miles below Franklin's Crossing. Halfway between the Rappahannock and the wooded heights where the Confederates waited, running parallel to the Rappahannock, was the Bowling Green Road, down which the Wisconsin and Indiana soldiers had marched in their abortive move to Richmond in May. Beyond the road, and running parallel to it at the foot of the heights, was the Richmond, Fredericksburg, and Potomac Railroad. In addition to these markings, the plain, largely composed of cultivated ground, contained wooded areas and was intersected by ravines, ditches, and hedges. With his left at the Rappahannock west of Fredericksburg and his right extending to the Massaponax, Lee could hardly have wished for a more advantageous defensive position. Longstreet's Corps held his left, west of Fredericksburg and opposite the town, while Jackson's men faced the plain in front of Franklin's Grand Division. To Jackson's right, Stuart's cavalry and horse artillery, with infantry support, anchored Lee's line in the valley of the Massaponax, occupying ground both east and west of that river.[31]

Another foggy winter's day awaited the soldiers on December 13th. Having deployed his army in two basic assaulting forces with Hooker's Grand Division as the reserve, Burnside ordered an attack from the left against Jackson. Meade was directed to lead off, supported on the right by Gibbon and with Doubleday assigned to cover the left. At eight-thirty, having moved slightly to his left, Meade formed his lines opposite Smithfield, faced the Bowling Green Road, and began the advance. As the blue columns crossed the road, the Confederate artillery opened from the wooded heights beyond. Their fire was countered by the Federal batteries that advanced to the open ground between the road and the railroad and engaged the enemy guns for half an hour while the infantry hugged the ground. Then the Confederate fire slackened, and under cover of the Federal artillery Meade and Gibbon moved out to the railroad and Jackson's wooded heights. As the lines became engaged, Doubleday's Division, which had followed Meade, was faced to the left and advanced directly down the river toward Stuart, who was already pouring a destructive artillery fire into Meade's flank and rear.[32]

In four lines of battle, and with the Iron Brigade and Battery B on the left, Doubleday's Division moved downriver, driving the Confederate skirmishers while the hostile artillery sought the range. Half a mile from its starting point, the brigade confronted a pine wood extending from the bank of the Rappahannock, from which Stuart's horsemen and artillery were raking the Federal advance. Halting his line, Doubleday ordered Battery B to the front to remove this obstruction to the Federal sweep of the riverbank. After the woods had been shelled, Meredith was ordered to storm the place.[33] The Twenty-fourth Michigan "were exceedingly anxious to go always to the front, and, resting upon our hard earned laurels, we were generously willing that they should do so," wrote an Iron Brigade veteran,[34] and the ambition of the new regiment was now to be accommodated. Deployed in two lines, with the Michigan regiment and the Seventh Wisconsin in the front line, the brigade stepped off, preceded by skirmishers from the Second United States Sharpshooters of Phelps' Brigade. At the woods the Michigan soldiers overtook the Sharpshooters, who had hesitated at a fence along the edge and were absorbing the fire from the invisible enemy. Responding to an order from the Sharpshooters' commander to "kick his men over the fence," the Michigan newcomers surged forward and,[35] in Doubleday's words, "carried the wood in gallant style, taking a number of prisoners and horses." Although there was nothing particularly remarkable about the assault on the wood, apparently but lightly held by the Confederates, there must have been something remarkable about the manner of the Twenty-fourth's advance which prompted the division commander to report that "in this affair my attention was particularly directed to the Twenty-fourth Michigan Volunteers, a new regiment, for the first time under fire. I was pleased to see the alacrity and courage with which they performed the duty assigned to them."[36]

Continuing its advance beyond the pine wood, the brigade moved to within three-quarters of a mile of the Massaponax. There, having driven the Confederates on the left beyond the river.[37] Doubleday established a line to secure the flank of the army while the assault of Meade and Gibbon proceeded. With the Iron Brigade on the left, its line extending on an angle from the Bowling Green Road to the Rappahannock, Doubleday wheeled his remaining brigades to their right to a position along the road. Here, though the ditches and embankments provided adequate cover against the enemy's pickets beyond the road, they gave little protection against the enemy's artillery firing from the heights and from beyond the Massaponax.[38] To counter this, Battery B had moved to the right of the brigade and was laboring mightily to drive off the Confederate guns. Out in the open, without protection against either artillery or musket fire, the men and horses of the battery began to go down.[39] To the left of the brigade another Federal battery was at work, and the Twenty-fourth Michigan was again sent forward, to rout the enemy sharpshooters harassing the gunners. Advancing from their sheltered position, the Michigan men now suffered their first battle casualties as a solid shot swept off the arm of one soldier and severed the head from another. "The casualty was soon known along the line and created some unsteadiness in the execution of orders . . . as cannon balls ploughed through the ranks, and shells shrieked like demons in the air," reported the candid historian of the regiment. What happened then, a classic moment in the career of the regiment, was inscribed in the record: "Colonel Morrow saw the wavering lines and was quick to discern that no troops would long stand in such a fire unemployed, without the privilege of returning a single shot. To bring the men to themselves he halted the regiment and put it through the manual of arms drill. His sonorous orders: 'Attention, battalion! Right dress! Front! Support arms . . .' were heard over the field, and with all the precision of a parade, the orders were obeyed . . . while the air was torn with cannon balls and the very hills seemed to rock under the reverberations." Then, still suffering casualties, the Twenty-fourth proceeded to accomplish its mission before returning to the friendly ditches where the brigade waited.[40]

It was now early afternoon, and the men of Meade and Gibbon, having pierced the first Confederate lines on the heights, were being driven back by heavy blows from Jackson's reserves. To their right, the Iron Brigade heard the crashing musketry and the wild yells as the disordered Federals retreated. Although Doubleday started to the right to check the enemy's advance, Birney, followed by Sickles, came up behind Gibbon and Meade, counterattacked, and stabilized the

Federal line. The immediate danger over, Doubleday's infantry resumed its position and waited to see if the repulse of Meade and Gibbon was to be followed by a Confederate counterstroke. As if to forecast a Confederate thrust, the enemy guns began what Doubleday described as "a furious cannonade, apparently from more than forty pieces of artillery, . . . sending an incessant shower of shot, shell, and case shot through our ranks. . . ."[41] The fury of the Confederate fire was also described by Rufus Dawes: "I have never known a more severe trial of nerve upon the battlefield, than this hour under that infernal fire . . . our eyes were riveted upon the cannon on the hill firing point blank at us. . . . There would be a swift outburst of snow white smoke, out of which flashed a tongue of fire, and the cannon would leap backward in its recoil; then followed the thundering report, in the midst of which the missile fired at us would plow deep into the ground, scattering a spray of dirt and bound high over us or burst in the air, sending fragments with a heavy thud into the ground around us."[42] While the cannonade continued, there was nothing for the infantry to do but lie in the ditches, an experience which a Wisconsin veteran explained in a letter to his father: "When a man has to choose between laying in a ditch half full of water or getting his head blown off he will generally lay contented in the mud. . . ." But the Federal artillery was not permitted even this luxury, and the gunners stood to their work, directing their fire against the Confederate guns as these were disclosed by their own fire. Again Battery B distinguished itself, Doubleday reporting that "Stewart . . . was fully equal to the occasion; nothing could exceed the accuracy of his fire and the sound judgment which regulated the discharges to suit the character of the attack. He blew up another of the enemy's caissons, disabled their pieces, and strewed the earth with the slain."[43]

Still anticipating a Confederate counterattack, and believing that it would be directed against the center of his concave line, Doubleday now concluded that the line of the Iron Brigade, extending on an angle to the Rappahannock, was too prolonged. At four-thirty he directed General Meredith and Colonel Rogers, whose brigade was next in line, to withdraw to a ditch and embankment behind them, leaving pickets out. This order was the background of an incident the division commander later described in his report: "There was unusual, and, I deemed, unnecessary delay in obeying . . . on the part of General Meredith, and finding after two hours had elapsed, that my instructions had not been carried out, I felt it my duty to relieve him of command. I therefore placed the brigade under Colonel Cutler. . . ."[44] Whether Meredith was at fault is uncertain. Both the newspapers and the historian of the Twenty-fourth Michigan attributed the incident to conflicting orders delivered to the brigade commander. In any event, although Long Sol was to be reinstated immediately after the battle,[45] Lysander Cutler was now in charge, and he formed the brigade as Doubleday had directed, slightly advancing its left so as to form a line diagonal to the Bowling Green Road and thus avoiding the enfilading fire from the enemy's batteries on the heights. As darkness fell, the Confederates' cannonade continued. But though their batteries had gradually advanced to within canister range of the Federal positions, the blue lines were strongly held[46] and the Iron Brigade never was called on to deliver the "little touch of Northwestern hell" which one of the Wisconsin men promised a Confederate infantry assault.[47]

At last the day was over, an extremely bad day for the Union. The action on the Federal left had been but a small part of the story. On the right, Sumner's Grand Division and parts of Hooker's, attacking again and again over impossible ground, had been torn to pieces by Longstreet's Corps at Marye's Hill. To add to the horror for the wounded of both sides, the night was again mercilessly cold, so cold that the soldiers of the Iron Brigade, still deprived of fires, resorted to a highly original maneuver. "We formed long lines of officers and men together, who would lie down on their oil cloths, spoon fashion to keep each other warm." To the discomfort of the night were added both heavy picket firing and canister from the Confederate guns, an experience recalled by one of the brigade in these words: "At short intervals the rebel battery would blaze away with its horrible shot rattling on the frozen ground. The shot seemed to fly about one foot above us, so that, while one was freezing as he lay down, he was tortured with the fear of being torn to pieces if he ventured to stand up or walk around."[48]

Although his army had been decisively defeated, Burnside continued to occupy the south side of the river through the 14th of December. At headquarters, the question of whether to renew the assault was debated. In the meantime the soldiers waited during a day that saw occasional artillery and picket firing, interspersed with periods of informal truce during which the enemies, mingling freely, buried the dead and cared for the wounded. There was quiet in Doubleday's front on the night of the 14th because the Second Wisconsin, on picket for the division, thoughtfully arranged a truce with the Confederates opposing them so that the soldiers of both sides could get some rest. Relieving the Second at daylight the next morning, and unaware of the agreement to give a warning signal before resuming hostilities, the Twenty-fourth Michigan opened fire on the exposed and unsuspecting enemy, shooting down a number of them. "This irritated the Confederates," wrote an Iron Brigade soldier in what was surely a remarkable understatement, and they responded in kind. Late in the afternoon the truce was reinstated when a Confederate challenged a Sixth Wisconsin soldier to a fist fight on the Bowling Green Road. Putting aside their weapons, both sides watched while the combatants fought to what was generally declared a draw. Following the fight, the cheering sections shook hands all around, traded tobacco and coffee and agreed that there was to be no more firing until either side ordered an advance.[49] The 15th was also marked by two movements involving the brigade. At the direction of the corps commander, Colonel Morrow led two of his companies in what Doubleday called "a daring and well executed reconnaissance" to the Massaponax. Late in the day, Lieutenant Colonel Williams advanced the Nineteenth on picket duty down the river to a point a mile beyond the line of the brigade.[50] Then night came on, and with it the Union's decision to withdraw.

Although the risk of detection was lessened by a favorable wind blowing away from the Confederate lines, and by the picket-line truces, which had relaxed the Confederate outposts, the crossing of the river in the presence of an alert and aggressive enemy was a perilous undertaking. Advised of the move at 7:00 P.M., Reynolds first sent his artillery off.[51] For many of the batteries, stationed toward the rear and protected by the infantry, the retirement was easily accomplished. But for Battery B, advanced to within five hundred feet of the Confederate pickets and without close infantry support, withdrawal was another matter. As soon as the guns were limbered up, they would be substantially disarmed and at the mercy of a quick dash from the enemy. "Under these circumstances, the guns were limbered as silently as possible and hauled off, still shotted with double canister and primed ready for action if the enemy should attempt a rush," wrote the battery historian.[52] Once the artillery was safely across, it was the infantry's turn. Rather than risk disclosure of the general withdrawal, it was decided to sacrifice the pickets. This meant that the Nineteenth Indiana, a mile beyond the line of the brigade, was to be abandoned, a disaster Colonel Cutler proposed to avoid if at all possible. Approaching General Reynolds, who had issued the order, Cutler finally obtained permission to make an effort to save the Indiana regiment, if it could be done without jeopardizing the movement as a whole. At eleven o'clock it was the Iron Brigade's turn to march for the bridges. Silently the men moved away, led by Colonel Cutler, who now, in his own words, "sent an order to Lieutenant Colonel Williams . . . to call in his pickets at 4:30 o'clock, and to follow the brigade in silence to a new position up the river, without intimating to him that we were to recross. . . ."[53]

At four-thirty, therefore, after their comrades were safely across, the Nineteenth started its march upriver. Three miles separated the regiment from the bridges, and, according to a participant, each man had been told that "if we wanted to save ourselves, we must be quick and silent. . . ." As the march proceeded, the Hoosiers saw that the "fields which at night fall had been covered by our army were now deserted."[54] Unknown to the marching column, only a handful of pickets remained south of the river, and these were now being brought in and were crossing the bridges, leaving the Hoosiers alone in the presence of Jackson's Corps. Behind the Indiana men, Confederate cavalry and infantry skirmishers, having felt the places where the Federal lines had rested, had begun the pursuit. Although their isolated situation was now reasonably apparent, there was no panic or disorder as the Nineteenth raced for the crossing. At last the advance of the regiment reached the bridges, and crossed. But the rear guard was not yet up, and the engineers could wait no longer. The bridges were cut away from the south bank and were at once swept down the river. Now the Nineteenth's rear guard arrived, clambered into the skiffs which the engineers held ready for their own crossing, and paddled for the north bank. On their heels followed the Confederate cavalry, but they were too late. Not a single soldier of the Nineteenth Indiana was captured.[55] In his report Colonel Cutler acknowledged his "great obligations . . . to Lieutenant Colonel Williams, for the coolness and good judgment which he exercised in obeying my orders, and which resulted in saving one of the best regiments in the service." Looking beyond the regimental commander, Abner Doubleday marked the exploit in these words: "I cannot too highly praise the coolness and good order which marked the retreat of this regiment, and in all probability saved it from destruction." And a private of the Nineteenth, writing in his diary, had this to say: ". . . if we had been left as our head General at first designed terrible would have been our fate, for we would have known nothing of the retreat, and when the enemy advanced the 19th is not the Reg't to surrender without any fight, the consequences would have been a wiping out of the old 19th. . . ."[56]

Back on the north side of the river, the Iron Brigade went into camp two miles from Franklin's Crossing.[57] The campaign of Fredericksburg was over. Although it had cost the Federal army almost 13,000 men, for the Iron Brigade the battle had been almost a casual experience. Only 65 of the Western soldiers were casualties, 32 of whom were from the Twenty-fourth Michigan.[58] Battery B's losses were reported by Lieutenant Stewart, who understood that it took both men and horses to operate an artillery battery: "Killed, 2 men and 8 horses; wounded, 6 men and 5 horses." The lieutenant and the battery had again earned the praise of the army. "Lieutenant Stewart showed himself, as at all times, the thorough soldier," reported the corps chief of artillery, and Doubleday's report was extended in its acclaim of the battery.[59]

In the wake of Fredericksburg followed some of the harshest controversy of the war. The soldiers themselves were bitter, including the men of the Iron Brigade, although their personal suffering had been relatively slight. "I won't try to describe to you the perfect contempt I feel for the man or men that run us into such a place as we have just got out of," wrote an Iron Brigade soldier. "I have a damned poor opinion of those that led us into such a place . . . ,"[60] was the comment of one of the Wisconsin men. Most dismal was the summing up of the historian of Battery B: "Fickle as is the fortune of war, . . . the butchery of Fredericksburg transcended even the scope of that apology, and . . . the unfortunate men who shed their blood there had less glory to assuage their pangs than the victims of any other battle known to civilized history."[61] But with all its horror and futility, Fredericksburg accomplished something for the Iron Brigade. "The Twenty-fourth Michigan . . . showed themselves to be worthy of the praise they have received, and of association with the Old Iron Brigade," said General Meredith's report. To the eyes of Rufus Dawes "no soldiers ever faced fire more bravely, and they showed themselves of a fibre worthy to be woven into the woof of the 'Iron Brigade.' Col. Morrow was equal to all requirements, enterprising, brave, and ambitious, he stepped at once into a circle of the best and most experienced regimental commanders in the Army of the Potomac."[62]

There was to be added something more important than the words written into the records. Until Fredericksburg a marked condescension had characterized the attitude of the veterans toward the Michigan newcomers. That Morrow and his soldiers were sensitive to this was apparent from an incident that had occurred on December 12th, just as the brigade prepared to cross the river. When a shell had fallen near the Twenty-fourth, Morrow had enjoined his soldiers with, "Steady, men, those Wisconsin men are watching you." Throughout the battle, both the Wisconsin and Indiana soldiers had watched their untried comrades. They had not been disappointed. A private of the Second Wisconsin remembered that "never a joke or a word of abuse did I hear after the 24th had shown its mettle in the battle of Fredericksburg."[63] Another enlisted man, a member of the Sixth Wisconsin, citing the "soldierly qualities" and "sturdy loyalty to the old brigade" that the Michigan soldiers had shown, said that they were now "received and accepted, and became a part of the 'Iron Brigade' in the hearts of its old members, who never had cause to regret that the regiment was a part of our brigade."[64] The historian of the Michigan regiment recorded the new status in these words: "Previous to the late battle, the older regiments of the Iron Brigade refused all sociability with our regiment, regarding us with aversion and studiously keeping out of our camp. But its noble conduct on this occasion entirely destroyed this exclusiveness and the greatest cordiality ever after prevailed."[65]

Black hats were not yet available for the Michigan men, but at Fredericksburg they were *earned*, and the Twenty-fourth was now admitted to full membership in the Iron Brigade.

10

BELLE PLAIN:
WINTER QUARTERS AND HOPEFULNESS

"... take holt is a good dog but hold on is better. ..."
From an Iron Brigade soldier's letter to his father

On December 20th the Army of the Potomac marched away from the heights opposite Fredericksburg, bound for winter quarters along the Potomac, twelve miles away. The site selected for the winter encampment was the area around Belle Plain, located at the confluence of Potomac Creek and the Potomac River.* Moving in easy stages, the Iron Brigade arrived on December 23rd and was assigned to camp on the side of a steep knoll along the river.[1] Although one of the Wisconsin men wrote of the "infernalest"[2] irregularity of the ground, the brigade had a fine view of the wide river and of the constant water traffic busied in supplying the army.[3]

At Belle Plain it was again up to the soldiers to build their own quarters, and they set to work at once. The Michigan soldiers christened their area "Camp Isabella" in honor of Colonel Morrow's wife, who, together with Mrs. Meredith and others of the officers' wives, was soon to join the army for the winter.[4] A description of their housing, laid out in rows with streets between, was provided by the historian of the Twenty-fourth Michigan:

These army cabins had a variety of style. Some were dug out of the steep bank; others made of small logs. They were about eight by ten feet in size and five feet high, with shelter tents for roof and gable coverings. The hillsides furnished good fire-places, which were finished with stone, and had mud and stick chimneys. The spaces between the

* Belle Plain and the route of the "Mud March" may be seen on the back end paper and the map at page 48.

logs were plastered with mud which soon hardened. The hard ground answered for a floor, while bedsteads were fashioned from poles covered with pine and cedar boughs. The beds served for chairs and knees for tables. A bed was constructed on each side of the cabin, and the space between was kitchen, sitting-room and parlor in one. A hardtack box served for a pantry, . . . A bayonet stuck in the ground with a candle on top served for lighting the humble abode, which was usually occupied by three or four comrades.[5]

For the officers, slightly more elaborate quarters were erected, and the counterpart of the modern officers' club was also provided—"a large room . . . , the walls being of logs . . . for public gatherings and merry making," as described by Rufus Dawes, who also recalled that "here the young officers had periodical meetings, and there were hilarious songs, speeches and other amusing public performances."[6] Having completed what a Wisconsin veteran called their "city of huts,"[7] the soldiers proceeded to cut and store the winter's supply of firewood. Later in the winter each regiment constructed its own cemetery, neatly enclosed with a post-and-rail fence, ready for the inevitable deaths which disease and accident would bring. At last the work was done and the Iron Brigade settled in for the winter, as "independent as a hog."[8]

The routine life in camp was recorded in detail by Rufus Dawes:

Reveille is the first thing in the morning for the soldier. When it is sounded, the companies are formed in their streets and the roll is called, one commissioned officer to be in attendance. In one hour, comes the breakfast call. Next, the police call, when it is required that the whole camp shall be swept as clean as a floor. Next comes guard mounting at 8:30 A.M. A critical inspection is made by the adjutant of the men of the guard details, and slovenliness and carelessness is punished. Then comes a company inspection by the captains, and especial attention is paid to the personal cleanliness of the men. . . . Next, . . . a battalion drill which is over at ten A.M. . . . We rest then . . . until four P.M., when . . . [there is] . . . a theoretical drill of the officers of the line. At half-past five, . . . dress parade, and at half-past six, the captains conduct a company drill. At seven o'clock, the Retreat is sounded and guard dismissed. At nine P.M., Tattoo is sounded and the evening roll-call is made, and at ten P.M., Taps are beaten, all lights put out and the day is done.[9]

A soldier of the Twenty-fourth Michigan provided another detail: "The two cleanest and neatest men, and the two dirtiest and most

slovenly in each company, have their names read on dress parade."
According to the diary of a soldier of the Seventh Wisconsin, this
gentle incentive was necessary for at least one of his comrades. For
February 14, 1863, the diary entry reads only: "This day in Camp C.
Ford changed his shirt, great rejoicing in camp."[10]

Besides housekeeping details and drill, the principal military activity
consisted of picketing along the Rappahannock. The men of the
brigade took turns, with thirty men to a detail to cover three regular
posts. Since the detail at each post was relieved every two hours,
the duty was not very arduous. Although on the alert for Confederate soldiers, the pickets also watched for civilians engaged in
smuggling supplies to the South. Paradoxically, the Federal soldiers
carried on a brisk, unlawful commerce of their own with the Confederate pickets across the river. Thus an Iron Brigade officer reported that "there is no hostility and the men sit dozing and staring
at each other, and when there are no officers about, they exchange
papers and communicate with each other in as friendly a manner as
if there was no cause for enmity." Rufus Dawes' attitude was shown
in a letter describing his having "fined one incorrigible little scamp
for paddling across the Rappahannock on a slab and trading coffee
to the rebel pickets for whisky, with which he made half of our men
on picket drunk."[11]

On January 18th the winter respite was suddenly broken by orders
for a movement of the army to begin two days later. Rations and
ammunition were promptly distributed, and the Iron Brigade prepared to move. At noon on the 20th the brigade stepped off to the
west, toward Stoneman's Switch, on the railroad between Aquia and
Fredericksburg. There was nothing noteworthy about the march until
the late afternoon when a heavy rain began to fall, "a cold and
driving storm which aided by the gale penetrated the clothing and
cut the faces of the men as they staggered along." Reaching the
railroad after dark, the troops went into bivouac while the unabating
rain turned the poor Virginia soil into a vast quagmire. In the
morning, despite the continuing storm, the march was resumed, but
the mud reduced the column's speed to an agonizing one mile an
hour. To the chaplain of the Michigan regiment, the "scenes on
the march defy description. Here a wagon mired and abandoned;
there a team of six mules stalled, with the driver hallooing and
cursing; dead mules and horses on either hand—ten, twelve and

even twenty-six horses vainly trying to drag a twelve-pounder through the mire." By midafternoon, exhausted and hopeless, the Iron Brigade had struggled over the remaining five miles to the Rappahannock and went into camp in the woods west of Falmouth. Behind the infantry were strewn the army's trains and artillery, utterly disabled.

In its muddy bivouac the army remained until midnight on January 22nd. Then Burnside, defeated this time by the elements, surrendered and ordered a return to Belle Plain. While thousands of their comrades labored to corduroy roads on which to extricate the trains and artillery, the Iron Brigade began their return march at 8:00 A.M. on the 23rd.[12] Following on the heels of the exhausting movement to the river and the exposure at the river's edge, the march back to Belle Plain was a nightmare. Many of the Westerners were sick and there was but one ambulance for the entire brigade. A typical incident was reported by a Wisconsin soldier: "As the column was about to move, a man came out of the ranks . . . and declared himself too sick to march. The Surgeon put his knapsack, gun, and all his load into the ambulance, but could not displace sick men who were already in the overloaded vehicle. The poor fellow succeeded in marching about half the distance to our camp, when he laid down in the mud in a fence corner and died."[13]

Late at night on the 23rd, the Iron Brigade stumbled into its camp at Belle Plain. There a new insult awaited the men. During the brief absence of the brigade, a group of Ohio and Connecticut regiments had appropriated their huts, occupying most of them and dismantling others for firewood. The reaction of the bedraggled Westerners was not surprising. "We were just a little bit hot to find someone occupying our nests, and felt rather disposed to throw the intruders out," was the restrained comment of a veteran of the Sixth Wisconsin. But the squatters were fortunately unwilling to debate the issue. Indeed, "pitying our forlorn condition, [they] gave up the best they had for supper," recalled one of the Iron Brigade soldiers. Another recorded of the trespassing Ohioans that "a more friendly lot of fellows we never met."[14] Bloodshed having been avoided, the other regiments withdrew on the following morning[15] and the Iron Brigade was again in undisturbed possession of its camp.

So ended the "Mud March," as even the official records were to denominate Burnside's effort. Although the brigade's casualties went unreported, Rufus Dawes testified that "the ignoble 'mud campaign' will ever hold its place in the memories of all the soldiers of the Army of the Potomac as firmly as the hardest fought battles." Another of the Wisconsin men went into more detail and found a moral in the effort: "We were out four days and four nights and we never suffered so much in the same length of time since coming into Service, i would like to of had every Northern man that says a campaign can be successfully carried on here in the winter time with us. I would like to have had them here, had them each take his sixty rounds cartridges, three days rations, blanket, half tent and rubber blanket, and in that condition been forced to made that march. . . ."[16] But the men could also be wryly humorous about the affair, and soon "Dixie" was being sung in the camp of the Iron Brigade, beginning with these new words: "On 'Dixie Land' we would like to stand, if it was not mud, instead of land."[17]

Despite the resourceful humor of the soldiers, the "Mud March" coincided with a new crisis in the war for the Federal Union. At Antietam, Perryville, and Corinth, the Confederates' fall offensives had been reversed. But Antietam had been followed in the East by the disaster at Fredericksburg and in the West by Sherman's December repulse at Chickasaw Bluffs before Vicksburg. In the "middle" theater the battle of Stone River, late in December, was a Federal victory, but a narrow and extremely costly one. By any measure, all of these events represented a worsening of the Union's chances, and Federal morale suffered, both at home and in the field. The Iron Brigade was not excepted from the decline of the Federal spirit. One of its officers wrote in a letter that the army was "discontented, discouraged and humiliated under the stigma of defeat." Another soldier noted that "even the capability of enthusiasm seemed to have died out of the army at this time," while a third saw Belle Plain as "a vale of mud and misery."[18] Even Rufus Dawes wrote of this winter as "the Valley Forge of the war." Still in charge of courts-marital, Dawes admitted that there was ". . . no difference between this winter and last winter in the character or number of offenders . . . ,"[19] indicating that his allusion to the winter of 1777-1778 was perhaps exaggerated. But over the Federal camps there hung an unmistakable cloud of pessimism, a cloud that had to be dispelled if the war was to continue.

A lack of confidence in the unfortunate Ambrose Burnside was one sure source of the pervading gloom. "The rank and file of the Army of the Potomac had begun to consider themselves better soldiers than their commanders," recorded a member of Battery B,[20] and however appealing such an attitude may have seemed to romantic civilians, it was in fact deeply destructive of the soldiers' morale. On January 26th this problem was remedied when General Joseph Hooker replaced Burnside as commander of the army. Known to the soldiers of the Iron Brigade as their First Corps commander at Antietam, "Fighting Joe" Hooker, whatever his faults, was a great quarter-master, and he had the "true Napoleonic idea of the power of an 'Espirit de Corps,'" to quote Rufus Dawes. Now Hooker at once directed himself to the reorganization of the army and to what one of the Iron Brigade soldiers aptly called its "re-inspiration."[21] Four days after his appointment, the soldiers were cheered by the issuance of a detailed order providing a system of furloughs. Pack mules were also widely introduced to lighten the soldiers' burdens.[22] More subtle than these innovations was the institution of corps badges, a device that had been previously instituted on a limited basis by General Kearny; it now became "regulation." To each corps was assigned its peculiar cloth insignia, to be affixed to the hat or cap, with each division within the corps designated by the red, white, or blue color of the insignia. The insignia of the First Division of the First Corps was a red circle which the men of the Iron Brigade attached to their battered hats, to become what one of them called "the almost wor-shipped symbols of a glorious service."[23]

A more direct attack on the general discouragement and lack of spirit was instituted during Hooker's command. Apparently prompted by rumors about the attitudes and condition of the army, this took the form of soldiers' resolutions on the issues of the war and the propriety of the Union's objectives. In the Iron Brigade, regimental committees of officers were first appointed to draft and present the propositions. Covering a variety of related subjects—insisting on war without compromise, calling for conscription, denouncing the North-ern dissenters, and denying the existence of army demoralization—the propositions were then enacted by the soldiers of the regiments. The regimental pronouncements were followed by a series of Iron Brigade resolutions. These were presented by General Meredith to each of the regiments, assembled without arms. More colorfully worded than the regimental resolutions, the brigade's manifesto covered the same general subject matter: war ". . . until the last rebel in arms has vanished . . . ," harsh words for ". . . the traitors in [the] midst . . . [of] . . . our friends at home . . ." and a demand for conscription with the slogan of "fight, pay or emigrate." In a typical scene recorded by the historian of the Twenty-fourth, "the resolutions were adopted with such a tremendous 'aye,' that it sent the horses of the General and his staff plunging away from the thunder of half a thousand voices, cheering for Generals Meredith and Hooker, and for the Union." Later disseminated to the public through the newspapers, the resolutions served the purpose of marshaling the soldiers' attitudes as well as influencing the public mind. But as evidence that there was still some strong feeling in the brigade against emancipation, the resolutions were obscure on this central issue. In general terms they applauded the administration and endorsed "all its acts or measures having for their object the effectual crushing out of this rebellion."[24]

Hooker's program could not have been accomplished by these means alone. To them was added a more tangible benefit—good food. Even on Christmas Day, 1862, the Iron Brigade had feasted on hardtack with "plenty of bugs in them," salt pork and tough beef. Now the soldiers' crude diet was supplemented by such delicacies as fresh bread, onions, potatoes, and fresh beef. These were available regularly, and an occasional ration of ham was added, inspiring one of the men of the Nineteenth to exclaim "Hurra for our side" to his diary.[25] And although Joe Hooker could not claim credit for it, the inaction of the army permitted the receipt at Belle Plain of the greatest of all soldiers' gifts, the package of food from home. Three wagonloads of boxes arrived for the Michigan regiment, containing cakes and other eatables, along with gloves, shoes, and similar comforts. The Wisconsin soldiers received such luxuries as "magnificient" canned peaches, and jelly, dried apples and catsup.[26] With such assists from home, Hooker's "re-inspiration" program gradually began to show its effect, and the spirit of the army turned again to hopefulness. Thus an Iron Brigade veteran found himself writing ". . . i yet think . . . we will whip them out of their boots. . . ." And one of his kinsmen in Battery B had this to say about the situation:

"The men reasoned that 'the old flag was still there,' and would be found there at the finish right side up and on top, and that . . . we were going to whip the Rebels and restore the Union some way, sometime and somehow in spite of poor commanders, silly editors, scheming politicians, and thieving contractors!"[27]

The winter also saw significant changes in personnel in the First Corps. Meade's Pennsylvania Reserves left the Third Division, to be replaced by two brigades of newly raised Pennsylvania volunteers, and Meade himself vacated the division command to move up to command of the Fifth Corps. The Second Division also had a new commander, General John C. Robinson, who assumed command in place of the wounded John Gibbon. More immediate to the Iron Brigade was Abner Doubleday's departure from First Division command, to return briefly to the leadership of his old brigade before replacing Meade as commander of the Third Division. Doubleday was replaced by Brigadier General James S. Wadsworth of New York,[28] who now followed McDowell, King, Hatch, and Doubleday, as commander of the Iron Brigade's First Division. Alluding to Wadsworth's recent defeat as the administration's candidate for governor of New York, one of the cynical Wisconsin soldiers wrote that "he could not be elected Governor . . . , so he must have a place in the army." But Rufus Dawes' description of the division's new commander was more realistic: "General Wadsworth was a strong character, and his command of our division left a deep impression on its history. . . . He was an intensely practical commander, indefatigable as a worker, and looking closely after details. No commander could do more for the personal comfort of his men."[29]

Within the First Division there were also interesting changes of troops and commanders during the winter. Phelps' First Brigade and Meredith's Fourth Brigade remained intact. But a new Third Brigade, commanded by General Gabriel R. Paul and composed of New Jersey and Pennsylvania regiments, replaced Patrick's New Yorkers. Doubleday's old brigade, numbered the Second, listed a new commander in the person of Lysander Cutler, newly commissioned a brigadier general of volunteers. Cutler doubtless regretted leaving the Iron Brigade, and the fact that Solomon Meredith had pre-empted the command of the Westerners. But in addition to a newly assigned regiment, the 147th New York, Cutler's Brigade included at least

one Western regiment, the distinguished Seventh Indiana, as well as
the New York and Pennsylvania organizations which had shared
in the furious fight at Brawner Farm. As his adjutant Cutler selected
the Sixth Wisconsin's Captain John A. Kellogg, thus providing another familiar face in his command.[30]

The army's Belle Plain sojourn also witnessed a number of changes
among the field officers of the Iron Brigade itself. Cutler's promotion
had left open the colonelcy of the Sixth, and Lieutenant Colonel
Bragg was quickly advanced to fill the vacancy. Rufus Dawes received
his lieutenant colonel's commission on the same day that Bragg was
made colonel. Among the principal contenders for the majority left
open by Dawes' promotion were Philip W. Plummer of Prairie du
Chien, captain of Company C, and John F. Hauser of Buffalo
County, captain of the German Company H. Foreign born, trained
at Thun in Switzerland, and distinguished by his association with
Garibaldi, Captain Hauser was famous in the regiment for his difficulties with the English language. On one memorable occasion when
his company had erred in drill, the German had upbraided the men
as "one damn herd of goose." But Hauser was also a brave and
accomplished soldier and the senior captain, and he prevailed in the
contest for the commission.[31] The Second Wisconsin also boasted
a new major, the result of a chain of events which began when
Lieutenant Colonel Thomas S. Allen was transferred. Although
bound to the regiment by strong ties, Allen, like other officers, was
willing to move elsewhere in order to obtain a higher rank. In
January the colonelcy of the Fifth Wisconsin was available, and
Allen was promoted to it. Major George H. Stevens was at once
advanced to replace Allen, leaving the Second's majority open. Again
there were several candidates, of whom the leading men were Captain
John Mansfield of Portage City and Company G and William L.
Parsons of Racine, survivor of wounds at First Bull Run and Antietam
and captain of Company F. After a brief period of doubt, Mansfield,
the senior man, prevailed.[32] The Seventh regiment also saw changes.
Badly wounded at Brawner Farm, Lieutenant Colonel Hamilton, the
grandson of Alexander Hamilton, at last limped home to be discharged
in March, 1863, still carrying in his thigh a bullet the doctors were
never able to remove. The veteran John B. Callis moved up to the lieutenant colonelcy[33] in Hamilton's place and the company officers vied

for Callis' vacant majority, a rivalry that was strictly democratic because Colonel Robinson insisted that the matter be determined by an election among the officers.[34] The principal candidates were Mark Finnicum of Fennimore, captain of Company H, and the colonel's son-in-law, Hollon Richardson of Company A, erstwhile district attorney of Chippewa County, who had been twice wounded at Fredericksburg and now wore a captain's shoulder straps. When the votes were counted, Captain Finnicum was the winner and the governor promptly accepted the result and issued Finnicum's majority. The last of the brigade's new field officers was the Twenty-fourth Michigan's Edwin B. Wight. Although not to be formally discharged until April, Major Nall had left the field because of illness immediately after Fredericksburg. Captain Wight was assigned as acting major, a rank that became official on June 1st, when the youthful alumnus of the University of Michigan finally received his commission.[35]

The slow winter days afforded much leisure time, time that was passed in a variety of ways. Not the least of the soldiers' pastimes was talking, a fine art Americans had not yet replaced with more complicated inventions. According to Battery B's historian, "Every company or battery camp was a community of American citizens, and every log hut in the Winter quarters was an improvised 'debating society' of bright, smart young men and boys, for the most part fairly educated, and retaining, despite military discipline, the habits of free thought and free speech which had been bred in their flesh and bone in the peaceful days gone by."[36] The principal topics were political, which was natural for a group of soldiers fighting a civil war in a democratic community. In terms of political partisanship, the men were unequally divided. In the Seventh Wisconsin the Democrats had polled but 20 votes to 181 for the Republicans when the regiment had voted in the field in October of 1862. In the 1863 spring canvass among the soldiers of the Sixth regiment the Democrats had done much better, listing 108 votes as compared to the Republicans' 292.[37] But in addition to simple partisan issues, there were deeper questions, questions that cut across the traditional party lines. Slavery and the Emancipation Proclamation were among these, and lively argument invariably ensued whenever these issues were introduced. Although Dawes reported that the opponents of the proclamation became fewer and fewer, surely few of the Westerners shared the fervor for the abolition cause that marked Dawes' journal and letters: "Do not let us stop short of our destiny, the entire destruction of slavery. . . ." Whatever ranks were divided by the soldiers' slavery discussions were quickly closed when the new draft law was discussed. Like most soldiers of any period, the men of the Iron Brigade had great contempt for civilians, indiscriminately denouncing the non-soldiers as either Copperheads or "the cowardly sneaks who stay at home." To force these men to fight seemed not only just but necessary, as the empty ranks of the brigade plainly testified.[38]

Citizens unwilling or psychologically unsuited for fighting were not, unfortunately, confined to the civilian population. Like all other organizations, the Iron Brigade had a handful of men who did not have whatever it took to succeed as Civil War soldiers. Shortly after Fredericksburg, twenty-five members of the Michigan regiment were absent without leave. Most of them were rounded up from the surrounding countryside by a guard detail sent out under Lieutenant Colonel Flanigan.[39] Nine soldiers of the brigade were dishonorably discharged early in the winter, convicted of cowardice at Fredericksburg.[40] A lieutenant of the Twenty-fourth Michigan suffered a similar fate, his cowardice having taken the form of tendering his resignation just as the bullets started to fly.[41] On the 21st of February, court-martial sentences were publicly meted out to seven more of the brigade, five of whom, for "misbehavior before the enemy," were to forfeit all bounty and pay, to have their heads shaved, and to be drummed out of the army. To witness their disgrace, the brigade assembled under arms, forming a hollow square within which the prisoners were brought under guard. General Meredith then read the sentences. According to the diary of a Hoosier private: "their hair was trimmed, their heads lathered all over, and shaved smooth and bare, the troops were then formed in two long lines, and the deserters were marched down between the two lines at double quick, to the tune of the 'rogues March,' in front of the prisoners were 8 guards with reversed arms, in the rear was 8 guards with guns at a charge bayonet, behind these came the Music about 20 drums and fifes. . . ."[42] Although one of the Wisconsin witnesses confided to his diary that "I should much rather face the enemy than to witness another such scene,"[43] there was a re-enactment six weeks later when two deserters from the Twenty-fourth were apprehended. An interesting insight into the character of Colonel Morrow was provided by one of the Michigan soldiers who noted that the colonel invariably extended himself to obtain mitigation of the punishments of deserters and "works as hard to help them from being disfigured as though it was his own person. He seems to feel worse than the prisoners themselves and cries while their sentences are being read."[44] But despite the colonel's feelings, the sentences were getting stiffer, and several weeks later a private of the Nineteenth, convicted a second time of desertion, was executed by twelve of his comrades, the grisly event taking place before the eyes of the entire brigade.[45]

If the deserters and misfits of the brigade were objects of scorn, imprisoned and wounded comrades were objects of pity and concern. On January 16th seven men of the Twenty-fourth captured at Fredericksburg were exchanged after a mercifully brief stay at the Libby and Belle Isle prisons at Richmond. Others of the brigade's captured men were not so fortunate. Counting the stragglers seized during the Frederick's Hall Raid and the men captured at Brawner Farm, Second Bull Run, South Mountain, and Antietam, almost two hundred of the Iron Brigade were now Southern prisoners, and as many more were later to meet this fate.[46] The prisoners at one time or another were inmates of almost all of the well-known Confederate prison camps, Florence and Charleston, South Carolina; Salisbury, North Carolina; Libby, Belle Isle, Lynchburg, and Danville, Virginia; Macon, Georgia; and, later in the war, Andersonville.[47] Some of the Western soldiers were paroled or exchanged, but others stayed to die, including 47 men of the Twenty-fourth Michigan,[48] probably a representative statistic for the brigade as a whole. Only Captain John A. Kellogg avoided the alternatives of parole, exchange, or death. Fighting in the Wilderness with the remnants of the brigade, Kellogg was captured on May 5, 1864. After a prolonged period of captivity, in October he jumped from a rapidly moving prison train while en route from Charleston to Columbia, South Carolina, and made his way over many miles and many days into the Federal lines. But without either the opportunity or the spirit of the intrepid Kellogg, the rest of the brigade's prisoners languished under impossible conditions made known to their comrades through pitiful letters asking for food and manfully sending "compliments to all our friends."[49]

The Iron Brigade's wounded were also scattered over a wide area. In addition to temporary field hospitals and other hospitals established at battle sites in such buildings as churches and schools, the North had developed extensive permanent installations, including the United States Army general hospitals at Wilmington; Satterlee in West Philadelphia; De Camp on Davids Island, New York; and Washington. All of these were occupied by Iron Brigade personnel, as were the convalescent camps at Alexandria and Annapolis. There the soldiers often found that "the examination is much more painful than the infliction" of the wound,[50] but they were as well cared for as the facilities and knowledge of the day permitted. That this was not good enough to satisfy the wounded men appeared from their persistent correspondence with the authorities, seeking transfer to hospitals in their home states, and from the astonishing fact that two wounded men of the Sixth Wisconsin actually *escaped* from a hospital in Washington in October, 1862, and walked back to the brigade's Maryland camp and resumed their duties.[51] Tragic as these wounded soldiers were, they were the least so to their comrades assigned to temporary nursing duty in the field. Thus one of the Wisconsin men, detailed as a "nurse" just after Chancellorsville, was to leave in his diary this picture of his experience: "Nursing wounded soldiers is awful hard and tiresome work. One says Jim turn me over. Another says James I want to P. Here one says nurse give me a drink there and another says wet my wound it is awful painful. One says please loosen the bandage around my wound and see if I cannot get a little relief from the severe pain. Another says Oh! wish I could go to sleep another says I wish I could change my position. I am so tired."[52]

As in the other regiments of the army, the winter at Belle Plain saw a religious revival among the soldiers of the Iron Brigade. A typical Sunday scene was recorded by the historian of the Twenty-fourth Michigan: "The several companies were drawn up in line, and such as were of a different worship were told to step out of the ranks, while the rest were marched to the 'meeting ground,' where a short discourse was preached by the Chaplain." Despite the revival, Colonel Robinson, a man with a sense of humor, could write, one Sunday morning, to the brigade adjutant: "Sir— There is a large crowd of soldiers in the grove below, engaged in the interesting game called

'Chuck-or-Luck.' My chaplain is running his church on the other side of me, but 'Chuck-or-Luck' has the largest crowd. I think this unfair, as the church runs only once a week, but the game goes on daily. I suggest that one or the other parties be dispersed."[53]

In addition to conducting religious services and funerals, the chaplains engaged in hospital chores behind the lines during battle, supplied the soldiers with reading material, and sometimes provided what would today be called "counseling" services for troubled soldiers. The chaplains were men of varying qualifications. The Twenty-fourth Michigan's William C. Way, who also served in the field as war correspondent for a Detroit newspaper, was a man of both physical stamina and spiritual influence who contributed much to the betterment of the lot of the men under his charge. Significantly, he was the only Michigan chaplain who remained in the service from the muster-in to the muster-out of his regiment.[54] The Nineteenth Indiana was not so fortunate. Its first chaplain, a Muncie man, was alleged in a letter to have "had no room in his carpet sack for a hymn book, but he could carry Blackstone's Commentaries. . . ." That this was a credible allegation appeared from the fact that the chaplain resigned at Belle Plain and returned to Indiana to seek the office of Clerk of Henry County at New Castle. Running as an "independent" against a regular Republican, the chaplain was defeated although he had "courted the Butternuts, Copperheads, anti-war and anti-administration party of the county," according to a letter to Governor Morton from a New Castle resident, who also pronounced the candidate as "lost to principle politically if not religiously." The Nineteenth's second chaplain, Thomas Barnett, joined the regiment at Belle Plain in April of 1863. Like Colonel Williams, the new clergyman was from Selma, Indiana, and was the personal choice of his fellow townsman. In addition to the usual functions of his office, Barnett lent some money to Colonel Williams, a sum the colonel had difficulty in repaying, and this fact strained relations between the two and even caused the creditor to complain to Indiana's adjutant general. The clergyman was to resign in July of 1864, "on account of failure of voice," according to his own account, a disorder fatal to his calling and one indicating that he had pursued a vigorous preaching schedule. Later in the war Barnett again sought a chaplain's post, but the Nineteenth was entirely without such an officer from the date of Barnett's discharge.[55]

The Wisconsin regiments in the Iron Brigade had varying experiences with their chaplains. The Seventh fared the best. Having lost its original chaplain through resignation on March 24, 1862, the Seventh acquired Samuel W. Eaton on July 10th of the same year, who served until the regiment was mustered out in 1865. At the other extreme was the experience of the Second Wisconsin, whose chaplain was discharged in May of 1862 and was never replaced. The Sixth listed a total of three chaplains, each of whom served for only a brief period. The first officer, imposingly named Nahor A. Staples, resigned in November, 1861.[56] Although little else is known about him, the regimental surgeon described Staples as "a very kind man [who] tried to improve the moral and social character of the men." But the surgeon had his reservations: "How much I wish he was one who respects Christ as a saviour and redeemer."[57] Following Staples' resignation, the Sixth was without a chaplain until 1864, when the regiment recruited a new volunteer whose father, Warren Cochran, was a minister. The father accompanied the son to war and occupied the chaplain's post from April 14 to August 26, 1864. Then he resigned, and it was not until after the end of hostilities that the third chaplain was provided. Commissioned on July 11, 1865, John Berk was mustered out just three days later, a curiosity which the records do not explain.[58]

In the words of a Nineteenth Indiana diarist, the Belle Plain winter was "spiced up occasionally with rumors of marching orders."[59] Additional spice resulted from the several occasions when the rumors turned out to be true and elements of the Iron Brigade were dispatched on military missions. One such expedition took place in mid-February and involved five hundred men of the Second and Sixth Wisconsin regiments. Led by the Second's Colonel Fairchild and with Dawes of the Sixth as second in command, the force embarked on February 12th on the steamer *Alice Price* and steamed down the Potomac to the mouth of the Coan River.* Arriving at the Coan on the 13th, the boat was secured and Dawes was left in charge with two hundred men while Fairchild moved the rest of the force overland to Heathsville in Virginia's Northumberland County, seizing horses, mules, foodstuffs, and other stores along the way.

While Fairchild's group was on the way to Heathsville, a squad

* The route of this raid may be followed by reference to the back end paper.

assigned to the Second Wisconsin's Major Mansfield foraged near
the steamer's landing. At a plantation on the bank of the Coan,
Mansfield's party discovered an enormous quantity of food, including
ten thousand pounds of bacon. Believing that this meant that the
plantation owner was either engaged in blockade running or was
smuggling food from Maryland, the major seized the stores and
arrested the owner, acts which Dawes confirmed when he arrived on
the scene. While riding over the plantation, Dawes, by his own
account, was approached by "an old negro slave with his hat under his
arm, his voice tremulous with fear and excitement, [who] said: 'Massa,
is you the big ossifer? . . . We heard you'uns would make us colored
people free. The people want to go with you. Some says we can go
and some says we can't go.' " Advised by Dawes that the Negroes
could go with the soldiers if they wished, the old man quickly spread
the word. Seventy people, from infants to aged men and women,
soon gathered at the landing, bearing their meager belongings and
anxious for passage on the Yankee boat. But the Negroes were followed by the mistress of the plantation, who was intent on retaining
her "property." Fairchild having by this time returned, the woman
was told that the Negroes would not be taken against their will and
that she was free to try to induce them to remain. Then ensued a
strange debate, reported in the words of one of the Wisconsin witnesses:

The lady went among the slaves with tears in her eyes and implored
them by every recollection and attachment of a life-time, and by the
sacred memories of their dead, not to go away, and she painted in high
colors the miseries that would be inflicted upon them when they become
"free niggers" up north. The slaves regarded her with affection and the
highest respect, and they were deeply moved. But there were friends of
freedom and fair play among the men who carried muskets. They warned
the negroes that before the steamer was out of sight the chains would
be on them, and they would be driven south. They told them that their
liberty was here, to take it. I remember the squeaking tenor voice of
private Edwin C. Jones, of Company "E," asking, "Shall these babes
be slaves? Almighty God forbid it!" The negroes all went on the boat.
The lady's maid hung weeping upon her, but she went with her people
to be free.

Having dispatched a small force overland with the horses and mules,
Fairchild's command embarked on the 14th, steaming to Nomini

Bay and to the Mattox River and destroying five small and unoccupied vessels en route. On the 15th the expedition returned to Belle Plain, having afforded an agreeable and bloodless outing for the participants.[60]

In March it was again the Second Wisconsin's turn as they were carried downriver by steamer for a raid on Westmoreland County, Virginia, where, as one of the Wisconsin men proudly wrote, the soldiers obtained horses "derived from the plantation of Hon. Willoughby Newton member of the Confederate Congress," along with other valuable stores.[61] Later the Sixth and Seventh Wisconsin had brief and novel employment when they were summoned from camp to quell a mutiny among soldiers of the Twenty-fourth New York, who claimed that their enlistments had expired. The men of the Iron Brigade stood sternly by with loaded rifles but were happily spared further efforts when the New Yorkers responded to what one of the Wisconsin men called "a few pointed remarks" from General Wadsworth.[62]

April 22nd saw the last of these outings for the brigade when the Twenty-fourth Michigan joined the Fourteenth Brooklyn from Phelps' Brigade and one gun from Battery B in an expedition to Port Royal on the Rappahannock.* At the express suggestion of Corps Commander Reynolds, Colonel Henry A. Morrow was in charge of the expedition, which left Belle Plain at 2:00 P.M., equipped with sixteen unassembled wood and canvas pontoons. Despite difficult roads, the soldiers reached the river at 10:00 P.M. and encamped near Port Conway, directly across from Port Royal. At dawn on the following morning the pontoons were assembled in the midst of a drenching rain. Then volunteers were called for, twenty-five men to a boat, and under the immediate command of Lieutenant Colonel Flanigan headed for the opposite shore, 350 yards away. As strong oars pulled the boats quickly through the water, soldiers strained their eyes through the mist to see whether the dimly visible rifle pits and gun emplacements were occupied by the enemy. If they were, the defenders had a heavy advantage and many of the assault group would surely die in forcing a landing. But even as the Federals waited for the first shot, the boats struck the bank and the men quickly swept by the empty defenses and entered the unwary village, flushing a small band of Confederate horsemen. Royally welcomed by the

* The route may be followed by reference to the back end paper.

Negroes, who also assisted in gathering stores for them, the soldiers quickly and systematically searched the town, seizing six Confederate soldiers, fifteen horses and mules, and Confederate mail. Also included in the conquest were two Virginia women of Union sentiments who were accommodated in their request for transportation across the river. With all of this baggage the party again boarded the boats and set forth, swimming the captured animals behind. Just before the northern bank was reached, a large force of Confederates appeared on the south shore and opened fire, but before any damage was done the Federals had taken cover. Excited by their brief and bloodless success, the soldiers returned to camp, there to regale their comrades with tales of the reconnaissance.[63]

April was also the month of reviews. On April 2nd the First Division turned out to parade for General Hooker and Division Commander Wadsworth. Still pursuing his "re-inspiration" program, the army commander published a congratulatory order following the review, addressed to the "Soldiers of the Iron Brigade" and praising their "soldierly bearing and general fine appearance!" Not to be outdone by General Hooker, General Meredith also published an order of his own. Directed to Colonel Morrow, the brigade commander referred in passing to the excellent conduct of all of his regiments but singled out the Twenty-fourth, whose performance "richly entitles them to the position they now hold in the Iron Brigade."[64]

A few days after the army commander's compliments were bestowed, the entire First Corps paraded before President and Mrs. Lincoln, identified in a soldier's letter as "Old Abe and Mrs. Abe."[65] Also with the Lincolns was their young son Tad. The chaplain of the Twenty-fourth Michigan has described the spectacle:

Looking to the left we saw a cloud of dust, and all eyes were bent in that direction. The expected ones round a curve in the road and gallop past us. President Lincoln was mounted on a splendid bay, richly caparisoned, while General Hooker rode his pet gray on his left. They were followed by a host of officers in gay uniforms, and these in turn by lancers with fluttering pennants. . . . Having reached the right of the column the cortege rode down the front in review. The numerous banners dipped gracefully, the bands playing while the bugles sounded their flourish of greeting. The President rode down the front with head uncovered. He next took a position with the generals in front, and then commenced the almost ceaseless tramp of the regiments by him. . . . As each regiment passed, its banners were dipped gracefully, which was acknowledged by the President by lifting his hat. Mrs. Lincoln accompanied the President, riding in a carriage drawn by four bays. . . .[66]

That the Iron Brigade was known to Lincoln was evidenced by a story from a correspondent of the *Cincinnati Gazette* who was near the President at the review: "When . . . the 'Iron Brigade' . . . marched up, there was a universal manifestation of admiration and applause. . . . 'This,' remarked General Hooker to the President, 'is the famous fourth brigade.' 'Yes,' rejoined the President, 'it is commanded by the only Quaker General I have in the army,'" an allusion to Solomon Meredith's religious background. Following the review, Battery B's Lieutenant Stewart had an encounter with the President, who requested to see Stewart's horse Tartar, which had lost its tail at Second Bull Run and was well known among the soldiers for a long and distinguished military career, stretching all the way back to the Utah Territory and including a winter of ownership by the Indians. Although the President was satisfied briefly to examine the animal, Stewart later recalled that another member of the Lincoln family was not so easily accommodated. "His little son 'Tad,' mounted on a pony, followed me and insisted on trading horses. I told him that I could not do that, but he persisted in telling me that his papa was the President, and would give me any horse I wanted in trade for Tartar. I had a hard time in getting away from the little fellow."[67]

At last the long Virginia winter drew to a close. Including the Twenty-fourth Michigan, already reduced to 625 officers and men, the Iron Brigade claimed 2,000[68] ready-for-duty soldiers. This did not, of course, include seventeen men from the Seventh Wisconsin and twenty-two men from the Twenty-fourth who had entered Battery B in February, replacing two-year men from the New York regiments, most of whom would not re-enlist.[69] Whatever its numerical strength, the morale of the brigade was unquestionably excellent, the men "fat, healthy and contented," according to one of the officers. Only a few details remained to be disposed of before the winter encampment was abandoned. Colonel Bragg took care of one of these when he returned the Sixth's bullet-riddled flag to Wisconsin's governor, in exchange for a new regimental color. Along with the old flag, the colonel sent a letter to the chief executive: "When we received it, its folds, like our ranks, were ample and full, still emblematical of our condition, we return it, tattered and torn in the shock of battle." The colonel's letter concluded: "If the past gives any earnest of the future, the 'Iron Brigade' will not be forgotten when Wisconsin makes up her jewels."[70]

The soldiers, too, wound up their letter writing as the April days rolled by, bringing fighting weather to Virginia. But despite almost two years of warfare, the spring weather somehow reminded the soldiers of other things. It was "on just such bright warm Sunday mornings that we always used to gather flowers together and I always endeavored to surprise you with the very first that were in bloom," wrote one of the Iron Brigade to his wife.[71] As he was writing, General Joseph Hooker was putting the finishing details to his order for the battle of Chancellorsville.

11

CHANCELLORSVILLE AND THE MARCH TO PENNSYLVANIA

"General Hooker . . . was outgeneraled and defeated . . . but in Pennsylvania, everybody . . . is overjoyed at the coming of our banners."

From the letters of an officer of the Iron Brigade

While the Army of the Potomac had rested at Belle Plain, Robert E. Lee's soldiers, except for Longstreet and part of his corps, had wintered around Fredericksburg, scene of their spectacular December victory. Between the two armies ran the Rappahannock, which, ten miles west of Fredericksburg, divided into two rivers, the Rapidan, extending almost directly west, and the Rappahannock, to the north of the Rapidan, and continuing in a northwesterly direction. Like his predecessor, General Hooker's initial problem was to cross these natural barriers.*

West of Fredericksburg, and before the point at which the Rappahannock divided to form the two rivers, there were two principal fords, Bank's Ford and, farther west, United States Ford. Beyond these and beyond the junction of the two rivers were Ely's Ford and Germanna Ford on the Rapidan. Due north of Germanna, on the Rappahannock, was Kelly's Ford. These fords were the natural river crossings available to the Federals. Accordingly, they were under surveillance by the Confederates; and those most convenient to Fredericksburg, Bank's Ford and United States Ford, were strongly defended. This meant that Hooker had to look elsewhere if he was to avoid forcing a disputed crossing of the rivers.

* For the Chancellorsville campaign, see map at page 48.

Hooker's infantry was composed of seven corps, the grand divisions of Burnside having been abandoned,[1] and the Federal commander's plan was a complicated one. Three of his corps were to march up the Rappahannock and cross at Kelly's Ford. They were then to march rapidly south to the Rapidan, crossing that river at Germanna and Ely's fords, west of the Confederate forces, and threatening Lee's rear. As the Confederates fell back from the Rappahannock to defend against this thrust from Germanna and Ely's fords, United States and Bank's fords would be uncovered, leaving these avenues open to the balance of the Federal army.

To distract Lee and mask the Federal plan, Gibbon's Division of the Second Corps was left in its camps in front of Fredericksburg, while three corps were to demonstrate below the town. Reynolds' First Corps and the Third and Sixth corps were assigned to the diversion below Fredericksburg. There, with the Third Corps in support, the Sixth Corps was to cross on pontoon bridges at Franklin's Crossing, re-creating its movement of the previous December, and the First Corps was to make a similar passage below the Sixth, at Fitzhugh's Crossing, approximately four miles below Fredericksburg and almost directly opposite the Smithfield plantation, also a landmark of the December fight.[2]

At noon on April 28th, while the rest of the army began its movement, the Iron Brigade stepped off to the southwest, following the First Corps' line of march toward the Rappahannock. Passing through White Oak Church, the column proceeded to within a mile of the river, to the grounds of the once-grand Fitzhugh house, where a halt was called in the late afternoon. As the Western soldiers rested and some of them casually investigated the abandoned and dilapidated house,[3] the officers were briefed on the plan for the crossing. The river nearby was nearly two hundred yards wide, with steep banks. The southern bank, but not the northern, was marked with a heavy undergrowth, and to this natural cover the Confederates had added rifle pits and an abatis of felled trees, works that commanded the river and the open northern bank.[4] If the Federal bridgebuilding was to succeed, these works had to be taken. The Federal plan was to cross one brigade in pontoon boats during the night, to seize and hold the entrenchments while the engineers did their work. For this duty the Iron Brigade had been selected, and at 11:00 P.M. Colonels

Williams, Morrow, Fairchild, Bragg, and Robinson gathered at General Meredith's headquarters, where the plan was detailed. Although the crossing, to begin at 2:00 A.M., involved some hazard, darkness would be the brigade's ally and quick work by the engineers, permitting prompt reinforcements, was expected to limit the Westerners' isolation south of the river.

Immediately following their leaders' meeting, the Iron Brigade advanced noiselessly to the river, prepared for their amphibious effort. All was quiet, but the boats were not there. The men stood by under arms, waiting, but the boats did not arrive. The hour for the assault passed and still the boats did not come. Slowly the time ran out, and finally the day dawned. With it came the end of the opportunity for the crossing, although the boats were at last available.[5]

Abandoning any effort to prevent Confederate interference with the bridgebuilding, at 5:00 A.M. the Federals sent the pontoon wagons down the bank to the river's edge and the engineers set to work unloading the cumbersome boats. But now the enemy was alerted and but a few boats had hit the water when a heavy rifle and artillery fire opened on the bridgebuilders. At a range of two hundred yards, the Confederates could hardly miss: "There was a grand skedaddle of mules" pulling the pontoon wagons, and the unprotected pontooners began to fall.[6] Recalling the engineers from their hopeless position, the Federals sent forward the Twenty-fourth Michigan, the Sixth Wisconsin, and the Fourteenth Brooklyn, charged with driving the Southerners from their works. The infantry line promptly descended to the river and, partially protected by a stone wall that ran at an angle from the water, the men "hit the dirt" and opened fire as the Federal cannon joined in from the crest behind. The morning fog was now slowly lifting, and the Confederate works were vaguely visible in the undergrowth beyond. But despite the Federals' fire, the enemy assigned to defend the crossing—among them the Sixth Louisiana, Twentieth Alabama, and Twenty-third Georgia—stood to their work, taking full advantage of their advantageous position.[7]

After an hour of trading fire with the enemy, during which at least one of the Michigan men had been killed, the Federal infantry line was withdrawn.[8] General Reynolds now realized that something else would have to be done if the First Corps, already hours behind schedule, was to make the crossing assigned. And there seemed but one remaining alternative, a storming of the Confederate position, an attack Reynolds believed would succeed, but only in the face of the present limited Confederate strength. For the soldiers who were to make the assault, the corps commander turned to the First Division, and General Wadsworth, confirming the earlier arrangement for the night crossing, looked again to the Iron Brigade.[9] As one of the Western men confided in a letter written two days later, "It now seemed that the Rappahannock must be reddened with our blood if the crossing was to be forced."[10]

The Federal plan, an adaptation of the night crossing, was quickly communicated to the Western soldiers. "I confess that a shrinking from the proffered glory came over us," wrote one of them, "to be shot like sheep in a huddle and drowned in the Rappahannock appeared to be the certain fate of all if we failed and of some if we succeeded."[11] The Twenty-fourth and the Sixth were to lead the way, assisted by companies B, E, and D of the Second, which were charged with running the pontoon wagons down the bank and launching the boats. Accompanied by the Fourteenth Brooklyn, the remaining regiments were to follow the leaders, first to deliver a covering fire from the edge of the river, to which the Federal guns were also to contribute, then to follow the Sixth and Twenty-fourth across the water. One company was assigned to each boat, and four oarsmen to a boat were selected. Except for the men assigned to row, the others were to lie down in the boats. Removing their haversacks, packs, and canteens, the soldiers formed in line. Just after nine o'clock the command was given, "To the front! Double Quick! March!" and with a ringing yell the soldiers in the black hats raced down the bank, swept at once by the fire of the enemy, and leaped into the boats. As the other regiments and the artillery opened "an incessant roar" of fire behind them, the oarsmen of the Sixth and Twenty-fourth, straining every resource, quickly drove the boats from the shore and into the hail of death emanating from the Confederate works. With them went the gallant Wadsworth, who sent his horse into the river and leaped himself into one of the boats, the horse swimming nearby.[12]

Although the water passage took but a few minutes, its scenes were recorded forever by the participants. Dawes counted fifteen of his men shot down almost before the boats had moved.[13] In the tension of the moment, some of the men could not lie still and rose to fire at the enemy. Excited almost out of his wits, another soldier stood up in the boat and cheered at the top of his voice, the bullets whizzing about him. Looking to his left, a Wisconsin man watched Colonel Morrow, riding nearby, "so impatient . . . [he] could hardly keep himself on the boat." The same soldier saw a comrade "tipping forward, a stream of blood rushing from his temple down over his face. . . . He sank but did not rise."[14] Gingerly poking his fingers into his cap, Wadsworth found two holes just provided by the rifles ahead.[15] As the boats neared their destination, the men saw the enemy clearly as some "shaggy-backed butternuts began to climb for the top of the rugged bank, but some came rolling down," victims of the Federal fire.[16]

"As soon as the boats touched the shore, the men sprang from them and scrambled up the steep hill, every man for himself—and a Rebel," wrote one of the Badger soldiers.[17] Another wrote: "When we got across . . . , we jumped into the mud and water, waist deep, waded ashore, crawled and scrambled up the bank, laying hold of the bushes." Bayonets fixed, the Wisconsin and Michigan men swept over the abatis into the arms of the enemy, but "very few shots were fired before the rebels were throwing down their arms or running." Quickly the officers gathered their excited men together, formed a line of battle, and advanced to the top of the bluff. There they beheld the plain beyond, over which the enemy was now rushing in headlong flight.[18] Then the Federals turned their attention to a brick house on their right, also a Confederate strong point, which was quickly overrun by the Sixth Wisconsin as the two regiments fanned out to the right and left while the remaining Western regiments, now also across the river, moved up the bluff. The Iron Brigade then established a line while the bridging proceeded. By ten-thirty the pontoons were laid and the remainder of the First Division crossed, securing a bridgehead for the corps. The Westerners were assigned to the left flank along the high bluff downriver from the crossing, and Cutler's men occupied the right. The remaining divisions of the corps advanced to, but did not cross, the river.[19]

"Without discredit to any regiment, I have the honor to report, without the fear of contradiction, that the Sixth Wisconsin Volunteers first scaled the bank and their colors first caught the breeze on the southern bank of the Rappahannock on the morning of April

29." So wrote Edward S. Bragg in his official report.[20] Regardless of the Wisconsin colonel's fears of contradiction, "the Twenty-fourth Michigan was in the lead, its flag landing first . . . ," recorded the historian of the Michigan regiment. But the latter wisely added that "there is a dispute as to which regiment belonged the boat first to land. It matters not. It was a neck and neck race, between two friendly regiments of the Iron Brigade . . . and there were bullets and glory enough for both."[21] Years later a Sixth Wisconsin participant remembered the affair: "The grandest fifteen minutes of our lives! *Worth one's life* to enjoy."[22] It had indeed cost the lives of several of the brigade. The Michigan regiment led the list, twenty-one of its men having been killed and wounded. As befitted the competition, the Sixth Wisconsin claimed sixteen casualties, while the Seventh and Second regiments listed, respectively, nine and six, men who had apparently been shot down with five men from the Nineteenth Indiana while occupying the north bank of the river during the crossing. For these losses the brigade had more than ninety prisoners, along with the guns that had been abandoned by the Confederates.[23]

Once the Federal bridgehead was established, it looked for a time as if the crossing of the river had led the First Division into a full-scale battle. Shortly after the bridges were completed, the Confederates reappeared, this time in great force, moving into the entrenchments they had successfully occupied the preceding December and throwing skirmishers forward to the railroad track and the Bowling Green Road. On the Federal left, the Iron Brigade was ready, but the enemy did not advance and soon the soldiers had worked out one of their informal picket-line truces, permitting both sides a restful night. Since such a truce could not be depended on if the officers decided otherwise, the Federals spent the next day digging in, and throwing up breastworks, the latter constructed in part from the farm equipment, mowers, reapers, and plows, from the Fitzhugh outbuildings, along with sticks and mud. Late in the day, the enemy loosed its artillery on the Federal bridgehead, and a solid shot found the Michigan regiment, killing and wounding four more of its men. Battery B was then brought over the river and, together with the guns left on the north side of the river, responded to the Confederates. That night the engineers were directed to remove one of the bridges and take it to Bank's Ford, west of Fredericksburg, auguring the success of Hooker's plan to uncover that crossing; and the following morning, May 1st, presented evidence of a Confederate withdrawal, although the artillery and the pickets, at least, were still there. The day also afforded an opportunity for a squad from the Michigan regiment to visit the scene of their December action where the bodies of two of their comrades were disinterred for removal to the north side of the river.[24] Again there was an artillery duel, during which two of the men of Battery B were hit.[25] And in the evening a Federal demonstration was mounted, with skirmishers from the First Division sent briefly to the left and with the appearance to the right of a division of the Sixth Corps, which had crossed at Franklin's and moved down the river. Then the day ended at Fitzhugh's Crossing, with the Iron Brigade still in its entrenchments.[26]

Elsewhere along the line of the Rappahannock and the Rapidan, Joe Hooker's complicated plan had also worked well. Although minor variations had been initiated and the timing was slightly behind schedule, by the evening of April 30th four Federal corps, less Gibbon's Division of the Second, had crossed the Rappahannock and concentrated in Lee's rear, at the Chancellor House, located ten miles west of Fredericksburg on the Orange Turnpike. The Third Corps, withdrawn from the diversionary force below Fredericksburg, was en route westward to United States Ford and was to join Hooker's main body on the following day. Convinced now that this was the direction of the Federals' real blow, Lee had also turned to the west, leaving only a holding force at Fredericksburg and in front of the Sixth and First corps below the town. Moving eastward over several roads, the Federals had collided with the enemy in the late morning of May 1st, near Tabernacle Church just below the turnpike running from Fredericksburg. The action had developed quickly. Although Joe Hooker's forces outnumbered the Confederates and were meeting them on almost precisely the terms and ground the general had anticipated, he had unaccountably wavered, suspended the Federal attack, and withdrawn to positions nearer the Chancellor House. On the morning of May 2nd the Federal line ran from the Rappahannock, near United States Ford, to the Chancellor House, and from there to the west for approximately three miles, to just beyond the point at which the Orange Turnpike and the Plank Road divided. There the Eleventh Corps held the Federal right along the turnpike. In this position, Hooker now awaited Lee's attack.

At 7:00 A.M. on May 2nd, while the rest of the army maneuvered near Chancellorsville, Reynolds was directed to recross the river and march to Chancellorsville, taking the remaining pontoon bridge with him. Before this could be accomplished, the First Corps was shelled by Confederate batteries and the Federal guns again responded. Reynolds then put the divisions of Doubleday and Robinson in motion up the river and directed Wadsworth to recross the river and follow the same route. As soon as the Federal move was apparent, the enemy guns again opened, firing at the bridge and inflicting some damage to one of the boats. Repairs having been effected, Wadsworth's men crawled from their fortifications and headed for the river. Following the familiar pattern, the Iron Brigade was the last to move, and constituted the rear guard for the division. And as had been true in December, some of the brigade's pickets—this time from the Twenty-fourth Michigan—did not cross until the bridge was withdrawn, and had to effect their passage by boat. Leaving two companies of the Seventh Wisconsin to cover the engineers loading the pontoons, Wadsworth then formed the division and began the march, pursuing a river road to Franklin's Crossing, where the Sixth Corps was across and from which point that corps was soon to march on Fredericksburg. After halting briefly in the late morning, Reynolds' men resumed their journey, through Falmouth and Hartwood Church, to camp, at 10:00 P.M., two miles from United States Ford.[27]

While the Iron Brigade marched north of the river to join the army at the Chancellor House, a vastly more significant march, and Stonewall Jackson's last, was taking place south of the river. Again assuming the risk, Lee had withdrawn Jackson's Corps from the Federal front and had sent the gray column far to the left, to fall on Hooker's right flank. Although the movement was plainly seen and frequently reported, an inadequate defense was established, and Hooker, like John Pope at Manassas, fatuously assumed that the Confederates were retreating. In the late afternoon Jackson at last reached the Orange Turnpike, organized his column, and fell on the Eleventh Corps with irresistible force. In the gathering darkness the Confederates drove relentlessly forward, routing the Federals and plunging to within a mile of the Chancellor House. There the assault was halted by a combination of Federal resistance, the disorganization and fatigue of the attackers, and the total darkness, in the midst of which Jackson received a fatal wound.

Although dealt a heavy blow, the issue of Hooker's campaign was by no means decided by Jackson's famous march. The Federals still outnumbered their foe and were now advantageously between the two wings of Lee's army. The Eleventh Corps was, of course, severely hurt, but as the eminent Kenneth P. Williams has written: "The advent of the fine First Corps under Reynolds, with the renowned Iron Brigade, more than compensated for the broken Eleventh."[28] And apparently with this premise in view, army headquarters aroused the First Corps at 2:00 A.M. and directed it to the battlefield. Crossing on pontoon bridges at United States Ford, Reynolds' men headed westward, to replace the Eleventh Corps on the Federal right, now recessed in the direction of the river. In the darkness the soldiers followed a road that ran southwest from United States Ford and, less than a mile above the Chancellor House, formed a junction with the road from Ely's Ford. At this junction the men turned northwest, on the Ely's Ford Road. It was a circuitous and crowded route and progress was slow. But at sunrise the column reached the destination, the army's right, posted along the Ely's Ford Road and extending toward the river. Here, next to the Fifth Corps, the First Corps went into position facing southwest, its right prolonged to the riverbank. Closest to the Fifth Corps was Wadsworth's Division, and his men at once dug in, throwing up strong works in anticipation of what the day would bring.[29]

With his line reorganized and reinforced, the Federal commander continued to stand on the defensive on May 3rd, awaiting a Confederate attack. He was not to be disappointed, as the enemy furiously assailed the Federal salient around the Chancellor House, to the left of the Iron Brigade's position. Gradually the Federals were driven northward, beyond the Chancellor House, permitting the two wings of the Confederate army to reunite. Although a stray artillery shot wounded one of the Michigan men, the Western soldiers did not participate in the day's action, their position permitting only the sounds of the sharp fire on their left.[30] And farther away, the Western men may also have heard other firing, that of the Sixth Corps and Gibbon's Division. Under General Sedgwick, these commands had entered Fredericksburg and, spearheaded by the Fifth Wisconsin under Iron Brigade alumnus Colonel Thomas S. Allen, had carried Marye's Hill and were marching for Lee's rear. As May

3rd came to a close, Sedgwick's column reached the vicinity of Salem Church on the Plank Road, almost halfway to Chancellorsville from Fredericksburg. There, on the following day, aware that Hooker at Chancellorsville posed no real threat and would continue simply to defend himself, Lee was to turn on Sedgwick and drive him to the river. Near Bank's Ford, Sedgwick was to cross on the morning of May 5th, thus ending one phase of the campaign.

In their entrenchments beyond the Chancellor House, the Iron Brigade spent the uncomfortable night of May 3rd, a night full of alarms and picket firing. Fires were prohibited, and the men were not allowed to remove their blankets, carried in a roll over the shoulder. As was the custom in the brigade, the officers shared the hardship and slept on the ground without blankets. In the Sixth Wisconsin, Dawes and Colonel Bragg shared a single oilcloth. Both men were booted and spurred, and Dawes long remembered that his commander had kicked in his sleep.[31] On the following morning, as the Confederates continued their probing, there were more alarms, and the Twenty-fourth Michigan was detached and sent to picket below Ely's Ford, in advance of the army's right on the Rapidan.[32] The otherwise uneventful day at length drew to a close, to be followed by a similar day on May 5th, during which the brigade was again out of action. But as darkness came, bringing with it a heavy thunderstorm, the appearances of a Federal withdrawal manifested themselves as the mules were loaded up and sent to the rear along with other baggage.[33] Unknown to the soldiers, at midnight General Hooker held a council of war. Although General Reynolds joined Generals Meade and Howard in voting against it, the army commander there confirmed his decision to recross the river, and at 3:30 A.M. on May 6th, in a drizzling rain, the First Corps began its movement for United States Ford, the Iron Brigade bringing up the rear. At 5:00 A.M., the river was reached, but the bridges were choked with men; Wadsworth's Division, in the meantime forming a line of battle to protect the crossing, waited until 8:00 A.M. to cross.[34]

Once across the river, the Army of the Potomac moved eastward, in the direction of Fredericksburg.[35] The rain continued to fall, and an Iron Brigade veteran left this picture of the march: "One hundred thousand miserable and discouraged men . . . wading through this terrible mud and rain." The writer also added this description of the soldiers' state of mind: "We cannot understand it in any other way than as a great disaster,"[36] surely an apt characterization of the latest Union effort. But even as they marched away, the men were able to choke down despondency and, aided by the usual soldiers' badinage, masked their discouragement behind a brave and buoyant appearance. Following a hilly road near the river, the First Corps passed other organizations that had been ordered off the roadway. Among them was Berdan's Sharpshooters, one of whom remembered this scene:

Loud cheers were frequently given when some particular regiment or brigade passed by. Especially when, while resting on the roadside . . . , the 1st corps came along with the "full moon" on its banners, and as the great Western or Iron Brigade passed, looking like giants with their tall black hats, they were greeted with hearty cheers. . . . And giants they were, in action. . . . I look back and see that famed body of troops marching up that long muddy hill unmindful of the pouring rain, but full of life and spirit, with steady step, filling the entire roadway, their big black hats and feathers conspicuous. . . .[37]

Reaching a point directly north of Falmouth, fifteen miles from United States Ford, the brigade encamped. And regardless of assumed appearances, according to one of the Western soldiers they were "despondent . . . wet, hungry and so fatigued that in ten minutes the men fell asleep in some pine woods, each one where he happened to be." On the 7th the Westerners accompanied the First Corps through Falmouth and on to the Fitzhugh house just below White Oak Church, where the brigade reoccupied its camp of April 28th.[38]

For "this most unfortunate Army of the Potomac"[39]—the words are those of a soldier of the brigade—the campaign of Chancellorsville was over. In their camp at the Fitzhugh house the soldiers of the Iron Brigade awaited developments. Examination proved that the camp site was a fortunate one, "wood and water handy," and surrounded by tall and beautiful pine trees.[40] In addition to its scenic characteristics, the Fitzhugh tract had historical associations, once having belonged to the Washington family. The men liked this aspect, and they journeyed to the nearby Rappahannock to duplicate Washington's feat of throwing a dollar across, except that the soldiers used stones. A few days following their arrival, the men received a welcome instruction to fix up the camp, an order implying that they were to remain for a time. Tents were promptly unpacked and erected, streets laid out and graded, and ditches dug. The soldiers also went further and "ornamented . . . the streets . . . with evergreens from the groves, forming fine walks and arbors."[41] Having completed these labors, the Western men again settled down to camp routine, with regular drill and picket duty as their principal functions.[42] The latter detail again permitted a resumption of trading across the river with the Confederates, who were "first rate friends of the Iron Brigade at present," according to one of the Wisconsin pickets. To effect their exchanges of Northern coffee for Southern tobacco, the soldiers now constructed miniature boats that regularly plied the waters of the river, carried by the current and their tiny sails.[43]

Camp life also afforded the soldiers time to think and talk about the rumors that were always running through the army. One of these announced that the First Corps was to be withdrawn from the front and sent to Baltimore for garrison duty, an interesting report, but one that was hardly believed. There was also news from Vicksburg, reliable news, that Grant's army had crossed to the east side of the Mississippi and in a series of lightning battles had taken Jackson, the capital of Mississippi. Indeed, the conquest of Vicksburg was shortly expected. This was, of course, all to the good, but it was hardly of as much concern to the soldiers of the Army of the Potomac as speculation about their own future. And in this department there was a new and exciting report that Lee was planning to invade the North, to attack Washington and Baltimore.[44]

On the 20th of May the soldiers' reveries were suddenly interrupted. On that day, General Reynolds was directed by Joe Hooker to send a force down Virginia's Northern Neck toward Heathsville, previously the destination of Colonel Fairchild's amphibious expedition.* The object was the relief of the Eighth Illinois cavalry, which had been sent on a foraging raid and was believed to be threatened by Confederates crossing to the north side of the Rappahannock. Hooker's order to Reynolds was significant: "Send down three good regiments, under the command of Colonel Morrow, or some officer of equal energy, courage and discretion, in whom you have full confidence."[45] Having selected Morrow as the commander, Reynolds designated the "three good regiments" that Hooker had specified: the Twenty-fourth Michigan, and the Second and the Sixth Wis-

* For this expedition, see back end paper.

consin. Orders were to proceed at daylight past Port Conway to Leesville, opposite Port Micou on the Confederate side of the river. There
the Federals were to "capture or destroy any party of the enemy who
may cross or attempt to cross," and to find the Illinois cavalry regiment and escort it safely back to White Oak Church.[46]

Colonel Morrow added the Nineteenth Indiana and the Eighth
New York Cavalry to his command and moved at daylight on the
21st, along the road nearest the Potomac, "the weather . . . uncommon warm & sultry, the dust near shoe mouth deep," according to
a Hoosier participant.[47] Two miles beyond King George Court House,
the road divided. Leaving Dawes and 160 men at this fork, Morrow
and the rest of his force proceeded onward. Dawes at once put his
men to work constructing an earthwork at the crossroads. But it was
not to be the enemy that distracted the conscientious lieutenant colonel. Instead, by his own admission, it was his "chicken-hungry boys
. . . in a land replete with pigs and poultry. I established a guard
around my post, and still the men slipped out. . . . Finally, exasper-
ated at the depletion of my force, I sent out a patrol with strict
orders to arrest every man or officer found." Unexpectedly, the first
culprit seized by the patrol was a captain of the Nineteenth Indiana.
The captain, of course, had a pass, but this did not mitigate Dawes'
chagrin or the soldiers' great amusement at the sight of the officer
being brought in under the bayonets of the guard.[48]

While Dawes was wrestling with the appetites of his soldiers,
Morrow led his men past what a Hoosier private called "fine farms
and tasty mansions,"[49] to Millville, inland from Port Conway and
twenty-five miles from the Fitzhugh house camp. Despite their tradition against straggling, the heat and dust had accounted for more than
one of the Western soldiers, who had fallen exhausted by the roadside. On the following morning the Federals proceeded to Mattox
Creek, which was bridged and crossed, and a small detachment was
left there. From this point the column turned southward to the
Rappahannock, striking the river at their destination, Leesville,
where Morrow decided to cross a small force for the purpose of
burning boats, an expedition that was canceled when enemy horsemen appeared on the opposite bank and exchanged shots with the
Federals.

Having found neither the Eighth Illinois nor Confederates at
Leesville, Morrow determined to look elsewhere. Again dividing his

force, he sent horsemen to Leedstown, down the river, while the rest of the column turned to the north and marched for Oak Grove. While the main column advanced to Rappahannock Creek, a detachment was left at Oak Grove and another cavalry party was dispatched, this one commanded by the Nineteenth Indiana's Lieutenant Colonel Dudley, and ordered to Westmoreland Court House. On the 24th, just as the Federals were planning to march again in search of the enemy and the missing Illinois troopers, the latter rode up, led by Morrow's scouts, "with an immense train of wagons, carts, horses, mules and contrabands," as Morrow phrased it, together with approximately fifty Confederate prisoners. After collecting the scattered outposts, the Federal column started for camp on the following day, picking up Dawes and his men on the way and arriving at White Oak Church on May 26th after five and one-half days and more than one hundred miles of marching.

In addition to bringing in the Eighth Illinois, the Michigan commander was able to report the absence of any significant enemy force north of the river. He also noted evidence of wholesale smuggling from Maryland to Virginia and the fact that the mouth of the Rappahannock was an active avenue for blockade runners. But the former judge of the Wayne County Recorder's Court reserved his most extensive comments, all gratuitous, for the Federal cavalry:

The wholesale plunder and pillage of our cavalry has done more to weaken the affection of the people for the Government than all other causes combined, and . . . the cavalry have left the inhabitants very little cause to respect them as men and soldiers. . . . These men, pretending to be representatives of our Government, and to act under and by virtue of its orders, have stripped helpless women and children of their last horse, and in many instances of their last article of food, and have then grossly insulted them. . . . I do not believe the general commanding the Army of the Potomac is aware of the utter want of every principle of true soldiers which characterizes the intercourse between the cavalry and the inhabitants. . . . The right of the United States Government to take from the people anything and everything which they may possess is beyond dispute, and is, perhaps, in many instances wise and politic; but to permit individual and unlicensed plunder, while it does not benefit the Government, does much lower the standard of our army in the estimation of our enemy, and must lead to demoralization among such troops as are allowed to practice it.[50]

In addition to "energy, courage and discretion," the attributes which
General Hooker had noted, and the sensitive and sympathetic spirit
which had been apparent to his soldiers when disciplinary problems
arose, Henry A. Morrow knew the difference between theft and foraging, and was willing to say so.

As May drew to a close, amidst continuing gossip about a Confederate thrust into Maryland and Pennsylvania, the Twenty-fourth
Michigan at last received their coveted black hats, earned almost six
months previously at Fredericksburg. But although the hats were
late, they were received just in time for a visit from Governor Blair
and his wife, who watched their constituents on dress parade, at last
bearing the unique trade-mark of the brigade. The soldiers of the
Twenty-fourth also wore their hats two days later when the First
Corps was reviewed by General Reynolds. On the following day, May
31st, the Michigan men learned that new hats provided no exemption
from the usual routine, as the regiment was sent to Franklin's Crossing on picket duty. There the soldiers witnessed a grand review of
twenty-five Confederate regiments parading on the December battleground, an event that increased the speculation that the Southerners
were preparing for a new campaign.[51]

While all of these events were transpiring along the Rappahannock,
something much more significant was happening in the Federal army.
When Wisconsin and Indiana had enlisted three-year regiments in
May and June of 1861, some of the other states had raised two-year
organizations. The terms of these units were now expiring and the
regiments were going home, in many cases to muster out and disband.
In the First Corps, the present-for-duty equipped strength of the infantry dropped from 14,361 just after Chancellorsville to 9,403 by
the end of June,[52] a stunning loss largely accounted for by the mustering out of two-year regiments. The shrinking of the brigades required
wholesale reorganization, a process which began during May and
which, by June 30th, had radically altered the structure of the First
Corps.

Wadsworth's First Division, reduced from nineteen to eleven regiments, was now divided into two brigades, instead of the four that had
previously existed. Meredith's Iron Brigade, which retained its integrity, was renumbered as the First Brigade, and Cutler's Brigade

became the Second, composed of its old members, the Seventh Indiana, Fifty-sixth Pennsylvania, Seventy-sixth New York, and Ninety-fifth New York, along with the 147th New York, which had joined the brigade in February, and the Fourteenth Brooklyn, fighting Zouaves, previously of Phelps' First Brigade. The Second Division, General John C. Robinson's, experienced a similar consolidation, having dropped from thirteen regiments in three brigades to eleven regiments, which were now organized into two brigades. General Gabriel R. Paul, formerly of the First Division, took over the first of these reorganized brigades, while the other was assigned to General Henry Baxter, who had also previously commanded a brigade in the Second Division. In Doubleday's Third Division, composed of but two brigades, the necessity for reorganization was limited, a result of the fact that it had been reorganized earlier in the year from newly raised regiments. Although the Eightieth New York Volunteers replaced the 135th Pennsylvania in Rowley's First Brigade, that brigade continued to claim four regiments, and Stone's Second Brigade maintained its three-regiment strength. The artillery, too, was not exempt from the shake-up in the First Corps. Reduced from ten batteries at Chancellorsville to five batteries by June 30th, the artillery was now organized into an artillery brigade, which included, of course, Lieutenant Stewart's reliable Battery B, now composed almost entirely of "old regulars" and Iron Brigade volunteers.[53]

Although doubtless aware of the effect on their corps' efficiency of the loss of almost 5,000 infantry, the Iron Brigade was consoled by its newly acquired designation as the *First* Brigade of the *First* Division of the *First* Corps. The men remarked that "if all the Armies of the United States were in one line, the Iron Brigade would now be on the extreme right."[54] So far as the soldiers were concerned, this was no mere coincidence resulting from a convenient army numbering system. Even Rufus Dawes naïvely recorded that "we . . . deserve the title," observing accurately that "as a brigade, we are one of the oldest in the army."[55] And as the division's First Brigade, the Westerners became the custodians of the flag of the First Division, a large white triangular flag with a red sphere in the center.[56]

For General Robert E. Lee the period after the battle of Chancellorsville was one of fateful decision. In addition to Jeb Stuart's division of cavalry, Lee's army, to which Longstreet had returned, had been reorganized into three corps, each composed of three divisions. Longstreet, of course, continued as one of the corps commanders, and two new ones had been selected, A. P. Hill and Richard S. Ewell, the latter just returned to duty with a new wooden leg in place of the one accounted for by the Iron Brigade at Brawner Farm. Lee's question was what to do with his army. At least a part of it could have been sent to the West, to relieve the rapidly worsening Confederate position before Vicksburg. Or it could have remained where it was on the line of the Rappahannock, awaiting a third successive Federal effort to break that line. But there was a third alternative, bold and dashing, the long-rumored invasion of the North. It was this alternative which Lee at length selected, motivated by the interplay of a variety of considerations, including the value in Europe of a Southern victory on Northern soil, the availability of provisions on the unspoiled Northern farms, and the blow to Northern morale a successful invasion would effect.

On June 3rd the momentous Confederate movement began. Led by one of Longstreet's divisions and followed the next day by Ewell's Corps, the Confederates moved westward, crossing the Rapidan west of Germanna Ford and aiming for Culpeper. By the 6th, only Hill's Corps remained in the Fredericksburg lines. That the Confederates were moving was signaled by the disappearance of their camps across the river, which was noticed by the Federals on June 4th. Reacting promptly, General Hooker issued a warning order on the 5th and directed on the same day that the bridges be thrown across at Franklin's Crossing so that the Sixth Corps could reconnoiter the south side of the river. But despite the knowledge that the enemy was in motion, there was continuing uncertainty as to his destination. At midnight on June 4th the First Corps was instructed to break camp, preparatory to moving out, and the men of the Iron Brigade struck tents and packed their gear. But morning brought a countermanding order, and the day was spent in rebuilding "our canvas cities," as one of the men called the encampment. On June 6th the brigade was advanced to Franklin's Crossing where a battle line was formed at the bridges, in support of elements of the Sixth Corps across the river. There was an artillery cannonade on the south side of the Rappahannock, but the Federals there did not cross the Bowling Green Road for fear of bringing on an engagement with A. P. Hill's

Confederates. After "roasting in line of battle for two days in the hot sun"—the words are those of an Iron Brigade officer—the brigade was withdrawn and sent back to the Fitzhugh estate camp.[57]

What a Wisconsin veteran called "excessive readiness" continued to discommode the soldiers for two more days. As described by one of the Westerners, "The men would lie hour after hour on the ground in the hot sun with everything packed for marching," only to be ordered at length to fall out. This order was then followed by another series of "alarms, orders and counter-orders."[58] But on June 11th the Federal commander began to move his army westward, up the Rappahannock. And at last, on June 12th, the First Corps and the Iron Brigade got into the campaign and marched to the northwest from the Fitzhugh house.[59] Just before they left, Lieutenant Colonel Dawes posted a letter to his sweetheart in Marietta, Ohio. "You are mustered into service now," the officer wrote, "and must endure your trials and hardships as a soldier, and I doubt not that they will be harder to bear than mine, for you see, you are a raw recruit." Alluding to the fact that Colonel Bragg had left the field as a result of a disabling kick from a horse, the lieutenant colonel commanding the regiment also wrote that "it has been my ardent ambition to lead it through one campaign, and now the indications are that my opportunity has come. If I do anything glorious I shall expect you to be proud of me."[60]

Crossing the Aquia to Fredericksburg railroad at Stoneman's Switch,* the First Corps' line of march proceeded for twenty miles under a scorching sun and through suffocating clouds of dust to Deep Run, north of the Rappahannock near Barnett's Ford. On the 13th, with all elements of both armies now in motion, the First Corps advanced to beyond Bealeton Station on the Orange and Alexandria Railroad, another grueling performance under a merciless sky. The next day was Sunday, but there was no respite for the Iron Brigade. The men plunged on through the heat and choking dust, spurred forward by their officers' inaccurate but meaningful report that they were racing with the Southerners for the heights around Manassas. The route now followed the line of the railroad, to Warrenton Junction, Catlett's, and then to Bristoe, where the column halted briefly for supper before resuming the march. Crossing Broad Run in the

* For the march to Gettysburg, follow maps at pages 48, 73, and 116.

night, the bridge lighted by torches and bonfires on the bank, the soldiers hastened on through the darkness. Just before sunrise on Monday morning, the weary column halted at Manassas Junction, the Iron Brigade selecting the same place along the railroad track in which it had encamped on the morning after Brawner Farm. But the veterans now had little opportunity to reminisce or to recall the earlier bivouac for the benefit of their Michigan comrades. As soon as four hours had passed, the soldiers were again on their feet and moving forward to Blackburn's Ford on Bull Run itself, where the Second Wisconsin, then in Sherman's Brigade, had appeared two years previously on the eve of First Bull Run. The recollections of the "old soldiers" were again cut short, however, as the men promptly crossed Bull Run and proceeded on to Centreville. There, at last, they halted in the afternoon to encamp southeast of the town, the men "tired, sore, sleepy, hungry, dusty and dirty as pigs." Although a few of the men had fallen by the roadside and all of them had at times been almost frantic from thirst, an officer reported that the brigade "came through without a murmur" during the continuous day-and-night marathon.[61]

"Our army is in a great hurry for something," wrote one of the Western soldiers from Centreville.[62] And at Centreville, where the First Corps was to rest on the 16th of June, the soldiers learned what that "something" was. Now leading Lee's infantry, Ewell's Corps, closely followed by Longstreet and Hill, had crossed the Potomac at Williamsport and had moved on to the vicinity of Boonsborough, Hagerstown, and Sharpsburg, near the Pennsylvania line. Accordingly, on the morning of June 17th, the First Corps moved out again, "hurrying . . . as I never knew the Army of the Potomac to hurry before," according to one of the brigade. Again "the sun was like a furnace, and the dust thick and suffocating," and General Wadsworth cleared the ambulances of officers' valises and loaded them with the knapsacks and muskets of the men. Although several soldiers in the corps actually fell dead on the road, an officer of the Iron Brigade wrote that "our boys have all come through so far, accepting the hardships as a matter of course, and remaining cheerful and obedient."[63] The brigade arrived at Herndon Station on the night of the 17th, on the railroad between Leesburg and Alexandria, where the men enjoyed another day's respite, marked by a heavy rain and by the arrival in camp of a Northern newspaper with the headline "Rebels in Pennsylvania—Another battle of Antietam on the taps." The Western soldiers already assumed that battle was forthcoming, but the newspaper's projected site was by no means suitable to them. "I never want to fight there again. . . . I dread the thought of the place," wrote one of the men, a sentiment all of the veterans must have shared.[64]

Resuming the march on June 19th, the Iron Brigade moved four miles up the railroad to Guilford Station and again went into camp, to remain until June 25th. Broad Run, a creek running northward to the Potomac, was nearby, and the soldiers had a much-needed opportunity to bathe. The long halt also afforded a chance to enrich the rigid diet of the march at the expense of "rebel chicken" from the adjacent farms. Except for these activities and the usual picket details, the soldiers rested while the officers inspected the ordnance and attended to the usual administrative tasks. On the morning of June 24th, Lieutenant Colonel Dawes was approached by the First Division's officer of the day and a guard detail, who brought with them one of the Sixth's privates, under arrest. The charge was that of sleeping while on picket, a capital offense when in the presence of the enemy. But Rufus Dawes, who had himself voted this penalty when assigned to courts-martial, could not quite bring himself to do what duty required. He lectured the "sadly frightened . . . boy" and warned him, and then released the soldier and sent him to his company. In a letter to his sweetheart he confessed that failing in his duty "gave me pleasure."[65]

While the First Corps rested at Guilford Station, the dramatic situation ahead continued to unfold. Ewell was now in Pennsylvania, his corps located around Chambersburg. With A. P. Hill's men close behind, Longstreet's Corps was at Hagerstown. Hooker's army, to which reinforcements and militia units were hastening, had also marched well. Already across the Potomac was Howard's Eleventh Corps, with the Twelfth and First corps close by. The remaining Federal units were behind these three, but all were within a day's march of the river. But the Federal army's performance was jeopardized by a developing controversy between its commander and General-in-Chief Halleck in Washington. Marked at first by an impudent and quarrelsome tone in Hooker's dispatches, and concerning insubstantial questions of command and procedure, the conflict had now settled around a bitter disagreement about the status of the Federal garrison at Maryland Heights. Fortunately for the Union, Joe Hooker was not the only general who was creating problems for himself. In another of the celebrated faux pas of the war, Robert E. Lee had entirely lost control of his cavalry. By permitting Stuart and three brigades to initiate a largely useless raid in Hooker's rear, and by failing to use his remaining horsemen, the Confederate commander continued his march deprived of intelligence of the Federal movements.

Unaware of Lee's handicap and of the dispute between the generals, the First Corps started at 8:00 A.M. on June 25th, bound for Maryland. Edwards Ferry was promptly reached, and the soldiers crossed the Potomac at noon, "out of the barren desert of Virginia into this land of thrift and plenty."[66] Again in Union territory, another of the Western soldiers wrote that they were "welcomed all along the route, by fair women and glad children,"[67] although at least one Wisconsin veteran felt that the reception was not quite so enthusiastic as in the fall of 1862.[68] Passing through Poolsville, the homesick soldiers saw "a most beautiful sight . . . a large school of children . . . who gazed upon the soldiers as they marched by." "One cannot imagine . . . the cheerful feeling such a sight induces," wrote one of the marching men, but he also recalled that "this reminder of home brought tears to many an eye."[69] The night of the 25th was spent at Barnesville, and the next day took the men through the rain across the Monocacy and the Catoctin Mountains, to Jefferson. From the latter town the column moved to Middletown, just east of Turner's Gap, where camp was made on the evening of the 27th.[70] Visiting again another of the scenes of their past, this time the rugged field on which their proud name had been acquired, the Western soldiers saw with sorrow that "the grass has grown green over the graves of our . . . boys. . . . The inscriptions on the head boards are already scarcely legible and with their destruction seems to go the last poor chance that the sacrifice these men have made . . . shall be recognized and commemorated."[71] But there was little time for thoughts of memorializing fallen comrades, as the column was again in motion on the following morning, marching directly eastward for Frederick by means of a rough road to the north of the National Road. At Frederick the brigade learned the big news and the upshot of the dispute between Hooker and Halleck. Pennsylvania's George

G. Meade, who was also at Frederick, now commanded the Army of the Potomac, replacing Hooker, whose resignation Lincoln had accepted.[72] Armed with this information, and wondering at its meaning, the men of the First Corps turned northward from Frederick, advancing through Lewiston and on to Emmitsburg. There the students of St. Joseph's College welcomed them, briefly marching along with them and confiding what they had seen of the "rebels." At last, on June 30th, the Pennsylvania line was crossed, where "everybody, great and small," was out to greet the Federal column. And at noon the weary soldiers stopped at Marsh Creek and established camp.[73]

Although the men of the Iron Brigade were doubtless unaware of the privilege, their corps, 9,400 infantry and thirty guns, was now in advance in the Federal march to meet the Confederates. Behind the First Corps, on both sides of the Pennsylvania line, lay the remaining Federal corps, the bulk of Meade's army of 83,000 men of all arms. And ahead rested Lee's 75,000-man army.[74] It had been widely scattered but a few days before, with detached commands at Carlisle, York, and all the way to the Susquehanna, in front of Columbia and Harrisburg. Although still without accurate knowledge of the Federals' whereabouts, the Confederates were now gathered around Chambersburg, twenty-five miles north and west of the position of the Iron Brigade. Between the two great armies, seven miles ahead of the camp of the Iron Brigade, was the little town of Gettysburg, the center of a complex of roads extending in all directions like the spokes of a wheel. One of these, running into Gettysburg from the southwest, was the road from Emmitsburg, the road the First Corps was traveling and which passed beside the Iron Brigade's bivouac at Marsh Creek. Next to the Emmitsburg Road, to the north, was the road from Hagerstown, which entered Gettysburg almost directly from the west. Above the Hagerstown Road was another, the Chambersburg Pike, extending from the northwest into Gettysburg. And north of the road from Chambersburg were the Mummasburg and Carlisle roads, the first above but almost parallel to the Chambersburg Pike, the other approaching Gettysburg from the north. In addition to its roads, Gettysburg claimed two ridges, Seminary Ridge, running north and south on the west side of the town and surmounted by a Lutheran seminary, and farther to the east, Cemetery

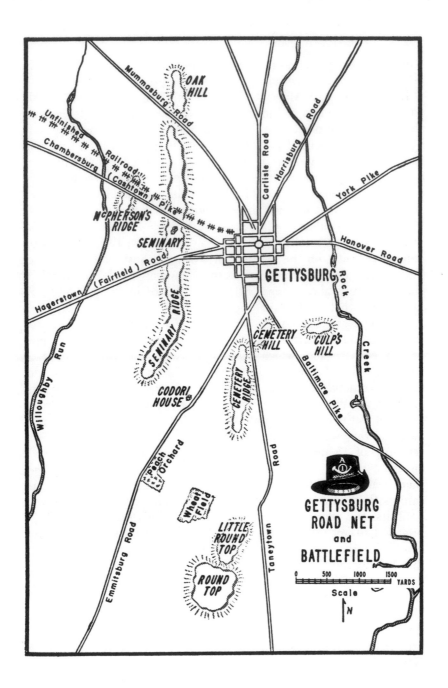

OAK HILL

Mummasburg Road

Unfinished

Railroad

Chambersburg ("Cashtown") Pike

Carlisle Road

Harrisburg Road

York Pike

McPHERSON'S RIDGE

SEMINARY

Hanover Road

GETTYSBURG

Hagerstown (Fairfield) Road

SEMINARY RIDGE

Willoughby Run

Rock Creek

CEMETERY HILL

CULP'S HILL

CODORI HOUSE

CEMETERY RIDGE

Baltimore Pike

Peach Orchard

Taneytown Road

Emmitsburg Road

Wheat Field

LITTLE ROUND TOP

ROUND TOP

GETTYSBURG ROAD NET and BATTLEFIELD

0   500   1000   1500   YARDS

Scale

N

Ridge, also extending north and south but terminating on the southern outskirts of the town.

In their camp at Marsh Creek, the soldiers of the Iron Brigade passed the afternoon of June 30th in the usual light details. As they were drawing rations in the late afternoon, a brigade of cavalry rode by. These were General John Buford's men, who had been back and forth in front of the infantry, seeking out the enemy, and who were again heading north on the Emmitsburg Road. As the horsemen passed up the road, they "sang out" to the foot soldiers and joined their usual banter with the arresting news that they had found the "Johnnies," just ahead and in great numbers.[75] Perhaps some of the Western soldiers recalled a similar encounter with Buford's men on August 28, 1862, on the Warrenton Turnpike, just west of Brawner Farm. The circumstances were in some respects similar. As in 1862, the enemy was ahead, apparently concentrated in strength and outnumbering that portion of the Federal force to which the Iron Brigade was attached. As in 1862, that Federal force also included Battery B and the three Pennsylvania and New York regiments, now of Cutler's Brigade, which had stood with the Iron Brigade at Brawner Farm. There was even a fair comparison of the numbers of the Western brigade, 2,100 on the Warrenton Turnpike as against 1,883 now.[76] But whether or not they saw these similarities, the news from the cavalrymen was understood and the Western soldiers realized that they were again on the eve of combat. To one observer "the certainty of an immediate battle . . . began to have a perceptible effect on the men. They were a little more serious than usual, and there was less chaff and badinage among them."[77] Gradually the camp settled down for the night. The last to leave the campfires were doubtless the officers: General Meredith, under whose command the brigade had not yet fought a full-scale battle; Williams, Dudley, and Lindley of the Indiana regiment; Morrow, Flanigan, and Wight of the Twenty-fourth Michigan; Fairchild, Stevens, and Mansfield of the Second; Dawes and Hauser of the Sixth; and Robinson, Callis, and Finnicum of the Seventh. Like the soldiers they commanded— "looking like giants with their tall black hats," according to one of Berdan's men—these officers were veterans, and combat wise. And it was well that they were, for the next day was to be July 1, 1863, at Gettysburg.

12

GETTYSBURG: THE LAST STAND

"Thar comes them blackhats! It ain't the militia, its the Army of
the Potomac!"

Shouts of the Confederates along McPherson's ridge

The soldiers of the First Division were up at dawn on July 1st, busy
preparing a frugal breakfast of hardtack, pork and coffee. In the
Twenty-fourth Michigan, the day's events were forecast by Chaplain
Way's calling the men together for prayer, an occasion that acquired
solemnity from the fact that ammunition was distributed to the
soldiers as they prayed. Shortly after 8:00 A.M., the division organized
for march. According to the custom of alternating the leading
brigade, Cutler's Brigade went first, less the Seventh Indiana, which
was detached to Emmitsburg for duty with the trains. Behind Cutler's
men came the Second Maine Battery, and then it was the Iron
Brigade's turn. The Second Wisconsin was its leading regiment,
followed by the Seventh, the Nineteenth, the Twenty-fourth, and the
Sixth. In the rear was the brigade guard, one hundred men, twenty
from each of the five regiments, led by a lieutenant from the Sixth
and another from the Seventh Wisconsin. Riding with the First
Division was General John F. Reynolds of Pennsylvania, commanding the army's advance wing, composed of the Third Corps, the
Eleventh Corps, and his own First Corps. With orders from Meade
to occupy Gettysburg, Reynolds had directed Doubleday to bring up
the other divisions and guns of the First Corps and had ordered up
Howard's Eleventh Corps from Emmitsburg. Now he proposed to
lead the First Division into Gettysburg.[1]

Despite the expectation of battle, in the column that followed
General Reynolds "all were in the highest spirits," according to an

officer of the Iron Brigade. Rufus Dawes placed the drums and fifes at the head of the Sixth Wisconsin and ordered the colors unfurled. The musicians struck up "The Campbells Are Coming" as the regiments closed up and swung into route step on the Emmitsburg Road. Although Dawes had intended his display "to make a show in the streets of Gettysburg,"[2] the first spectators were the men of Battery B, which had crossed Marsh Creek and pulled off the road to wait for the remaining divisions of the corps. A recollection of the marching men was left by the historian of the battery:

No one . . . will ever again see those two brigades of Wadsworth's Division—Cutler's and the Iron Brigade—file by as they did that morning. The little creek made a depression in the road, with a gentle ascent on either side, so that from our point of view the column, as it came down one slope and up the other, had the effect of huge blue billows of men topped with a spray of shining steel, and the whole spectacle was calculated to give nerve to a man who had none before. Partly because they had served together a long time, and, no doubt, because so many of their men were in our ranks, there was a great affinity between the Battery and the Iron Brigade, which expressed itself in cheers and good-natured chaffing between us as they went by. "Find a good place to camp . . . tell the Johnnies we will be right along," were the salutations that passed on our part, while the infantry made such responses as . . . "better stay here . . . the climate up there may be unhealthy just now for such delicate creatures as you!"[3]

Soon the cheers and shouts of the artillerymen were replaced by the distant sounds of firing ahead. Wadsworth's soldiers quickened their pace, and the noise became gradually louder as the miles to Gettysburg passed by.[4] The firing the Western soldiers heard was that of General John Buford's sturdy troopers, opposing the men of A. P. Hill's Corps on the Chambersburg Pike. Heth's Division, followed by Pegram's artillery battalion of five batteries and Pender's Division, had started from Cashtown at 5:00 A.M., bound for Gettysburg. Unaware of the nearness of the Federals in force—"It may not be improper to remark that . . . I was ignorant what force was at or near Gettysburg," was Heth's acid report—the Confederates sought a store of shoes reportedly available in the town. But at eight-thirty they had run into Buford's men three miles west of the town, where the cavalry was picketing the pike in advance of Seminary Ridge. Despite the strength of the Confederate column, Buford's regiments had not been inclined to withdraw. Supported by Calef's four-gun Battery A of the Second United States Horse Artillery, the blue-clad troopers had dismounted, formed a line of battle, and opened fire. The enemy had promptly responded and heavy skirmishing had begun, but the cavalry had only grudgingly given ground and, apparently disconcerted by the unexpected opposition and wary of the possibility of strong Federal supports, the Confederates had been reluctant to unleash their overwhelming force of numbers.[5]

After an hour's fighting, during which his force had slowly backed toward the town, John Buford rode back to Seminary Ridge. Mounting the stairs to the cupola of the seminary building, he was joined by General Reynolds who had ridden ahead of the First Division toward the firing.[6] From their vantage point Reynolds and Buford now examined the ground. Two hundred yards to the right of the seminary was the pike, and beyond it, perhaps another 100 yards, was a railroad grading that ran roughly parallel, forming deep cuts through Seminary Ridge and the ridge to the west. The latter ridge, 500 yards from the seminary, was McPherson's ridge. Beyond it the ground dipped down to Willoughby Run, 500 yards from McPherson's ridge. Both the run, which extended north and south, and the slope descending to it were partially obstructed on the left of the pike by a small wood that crowned McPherson's ridge for several hundred yards to the south. While Reynolds considered this terrain, Buford doubtless told him of the Confederate forces opposed. Heth's Division and Pender's were in front of them, almost 16,000 men and seventeen batteries, counting the artillery reserve from A. P. Hill's Corps. Nearby were two more divisions, Rodes' and Early's from Ewell's Corps, an additional 16,000 infantry and eight more batteries. Against these numbers Reynolds could throw his nearby First Division, almost 4,000 men. With it and the rest of his own corps, he would have 9,500 men and five batteries. The Third Corps was not within supporting distance, but the Eleventh was expected, an additional 9,000 men and five more batteries.[7] Eighteen thousand against almost 32,000. The odds were certainly against the Federals, who would also be outgunned. But the ground in front of the seminary—this *Pennsylvania* ground—was defensible, and behind it, through the town, loomed Cemetery Hill, another natural point of defense if a battle at Seminary Ridge went against the Federals.

John F. Reynolds decided to fight. Dispatching a rider to tell General Meade of the situation, Reynolds rode back to hasten his men along.[8]

While their corps commander was making his decision at the seminary, Wadsworth's Division, hastening now, continued its march up the Emmitsburg Road. Directly west of the seminary, General Heth was preparing his move. Archer's Brigade, 2,000 Tennessee and Alabama veterans, was deployed on the right of the pike, facing McPherson's woods. To the left were three Mississippi and North Carolina regiments composing Davis' Brigade, another 2,000 men.[9] At ten-thirty,[10] just as the Confederates moved forward, Wadsworth's column reached the Codori house,* a mile from Gettysburg. There the Federals left the road, turning to the west, toward the sounds of battle. As scattered artillery projectiles crashed through the nearby treetops,[11] the column halted briefly while the regimental officers dismounted, baggage was dropped, and the brigade guard joined the Sixth Wisconsin, organizing as the right and left companies of Dawes' regiment.[12] Then the division was again in motion, the men feverishly loading and fixing bayonets while advancing at the double quick, up the eastern slope of Seminary Ridge, then north along its crest, across the Hagerstown Road and to the seminary. Without a pause, Cutler led the Seventy-sixth and 147th New York and the Fifty-sixth Pennsylvania across the Chambersburg Pike and over the railroad cut while the Second Maine battery prepared to unlimber between the pike and the cut, with the Fourteenth Brooklyn and the Ninety-fifth New York in support, south of the pike. Behind them, also south of the pike, was the Iron Brigade, less Dawes' regiment which was detached at the seminary as the reserve.[13] As Cutler's advance became engaged on the right, Sol Meredith's four regiments faced left at the seminary and, responding to the command "Forward into line!" formed line of battle from line of march and raced *en echelon* up the slope of McPherson's ridge, through the ranks of John Buford's cavalrymen.[14]

At the crest of the ridge, the leading Second Wisconsin crashed head on into Archer's Tennessee and Alabama regiments, also advancing in McPherson's woods. "It was . . . the unadorned, long-drawn-out line of ragged, dirty blue against the long-drawn-out line of dirty, ragged butternut,"[15] according to one of Meredith's soldiers,

* See map at page 231.

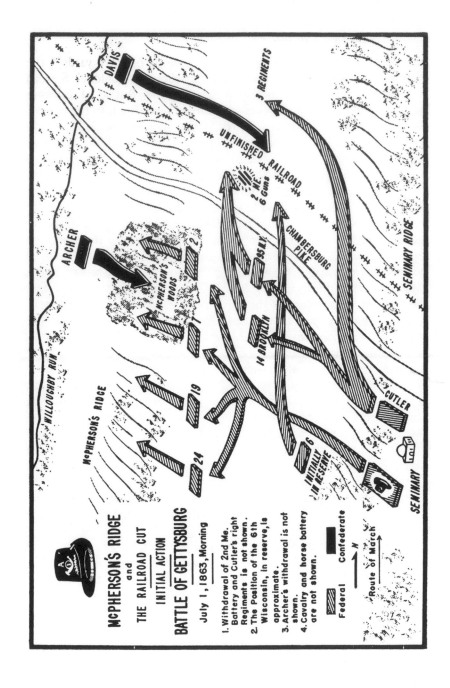

McPHERSON'S RIDGE
and
THE RAILROAD CUT
INITIAL ACTION
BATTLE OF GETTYSBURG

July 1, 1863, Morning

1. Withdrawal of 2nd Me. Battery and Cutler's right Regiments is not shown.
2. The Position of the 6th Wisconsin, in reserve, is approximate.
3. Archer's withdrawal is not shown.
4. Cavalry and horse battery are not shown.

Federal   Confederate

N

Route of March

and both lines exploded at impact. At a range of forty yards,[16] the first furious Confederate volley killed Lieutenant Colonel Stevens and opened telling gaps in the Wisconsin line. But as at Brawner Farm, the Second plunged forward, pouring a hot fire into the enemy. Leading the charge, Colonel Fairchild was now struck down, bleeding heavily, his left arm shattered at the elbow. Still the regiment advanced, directly into the enemy, shredding Archer's line and moving toward the western slope of the ridge and Willoughby Run beyond. To the left of the Second Wisconsin, outside the woods, the Seventh Wisconsin had also reached the crest of McPherson's ridge and paused while the Indiana and Michigan regiments caught up and formed on its left. Peering into the smoky confusion in the depressed ground ahead, Colonel Robinson of the Seventh hesitated. Then he saw the enemy's battle flags, and with a shout the Westerners swept into the ravine, firing rapidly into Archer's right regiments. At first the Confederates returned the fire, grievously wounding Lieutenant Colonel Flanigan and killing Color Sergeant Abel G. Peck of the Michigan regiment. But Meredith's left overlapped Archer's right, and the black-hatted soldiers poured a merciless enfilading fire into the enemy's line. In a matter of minutes, the Confederates were overpowered, Robinson grimly reporting that "the enemy—what was left of them able to walk—threw down their arms" or fled. Among seventy-five Confederate prisoners was General Archer himself, captured by Private Patrick Maloney of the Second.[17] Leaving the Second in the woods behind, the Seventh, Nineteenth, and Twenty-fourth followed the fleeing enemy across Willoughby Run and up the slope on the other side, where they were halted. In the first furious onslaught, the Western soldiers had swept the enemy entirely from the field, and the remnants of Archer's line disappeared into the woods beyond.[18]

Elsewhere along McPherson's ridge the Federals were losing. The man who had decided to fight, the magnificent John F. Reynolds, was dead, victim of a sharpshooter's bullet. To the north of the pike, beyond the railroad cut, Cutler's three leading regiments had been roughly handled by Davis' Brigade. Striking Cutler obliquely on the right flank, the Confederates had stopped the Federal advance with a sharp enfilade. Although the New York and Pennsylvania men had "fought as only brave men can," according to General Cutler, they

In the Field

SECOND WISCONSIN HEADQUARTERS STAFF at mess in winter quarters, Arlington Heights, spring of 1862. Left to right, foreground: Surgeon A. J. Ward, Major Allen, Lieutenant Colonel Fairchild, Colonel O'Connor.

State Historical Society of Wisconsin

Non-Commissioned Officers of Company E, Second Wisconsin. Nothing is known about the date and place of this photograph, which shows interesting details of uniforms and camp life.

State Historical Society of Wisconsin

COMPANY STREET of Company I, Seventh Wisconsin, at Upton's Hill, Virginia. The photograph was probably made in September, 1862, between Second Bull Run and South Mountain.

OFFICERS OF THE SECOND WISCONSIN at Falmouth, Virginia. Taken in July, 1862, this photograph shows (left to right) Lieutenant J. D. Ruggles, Surgeon A. J. Ward, Major Allen (standing), Lieutenant Colonel Fairchild, Adjutant C. K. Dean (standing), and Colonel O'Connor. The national color of the regiment is in the center foreground. The other flag identifies the regiment as the second regiment in Gibbon's brigade.

BRAWNER FARM TODAY. Photograph taken from the Warrenton Turnpike. The view is toward the north. The Brawner house and barn may be seen at the crest of the ridge at the left. The rectangular wood appears at the right. The Second Wisconsin and, later, the Nineteenth Indiana and Seventh Wisconsin advanced up this field to the crest of the ridge on which the fight occurred.

COMPANY C of the Second Wisconsin.

COMPANY I of the Seventh Wisconsin, Upton's Hill, Virginia, September, 1862.

THE DUNKER CHURCH at Antietam. The photograph is taken from slightly to the south of the church and looking toward the west. The West Woods, which extend to the north of the photograph (the right), appear behind the church. The Hagerstown Turnpike may be seen in front of the church. The action of the Iron Brigade was to the north, toward the right of the photograph.

THE FIRST DAY'S FIELD at Gettysburg. Taken by the Tyson brothers in 1863, this photograph looks west along the Chambersburg Pike, from the western edge of Gettysburg, toward the scene of the first day's battle. The seminary is plainly visible on the left. McPherson's Ridge is in the background, the horizon of the photograph. The railroad cut through the ridge is in the right background.

Kean Archives, Philadelphia

FROM THE CREST OF MCPHERSON'S RIDGE, looking west. An 1880's Tipton photograph along the Chambersburg Pike, looking west toward Herr Ridge. In the initial action, the Iron Brigade drove the Confederates westward from McPherson's Ridge and pursued them into the low ground between Mc-Pherson's and Herr Ridges, on the left of the photograph.

National Park Service

CONFEDERATE VIEW of the initial battleground at Gettysburg. The photograph looks toward the southeast and pictures the area south of the Chambersburg Pike, including the northern face of McPherson's Woods at the right. The cupola of the seminary may be seen in the background. In the initial action, the Iron Brigade advanced from the seminary into McPherson's Woods. There it met Archer's Brigade.

National Archives

FROM THE CREST OF MCPHERSON'S RIDGE, looking east. A late-nineteenth-century Tipton photograph looking eastward on the Chambersburg Pike, toward Gettysburg, from the crest of McPherson's Ridge. Seminary Ridge is visible just beyond the horse and carriage. During the afternoon of July 1, the Iron Brigade fought on the right side of the photograph, between the two ridges, ultimately making its final stand near the seminary, hidden by trees in this photograph.

THE RAILROAD CUT, LOOKING EAST. Taken many years after the battle, this photograph looks eastward, toward the town, and shows the railroad cut through McPherson's Ridge, north of the Chambersburg Pike. Davis Brigade of North Carolina and Mississippi regiments were trapped in the cut by the Sixth Wisconsin and the Iron Brigade Guard.

had then given way and had been pulled back by Wadsworth to Seminary Ridge, to re-form before facing the enemy again.[19]

The withdrawal of Cutler's regiments to the right of the railroad cut immediately endangered the entire Federal position. Between the pike and the cut the Second Maine battery was uncovered and soon virtually surrounded. "Feeling that if the position was too advanced for infantry it was equally so for artillery," the laconic report of the battery commander, the battery was retired to Seminary Ridge through a murderous fire from the railroad cut, which forced the abandonment of one of the Federal guns. Cutler's withdrawal on the right also opened the way to the rear of the regiments below the pike, the Fourteenth Brooklyn and the Ninety-fifth New York, which were already falling back, and the Iron Brigade, still farther to the left, and occupied with Archer's men. Davis' Brigade now seized this opening, pivoting on the pike and swinging to its right, toward the Federal rear. But Rufus Dawes' command was still available, 442 men representing all five of the Iron Brigade regiments,[20] posted at the seminary as the only reserve. On Doubleday's order, Dawes marched by the right flank at the double-quick, advancing directly toward the wheeling gray line. Riding at the head of his column, Dawes saw Cutler's men above the pike, "manifestly in full retreat," and the Maine battery driving for the rear. Then his horse was shot, and he was dashed to the ground in front of the regiment. But he was not hurt and, apparently inspired by his escape, the men loosed a mighty cheer as he scrambled to his feet and resumed his place at their head. And as the new blue line approached the pike, the veterans of the Ninety-fifth New York and the Brooklyn regiment saw it coming and, checking their backward movement, formed on the left of Dawes and moved with him toward the enemy.

Despite the heavy enemy fire, Dawes reported that his regiment held its fire and "kept up a steady double-quick, never faltering or breaking." At last reaching a fence along the pike, the Federals opened on the enemy, now but 175 yards away. Stung by this volley, Davis' men leaped for cover into the railroad cut. There the "kowardly sons of bitches"—the opinion of a charging Wisconsin soldier—joined others of their number who had used this route to outflank the Maine battery. From the cut the protected gray infantry poured a telling fire into the Federals, but, perhaps remembering the "something glorious" he had suggested to his sweetheart, Dawes ordered a charge and led the line over the fence and into the hail of bullets from the cut.

In the 150 yards between the pike and the cut, 160 of Dawes' men went down, among them the sleeping sentry whom Dawes had saved from a court-martial on the march to Pennsylvania and who now died in the advance. Down, too, went the colors of the Sixth, to be swept up each time and held aloft at the head of the line, where Dawes' urgent command, "Close up on the colors! Close up on the colors!" rang out over the hideous battle din. Behind the colors Dawes' men did close up, braving the terrible fire. At the cut they quickly extended their line along the edge, effectively trapping the enemy. At first the Confederates would not give up, and Dawes reported a "murderous skirmishing." He also described the frenzied struggle for possession of the flag of the Second Mississippi: "The rebel color was seen waving defiantly above the edge of the railroad cut. A heroic ambition to capture it took possession of several of our men. Corporal Eggleston . . . sprang forward to seize it, and was shot and mortally wounded. Private Anderson of his company, furious at the killing of his brave young comrade, recked little for the rebel color, but he swung aloft his musket and with a terrific blow split the skull of the rebel who had shot young Eggleston. . . . Lieutenant William N. Remington was shot and severely wounded . . . while rushing for the color. Into this deadly melee came Corporal Francis A. Waller, who seized and held the rebel battle flag." To him a Congressional Medal of Honor was later awarded. At last Davis' men, like Archer's before them, began to throw down their arms in surrender. To Dawes the commander of the Second Mississippi tendered his sword, and the youthful Federal later recorded that "I took the sword. It would have been the handsome thing to say, 'Keep your sword, sir,' but I was new to such occasions, and when six other officers came up and handed me their swords, I took them also." More important than the swords were the seven officers and 225 enlisted men who were taken, besides the gun of the Second Maine battery, which was restored to ownership of the United States.[21]

Hurled back on the right and on the left, the Confederates now were forced to reorganize, and the battle along McPherson's ridge died down. The Federals also re-formed. Buford's cavalrymen, some of whom had stayed to fight with the First Division, were placed on the extreme Federal left, toward the Hagerstown Road. Beside the Chambersburg Pike, Solomon Meredith withdrew his regiments, back across Willoughby Run and into McPherson's woods, with the Nineteenth Indiana now on the left and the Twenty-fourth, Seventh, and Second, respectively, extending the line along the western and northern fronts of the woods.[22] Farther north, Calef's horse battery again came forward, unlimbering between the pike and the railroad cut, where his guns were joined by the remnants of Dawes' regiment and the Fourteenth Brooklyn and Ninety-fifth New York from Cutler's command. Cutler's other three regiments also resumed their original position, completing the First Division's line along McPherson's ridge,[23] where the opening engagement had been so decisively settled in favor of the Union. Fighting on even terms numerically— except for artillery—the two Federal brigades had suffered severely. In the Iron Brigade, the Sixth and the Second Wisconsin had been badly hurt; 116 of the 302 men of the Second had been killed or wounded in McPherson's woods. But Archer's men had been decimated and driven from the field, and Division Commander Heth candidly described the condition of Davis' Brigade: "Every field officer save two were shot down, and its ranks terribly thinned . . . from its shattered condition it was not deemed advisable to bring it again into action on that day."[24]

In spite of their defeat, the activity of the Confederate artillery and skirmishers made it plain that the enemy had no intention of quitting the contest. But there was to be a lull of more than two hours before the battle was again joined.[25] During this period, it was up to Abner Doubleday, now commander on the field, to decide what the Federals should do. Despite the spectacular opening success, the tactical situation confronting Doubleday was much like that which Reynolds had earlier considered. In the likely event of a general engagement, the same numerical disadvantage existed and the same ground was there to defend. "Upon taking a retrospect of the field, it might seem, in view of fact that we were finally forced to retreat, that this would have been a proper time to retire," was Doubleday's later report. But although not a Pennsylvanian, Doubleday was a fighter, and he also recorded that he was influenced by the fact that "as General Reynolds, who was high in the confidence of General Meade, had formed his lines to resist the entrance of the enemy into Gettysburg, I naturally supposed that it was the intention to defend the place." And before the battle was renewed, General Howard arrived in the town, superseding Doubleday, but confirming his decision to stay and fight. With Howard came the Eleventh Corps, and the rest of the First Corps—the divisions of Robinson and Doubleday and four batteries. With instructions from Howard to hold Seminary Ridge at all hazards if driven from McPherson's ridge, the Federals reinforced their meager line, already threatened by the enemy's galling artillery and sharpshooter fire.[26]

Posting one division and three batteries of the Eleventh Corps on Cemetery Hill, to which place the Second Maine battery had already retired, Howard sent the First and Third divisions, each with a battery attached, to form along the semicircular extension of Seminary Ridge, north and northwest of the town. His left reached the Mummasburg Road, there forming an angle with the line of the First Corps, extending to the south. To the strengthening of this line, Doubleday now attended. He detached Robinson's Division and the Fifth Maine battery at the seminary as the corps reserve, with instructions to the infantry to prepare entrenchments in case the battle line should be retired. Dividing his own division, Doubleday sent Stone's Brigade, to which one of Rowley's regiments was shortly to be transferred, to Meredith's right, along the pike. Rowley's Brigade was placed on Meredith's other flank, to the left and rear of McPherson's woods, toward the Hagerstown Road. The remaining First Corps batteries were distributed along the line: the First Pennsylvania with Rowley on the left, Reynolds' New York guns to the relief of Calef's, between the pike and the railroad cut, and Battery B, behind Reynolds', directly north of the seminary, a half-battery on either side of the cut and positioned so as to sweep the pike.[27]

Once the new arrivals were in line, the Federals could only wait for the obviously mounting Confederate assault. For the Iron Brigade, this nerve-racking trial was relieved by the arrival in their midst of a curious recruit, John Burns, a resident of Gettysburg. Apparently a veteran of the War of 1812, this aged gentleman came out of the town carrying his own gun. His uniform was also his own, perhaps in part that of the earlier war, a dark, swallowtail coat with brass buttons and a curious hat remembered by the soldiers as "a high black

silk hat" or "bell crowned hat." Despite the soldiers' taunts and warn-
ings, old John Burns was not simply to be an onlooker. He had come
to fight. Directed to McPherson's woods, "I pitched in with them
Wisconsin fellers," he later told Frank Haskell. Whatever the humor
or quaintness of the event, a soldier recorded that John Burns' arrival
and the fact that he intended to stay "did much to create good feeling and stimulate the courage"[28] of the soldiers waiting for the
battle to resume.

The coming of John Burns did not, of course, have any influence
on the enemy organizing in front of the Federals. Rodes' Division of
Ewell's Corps was arriving opposite the Eleventh Corps. On the left
of Rodes, Early's Division was also coming up. In front of the
First Corps, the brigades of Heth's Division, minus Davis' remnants,
were disposed south of the pike, from left to right, Brockenbrough's
Virginians, Pettigrew's North Carolinians, and the survivors of
Archer's Brigade. Behind Heth's brigades were those of Pender's
Division, Thomas' Georgians north of the pike, and the brigades of
Scales, Perrin, and Lane, from left to right south of the pike.[29] And
at last, at 3:00 P.M., heralded by a sharp rise in artillery fire, the Confederate host began to advance all along the line. From their position
in the woods, the Western soldiers saw the enemy coming, "yelling
like demons," according to Colonel Morrow, two and three lines deep
and far outflanking the left of the Iron Brigade.[30] Although this overlapping line was bound to mean that the brigade's position was an
untenable one, General Meredith passed along Abner Doubleday's
stern mission: "The Iron Brigade would hold the woods at all
hazards."[31]

With the restraint of veteran soldiers, the Iron Brigade held its
fire as the onrushing Confederates swept forward. When they reached
Willoughby Run, the Western rifles opened, and the Confederates
at once responded, pouring a converging fire into the woods. But in
front of the Iron Brigade, "no rebel crossed that stream and lived,"
recorded the Nineteenth's Lieutenant Colonel Dudley, who was to
lose a leg in the initial onslaught. Solomon Meredith was also an
early casualty, crushed beneath his horse, which had been shot dead.
Another Hoosier officer, the Nineteenth's ambitious major, John M.
Lindley, was severely wounded, leaving Colonel Samuel J. Williams
alone among the field officers of the regiment, anchoring the brigade's

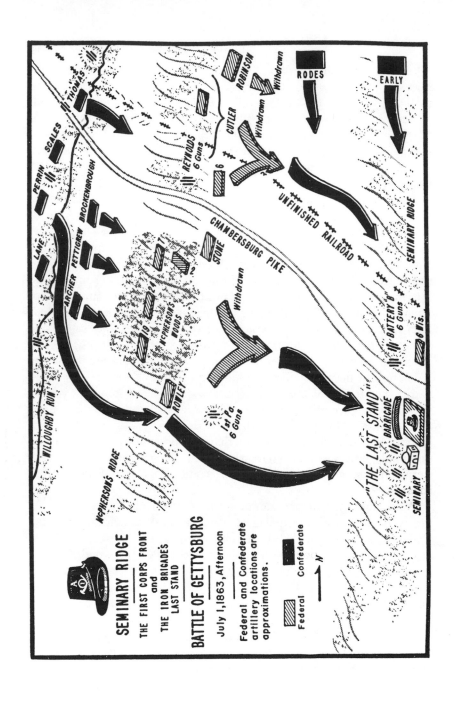

SEMINARY RIDGE

THE FIRST CORPS FRONT
and
THE IRON BRIGADE'S LAST STAND

BATTLE OF GETTYSBURG

July 1, 1863, Afternoon

Federal and Confederate artillery locations are approximations.

Federal

Confederate

N

left in the woods.[32] Still the Iron Brigade fought on, their front apparently impregnable, as the enemy's second line gradually passed farther to the Federal left, overpowering Rowley's regiments[33] and at last opening the Indiana regiment to a fatal enfilade. Losing heavily, "their dead . . . thick upon the ground," the Hoosier line was gradually bent backward, and the raking enemy fire spread to the right, into the flank of the Twenty-fourth Michigan, the Seventh, and the Second. Down went the Seventh's Lieutenant Colonel Callis, severely wounded, as did the old volunteer John Burns, who was to be three times wounded before the day was done and to whom Doubleday's official report would extend "thanks . . . especially due."[34]

Unable to resist the Confederates now in front and around their left, the Westerners were ordered to withdraw to a line in the eastern edge of the woods, where they again stood to face the overwhelming foe, "every tree . . . a breastwork, every log a barricade, every bush a cover," according to a Wisconsin soldier. The commander of Pettigrew's Confederates described the renewed resistance: "On this second line, the fighting was terrible—our men advancing, the enemy stubbornly resisting, until the two lines were pouring volleys into each other at a distance not greater than 20 paces." But again the combined frontal and flank assault was too much, and another backward movement was ordered from the line which, according to General Heth, the Iron Brigade's dead "marked . . . with the accuracy of a . . . dress parade."[35] Withdrawing "step by step, contesting every foot of ground," the black hats moved this time to a ravine in the low ground between McPherson's and Seminary Ridge. Again the enemy advanced, out of the woods which they had so dearly purchased, down the slopes in front of the Iron Brigade. Changing fronts between rounds so as to cope with the flank assault as well as that from the front, the Westerners fought on, every minute increasing the devastation in their ranks.[36] In the Twenty-fourth Michigan, Morrow now saw Major Wight fall, leaving the colonel alone among that regiment's field officers. Three of his color-bearers were already dead and almost three-fourths of all of his men killed and wounded. Momentarily doubting the survivors' staying power—out in the open and caught between the Confederates' fire—Morrow directed the fourth color guard to plant the flag so that his remnants could rally around it. At once the willing soldier was shot down, and Morrow himself seized the riddled banner. Insisting that while he was alive the colonel would not carry the flag, an eager private now took the staff from Morrow. He was immediately shot dead, and Morrow again held the flag aloft until another soldier took it. But he, too, was shot, and again the flag became Morrow's precious burden as the storm continued and the Westerners held on in their hopeless position between the ridges.[37]

While Meredith's soldiers were battling south of the pike, the fighting to the north had been just as furious. There Rodes' and Early's divisions had been hurled against the Eleventh Corps and the right flank of Doubleday's line, to which place both brigades of Robinson's Division, the First Corps reserve, had been sent. Although suffering tremendous loss, the Confederates had maintained their attack, driving south through the Eleventh Corps, through Robinson's Division, and into the flank of the brigades of Cutler and Stone, who were also contending manfully in their front with Pender's left flank along the pike. Against immense odds the Federals fought with desperation, but they were slowly overpowered and, the Eleventh Corps having given way, Doubleday was forced to withdraw his right to Seminary Ridge as the enemy swept over the railroad cut and reached the pike. Now the Iron Brigade was flanked on its right as well as its left, compelling Wadsworth's order for the withdrawal to Seminary Ridge.[38]

Despite their appalling losses and the increasing pressure from three sides, the Western survivors were still soldiers, and organizationally intact. In the midst of the hellish gunfire, they received the order to withdraw, and Colonel Robinson reported that the regiments "retired by the right of companies to the rear some . . . yards, halted, and wheeled into line again. . . . Then again retired about the same distance, and again wheeled into line, and so on until . . . [they] reached the foot of Seminary ridge." As they moved up the ridge, presenting an open target to the enemy, their casualties increased, among them Colonel Morrow, acting color sergeant for the Twenty-fourth, whose loss left Captain Albert M. Edwards in command.[39] But near the crest, north of the seminary and forty yards south of the pike, was a barricade of rails which Robinson's Division had earlier prepared. Nearby was the Fifth Maine battery, and to its left, supported by Rowley's infantry survivors, were other guns from the First Pennsylvania and Reynolds' New York batteries which had preceded the infantry in the withdrawal.[40] Ordered to hold the ridge as long as possible, "the shattered remnants of the Iron Brigade"—Doubleday's description—moved in behind the barricade to face the onslaught to come.[41]

The enemy's advance was not long delayed, with Confederates from Heth's, Pender's, and Rodes' divisions, on both sides of the pike, again striking obliquely against both flanks as well as the front of the Iron Brigade's position. Marshaling their depleted energy and ammunition, the Western men and the Maine cannoneers held their fire until the Confederates had begun their ascent of the ridge. Then they fired, the artillery booming "as if every lanyard was pulled by the same hand."[42] To one of the onrushing enemy, the Federal barricade seemed "a sheet of fire and smoke, sending its leaden missiles . . . in the faces of men who had often, but never so terribly, met it before." To the eyes of Colonel Robinson, the Confederate "ranks went down like grass before the scythe."[43] An advancing North Carolina lieutenant had a similar impression: "The earth just seemed to open and take in that line which five minutes ago was so perfect." And Scales confessed that "our line had been broken up, and now only a squad here and there marked the place where regiments had rested."[44]

But despite their losses, the enemy's advance was only checked. Quickly re-forming, the gray soldiers again pressed forward, always compressing their line and forming what Colonel Robinson, with the Seventh Wisconsin on the left flank, saw as "three sides of a square around us." On the brigade's other flank, Major Mansfield, commanding the Second Wisconsin, joined the ranks of the wounded, reporting almost apologetically that "being unable to remain standing, I was taken to temporary shelter." This left Captain George H. Otis in command of the Second. Beside him Private Patrick Maloney, General Archer's captor, was shot dead.[45] Between the Wisconsin regiments, standing among their fallen, were the Indiana and Michigan survivors. The flag of the Michigan regiment had disappeared in the uproar, but Captain Edwards found it inside the barricade, gripped in the arms of a dying soldier. Close at hand was another wounded man from Michigan, a sergeant, disabled so that he could not hold a rifle. But with one hand and his teeth, he was still in the fight, tearing cartridges for his comrades still able to fire.[46] Nearby, too, was the Seventh's Captain Hollon Richardson, attached to Meredith's staff and representing the brigade command on the field. Mounted and waving the Seventh's flag, the man whom Colonel Robinson had not wanted in his family rode calmly up and down the line, presenting himself as an open target above the barricade.[47]

In Abner Doubleday's words, "From behind the feeble barricade of rails these brave men stemmed the fierce tide which pressed upon them incessantly, and held the rebel lines . . . at bay until the greater portion of the corps had retired." The Maine guns were surely a large factor in this performance, but to Confederate Colonel Abner Perrin it was also "the most destructive fire of musketry I have ever been exposed to." Of his own South Carolina regiment, Perrin wrote that it "was staggered . . . by the severity and destructiveness of the enemy's musketry. It looked . . . as though this [my] regiment was entirely destroyed."[48] But Doubleday knew that "it was no longer possible to answer" the growing assault on the left of the brigade, and in Wadsworth's words, "Outflanked on both right and left, heavily pressed in front, and my ammunition nearly exhausted, . . . I ordered the command to retire." Although in the very face of the enemy, again the withdrawal was orderly. All but one gun of the artillery was drawn off,[49] the infantry following by the right of companies to the rear, then by the right flank by file left into column, onto the pike. The last to go was the Seventh Wisconsin, and by the time it reached the road the Confederate flanking columns had closed along the pike, extending parallel to it and creating a gauntlet of fire. Sadly Colonel Robinson saw his brave survivors cut down, "men falling at every step, [and] many . . . taken prisoner." Among the last-minute casualties was the regiment's color sergeant, struck by a charge of grape and canister at the edge of the town, the flag staff splintered to pieces in his hands. The tattered emblem was the original regimental flag, and the sergeant, who had borne it in every battle from Brawner Farm, would not give it up now. The shattered soldier was picked up by his comrades and placed on a caisson moving ahead of the regiment. He continued to wave the banner as the regiment moved through the town.[50]

While their comrades south of the pike had been engaged in their desperate struggle, Battery B and the Sixth Wisconsin had been in the second line above the pike. On Seminary Ridge, astride the railroad cut directly north of the Iron Brigade's final barricade, the artillerists had seen the First Corps slowly overpowered and, as Doubleday withdrew his right, they had been joined by the Eleventh Pennsylvania and the Sixth Wisconsin, who had retired through the railroad cut to their support. Then the gunners had suffered the agonizing wait while the Confederates re-formed. At last, with its heavy line extending in an arc that would surely flank the guns on both sides, the enemy came on and "the old Battery's turn had come again," as its historian recorded.[51]

"First we could see the tips of their color-staffs coming up over the little ridge, then the points of their bayonets, and then the Johnnies themselves, coming on with a steady tramp, tramp, and with loud yells." Waiting for effective range, the men of the battery also began to shout at the advancing enemy and at each other, words of encouragement passing from gun to gun. Then came the command: " 'Load—Canister—Double!' There was a hustling of Cannoneers, a few thumps of the rammer-heads, and then 'Ready!—By piece!—At will!—Fire! !' " Like "chain-lightning . . . in one solid streak" the guns opened and the approaching gray lines staggered and broke in fragments. But quickly re-forming, they advanced again, breasting the canister and the rifles of Dawes' regiment and their Pennsylvania comrades, and pouring a terrible converging fire into the guns. Forced to change front frequently because of the alternating thrusts, the cannoneers worked furiously, one man taking over a comrade's duties as the latter slumped to the ground. An early casualty was Lieutenant James Davison, commanding the left half-battery and responsible for the defense of the Chambersburg Pike. Bleeding from two desperate wounds and with one ankle shattered, Davison stayed erect, held up by one of his soldiers, "his eagle face lit with the battle flames, his arm outstretched, and his strong voice still ringing out above the crash." Under his urgings the gunners continued to rake the slowly encircling enemy line and wheeled to protect the pike which "from our second round on a gray squirrel could not have crossed . . . alive."

The historian of the battery has described the climax:

How those peerless Cannoneers sprang to their work! . . . "Old Griff" [Wallace], his tough Irish face set in hard lines with the unflinching resolution that filled his soul . . . he sponged and loaded under that murderous musketry with the precision of barrack drill; . . . the burly corporal, bareheaded, his hair matted with blood from a scalp wound, and wiping the crimson fluid out of his eyes to sight the gun; . . . the steady Orderly Sergeant, John Mitchell, moving calmly from gun to gun, now and then changing men about as one after another was hit and fell, stooping over a wounded man to help him up, or aiding another to stagger to the rear; . . . the dauntless Davison on foot among the guns, cheering the men, praising this one and that one, and ever anon profanely exhorting us to "Feed it to 'em, God damn 'em; feed it to 'em!" . . . Up and down the line men reeling and falling; splinters flying from wheels and axles where bullets hit; in rear, horses tearing and plunging, mad with wounds or terror; drivers yelling, shells bursting, shot shrieking overhead, howling about our ears or throwing up great clouds of dust where they struck; the musketry crashing on three sides of us; bullets hissing, humming and whistling everywhere; cannon roaring; all crash on crash . . . , smoke, dust, splinters, blood, wreck and carnage indescribable; but the brass guns of old B still bellowed and not a man or boy flinched or faltered![52]

This incredible effort had its effect, repeatedly driving the Confederates back and piling up their dead around the battery. Electrified by the frenzy around them, the Sixth Wisconsin poured in volley after volley, screaming, "Come on, Johnny! Come on!" at the surging foe each time that a charge was dashed to pieces. But overwhelmed by numbers and with their rear opened by the Eleventh Corps' defeat, time, not victory, was all that the Federals could gain, and at last the Sixth Wisconsin and the battery were ordered to withdraw.[53]

Except for one of his men who had moved into the battery and was serving a gun, Dawes faced his regiment to the rear and marched in line of battle over the open fields toward the northern outskirts of the town, the men turning and firing at will at the Confederates who undertook pursuit.[54] For Battery B, forced to limber up when almost surrounded, the moment was as critical as Antietam. But, apparently stunned by the fire and not realizing that the guns were without infantry support, the Confederates refrained from charging, and concentrated instead on pouring in a bitter fire. Although horses, drivers, and cannoneers were falling on all sides, Davison's left half-battery finally got away, careening through the hail of bullets to the pike. On the other side of the railroad cut, Stewart directed the right half-battery, the men cutting wounded horses out of the traces and at last driving east across the field north of the cut, crossing the grading where it ran on level ground, and reaching the pike in the rear of the left half-battery. Stewart stayed on the field until the last gun of his half-battery was away. Unaware that Davison had extricated his guns, Stewart then rode to his left to help Davison, and found himself among the Confederates who now occupied the ground where the left half-battery had been. Called on to surrender, Stewart spurred his horse instead, surged through an opening in the encircling enemy line, and jumped a fence. As he did so, a shell fragment found him, inflicting a painful wound in the thigh. A hundred yards farther on Stewart dismounted, overcome by nausea and almost unconscious. But after bathing his face in a puddle of water, the artilleryman was again able to mount, and rode to the pike and headed for the town. On his way he found one of his caissons wrecked in the road, its rear axle broken. There, too, was one of his men, a private, who was still fighting according to the regulations, destroying the charges in the ammunition so that the enemy could not use it. The commander stayed with the enlisted man until the demolition was done; then the two mounted Stewart's horse and caught up with the battery in the outskirts of Gettysburg.[55]

As Battery B entered the town, the artillerymen sighted an old friend, Colonel Lucius Fairchild, seated on the porch of a house beside the pike. The colonel's left arm had been amputated since the morning, but he waved his other arm and cheered the gunners as they rode by. Passing through the mass of infantry moving into the town, the battery proceeded up Cemetery Hill. There General Hancock, now the commander on the field, personally directed Stewart to place his guns in front of the cemetery gate and to remain there until he himself relieved him. In the turmoil of the next two days Hancock doubtless forgot the order, and he never relieved Stewart, whose guns were to remain where they were until the morning of July 5th.

Although all six of "old B's" Napoleons had reached Cemetery Hill, the battery had suffered severely, its casualties surpassed by only one other Federal battery in the three-day fight. Out of ninety men, seven were dead or dying and, counting several who had "tied up their own wounds with tent-cloths, or whatever rags they could get," twenty-nine more were wounded. Of the horses, twelve had been killed outright and several others were so badly hurt that the soldiers had to destroy them, for which unpleasant duty the battery historian remembered that his mates borrowed pistols because their own had been emptied in defending the guns during the withdrawal. Of the

six guns, two were disabled and out of action, and four caissons had
been abandoned with axles or wheels shot off. But all of this was
simply evidence of the glorious ordeal on Seminary Ridge. Years later
the battery historian indignantly refuted a then current anecdote
which reported that a Confederate officer had actually put his hand
on one of Battery B's guns: "No Rebel hand was ever laid on any gun
of Stewart's Battery in any battle . . . , from Bull Run to Appomattox.
. . . It was always our proudest boast that she was a virgin battery!
Because, though in battle many times, and in the wide-open jaws of
death more than once, not one of her bright guns had ever been
defiled by the touch of a Rebel hand!" The battery historian also
proudly recorded of that terrible first day at Gettysburg: "It [the bat-
tery] stood its ground till all the rest were gone, and . . . Stewart
was the last man to leave the Union position on Seminary Ridge,
anywhere west of the Seminary itself."[56]

While Battery B was moving to the cemetery, the Iron Brigade,
with the Seventh's Colonel Robinson in command but still minus
the Sixth Wisconsin,[57] was making its way through the town, now a
bedlam of confusion. Early's Division and a portion of Rodes' Division had already entered the town in pursuit of the Eleventh Corps,
and Heth's and Pender's battered regiments were also streaming in
from the west and northwest. "The streets were jammed with crowds
of retreating soldiers, and with ambulances, artillery, and wagons,"
but there was no disorganization in the ranks of the Iron Brigade,
which threaded its way through the mass, occasionally losing a man
to the scattered enemy skirmish firing while others, wounded or exhausted, were cut off and captured.[58] At the center of the town,
Robinson turned his column to the south and proceeded by way of
the Emmitsburg Road to Cemetery Hill. There the men promptly
re-formed and were ready for service, as Abner Doubleday, who was
feverishly organizing a line to defend the hill, has recorded. The
brigade was at first a part of this line, in front of the Emmitsburg
Road and facing to the west. But as the enemy prolonged his left,
the Westerners were dispatched to Culp's Hill, east of the cemetery,
in support of a battery defending that ground.[59]

Although the survivors of four of the Iron regiments had reached
the new Federal position, the Sixth Wisconsin was still not accounted
for. Marching north of the pike, Dawes had run directly into the

Confederates sweeping in wild pursuit against the Eleventh Corps. Just in time, he had realized the situation and turned away from the enemy. Despite the fire of the gray sharpshooters and the great fatigue of his men, Dawes kept them together around the colors as they entered the town, proceeding due east until met by a heavy enemy column. Then the Sixth turned south, only to find the first cross street swept by the rifles of the enemy. This required a unique maneuver which Dawes was later to describe: "There was a close board fence, enclosing a barnyard, on the opposite side of the street. A board or two off from the fence made what the man called a 'hog-hole.' Instructing the regiment to follow in single file on the run, I took a color, ran across the street, and jumped through this opening in the fence. Officers and men followed rapidly. Taking position at the fence, when any man obstructed the passage-way through it, I jerked him away without ceremony or apology . . . to keep the track clear for those yet to come. Two men were shot in this street crossing." Re-forming in the barnyard, the regiment again started for the hill beyond, now harassed by rifle fire from the houses and cross-lots. Dawes' men attempted to reply to this fire, but fearful that his exhausted survivors would never escape, Dawes drove them on. Here another volunteer appeared, a man as old as John Burns, but armed with buckets of fresh water instead of a gun. Thus refreshed (Dawes long remembered "the inestimable value of this cup of cold water"), the Sixth renewed its bid for safety, halting only once more, this time to give three hearty and defiant cheers for "the old Sixth and the good cause." At last arriving at Cemetery Hill, the Sixth was ordered by Wadsworth to rejoin the brigade on Culp's Hill, where, Dawes reported, "after a short breathing spell my men again promptly responded to the order to 'fall in'" and joined in the business of intrenching.[60]

From Cemetery Hill, the Federal survivors could look down on the field they had so bitterly contested, now the property of the enemy. But although in possession of the field, the Confederates had been severely hurt. As for the Iron Brigade's particular opponents, in Heth's Division, where that general was among the wounded, Archer's and Davis' brigades had been almost solely accounted for by the Western soldiers. Brockenbrough's Brigade had also suffered heavily, while in Pettigrew's two of four colonels were killed and wounded and one regiment, the Twenty-sixth North Carolina, closed the day with 216 survivors out of 800 men who had assailed the First Division. In Pender's Division the reports were equally sanguinary. Perrin's Brigade counted 500 men killed and wounded, and Scales' Brigade, also the victim of Battery B's fury, had seen General Scales himself shot down, "every field officer of the brigade save one," and a total of 545 killed, wounded, and missing. Reporting candidly on the condition of the brigade when he took command at the close of the day, Scales' successor found it "depressed, dilapidated, and almost unorganized . . . [with] but few line officers, and many companies . . . without a single officer."[61]

In Confederate hands below Cemetery Hill were most of the Federal wounded, now prisoners of war. The Seventh's Lieutenant Colonel Callis was overlooked by the enemy—he lay wounded on McPherson's ridge for forty-three hours—but Colonel Fairchild and Colonel Morrow were prisoners, although Morrow, acting as an unofficial assistant to the regimental surgeons, was granted freedom to work among the Federal wounded. In this capacity the gentle Morrow suffered the heartbreak of visiting his shattered soldiers, more than one of whom greeted him with the question, "Colonel, ain't you proud of the Twenty-fourth now?"[62] Another wounded man from the brigade, a sergeant of the Sixth, was the custodian of the captured flag of the Second Mississippi. Having fainted in the streets of the town before the Federal withdrawal, he was rescued by two young women who put him to bed in their house. When the Confederates entered the town, the sergeant was captured but his trophy was saved, secreted in the bed tick by the two young women. As in every disaster, there were beasts of prey at Gettysburg, including a farmer who charged twelve dollars to a group of wounded Indiana soldiers who begged a ride in the farmer's wagon. But the women who protected the captured Confederate battle flag were of a different sort. And after the Confederates had retreated, the wounded sergeant, released from captivity, was to salvage the flag and deliver it to Rufus Dawes on Culp's Hill. Other wounded Federals were also to be abandoned by the enemy and to trek wearily up Cemetery Hill after the Confederate withdrawal, to rejoin comrades who had given them up for dead. Among them were Colonel Fairchild and Colonel Morrow. Another was Dan Ackerman of the Seventh Wisconsin, detached to Battery B, and his welcome was no less affecting than those accorded the regimental commanders. Although his "own leg was so badly hurt he could hardly stand," when Lieutenant Stewart saw Ackerman limping up the hill on July 4th, the lieutenant struggled to his feet and "put his arms around Dan's neck and gave him a good hug in the presence of the Battery, or what was left of it!"[63] But many Western soldiers were not to rejoin their comrades. Fifty-seven from the Twenty-fourth Michigan were only an example of the men who were to be taken to the South as prisoners. On the way to the prison camps the Confederates were to lose at least one more Iron Brigade soldier, the drum major of the Sixth, who escaped in Virginia and rejoined his regiment by floating down the Shenandoah River on a saw log, hiding in the daytime and floating only at night.[64]

Despite their demonstrations in front of Cemetery Hill and Culp's Hill, the victorious Confederates did not assail the Federal survivors posted there, and at last the bloody day of July 1st drew to a close. During the night the rest of the Army of the Potomac was to arrive at Gettysburg, concentrating along what later writers were to picture as a "fishhook" turned upside down: from Culp's Hill and Cemetery Hill, down Cemetery Ridge, and to Little Round Top to the south. There on the next two days was to be waged the greatest battle of the war, during which Lee's army was heavily defeated in its assaults against the Federal positions. The Sixth Wisconsin was to be briefly engaged on July 2nd on Culp's Hill, losing two more of its men. Battery B was also briefly in action, and five more of the battery were struck by artillery and long-range rifle fire, and a caisson was blown up by a direct enemy hit.[65] But the storied fights at Culp's Hill, the Wheat Field, the Peach Orchard, Little Round Top, and "the little clump of trees" were to be but anticlimax to the men of the First Corps. For them the battle of Gettysburg was the first day. Fighting largely in the open, "with no other protection than the flannel blouses that covered their stout hearts," the First Corps counted casualties of more than 6,000 of its 9,403 men. This was 2,000 more than the losses of the Eleventh Corps, 2,000 more than Sickles was to lose the next day in the Wheat Field and the Peach Orchard, and 2,000 more than the Second Corps was to give up in defending the Federal center against Pickett's assault. Surely the veterans of the First Corps could be pardoned for feeling that too much emphasis was later placed on the last two days of the battle, when the Federals had the edge in manpower and the advantage of the ground.[66]

As was required by its proud name, leading the casualty list for the entire army during the three-day battle was the Iron Brigade, which had learned at Brawner Farm to stand and fight without regard to the odds. As the Seventh's Major Mansfield proudly reported, it had shown again "cool indifference to danger and long continued and stubborn resistance, resulting from hard-earned experience and thorough discipline." Wrote Colonel Henry A. Morrow, "The field over which we fought, from our first line of battle in McPherson's woods to the barricade near the seminary, was strewn with the killed and wounded."[67] This was not an exaggeration. Of the 1,883 Western men who had marched up the Emmitsburg Road that morning, 1,212 (65 per cent) were casualties, of whom the great majority were killed and wounded. The Second Wisconsin had lost 77 per cent of its numbers and the Nineteenth Indiana 72 per cent. In the Seventh and Sixth Wisconsin the percentages were 52 per cent and 48 per cent. But as if to make up for its late joining of the brigade with the black hats, the Twenty-fourth Michigan showed casualties of *80 per cent*, giving it the melancholy honor of the highest loss of any Federal regiment for the three days at Gettysburg.[68]

The casualties among the officers in Morrow's command were set forth in his report: "Col. Henry A. Morrow, scalp wound; Lieut. Col. Mark Flanigan, lost leg; Maj. Edwin B. Wight, lost an eye; Capt. William H. Rexford, severely in leg; Capt. William W. Wight, slightly in leg; Capt. William Hutchinson, contusion on leg; Capt. Richard S. Dillon, severely in leg; Capt. Chas. A. Hoyt, severely in leg; Lieut. John M. Farland, wounded by fall; Lieut. William R. Dodsley, slightly wounded; Lieut. Abraham Earnshaw, wounded in side; Lieut. Frederick A. Buhl, severely in thigh; Lieut. Edwin E. Norton, slightly; Lieut. Michael Dempsey, slightly. The officers killed were: Capts. William J. Speed and Malachi J. O'Donnell; Lieuts. Walter H. Wallace, Winfield S. Safford, Newell Grace, Reuben H. Humphreville, Gilbert A. Dickey, and Lucius L. Shattuck." All of this meant that of the twenty-five officers of the regiment, one captain and two lieutenants remained.[69] The officers of the brigade as a whole had not, of course, fared much better than the Michigan men. Solomon Meredith was a casualty, and of the fourteen field officers only five were left, Colonel Robinson and Major Finnicum of the Seventh, Colonel Williams of the Nineteenth and Dawes and Major Hauser of the Sixth. The fact that there were just enough officers on their feet to handle the skeleton remaining was of no comfort. But it was true. Thus in the Twenty-fourth Michigan, a total of 97 men stood together on Culp's Hill, about the strength of a company, while some companies in the brigade mustered exactly three men. Sadly, Major John Mansfield reported that "from such a record I may be spared from making what seems the usual commonplace remark, 'that both officers and men behaved well.' "[70]

Waiting for the night to close over the scene of their battle, the survivors of the First Corps maintained their morale and organization, in spite of the casualties and the Confederates' possession of the field. There were, of course, good reasons for the soldiers' equilibrium. As one of them later wrote, "The rawest recruit in the ranks could see that the new position was much stronger than the old one . . . the old First had covered itself with glory, and every man in its ranks knew it. They were not whipped or defeated; they did not feel that they had been beaten, because they knew that they had held their ground against superior numbers; that they had punished the enemy terribly, and that they had finally made an orderly and respectable retreat to a much stronger and better position." A spokesman for the Iron Brigade could also have said this for the Westerners: Although overwhelmed by force of numbers, *not a single backward step had been taken except on orders.* Summing up the spirit of the First Corps, the historian of Battery B reflected that they "were actually in better heart at the end of the first day than at the beginning. At all events we knew that we had done as desperate work as ever befell an army corps, and were almost as proud of the record as we would have been of a victory."[71]

There was independent evidence of the spirit of the First Corps that night on Cemetery Hill and Culp's Hill, evidence in addition to the words of the soldiers themselves. Thus the men were exceedingly and vocally annoyed when it was announced that General John Newton, a division commander from the Sixth Corps, was to supersede Doubleday in command of the First Corps. Although personally austere and unspectacular, the soldiers correctly understood that Doubleday, "in handling the corps that day . . . displayed skill and courage which the dullest private could not help commending; and he had, moreover, exposed himself all day in plain sight of the troops with a reckless gallantry." Doubleday was also a *First Corps man,* "entitled to command of the corps," so far as the soldiers were concerned.[72] Another incident went into the record to illustrate the indomitable mood of the Western soldiers. Commanding the Twenty-fourth Michigan, Captain Albert M. Edwards issued a formal address to his regiment, 97 strong. Perhaps the captain had read in a manual that this was the thing to do on the occasion of accession to command. Whatever the source of the idea, Edwards did a good job of it, in words that became a University of Michigan man with a newspaper background:

All the field officers of this regiment having been wounded, and the senior captains killed or wounded, I hereby assume command. . . . I congratulate you, brave soldiers, upon your splendid achievements of July 1. . . . The enemy's dead in front of your lines attest your valor and skill. Again you have merited a nation's gratitude; again you have shown yourselves worthy of the noble state you represent and the glorious cause for which you are fighting. Our joy in the glory of our arms is mingled with sadness for the heroic dead on the field of honor. Let the memory of our lamented comrades inspire your hearts with new life and zeal to emulate their heroic virtues and avenge their untimely fall.[73]

While the Federal army moved into position around them, the Westerners at last settled down on the uneven ground of Culp's Hill for the "troubled and dreamy sleep . . . that comes to the soldier on a battle field."[74] For them one of the troublesome questions concerned the future of their own organization. With only 600 men in its ranks could the Iron Brigade maintain its identity? Referring simply to the barricade of rails on Seminary Ridge, but unconsciously answering this question, Abner Doubleday reported that "the Iron Brigade here made their final stand." And what had the brigade accomplished in pouring out so much blood on July 1, 1863, at Gettysburg? In his report, General Meade was to write, "I determined to give battle at this point."[75] But it was John F. Reynolds, and later Abner Doubleday, who had decided to fight at Gettysburg, and it was the Iron Brigade and its First Corps comrades who had determined the matter, by their dogged, desperate fighting, which had permitted Federal possession of the key ground and had purchased the time for the Army of the Potomac to concentrate. These were the factors—superior numbers and position—that made the victory. Historians were later to debate the decisiveness of Gettysburg, made possible by the soaring Federal effort on the first day. But Gettysburg forever robbed Lee's army of its offensive power, and thereby fixed the ultimate Federal strategy, both East and West. And for at least one hundred years, the word *Gettysburg* was to have a unique meaning for Americans, rivaled only by two other names, *Lexington* and *Concord*, where the American story had begun. The Iron Brigade from the Old Northwest had been there, and there it had made its final stand.

"MINE EYES HAVE SEEN THE GLORY OF THE COMING OF THE LORD"

"The Iron Brigade has a record . . . and . . . with the inducement of pride, duty, patriotism and personal preservation, they will stand together till the last."

From the Journal of Rufus Dawes, 1863

EPILOGUE

There was celebration in the North on July 4, 1863. For the traditional occasion of Independence Day the Federal armies had contributed solid triumphs, at Gettysburg, Vicksburg and, of lesser renown, at Helena, Arkansas, where a Confederate assault had been repulsed. So bright were the prospects for the Union that the soldiers were thinking tentatively of peace. "If we can end this war right here, I will cheerfully abide the terrible risk of another battle," wrote a veteran of the Iron Brigade. But the war was far from ended, and on July 13th the Army of Northern Virginia recrossed the Potomac, an event which plainly foretold the continuation of the contest. The Army of the Potomac followed the Confederates, back to the familiar battlefields along the Rappahannock and the Rapidan. There for nine months the two great adversaries were to be often in close proximity and occasionally arrayed for battle. But until May of 1864, the war in Virginia was to be one of maneuver, unmarked by a major engagement.[1]

The Iron Brigade was part of the army in the pursuit of the Confederates from Gettysburg to Virginia. But the march had hardly begun when, on July 16th, at the Potomac River, a new regiment was incorporated into the brigade. Sentiment to the contrary, there was, of course, good reason for reinforcing the depleted Westerners, and the new regiment, with 800 men on its rolls, more than doubled the strength of the brigade.[2] But had the army tried its best, its selection could not have been more incongruous. From the Seventh Corps, previously stationed at White House, came the 167th Pennsylvania—*Easterners, nine months' men, draftees,* whose term was about to expire.[3] In addition to these disqualifications, the Pennsylvanians were a hopelessly undisciplined lot and mutiny was almost their first act of membership in the brigade. With the complicity of their officers —also conscripts and elected by the men—the Pennsylvanians refused to march on August 1st, claiming that their enlistments had expired. The Western soldiers were promptly assembled and the commands "Ready!" and "Aim!" were actually given before their new brothers-in-arms changed their minds. After this, the Sixth Wisconsin was placed behind the 167th, and Rufus Dawes was instructed to shoot any man who fell out of the ranks. Unwilling to exercise this authority, Dawes deployed one company which, in his words, "drove them up when they lagged," a maneuver which prompted the label "cattle," applied by the proud—and now deeply resentful—soldiers of the Iron Brigade. Fortunately for the Westerners the association with the new regiment was of short duration. In mid-August the Pennsylvanians were withdrawn from the brigade and, their term having by then expired, they were sent home and mustered out. But the place of the Pennsylvanians was at once taken by another organization, the First Battalion New York Sharpshooters, also from the Seventh Corps, three-year men who were to fight with the soldiers in the black hats throughout most of 1864.[4] Although some of the men of the Iron Brigade were to remain in the field until Appomattox, and the vaunted name of the brigade was to continue in use until the end of the war, the Iron Brigade was never the same after July 16, 1863, when its ranks were joined by the unlikely 167th Pennsylvania, the first in a succession of strangers whose presence forever destroyed the identity of the unique Western organization.[5]

In addition to the strange Eastern regiments, there were other newcomers during the period after Gettysburg. These were the recruits—volunteers, draftees, and substitutes—who began to report in heavy numbers and who were to continue to come until the end of the war. The draftees were broadly scorned by the old volunteers who saw them indiscriminately as "a sorry looking set," "hounds," and "thoroughly despised." In some cases these judgments were doubtless just, but a veteran of the Sixth Wisconsin was later grudgingly to acknowledge that the Sixth's drafted men fought courageously in the closing battles. The volunteer recruits were not, of course, treated with the scorn accorded to the conscripts, although the veterans drew invidious comparisons between the volunteers of 1861 and the volunteers of 1863. Among the latter the most unusual were fourteen Indians, "wild from the woods," who were assigned to the Seventh Wisconsin. Although they could not speak English, they were to compensate for this inconvenience in the Wilderness, an admiring officer reporting that they "covered their bodies very ingeniously with pine bows to conceal themselves in the woods," to which tactic they added a genuine war whoop delivered on appropriate occasions. But whatever their merits or shortcomings, the soldiers who joined the army after Gettysburg—even those from the West—were largely a different breed from the earlier "enthusiastic and eager volunteers"[6] who had become the Iron Brigade, and the wholesale arrival of the newcomers was only another aspect of the dissolution of the Western organization.

In spite of the formal demise of the Iron Brigade, the public reputation of the Western men was secure because of their accomplishments at Gettysburg. An enterprising music publisher brought forth the "Iron Brigade Quickstep," and although Rufus Dawes believed that the score "was not worthy of its name," the march was doubtless sounded "con spirito" on the pianos in Northern parlors.[7] More gratifying to the soldiers than the "Quickstep" was an Iron Brigade flag, commissioned in honor of the brigade by citizens from Wisconsin, Indiana and Michigan residing in Washington. September 17th, the anniversary of Antietam, was set aside for the formal presentation of the color, and elaborate preparations were made in the camps of the Westerners along the Rappahannock. As described by the historian of the Michigan regiment, "a large evergreen arch was erected with the words 'Iron Brigade' and 'Welcome Guests' underneath. To the rear of the arch ran an embowered hall, 100 feet, for the banquet, and the leaves and underbrush were cleared away for the . . . assemblage," which was to include prominent officers of the army and political notables from the three states. Even more appropriate was the plan for the participation of the enlisted men of the brigade, who were also to be feted, the officers having contributed $1,000 to pay the cost of the soldiers' party. But on the eve of the big day, the brigade was suddenly moved to Culpeper, where, on September 19th, the flag caught up and was presented in considerably curtailed ceremonies, featuring a speech by the spokesman for the donors, and a response by Colonel Robinson, the acting commander. The officers then repaired to a banquet where champagne was served amidst the speeches of General Newton and Colonels Morrow and Bragg. Although the enlisted men were not formally included in this impromptu festival, they ate and drank "what they could swipe, which was no small amount," according to one of their number. And in any event, the flag was acquired by the "First Brigade of the First Division, of the First Army Corps of the Army of the American Republic," the designation now applied to the brigade by one of its members.[8]

After Gettysburg the new faces among the enlisted men and the new brigade flag were matched by the new command arrangements. General John Newton, Reynolds' replacement, remained at the head of the First Corps and came to be accepted by the soldiers, despite their earlier feelings. But there was no such continuity in the leadership of the First Division. James F. Wadsworth, the permanent commander, went on extended leave on July 17th and, plagued by physical exhaustion and illness, was not to return until the spring of 1864. During most of this period, Lysander Cutler—who also shared command of the brigade with Colonel Robinson—and two Massachusetts soldiers, Generals James C. Rice and Henry S. Briggs, took the place of the Iron Brigade's Solomon Meredith, who would have been Wadsworth's substitute at the head of the division.[9] Badly wounded at Gettysburg, Meredith remained on leave in Indiana until October. Returning to the front, he commanded the division for two weeks in November, an assignment he surrendered when it became apparent that field service was too much for him. Long Sol then served as garrison commander at Cairo, Illinois, and in 1864 bid for the Union nomination for Congress, running as Governor Morton's man against a factional foe. Defeated in politics, but brevetted a major general, Meredith returned to duty to finish out the war as commander at Paducah, Kentucky.[10]

There were also wholesale changes among the field officers. The Nineteenth Indiana had forever been deprived of Lieutenant Colonel Dudley. After a second amputation of his mangled leg, Dudley was discharged, to turn to the law and politics in Richmond, Indiana. This left Major Lindley, recovered from his wound, as Colonel Williams' second-in-command, with the post of lieutenant colonel unfilled.[11] In the Twenty-fourth Michigan, to which Colonel Morrow returned on August 7th, the lieutenant colonelcy had also been vacated, the result of Lieutenant Colonel Flanigan's amputation. And having found that he could not keep the field with but one eye, Major Edwin Wight also departed. In place of these officers, Captain William W. Wight was commissioned lieutenant colonel, jumping the rank of major, and Captain Albert M. Edwards, the man who had addressed the regiment on the night of July 1st, was promoted to the majority.[12] The Second Wisconsin listed similar changes. Gone was Colonel Lucius Fairchild, permanently disabled by the loss of an arm. Resigning in October, shortly after the issuance of his commission as brigadier general, Fairchild was at once elected as a Republican to the office of Secretary of State, to be followed in 1866 by the governorship of Wisconsin. In the place of Fairchild and Lieutenant Colonel Stevens, killed at Gettysburg, the command of the regiment fell to Major Mansfield, recovered from his own Gettysburg wound and promptly promoted to lieutenant colonel and, in February of 1864, to the colonelcy. Moving up behind Mansfield was Captain William L. Parsons of Racine and Company F, who was appointed to the majority in September of 1863.[13] In the Sixth Wisconsin, Colonel Bragg returned to duty briefly in July, only to find ten days later that he was not yet ready to resume the field. Bragg was then absent until late in August, during which period Rufus Dawes continued to direct the regiment, backed up by the colorful Major Hauser. But in March of 1864, Hauser resigned, to accept the post of Consul to Switzerland, which made way for the promotion of Captain Philip W. Plummer of Prairie du Chien, whose majority came through in April of 1864.[14] In the Seventh Wisconsin, in which the grievously wounded Lieutenant Colonel Callis was to be discharged in December, Mark Finnicum was promoted to lieutenant colonel and Captain Hollon Richardson to major, effective in January, 1864.[15]

The period after Gettysburg also saw the raising of "the veteran question" in the Army of the Potomac. Having learned a lesson from their experience with the two-year regiments whose terms had expired between Chancellorsville and Gettysburg, in July of 1863 the Federal high command authorized the re-enlistment of the three-year regiments whose terms were to expire in 1864. The problem was to induce the veterans to volunteer again, for a term of an additional three years or the duration of the war. Most of the same motives still existed which had caused the typical soldier to volunteer in 1861, including love for the "old flag." But these motives were now accompanied by a stern knowledge, of death, wounds, captivity, and incredible deprivation and discomfort, for which the rewards offered to the soldiers were but token compensation: a bounty of $402 paid in installments during the period of the new enlistment, the title "veteran volunteer," and the right to wear a red and blue braided service chevron on the sleeve. To these was added the most influential prize, the promise of a thirty-day furlough. If three-fourths of a regiment re-enlisted, the re-enlisted men of the regiment were assured of their furloughs at the same time. In addition, if the three-fourths quota was met, the high command guaranteed that the regiment's existence would not be permitted to lapse. For purposes of the three-fourths requirement, each regiment was credited with the number of men it had in the Department of the Army of the Potomac, without distinction between effective and ineffective strength.[16]

Except for the Twenty-fourth Michigan—its original term was not to expire until 1865—the Iron Brigade regiments were due to muster out in the spring and summer of 1864. Accordingly, as the army moved toward winter quarters near Kelly's Ford* on the Rappahannock,[17] the Wisconsin and Indiana regiments were presented with the hard question of "veteranizing." That the issue was a close one was implicitly acknowledged even by such whole-souled officers as Rufus Dawes. Knowing that re-enlistment would literally condemn many of his men to death, Dawes showed considerably more restraint in his recruitment efforts than he had in 1861. Directed to submit the question to his men, Dawes left this description of the occasion: "I called the regiment together, and spoke to them for half an hour, explaining fully and as fairly as I could, the inducements offered by the Government . . . , the prospect of the continuation of war, and the especial advantages of re-organizing as the Sixth regiment. I submitted an agreement for as many as chose to sign, pledging themselves to re-enlist in the sixth Wisconsin, as a veteran volunteer organization . . . , provided the regiment should immediately upon

* See map at page 48.

the re-enlistment of three-fourths of its members now within the department, be sent home to Wisconsin for a furlough of at least thirty days."[18]

The cautious conduct of conscientious regimental officers did not, of course, reflect the official attitude. There was much at stake for the Union, and the veteranizing process was helped along by a variety of high-pressure and emotional tactics. It was also attended by much red tape and confusion, which tended to bewilder the soldiers. Thus a private of the Nineteenth Indiana reported on October 5th that "from a test vote taken this evening four fifths of the 19th will re-enlist." Two days later, the same diarist wrote that "9 out of ten of the 19th present have gone into the arrangement." Again, on December 23rd he recorded that "3/4 of the 19th and 12 men over have put down their names as veterans, the Regt. has been reported to Headquarters as ready for mustering." At last, on December 28th, he reported that "the history of the veteran re-enlistments in our Brigade gives rise to some queries, when Regts. comply with the orders on the subject why can they not get in? When they are about to be mustered in as veterans, why must another order come creating difficulties and who is to blame, etc. etc., two Regts. in our brigade have voted 3 times to re-enlist and have been repulsed each time."[19] Surely this confusion, together with the arbitrary establishment of regimental strength to which the three-fourths factor was applied, must have decided whether or not some regiments succeeded in mustering the required three-fourths.

The progress of re-enlistment can be gauged from the timetable of the Sixth Wisconsin, which was credited with a total of 290 enlisted men in the Department of the Army of the Potomac. To the Sixth, the agreement was first formally presented on December 20th. Eighty men enrolled at once. Within two more days a total of 148 had signed their names, a number which had increased to 195 by the end of the month. By January 2nd the quota of 217 men was reached, and was signaled by the unfurling of the regiment's color from the window of regimental headquarters. Even then the re-enlistment continued, finally totaling 227 men, and Rufus Dawes proudly announced the achievement, disclosing at the same time another aspect of the event: "Our detached men who have been cooks for officers, hostlers, clerks, and teamsters, of whom there are sixty-eight, nearly all decline to re-enlist, but the men who have stood by the old flag through fair and foul weather, and through many bloody battles, almost to a man dedicate their lives and service anew to their country."[20] Ultimately, among the four Iron Brigade regiments which met "the ever lasting veteran question"—the view of a Hoosier private[21]—enrollment of the necessary three-fourths was achieved by two regiments, the Sixth Wisconsin and the Seventh, 211 of the latter's 249 eligibles having responded. The much-reduced Second Wisconsin, in which 78 signed the new roll, and the Indiana regiment, which re-enlisted 213 men, fell just short of the goal.[22]

Shortly after January 1, 1864, the re-enlisted men received their richest reward. Leaving behind their comrades who had not re-enlisted, the veteran volunteers entrained for Wisconsin and Indiana and the promised thirty days at home. Even this happy occasion was attended with pathetic hardship. "We were all night on the Orange and Alexandria railroad without fires, and there was great suffering. One man was so severely frozen that he was left in the hospital at Alexandria."[23] But when at length the soldiers reached their destinations, their reception must have made it all worth while. Typical was the Milwaukee ceremony for the Sixth Wisconsin, as reported by the local newspaper: "The Sixth regiment proceeded from their quarters at Broadhead's Block, to the Chamber of Commerce, escorted by six companies of the thirtieth Wisconsin under Colonel Daniel J. Dill, —formerly a Captain in the Sixth,—and the Milwaukee Light Infantry under Captain Nazro. At a few minutes past one o'clock the cortege made its appearance, headed by Christian Bach's excellent band, playing: 'The Year of Jubilee.' The veterans marched into the hall and the escort was dismissed. As the regiment entered, they were greeted with salvos of cheers. They formed in the center of the room in close column by company, and at the command of Colonel Bragg, brought their pieces to an order with a thud that elicited rounds of applause." Former Governor Salomon, Lucius Fairchild, Milwaukee's Mayor O'Neill, and other prominent men then spoke before the regiment was dismissed.[24] Other formal gatherings greeted the companies as they dispersed to the county seats whence they had come. Then at last the men reached their homes, to find, as one of them later remembered, that "it was worth a lifetime of service to become the recipients of the loving welcome we received from mothers, fathers, sisters, brothers, [and] sweethearts. . . ."[25] For Rufus Dawes, the homecoming at Marietta, Ohio, was no exception. Indeed, he increased the warmth of the occasion by marrying the girl with whom he had so faithfully corresponded. While honeymooning in Milwaukee, Dawes enlarged the time of his furlough when his horse fell on the icy streets, injuring his ankle. Because of this accident—or "great piece of good fortune," as Dawes regarded it—he was left at home for an additional month when the Wisconsin and Indiana regiments returned to Virginia late in February.[26]

As the long winter of inactivity drew to a close along the Rappahannock, the attention of the soldiers turned from questions involving themselves to significant changes taking place in the Union high command. The immediate background was the course of events in Tennessee and Georgia, where the Federals had met a sharp defeat in a September battle at Chickamauga, and had then been trapped within strategic Chattanooga. To spring the trap, Lincoln had turned to U. S. Grant, appointed to command a new department embracing almost all of the territory west of the Allegheny Mountains. In vindication of his appointment, Grant's armies in November had routed the enemy at Chattanooga, matching the Union's successes at Vicksburg and Gettysburg with a comparable victory in the middle theater of the war. In March, 1864, "the President . . . let the contract of finishing up the rebellion to Ulysses S. Grant,"[27] as an Iron Brigade veteran phrased it. Commissioned lieutenant general, the resolute Westerner came to Washington as general-in-chief.

Establishing his headquarters with the Army of the Potomac, Grant set to work to plan the final Federal strategy, a synchronized movement of all the Federal armies: Meade's against Lee, Sherman's to Atlanta and then to the sea, Sigel's in the Shenandoah Valley, and Benjamin Butler's Army of the James from Fortress Monroe up the Peninsula. In the midst of these preparations the commanding general took occasion on March 29th to review Meade's army, still encamped in its winter quarters. Dawes described the first meeting between the regiments of the historic Iron Brigade and U. S. Grant:

The troops were drawn up in line of battalions en masse doubled on the centre. There was a cold drizzle of rain, and as General Grant, at the head of his staff and escort, rode slowly along in front of the line, regiment after regiment gave loud cheers in his honor as he approached. This had become customary in our army when the troops were reviewed by the commanding General. General Grant made no recognition of the intended compliment. I was in command of the regiment and observing this felt provoked. I turned to the regiment and said: "As General Grant does not seem to think our cheering worth notice, I will not call for cheers. Maintain your position as soldiers." When General Grant came to the sixth Wisconsin, the military salutes required were performed with exact precision and the men stood motionless as statues. He evidently expected us to cheer him as the others had; but when he saw us performing only our exact and formal duties as soldiers, he took off his hat and made a low bow to us, and to our colors dipped in salute to him as commander of the army.

The Western soldiers were highly pleased with this acknowledgment, remarking among themselves that "Grant wants soldiers, not yaupers." They also correctly understood that their new commander was a man who did not care for personal adulation.[28]

Another of the preliminaries to the coming campaign was the reorganization of the Army of the Potomac. On March 23rd Meade's force was consolidated into three corps. Among the eliminated corps was the "old First," which had never recovered from its great day at Gettysburg. Consolidated into two divisions—numbered Second and Fourth and each composed of three brigades—the men of the First Corps were absorbed in General G. K. Warren's Fifth Corps, a change which provoked much dissatisfaction among the First Corps veterans. To the Western soldiers, assigned to the First Brigade of the Fourth Division, the loss of the cherished First Corps numeral was especially disappointing. "It will be a swallowing up of the old first army corps," wrote one of the Wisconsin men, "which hurts our feelings very much." A Michigan soldier complained that "the brigade and corps disorganized would lose their identity purchased with blood and held most sacred." General Newton's farewell order only served to emphasize the resentments held by the soldiers: "Identified by its service with the history of the war the First Corps gave at Gettysburg a crowning proof of valor and endurance, in saving from the grasp of the enemy the strong position upon which the battle was fought. . . . Though the corps has lost its distinctive name by the present changes, history will not be silent upon the magnitude of its services."[29]

The chagrin at the destruction of the First Corps was salved to some extent by an order permitting the men to wear their old corps badges. And in spite of the reorganization, there were many well-known faces about. The command of the Fourth Division went to James S. Wadsworth, at last returned to duty. Lysander Cutler assumed command of the Westerners' brigade, which included the five Iron Brigade regiments, the now-familiar New York Sharpshooters, and the Seventh Indiana. Wadsworth's artillery brigade included the brass guns of "Bloody B," as the soldiers of the Iron Brigade called their favorite battery, also moved from the First to the Fifth Corps.[30] Many of the battery's Western soldiers had returned to their regiments—a process that was to be accelerated as the war continued —and only fifty-seven men from the original Iron Brigade remained with the guns. But Lieutenant Stewart was still the artillery commander, and the affinity between Battery B and the brigade was to continue.[31]

At midnight on May 3, 1864, "the bugle once more sounded . . . fall-in," and the Army of the Potomac embarked upon its final campaign.* It was to be like no other campaign that army had ever experienced. Gone were the years of sporadic fighting, the recurring episodes of great preparation, climactic battle, and prompt disengagement. The *constant* war had begun, war which the officers' reports could only identify by "epochs," during which "two great armies marched and fought for 11 months . . . without ever being out of gunshot." Moving from their winter encampments, Cutler's Brigade and its Fifth Corps comrades crossed the Rapidan at Germanna Ford and marched to Wilderness Tavern, near the scene of Jackson's assault at Chancellorsville. There on May 5th the Fifth Corps was met by veterans of Ewell's Corps, and the final "tale of blood" began.[32] For three hideous days the armies wrestled in the jungle of the Wilderness. Then the constant war swirled to Spottsylvania Court House where the Federals were hurled against the enemy entrenchments in probably the most ferocious fighting of the war. From Spottsylvania, the thrust was again southward, Meade's force marching by the left flank and Lee sliding to his right, always conforming his movement to that of his adversary. At the North Anna River, the armies again met head on, and again the Northerners swung to their

* Grant's final campaign may be followed by reference to the map at page 48 and the back end paper.

left, recrossing the river and moving to Bethesda Church and Cold Harbor, eight miles north of Richmond, where elements of the Army of the James joined in unsuccessful assaults against the Confederate works. Unwilling then simply to lay siege to the defenses of Richmond, the Federals crossed the Peninsula, bridged the James River, and moved to Petersburg, on the south side of the Appomattox River, twenty-three miles below the capital and focal point of the rail and wagon roads upon which Lee's army depended. There, assault tactics having ultimately failed on June 18th, the long siege of Petersburg began.[33]

"Completely holed, and ground-hogging," at Petersburg was a new experience for the Western soldiers, but the closeness of the enemy lines and the constant sharpshooting would permit of nothing else. Besides, lying in a hole in the ground was surely to be preferred to the pile-driving, ceaseless day-and-night fighting that had marked the trail from Germanna Ford. The onset of the siege also permitted an accounting of the results of the last six weeks of fighting. The Federal armies had lost more than 50,000 men, to which number the old Iron Brigade regiments, in the thick of the struggle except at Cold Harbor, had contributed 902 men killed, wounded, and missing.[34] Among the dead was General James S. Wadsworth, whose career had for so long been associated with the brigade. Wadsworth had fallen in the Wilderness, an event that had put Cutler at the head of the Fourth Division and left the brigade again under the temporary leadership of the Seventh's Colonel Robinson.[35] Also a fatality in the Wilderness was Colonel Samuel J. Williams of the Nineteenth Indiana, Virginia-born and Indiana-bred. Major Lindley reported that Williams, "while bravely leading his regiment against the enemies of his country was struck in the breast by a cannon ball and instantly killed."[36] The Wilderness had also finally accounted for the new Wisconsin major, Philip W. Plummer of the Sixth, mortally wounded on May 5th.[37] In addition to these fatalities among the field officers, the list of the wounded and disabled was woefully long. Colonel Henry A. Morrow had been wounded, this time severely, and Lieutenant Colonel Wight of the Twenty-fourth Michigan had left the field for good, the result of his Gettysburg wound. In the Second Wisconsin, Lieutenant Colonel Mansfield and Major Parsons were grievously wounded and permanently out of action, although Mansfield, as a noncombatant, was to appear again as a colonel in the Veteran Reserve Corps.[38] Completing the roll was the Seventh Wisconsin's Lieutenant Colonel Finnicum, wounded at Spottsylvania but returned to duty on May 31st.[39] But more significant in the history of the brigade than the casualties on the road to Petersburg was the formal detachment from it of the Second Wisconsin, the oldest regiment in the brigade and the first to leave its ranks. Reduced to fewer than one hundred men, and commanded by George H. Otis, now commissioned major, the Second had been detached at Spottsylvania to become provost guard for the division. Soon after that battle, on June 11, with the expiration of the regiment's three-year term, Otis and the nonveterans had been sent home to muster out, and the veterans and later recruits, remaining as provost guard, had been organized into two small companies under Captain Dennis B. Dailey of Company B.[40] In 1861 the Second Wisconsin had been the first three years' regiment to reach Washington. Thereafter, it had established a combat record that no Federal regiment would surpass. Indeed, the Second was to sustain the greatest percentage of loss of any regiment in the Union armies.[41] But Dailey's companies were now identified as the "Independent Battalion Wisconsin Volunteers," and the distinguished name "Second Wisconsin Volunteers" disappeared from the roster of the army.

Although deprived of the services of the Second Wisconsin, the Westerners' brigade remained in the trenches at Petersburg, participants in a deadly, close-range sharpshooting contest with the enemy. In addition to the constant sniping and the Battle of the Crater on July 30th—a disaster that the Westerners missed—the siege was marked by a series of Federal thrusts below the city, aimed at one or another of the rail or wagon roads which permitted the supply of the Confederate army. Among these, all involving bitter fighting, were four in which the brigade participated: the Battle of Globe Tavern in August, Boydton Plank Road in October, a raid on the Weldon Railroad in December, and the Battle of Hatcher's Run in early February, 1865.[42] In these engagements the brigade was led by Edgar S. Bragg, who had superseded Colonel Robinson on June 7th, and whose commission as brigadier general, dated July 2nd, assured him of the permanent command.[43] Whatever their success in gradually choking off the enemy, each of these engagements further dissipated

the strength of what remained of the once-powerful regiments, adding
247 more of the Western soldiers to the long lists of casualties.[44]
Again among the fallen were leaders long associated with the greatness
of the past, among them Division Commander Lysander Cutler, who
was shot down at Globe Tavern on August 21st and left the field,
to finish the war at draft rendezvous in New York and Jackson, Michigan.[45] Another casualty was Henry A. Morrow. Returned to duty on
November 13th and brevetted a brigadier, Morrow had been assigned
to command of the Third Brigade of the division to which the
Westerners' brigade was attached. At Hatcher's Run, Morrow assumed
his favorite role and with a familiar result, officially described in the
division commander's eyewitness account: "He held his command in
place against greatly superior numbers, until, while carrying the
colors of his brigade, he received a severe wound," his third and the
one which took him from combat for good.[46] And General Cutler
and General Morrow were not the only great names of the Iron
Brigade who left the war at Petersburg. Colonel Robinson resigned,
to return to Wisconsin before undertaking a twelve-year term as
Consul to Madagascar. The Seventh also lost Lieutenant Colonel
Finnicum, who resigned in December. And although at last commissioned colonel, the dauntless Rufus Dawes accepted a discharge
at Petersburg, and left the war.[47]

An insight into Dawes' conduct—and a probable explanation of
the resignations of the other officers—is provided by a letter from a
soldier of the Sixth Wisconsin. To a former comrade who had been
disabled and discharged, the soldier wrote: "About the most demoralized man I have ever seen in the army was Dawes before he got his
discharge. With him the Government was everything but what it
should be. And they is some more here yet that for the good of the
service they had ought to be discharged." That this observation was
pertinent was apparent from Dawes' own letters and journal. From
the North Anna on May 25th he had tried to write to his bride, but
"the bullets clip through the green leaves over my head as I lie
behind the breastwork writing. I have had no full night's sleep since
May 7th, when I took command of the regiment. Day after day, and
night after night we have marched, fought and dug entrenchments; I
have not changed my clothing since May third. We have not seen,
and seldom communicated with our wagon train. I have not com-

posure to write, as the bullets are coming so thickly . . . , and some poor wounded soldiers are near me." The colonel was also preoccupied with another aspect of his career, the fact that he almost alone among the officers of the regiment had never been wounded. Again and again his letters referred to this haunting fact, and he was apparently burdened with the feeling that any moment would be his last. To his wife he confided, "I wonder if a man can go forever without being hurt in battle," and it was obvious that he believed the answer to his question was in the negative. Toward the close of his career, a new note, a note of intense bitterness, inspired his pen. The war had become "a carnival of blood" and the death of a favorite soldier was now characterized as "murder."[48] So Dawes took the discharge to which he was entitled on August 10th, apparently victim of what later generations would call "battle fatigue," a disability just as crippling as the bullets that had accounted for his comrades.

Bullets and battle fatigue were not the only forces at Petersburg that struck at the remaining identity of the regiments of the Iron Brigade. There were added the frequent reorganizations and consolidations of the divisions and brigades to which the Western survivors were attached. On August 25th the Fourth Division, which Wadsworth and later Cutler had led from Germanna Ford, disappeared from the records, to be merged with the remaining divisions of the Fifth Corps. Bragg's men were absorbed into General Samuel Crawford's Third Division, henceforth to be identified as the First Brigade.[49] The terms of the Wisconsin and Indiana nonveterans had by this time expired and they had left the brigade to be mustered out, but three Pennsylvania regiments, the 143rd, 149th, and 150th Volunteers, had been added to the brigade. Also assigned to Bragg was the Independent Battalion Wisconsin Volunteers, which now returned to the line and on November 30th was formally merged with the Sixth Wisconsin.[50] Whatever satisfaction the Westerners gained from the return of these old comrades was to be offset by the fate of the Nineteenth Indiana. In August the Indiana regiments in the Army of the Potomac had begun to consolidate. The Fourteenth Indiana was the first to go, merged into the Twentieth Indiana Volunteers. On September 23rd the Seventh Indiana was transferred to the Nineteenth, increasing the latter's roll by 107 men. On October

18th it was ordered that the Nineteenth be consolidated with the Twentieth, with the latter regiment as the survivor.[51]

As a part of the Twentieth Indiana, the soldiers of the old Nineteenth joined the brigade of General P. Regis de Trobriand, in Mott's Third Division of the Second Corps. The Nineteenth's Lieutenant Colonel Lindley resigned, but command of the surviving Twentieth regiment went to a Nineteenth Indiana man, William Orr of Selma, Indiana, recently promoted to a majority and now commissioned as colonel of the Twentieth.[52] The Iron Brigade veterans doubtless found some comfort in the fact that one of "their boys" was at the head of the reorganized Twentieth Indiana, but the disappearance of the Nineteenth, and their transfer to the Second Corps, was far more bitterly resented than the detachment of the Second Wisconsin, whose remnants had after all remained in the same division as their Iron Brigade comrades. That this resentment was especially acute is apparent from the diary of an enlisted man of the Nineteenth, which described the "long faces and much murmuring among our boys" at the "astounding order" to report to the Second Corps. No less resentful were their former comrades, one of whom wrote that "it was a cruel act to separate and take them from the 'Old Brigade.' They left us, their hearts filled with sorrow over their forced separation from us. We . . . felt badly over their being taken away. . . . We all gloried in the . . . record of the 'Iron Brigade,' a record which they helped to make." That these records did not exaggerate the bitterness of the veterans of the Nineteenth was apparent from an incident after the October battle at the Boydton Plank Road, the first engagement following the Nineteenth's removal. On that occasion it was reported that "many men wearing black hats having a round red badge, could be seen coming back to the regiments of the old brigade. They swore they would never go back to their new command and did not until forced at the point of a bayonet."[53]

Four months after the disappearance of the Nineteenth Indiana, it was time for another regiment of the Iron Brigade to leave the war. On February 10, 1865, General Grant instructed Meade to send to Baltimore "some of your old reliable and reduced regiments . . . to go North to take charge of camps of drafted men." Apparently convinced that "reliable and reduced" was descriptive of Bragg's Brigade, Meade ordered it to Baltimore.[54] But Meade now had to reckon with

General Crawford, who eloquently objected. The division commander offered to compromise, at the same time disclosing the wishes of the Westerners themselves. To Meade he wrote: "If Bragg's brigade may not return, I earnestly desire to retain the Twenty-fourth Michigan, with the Sixth and Seventh Wisconsin. I have a surplus of regiments which can much better be spared. . . . The three regiments mentioned have served together from the beginning of the war, and are identified with the Army of the Potomac. They desire to remain and I ask the privilege of sending other regiments in their place." To Corps Commander Warren, Crawford sent a similar message: "I have many regiments better fitted for service out of this army . . . and have asked that I be allowed to . . . retain my Western regiments. They wish to remain."[55] General Crawford's feeling for organizational morale —which the army had so often ignored after Gettysburg—was only partially satisfied. The Sixth and Seventh Wisconsin were returned to him, but General Bragg and the Twenty-fourth Michigan, along with the three Pennsylvania regiments, marched away for good. From Fortress Monroe they moved to Baltimore, where Bragg was to remain until the end of the war, while the Twenty-fourth Michigan journeyed to the draft rendezvous at Springfield, Illinois, the last post of the fighting Michigan men.[56]

For a short time after the departure of the Michigan and Pennsylvania regiments, the Sixth and Seventh Wisconsin had the First Brigade all to themselves.[57] Although it was hardly like old times, the organization was all-*Western* once more, and surely the Badgers must have remarked on this fact. Again with them was the remarkable John A. Kellogg, who had at last completed a roundabout route back to duty from capture in the Wilderness. From Madison, Kellogg had brought several hundred drafted men to fill up the Sixth Wisconsin. He also carried his newest commission, a colonelcy, and this put him at the head of the now Wisconsin brigade. Reporting to Kellogg were other officers, some of them new to field command. In the Sixth Wisconsin, the commander was Thomas Kerr, before the war a carpenter in Milwaukee, who had started out in 1861 as a lowly private in the Sixth's Irish Company, the Montgomery Guards. Having survived four wounds, Kerr now wore the shoulder straps of a lieutenant colonel. His major was Dennis B. Dailey from the old Second Wisconsin, now second-in-command in the Sixth. Commander of the Seventh Wisconsin was Hollon Richardson, now a lieutenant colonel, and he was backed up by another former enlisted man, George S. Hoyt, who had made the long climb to the majority of the Seventh.[58]

The life of Kellogg's Wisconsin brigade was a short one. On March 3rd the Western men were joined by the Ninety-first New York Volunteers, a heavy-artillery organization that had been converted to infantry. Together with the Wisconsin recruits, the arrival of the New Yorkers increased the strength of Kellogg's Brigade to over 3,000 men.[59] It was none too soon, because the time had come for the final Federal thrust to break into Petersburg and at the same time block the routes by which the much-weakened enemy could escape. The Confederates anticipated the Federal effort and moved to the attack on March 25th, against Fort Stedman, a Federal stronghold east of the city. But this assault was but a forlorn hope and was followed by heavy Federal pressure all along the line extending now almost around the city. On April 1st, west of Petersburg, Sheridan's cavalry and the Fifth Corps overran the enemy at Five Forks, closing off the possibility of escape south of the Appomattox River, and on the following day a major assault on Petersburg itself effected the seizure of the critical Confederate works and forced the city's evacuation. Fighting on the Federal left, Kellogg's Brigade was a heavy participant in the assaults on March 31st and the advance to Five Forks, which, despite the late hour of the war, were fierce and sanguinary. Exactly two hundred more of the soldiers of the Sixth and Seventh Wisconsin were casualties, including the commanders of both regiments—Lieutenant Colonel Kerr and Lieutenant Colonel Richardson—and Major Dailey of the Sixth, who was hit on March 31st while temporarily assigned as the commander of the 147th New York in another brigade.[60]

From Five Forks, Kellogg's Brigade with the Fifth Corps followed in pursuit of the fleeing enemy, to Jetersville, then along the Appomattox River, past Farmville and, at length, on the night of April 8th, it went into bivouac a few miles from Appomattox Court House. On the following morning the brigade resumed its advance, noticing as the day wore on that the sounds of firing ahead had ceased. Not yet at Appomattox Court House, the column halted in the late morning, and the soldiers waited. As recorded by one of the original

Sauk County Riflemen: "In the afternoon, we saw an officer come riding down the lines, his horse wet and covered with lather; as he passed along we saw that the boys' caps went up into the air—the welkin rang with cheers. . . . As he came in front of us he shouted, 'Gen. Lee and army have surrendered to Gen. Grant.' . . . We yelled for joy, for we knew the war was ended." And, of course, it was true, "near Appomattox Court-House . . . the enemy, tired, dispirited, harassed, and surrounded, surrendered at discretion," according to Kellogg's final report. Although other Confederate forces were to hold out for a few more days or weeks, for the survivors of the regiments of the Iron Brigade the end had finally come.[61]

The Confederate armies were disbanded as they surrendered, to drift home to states that were but part of the United States, after all. But the soldiers of Meade and Sherman marched to Washington for the Grand Review, a final fanfare before the muster-out. On May 23rd the Army of the Potomac paraded, filling the whole length of Pennsylvania Avenue with the brilliant show, "the bronzed faces of the men, their muskets at right shoulder shift, and interspersed in the line were the commanders . . . above them floated the flags under which they had fought. . . ."[62] Moving with the artillery of the Fifth Corps was Battery B of the Fourth U.S., Brevet Captain James Stewart at its head. Although not since November of 1864 had the battery listed any of the Western volunteers on its roster, men from the Iron Brigade had served its guns for three years, and the records showed that more men had fallen there than in *any other field artillery battery in the armies of the Union*.[63] Also in the column were other marching men, soldiers who represented the Westerners even more directly than did their artillery kinsmen of Battery B. At the head of the First Brigade of Crawford's Division rode Brevet Brigadier General Henry A. Morrow, who had rejoined his Michigan comrades at Springfield and had then been sent East, after the surrender, to displace Colonel Kellogg as brigade commander.[64] Marching behind Morrow of the Twenty-fourth Michigan was the Sixth Wisconsin, whose ranks included the veterans of the Second Wisconsin, one of whom, Major Dennis B. Dailey, now commanded the Sixth. In step with the men of the Second and the Sixth was the Seventh Wisconsin, Lieutenant Colonel Hollon Richardson commanding. Elsewhere in the line were Hoosier veterans, disguised, to be sure, as men of the Twentieth Indiana but actually Sol Meredith's men of the old Nineteenth.[65] This had been the Iron Brigade, the unique brigade of volunteers from the Old Northwest. Surely it was appropriate for the brigade to be represented that day on Pennsylvania Avenue, because the records showed that a greater percentage of its men had been killed and mortally wounded than *in any other brigade in the Federal armies.*[66]

As they passed the reviewing stand, the Western soldiers could not see the homespun Western lawyer, whose own resolve had summoned them to arms and whose life had gone out in the ultimate nightmare of the whole ordeal. More than four years previously, in Indianapolis, on the way to his inauguration, he had put the question, Shall the Union and shall the liberties of this country be preserved? The Iron Brigade had answered, and the Union lived![67]

APPENDICES

1

The Iron Brigade Counties

When the regiments of the Iron Brigade were originally raised, a number of men crossed county lines to volunteer. In addition, later recruits to the regiments were assigned from various counties, and these counties cannot be fully identified. For these reasons it is impossible to determine all of the counties that contributed to the Iron Brigade. Despite these limitations, it is still possible to specify the counties in which the various companies were initially recruited and which contributed the bulk of the volunteers to the Iron Brigade. According to the adjutant generals' reports, these "Iron Brigade counties" are the following:

THE SECOND WISCONSIN VOLUNTEERS

Company		County
A	The Citizens' Guard	Dodge
B	The La Crosse Light Guards	La Crosse
C	The Grant County Grays	Grant
D	The Janesville Volunteers	Rock
E	The Oshkosh Volunteers	Winnebago
F	The Belle City Rifles	Racine
G	The Portage City Guards	Columbia
H	The Randall Guards	Dane
I	The Miner's Guards	Iowa
K	The Wisconsin Rifles	Milwaukee
K*		Dane and Milwaukee

* Replaced original Company K in January, 1862, after the original was detached and converted to heavy artillery.

THE SIXTH WISCONSIN VOLUNTEERS

Company		County
A	The Sauk County Riflemen	Sauk
B	The Prescott Guards	Pierce
C	The Prairie du Chien Volunteers	Crawford
D	The Montgomery Guards	Milwaukee
E	Bragg's Rifles	Fond du Lac
F	The Citizens' Corps Milwaukee	Milwaukee
G	The Beloit Star Rifles	Rock
H	The Buffalo County Rifles	Buffalo
I	The Anderson Guards	Juneau and Dane
K	The Lemonweir Minute Men	Juneau

THE SEVENTH WISCONSIN VOLUNTEERS

Company		County
A	The Lodi Guards	Chippewa and Columbia
B	The Columbia County Cadets	Columbia
C	The Platteville Guards	Grant
D	The Stoughton Light Guard	Dane
E	The Marquette County Sharp Shooters	Marquette
F	The Lancaster Union Guards	Grant
G	The Grand Rapids Union Guards	Wood
H	The Badger State Guards	Grant
I	The Northwestern Tigers	Dodge and Waushara
K	The Badger Rifles	Rock

THE NINETEENTH INDIANA VOLUNTEERS*

Company		County
A	The Union Guards	Madison
B	The Richmond City Greys	Wayne
C	The Winchester Greys	Randolph
D	The Invincibles	Marion
E	The Delaware Greys	Delaware
F	The Meredith Guards	Marion
G	The Elkhart County Guards	Elkhart
H	The Edinburgh Guards	Johnson
I	The Spencer Greys	Owen
K	The Selma Legion	Delaware

* These company names have been discovered since the 1961 edition. Contrary to that edition and the Indiana adjutant general, Company A was from Madison County, not Delaware. *History of Madison County, Indiana*, Samuel Hardin, Markleville, 1874; *A Twentieth Century History of Delaware County, Indiana*, G. W. Kemper (ed.), Chicago, 1908.

THE TWENTY-FOURTH MICHIGAN VOLUNTEERS

Recruited largely from Wayne County, the regiment also had a total of 123 original volunteers from Monroe, Washtenaw, Oakland, and Clinton counties.

2

Commanders and Officers

THE BRIGADE

The Iron Brigade originated on October 1, 1861, with the arrival in Washington of the Seventh Wisconsin Volunteers, *Wis.* A.G., 1861, p. 29. Pursuant to an order dated September 28, 1861, O.R., 107, 489, the Seventh reported to Rufus King, whose brigade, as of the Seventh's reporting, included the Second, Sixth, and Seventh Wisconsin and the Nineteenth Indiana. Thus Rufus King was the first commander of the Iron Brigade.

John Gibbon succeeded King as permanent commander on May 7, 1862, O.R., 107, 605. Disregarding temporary commanders, Gibbon was thus the second commander, and he retained this post until November 4, 1862, when he was advanced to division command, O.R., 107, 922.

Again disregarding temporary assignments, the third commander of the brigade was Solomon Meredith of the Nineteenth Indiana. Assigned on November 25, 1862, O.R., 107, 951, Meredith held the command until he was wounded at Gettysburg on July 1, 1863.

Since the Iron Brigade was formally destroyed on July 16, 1863, with the assignment to it of the 167th Pennsylvania, O.R., 45, 674-5, Solomon Meredith was the last commander of the brigade. But if the brigade that included the Iron Brigade survivors is traced, Meredith's successors were the following officers:

William W. Robinson, Seventh Wisconsin
From July 1, 1863, until March 25, 1864 (see Epilogue, Notes 9 and 30, for interruptions of Robinson's tenure), and from May 6, 1864, until June 7, 1864. (See Epilogue, Notes 30, 35 and 43.)
Lysander Cutler, Sixth Wisconsin
From March 25, 1864, O.R., 60, 737-8, to May 6, 1864. (See Epilogue, Note 35.)

Edward S. Bragg, Sixth Wisconsin
   From June 7, 1864, O.R., 67, 171, until February 10, 1865, O.R.,
   96, 519. (See Epilogue, Note 54.)
John A. Kellogg, Sixth Wisconsin
   From February 28, 1865, O.R., 96, 742, until April 27, 1865,
   O.R., 95, 882. (April 27 is the date of Kellogg's last report.)
Henry A. Morrow, Twenty-fourth Michigan
   From April 27, 1865 (See Kellogg's dates, above), until June 5,
   1865. (See Epilogue, Note 67.)

The foregoing table excludes temporary assignments.

The Regiments

According to the adjutant generals' reports of the three states, the
field officers of the Iron Brigade regiments and the communities from
which they enlisted were the following:[1]

Nineteenth Indiana

NAME	RESIDENCE	PERIOD OF RANK
Colonels		
Solomon Meredith	Cambridge City	July 29, 1861–Oct. 6, 1862
Samuel J. Williams	Selma	Oct. 7, 1862–May 6, 1864 (killed in action)
Lieutenant Colonels		
Robert A. Cameron	Valparaiso	July 29, 1861–Feb. 3, 1862
Alois O. Bachman	Madison	Feb. 6, 1862–Sept. 17, 1862 (killed in action)
Samuel J. Williams	Selma	Sept. 18, 1862–Oct. 7, 1862
William W. Dudley	Richmond	Oct. 7, 1862–April 9, 1864
John M. Lindley	Indianapolis	April 10, 1864–Oct. 24, 1864
Majors		
Alois O. Bachman	Madison	Aug. 2, 1861–Feb. 6, 1862
Isaac M. May	Anderson[2]	Feb. 6, 1862–Aug. 28, 1862 (killed in action)
William W. Dudley	Richmond	Sept. 18, 1862–Oct. 7, 1862
John M. Lindley	Indianapolis	May 1, 1863–April 10, 1864
William Orr	Selma	Aug. 4, 1864–Oct. 18, 1864

[1] The dates given are dates of the commissions, not issue dates or late muster
dates.

[2] Contrary to the Indiana adjutant general, May was from Anderson, not
Muncie. See Prologue, Note 56.

SECOND WISCONSIN

NAME	RESIDENCE	PERIOD OF RANK
Colonels		
S. Park Coon	Milwaukee	April 24, 1861–July 30, 1861
Edgar O'Connor	Beloit[1]	Aug. 3, 1861–Aug. 28, 1862 (killed in action)
Lucius Fairchild	Madison	Sept. 8, 1862–Oct. 20, 1863
John Mansfield	Portage	Feb. 9, 1864–Aug. 14, 1864
Lieutenant Colonels		
Henry W. Peck	Monroe	April 29, 1861–July 29, 1861
Duncan McDonald	Milwaukee	July 29, 1861–Aug. 9, 1861
Lucius Fairchild	Madison	Aug. 20, 1861–Sept. 8, 1862
Thomas S. Allen	Mineral Point	Sept. 8, 1862–Jan. 14, 1863
George H. Stevens	Fox Lake	Feb. 2, 1863–July 4, 1863 (killed in action)
John Mansfield	Portage	Aug. 13, 1863–Feb. 9, 1864
William L. Parsons	Racine	May 25, 1864–Dec. 19, 1864
Majors		
Duncan McDonald	Milwaukee	May 9, 1861–July 29, 1861
Thomas S. Allen	Mineral Point	Aug. 28, 1861–Sept. 8, 1862
George H. Stevens	Fox Lake	Sept. 30, 1862–Feb. 2, 1863
John Mansfield	Portage	Feb. 2, 1863–Aug. 13, 1863
William L. Parsons	Racine	Sept. 25, 1863–May 25, 1864
George H. Otis	Mineral Point	May 25, 1864–June 29, 1864

SIXTH WISCONSIN

NAME	RESIDENCE	PERIOD OF RANK
Colonels		
Lysander Cutler	Milwaukee	May 28, 1861–March 25, 1863
Edward S. Bragg	Fond du Lac	March 17, 1863–July 2, 1864
Rufus R. Dawes	Mauston (Marietta, Ohio)	July 5, 1864–Aug. 10, 1864
John A. Kellogg	Mauston	Dec. 10, 1864–July 14, 1865
Lieutenant Colonels		
Julius P. Atwood	Madison	May 28, 1861–Sept. 14, 1861
Benjamin F. Sweet	Chilton	Sept. 17, 1861–July 18, 1862

[1] Contrary to Wisconsin's adjutant general, O'Connor was from Beloit, not Milwaukee. See Prologue, Note 28.

Edward S. Bragg	Fond du Lac	June 30, 1862–March 17, 1863
Rufus R. Dawes	Mauston (Marietta, Ohio)	March 17, 1863–July 5, 1864
John A. Kellogg	Mauston	Oct. 19, 1864–Dec. 10, 1864
Thomas Kerr	Milwaukee	Dec. 10, 1864–July 14, 1865

Majors

Benjamin F. Sweet	Chilton	May 28, 1861–Sept. 17, 1861
Edward S. Bragg	Fond du Lac	Sept. 17, 1861–June 30, 1862
Rufus R. Dawes	Mauston (Marietta, Ohio)	June 30. 1862–March 17, 1863
John F. Hauser	Fountain City	March 17, 1863–March 18, 1864
Philip W. Plummer	Prairie du Chien	April 12, 1864–May 5, 1864 (killed in action)
John A. Kellogg	Mauston	Sept. 1, 1864–Oct. 19, 1864
Thomas Kerr	Milwaukee	Oct. 19, 1864–Dec. 10, 1864
Dennis B. Dailey	Lebanon, Ohio	Dec. 21, 1864–July 14, 1865

Seventh Wisconsin[1]

NAME	RESIDENCE	PERIOD OF RANK

Colonels

| Joseph Vandor | Milwaukee | June 24, 1861–Jan. 30, 1862 |
| William W. Robinson | Sparta | Feb. 3, 1862–July 9, 1864 |

Lieutenant Colonels

William W. Robinson	Sparta	Aug. 15, 1861–Feb. 3, 1862
Charles A. Hamilton	Milwaukee	Feb. 3, 1862–March 3, 1863
John B. Callis	Lancaster	March 9, 1863–Dec. 28, 1863
Mark Finnicum	Fennimore	Jan. 13, 1864–Dec. 17, 1864
Hollon Richardson	Chippewa Falls	Aug. 3, 1864–July 3, 1865

Majors

Charles A. Hamilton	Milwaukee	Aug. 15, 1861–Feb. 3, 1862
George Bill	Lodi	Feb. 15, 1862–Jan. 5, 1863
John B. Callis	Lancaster	Feb. 26, 1863–March 9, 1863
Mark Finnicum	Fennimore	March 9, 1863–Jan. 13, 1864
Hollon Richardson	Chippewa Falls	Jan. 13, 1864–Aug. 3, 1864
George S. Hoyt	Allen's Grove	Dec. 29, 1864–July 3, 1865

[1] For the status of Martin C. Hobart, commissioned major and lieutenant colonel, but never mustered, see Epilogue, Note 58.

TWENTY-FOURTH MICHIGAN

NAME	RESIDENCE	PERIOD OF RANK
Colonels		
Henry A. Morrow	Detroit	Aug. 15, 1862–July 19, 1865
Lieutenant Colonels		
Mark Flanigan	Detroit	Aug. 15, 1862–Nov. 21, 1863
William W. Wight	Livonia	Feb. 1, 1864–June 9, 1864
Albert M. Edwards	Detroit	July 17, 1864–July 19, 1865
Majors		
Henry W. Nall	Detroit	Sept. 4, 1862–April 17, 1863
Edwin B. Wight	Detroit	June 22, 1863–Nov. 17, 1863
Albert M. Edwards	Detroit	Feb. 1, 1864–July 17, 1864
William Hutchinson	Detroit	July 17, 1864–July 19, 1865

3

Biographical Note

Where available, the prewar careers of the prominent officers of the brigade are set forth in the text and amplified in the notes appended to the text. Despite diligent search, biographies of certain of the field officers have not been found. These men, who briefly achieved prominence one hundred years ago and then vanished from sight, are listed below:

SECOND WISCONSIN VOLUNTEERS

John Mansfield of Portage, Wisconsin, who was the last colonel of the regiment.

Henry W. Peck of Monroe, Wisconsin, the first lieutenant colonel.

William L. Parsons of Racine, who achieved the rank of lieutenant colonel.

George H. Otis of Mineral Point, Wisconsin, a major and last commander of the regiment.

SIXTH WISCONSIN VOLUNTEERS

Philip W. Plummer of Prairie du Chien, advanced to the majority on April 12, 1864, and killed on May 5, 1864, in the Wilderness.

Dennis B. Dailey of Lebanon, Ohio, who somehow volunteered in Wisconsin and served as a captain of the Second and major of the Sixth, the latter after these two regiments were merged.

SEVENTH WISCONSIN VOLUNTEERS

Mark Finnicum of Fennimore, Wisconsin, who reached the rank of lieutenant colonel, commanding.

Martin C. Hobart of Fall River, Wisconsin, who, while a prisoner of war, was promoted to the majority and lieutenant colonelcy of the regiment. See Epilogue, Note 58.

George Bill, Lodi, Wisconsin, first major of the Seventh.

George S. Hoyt of Allen's Grove, Wisconsin, the last major of the regiment.

The text does not make any extended effort to treat the postwar lives of the surviving officers. Except for Rufus King and John Gibbon, who are here discussed, the notes contain the postwar data, to the extent that it is available. Thus, the postwar facts about the following officers are contained in the following notes:

SECOND WISCONSIN

Lucius Fairchild, see Epilogue, Note 13.

Thomas S. Allen, see Chapter 10, Note 32.

SIXTH WISCONSIN

Lysander Cutler, see Epilogue, Note 45.

Edward S. Bragg, see Epilogue, Note 56.

Rufus R. Dawes, see Epilogue, Note 48.

John A. Kellogg, see Epilogue, Note 61.

Thomas Kerr, see Epilogue, Note 58.

SEVENTH WISCONSIN

William W. Robinson, see Epilogue, Note 47.

Hollon Richardson, see Epilogue, Note 65.

Charles A. Hamilton, see Chapter 10, Note 33.

John B. Callis, see Epilogue, Note 15.

NINETEENTH INDIANA

Solomon Meredith, see Epilogue, Note 10.

William W. Dudley, see Epilogue, Note 11.

William Orr, see Epilogue, Note 52.

TWENTY-FOURTH MICHIGAN

Henry A. Morrow, see Epilogue, Note 64.

Rufus King became Minister to the Papal States in 1863. There he was instrumental in the apprehension of John H. Surratt, allegedly one of the Lincoln conspirators. In 1867 Congress failed to appropriate funds for continuing the United States representatives at the Papal Court, and King resigned on January 1, 1868, and returned to the United States. He was appointed Deputy Collector for the Port of New York, a post he occupied until 1869, when ill-health compelled his retirement. He died on October 13, 1876.

King's son, Charles King, was the general's messenger during King's command of his division. Charles was with the division at Brawner Farm. After the war, Charles was a prominent officer in the United States Army, and a writer. Charles King spent many years in an effort to overcome the general impression of Rufus King's military career, which had arisen out of the incidents at Brawner Farm and the decision on the night of August 28th to march his division from Brawner Farm to Manassas Junction. *Dictionary of American Biography*, Vol. X, p. 400.

John Gibbon commanded his division at Fredericksburg and was severely wounded there. He also had a division of the Second Corps at Chancellorsville and Gettysburg, and was acting commander of the Second Corps during parts of the latter battle. He was also wounded at Gettysburg. On June 7, 1864, Gibbon was commissioned a major general of volunteers, and in January of 1865 he was assigned to command the Twenty-fourth Corps of the Army of the James. At Appomattox he was one of the commissioners appointed to arrange the details of the surrender, and his account of the surrender, appearing in his *Personal Recollections of the Civil War*, is a valuable source record. In 1866 Gibbon was mustered out of the volunteer force and was appointed a colonel in the regular army. His postwar duty was largely in the West, and he was among the prominent officers of the Indian Wars. In 1876 he commanded the expedition that rescued Custer's survivors and buried the dead at Little Bighorn. In 1877 he led the force that attacked and defeated the Nez Percé Indians commanded by Chief Joseph. On July 10, 1885, Gibbon became a brigadier general in the regular army. He was the commander of the Department of the Columbia in 1885-1886 and was active in restoring order in Seattle at the time of the anti-Chinese riots there. He retired in 1891 and became Commander-in-Chief of the Loyal Legion. He died at Baltimore on February 6, 1896, and was buried at Arlington. His monument at Arlington was purchased by donations from Iron Brigade veterans and is marked with the five-pointed Iron Brigade postwar insignia. *Dictionary of American Biography*, Vol. VII, pp. 236-7.

4

The Uniform of the Iron Brigade

The photographs appearing in this book presumably settle any questions that have existed about the uniform Gibbon ordered for the brigade, at Fredericksburg, shortly after his accession to command. Essentially this uniform originally consisted of the following distinctive features: the hat, the regular army frock coat, and white leggings. White gloves were also procured, but these were worn only for dress. Except for the hat, the frock coat, and the leggings, the soldiers of Gibbon's Brigade were uniformed and equipped like the majority of their comrades in the Army of the Potomac.

In addition to the story the photographs tell, other comments are appropriate on the Iron Brigade's distinctive dress.

The Hat   Certain of the Iron Brigade's contemporaries identified the hat as "Western" or "slouch" (see *The Cannoneer*, Augustus Buell, pp. 64-5), and after constant wearing the hat doubtless did tend to "slouch" and lose its shape. At times the soldiers also seem to have creased the crown of the hat, thus increasing its "Western" appearance. But the hat was, in fact, the stiff, black felt Hardee dress hat of the regulars, introduced in 1855 and associated with Captain William J. Hardee of Hardee's *Tactics* and, later, of the Confederate army. When worn by the regulars, the hat was turned up on the left side and fastened with a brass eagle pin, at least for dress (see Plate CLXXII, *Atlas to Accompany the Official Records*). From the photographs it is apparent that in the Iron Brigade there was a lack of uniformity in the manner of wearing the brim. It was worn down or turned up on either side, apparently at the wearer's discretion. It is significant, however, that the brass eagle was used by at least some of the soldiers, as shown in a photograph of the noncommissioned officers of the Second Wisconsin.

Just as the regulars wore a black plume in the black hat, so did the Iron Brigade. Consistent with their varied treatment of the hatbrim, the photographs indicate that the plume was worn on either side. It is true, of course, that these plumes were highly perishable and are not invariably visible in the photographs. But they appear frequently and are referred to at various times after the original issue of the uniform, which indicates that the plumes must have been replaced from time to time. Thus Dawes states that "the feathers in our hats were drooping" on October 9, 1862, when the Twenty-fourth Michigan joined the brigade (*The Sixth Wisconsin Volunteers*, p. 104), and Captain C. A. Stevens, the historian of Berdan's Sharpshooters, recalled the Iron Brigade just after Chancellorsville, "their big black hats and feathers conspicuous" (*Berdan's United States Sharpshooters*, pp. 277-8). Granted that these accounts were written after the war, the Arlington photograph of the Seventh Wisconsin, which must have been taken in early September, 1862, shows at least some of the hats equipped with plumes.

The remaining trimmings for the black hat included the traditional brass horn, the infantry insignia, which almost universally appears in the photographs. The light-blue infantry hat cord was also generally worn. The cord may be seen in at least some of the photographs, and its color was expressly identified, "a blue cord for a band," by R. K. Beacham of the Second Wisconsin in his book *Gettysburg*, p. 64. Another trimming for the hat was the cloth corps badge, issued throughout the Army of the Potomac during the early days of Hooker's command. In the Iron Brigade this badge was a circle, for the First Corps, and its color was red, designating the First Division. Both Dawes, p. 132, and Curtis (*History of the Twenty-fourth Michigan*, p. 117) specify the wearing of the corps badge. In addition, at the State Historical Society of Wisconsin, a faded red cloth circle has been carefully preserved in the *Young MSS*, a part of the *Warner MSS*. It is to be noted that this was the brigade's only corps badge, despite the merger of the First and Fifth corps, because the army permitted the men from the First Corps to retain their First Corps badges (see Note 30, Epilogue). Completing the hat trim was the brass company letter, visible above the horn in many of the photographs.*

How long the survivors of the brigade retained the black hat can-

* As indicated by the photographs in this book, a brass regimental identification was ordinarily worn in the center of the brass infantry horn. The red cloth corps badge was probably worn beneath the brass company letter, perhaps pinned to the hat in this way.

not be definitely determined. It may be seen, battered and misshapen, among the bodies of the Michigan soldiers in the well-known O'Sullivan photograph of the dead at Gettysburg.° Philip Cheek and Mair Pointon of the Sixth Wisconsin, who wrote from contemporaneous notes and letters, recorded two late references to the hat. Thus on January 7, 1864, while en route home on veteran furloughs, the soldiers stopped in Washington. There "many of the boys replenished their wardrobe with fine suits of clothes and new hat trimmings" (*History of the Sauk County Riflemen,* p. 86). "Trimmings" is a meaningful term in reference to the black hat, and surely did not signify that the men were wearing kepis. Much later, in October of 1864, after the battle at the Boydton Plank Road, Cheek and Pointon told of how the soldiers of the Nineteenth Indiana, transferred to the Twentieth Indiana in the Second Corps, sought to return to their former comrades. Thus "many men wearing black hats having a round red badge, could be seen coming back to the regiments of the old brigade" (p. 139).°°

The Frock Coat   Unquestionably this coat, dark blue and trimmed at the collar and cuffs with light blue, was originally issued as a part of Gibbon's uniform for his newly acquired brigade. Gibbon said as much (*Personal Recollections of the Civil War,* p. 93), and Cheek and Pointon (facing page 27) present a photograph of Pointon in a frock coat captioned "Uniform of the Iron Brigade." It also seems likely that this part of the uniform was not regularly replaced. Thus the photograph at Arlington in September of 1862 shows enlisted men in both the usual short blouse and the frock coat, with a minority wearing the latter. But much later than this, at Gettysburg, C. W. Okey of the Sixth Wisconsin wrote of a bullet passing through "my frock coat" at the railroad cut (*Echoes of the Marches of the Famous Iron Brigade,* Doc Aubery, p. 63), some evidence that the coat was reissued at least once after the original acquisition.

The Leggings   This item of the uniform is not depicted in available photographs. It was originally issued, since Dawes' journal for May 17, 1862, states "the regiment was fully supplied with white leggings" (p. 44), and goes on to describe the prank played on Gibbon, when his horse was equipped with the leggings. Dawes is also the authority for the final reference to the leggings, on October 9, 1862, when the

° A recent book suggests that this photograph has been erroneously identified and that the soldiers appearing in it are probably Confederate dead. *Gettysburg: A Journey in Time,* William A. Frassanito, Charles Scribner's Sons, New York, 1975.

°° An examination since the 1961 edition of the clothing records of the Nineteenth Indiana, available at the National Archives, establishes that the black hats were in fact issued throughout the war.

Twenty-fourth Michigan joined the brigade. At that time Dawes reported that "the white leggings, which, as protection to the feet and ankles, were now more useful than ornamental, had become badly soiled" (p. 104), a record that would also imply that the leggings were not simply worn for dress. In any event, without a further record or picture, it seems likely that the leggings were not reissued, and gradually disappeared.

Despite the distinction of the uniform of the enlisted men, the officers of the Iron Brigade apparently did not wear any unusual uniform. Thus all of the photographs show the typical officer's single-breasted coat, worn with either dark or light blue trousers, and one or another version of the traditional black felt officer's hat, sometimes worn with feathers, which was regulation.

It remains to discuss the Iron Brigade "cross" or insignia, displayed as a decoration in this book. There is no evidence that this insignia was developed before the end of the war. Indeed, the earliest written reference to it was in 1890, in a report of the Iron Brigade reunion in Detroit. On that occasion, Philip Cheek addressed his comrades, and said in passing, "I wouldn't give for those little badges of the Iron Brigade any possession I have or could have outside of my wife and children" (*History of the Twenty-fourth Michigan*, pp. 468-9). Despite this authority, it is probable the badge originated in 1880, when the Iron Brigade association was formed (see Note 67, Epilogue).

5

Source Materials for the Battle of Brawner Farm

As stated by G. F. R. Henderson in *Stonewall Jackson and the American Civil War*, p. 451, because Brawner Farm was "preceded and followed by events of still greater moment, it never attracted the attention it deserved." Henderson and others have mentioned it, but no one has published a detailed account or closely analyzed the *Official Records'* materials. Since this represents the first effort at a definitive account, a discussion of source materials is appropriate.

The Official Records There are many unfortunate gaps in the reports of the battle. Pope refers to it in both his preliminary and general reports, *O.R.*, 16, 14, 37, but he, of course, was not a participant. McDowell, also absent, mentions the battle in his report for the period of August 7 to September 2, 1862, O.R., 16, 377, but he makes no effort to detail the event.

At the division level, the competent Federal witness was General King, but no report from King is contained in the *Official Records*. Pope purported to transmit a report from King with his own report, O.R., 16, 38, when he stated as follows: "The report of General King, herewith appended, exhibits his high opinion of the conduct of this brigade, and of the officers who distinguished themselves in that action." But the editors of the *Official Records* inserted as a note to this statement from Pope, "King's report not found," O.R., 16, 38. Gibbon also took exception to Pope's purporting to transmit a report from King in a letter Gibbon wrote on December 4, 1863, to the adjutant general of the army, O.R., 16, 380. Gibbon noted in his letter that no report from King appeared in the published documents, and also stated that McDowell had said that he had not received a report from King. The remaining evidence on the question of King's report is a letter from King to Colonel Schriver, Pope's chief of staff, dated September 28, 1862, O.R., 18, 816:

> Yours of the 25th is at hand. When I turned over the command of the division to Hatch all the papers were left with him, including the reports of the several brigadiers as to the operations during the latter part of August, and the battles of the 28th, 29th, and 30th. Hatch, I understand, has made his report. Pray let me know what you have from our division, and I will endeavor to supply what is still lacking. I hope the general is well and bears up manfully under the outrageous attacks of his enemies. Time will vindicate him. I am much better, and hope to be entirely well again in a few days.

Neither Schriver's letter of the 25th nor any later correspondence between King and Schriver on the subject of reports has been found. In any event, from all indications, it is apparent that King's illness and almost immediate surrender of his command acted to prevent his submitting a report for Brawner Farm. Hatch's report as division commander in place of King, O.R., 16, 367, covers the days of August 29 and 30, but not August 28.

Concluding the Federal division commander reports are Ricketts',

O.R., 16, 383, but he was not in the battle, and Reynolds', O.R., 16, 392, which is of little value as to the events of the battle.

At the brigade level, Gibbon published two reports of the battle. The first of these, dated September 3, 1862, appears at O.R., 16, 377. The second, O.R., 16, 380, was written December 4, 1863, and is in the form of the above-mentioned letter to the adjutant general, U.S. Army, and was written "to correct" errors in Pope's report. Doubleday also published his report, O.R., 16, 369, although his enclosed table of casualties has not been found, but neither Hatch's nor Patrick's reports, if any, have been found, in spite of King's implication in his letter to Schriver that such had been rendered to him and turned over by him to Hatch.

Turning to the regimental level, only the Sixth Wisconsin of Gibbon's regiments has a report. It was rendered by Lieutenant Colonel Bragg, O.R., 16, 382. The casualties among field officers in the Second and Seventh Wisconsin doubtless account for the lack of reports from those regiments, but no such reason exists for the Nineteenth Indiana. Two of Doubleday's regiments have reports, the Ninety-fifth New York, O.R., 16, 371, and the Fifty-sixth Pennsylvania. Lieutenant Colonel J. William Hofmann of the Fifty-sixth submitted two separate reports, dated September 5, 1862, O.R., 16, 373, and September 10, 1862, O.R., 16, 372, which are in some respects in irreconcilable conflict. None of Hatch's regiments and only one of Patrick's, the Eightieth New York, reported, O.R., 16, 375. Neither Battery B nor any other Federal artillery or any cavalry unit has any report describing the event from the Union side.

In the Confederate reports, Lee mentions the battle in his brief report of September 3, 1862, O.R., 16, 559, and his formal report of the campaign, O.R., 16, 555. Jackson's report is also available and, since he was in personal command, is of value, O.R., 16, 644, 645. At the division level, General Taliaferro reported in spite of his wounds, O.R., 16, 656, but Ewell did not, and A. P. Hill's report is silent on the battle because he was not engaged, O.R., 16, 669. Stuart also reported for his cavalry division, and the brief reference is valuable at O.R., 16, 735.

At the brigade level, in General Taliaferro's Stonewall Division, reports are available for Johnson's Second Brigade, which was not engaged, O.R., 16, 664, and Starke's Fourth Brigade, written by

Colonel Stafford because of Starke's wound, O.R., 16, 668. But there is no report for Baylor's Stonewall (First Brigade) or Colonel A. G. Taliaferro's Third Brigade. In Ewell's Division, reports are lacking for Lawton's and Trimble's brigades, the two engaged, while Early has a report, O.R., 16, 710, as does Hays' Brigade, written by Colonel H. Forno, O.R., 16, 717. In A. P. Hill's Division, reports are available for three brigades, Archer's, O.R., 16, 700, Branch's, O.R., 16, 675, and McGowan's, O.R., 16, 679, none of which was engaged but each of which refers to the action of Taliaferro's and Ewell's brigades.

Of the Confederate infantry regiments, only those in Baylor's Brigade reported, but all of these did except one (the Fifth Virginia): Second Virginia, O.R., 16, 660; Fourth Virginia, O.R., 16, 661; Twenty-seventh Virginia, O.R., 16, 662; and Thirty-third Virginia, O.R., 16, 663.

For the Confederate artillery, Colonel Crutchfield, Jackson's chief of artillery, reported, O.R., 16, 651, as did Major Pelham of Stuart's horse artillery. Pelham has two reports of the action, O.R., 16, 753, 754. Hill's divisional chief of artillery, Lieutenant Colonel Walker, also has a report, O.R., 16, 674, but it is helpful only to confirm the lack of participation by Hill's guns.

In addition to Stuart's report, above-mentioned, the Confederate cavalry is also represented by a report from Colonel Rosser, O.R., 16, 750, which briefly refers to the engagement and locates the Confederate cavalry.

Eyewitness Accounts Among published accounts by participants, the most comprehensive is Rufus R. Dawes' in *The Sixth Wisconsin Volunteers*. Since Dawes was writing from his contemporaneous letters and a journal, his narrative, although published years after the war, is valuable. John Gibbon's version, appearing in his *Personal Recollections of the Civil War*, is generally compatible with his official reports, and is also a basic authority for the battle. *History of the Sauk County Riflemen*, Philip Cheek and Mair Pointon, also highlights the affair, but does not purport to describe the battle in any detail. Another Federal account is that of George F. Noyes, *The Bivouac and the Battlefield*. Noyes was on Doubleday's staff, and his book was published in 1863. It is the best authority for the action as it developed before Doubleday's Brigade, and is especially helpful with respect to the location and movements of Battery B.

In addition to the foregoing, there are four published letters from Wisconsin participants which describe Brawner Farm. The best of these is Lucius Fairchild's letter of September 2, 1862, in *Wisconsin Newspaper Volumes*, Vol. II, p. 295. John B. Callis also has a published letter, dated September 4th, *Wisconsin Newspaper Volumes*, Vol. IV, p. 14. Two other soldiers' letters are in *Wisconsin Newspaper Volumes*, Vol. II, p. 293, and Vol. III, p. 265.

The remaining Federal published eyewitness accounts are those of Solomon Meredith and Charles King. Meredith's appeared in his letter to the *Indianapolis Daily Journal*, published September 11, 1862, at page 2. It is not a valuable source and is confined to exaggerated descriptions of the action of the Nineteenth Indiana. Charles King's description appears in his article "Gainesville," published in *War Papers, Wisconsin Commandery, Military Order of the Loyal Legion*, Vol. III. Charles King was his father's messenger at the battle and is surely qualified as a witness. His narrative is vastly detailed and largely accurate, and was principally directed at mitigating the impression of his father's failure. Of special concern is the question of the withdrawal *after* the battle, and Charles King does not attempt to explain why the division was surprised and why Gibbon was substantially unsupported.

For the Confederates, the most comprehensive published accounts are William C. Oates', *The War Between the Union and the Confederacy*, and General Taliaferro's article in *Battles and Leaders*, Vol. II. Oates was a member of the Fifteenth Alabama of Trimble's Brigade, and his narrative is detailed for the action of this brigade. Taliaferro's story is also good, and in it he corrects errors his report contained. Completing the published Southern descriptions are those of W. W. Blackford, *War Years With Jeb Stuart*, and Poague's *Gunner With Stonewall*, of which the latter only briefly identifies the engagement.

The principal source of unpublished accounts by participants is the manuscript collection of the State Historical Society of Wisconsin, at Madison. Among the fairly detailed accounts there is Frank Haskell's, appearing in a letter of August 31, 1862, to his brother. Haskell also wrote of Brawner Farm on September 22, 1862, again in a letter to his brother. Another valuable account is that of George Fairfield of the Sixth Wisconsin, contained in his diary. Edward S. Bragg also gives a brief account, which appears in a letter to his wife, written September 13, 1862.

From the Second Wisconsin, Sydney B. Mead's letters are also valuable manuscript sources, as is the diary of William Noble, which was copied by Major George H. Otis and continued by Otis after Noble's death in 1864. Although not a contemporaneous account, Gilbert M. Woodward's letter of May 3, 1913, to Charles King, contained in *Hughes MSS*, is also a view of the battle from a member of the Second Wisconsin.

NOTES

Prologue (pages 3–28)

1. *Annual Report of the Adjutant General, State of Wisconsin,* 1861, pp. 13, 15, 16–17; *Annual Report of the Adjutant General, State of Wisconsin,* 1862–3, pp. 898–9. These reports are hereinafter identified as "Wis. A.G.," with appropriate dates. The fairgrounds situs of the camp is stated in *The Military History of Wisconsin,* E. B. Quiner, p. 60. For Wisconsin's quota of one regiment, see *War of the Rebellion, Official Records of the Union and Confederate Armies,* Series III, Vol. I (Serial No. 122), p. 69, abbreviated as O.R., 122, 69.

2. *Wisconsin Necrology,* Vol. IV, pp. 46–8; *The Bench and Bar of Wisconsin,* Parker M. Reed, p. 184; *History of the Bench and Bar of Wisconsin,* Vol. I, John Berryman, p. 442.

3. Wis. A.G., 1861, p. 16; *Register of Graduates and Former Cadets, United States Military Academy,* 1952 edition, p. 191. McDonald was a railroad clerk and ticket agent and an officer of the Phoenix Insurance Company. He had been treasurer of the Juneau Guards, a militia regiment, and was appointed the colonel thereof in 1859 by Governor Randall. At Milwaukee's first war meeting, April 15, 1861, McDonald was elected one of the secretaries. *History of Milwaukee, From Its First Settlement to the Year 1895,* Vol. I, p. 112; *Milwaukee Daily Sentinel,* Feb. 24, 1858, p. 1; May 31, 1859, p. 1; Feb. 14, 1860, p. 1; *Milwaukee City Directory,* 1854–5, 1856–7.

4. *Wisconsin Newspaper Volumes,* Vol. I, p. 71.

5. *Ibid.,* p. 81.

6. *Ibid.,* pp. 79, 81.

7. *Ibid.,* p. 78.

8. *Larke MSS.*

9. *Wisconsin Newspaper Volumes,* Vol. I, p. 81.

10. *Ibid.,* p. 78.

11. *Ibid.,* p. 79.

12. *Ibid.,* p. 82.

13. *Echoes of the Marches of the Famous Iron Brigade, 1861–1865,* Doc Aubery, pp. 8–9.

14. *Rollins MSS.*

15. *Wisconsin Newspaper Volumes,* Vol. I, p. 87.

16. *Larke MSS.*

17. *Wis. A.G.,* 1861, pp. 13, 15, 16–17; *Wis. A.G.,* 1862–3, pp. 898–9; *Rollins MSS.*

18. For an 1864–5 map of the Defenses of Washington, showing the location of Fort Corcoran and other forts constructed in 1861, see *Battles and Leaders of the Civil War,* Vol. IV, p. 496. This work is hereinafter identified as *B and L.*

19. *O. R.,* 2, 314; *Military Collector and Historian,* Vol. VIII, No. 1, Spring, 1956, p. 20; *O.R.,* 5, 561.

20. *Wis. A.G.,* 1861, p. 56.

21. *New York Tribune,* Nov. 15, 1861, p. 7; *Memoirs of General T. F. Meagher,* pp. 364, 378, 454–5; *New York Tribune,* April 24, 1861, p. 8. *Rollins MSS* evidences the reaction of the Second to the unusual types of men in Sherman's Brigade.

22. *Wis. A.G.,* 1862–3, p. 899; *O.R.,* 2, 310, 312; Sherman's report, *O.R.,* 2, 368–71; *O.R.,* 107, 17.

23. *Wis. A.G.,* 1862–3, p. 899.

24. Both the *History of the Bench and Bar of Wisconsin,* Vol. I, John Berryman, p. 442, and the obituary in the *Wisconsin Sentinel* for Thursday, Oct. 18, 1883, refer to the fact that Coon had a liquor problem. The latter publication attributes his resignation to this cause. Since sources like Berryman and the newspaper are based entirely on hearsay evidence, and in the light of General Sherman's express commendation of Coon at Bull Run (see text), the allegation that liquor caused Coon's resignation cannot be accepted. The most that can be said is that liquor may or may not have been involved.

25. *Rollins MSS.*

26. Sherman's report, *O.R.,* 2, 371; *Memoirs of General William T. Sherman,* 1875 edition, Vol. I, p. 180; *Wis. A.G.,* 1865, p. 1313.

27. *Wisconsin Newspaper Volumes,* Vol. I, p.105; *ibid.,* p. 108; *ibid.,* p. 123; *ibid.,* p. 109; *Wis. A.G.,* 1865, p. 1583. This authority states that Peck was commissioned a captain on Oct. 10, 1863, and discharged on June 20, 1865. *Wis. A.G.,* 1865, p. 1313.

28. *Register of Graduates and Former Cadets, United States Military Academy,* 1952 edition, p. 190; *Wisconsin Newspaper Volumes,* Vol. II, p. 293.

29. *Wisconsin Newspaper Volumes,* Vol. I, pp. 135–6, 129.

30. *Ibid.,* pp. 135–6.

31. *The Military History of Wisconsin,* E. B. Quiner, pp. 993–4.

32. *History of Winnebago County Wisconsin,* Vol. II, Publius V. Lawson, pp. 850–53; *Biographical Dictionary of Representative Men of Chicago, Wisconsin and the Columbian Exposition,* pp. 411–12; *Wis-*

consin Necrology, Vol. III, p. 140; *Soldiers and Citizens Album of Biographical Record*, Vol. I, pp. 695–7.

33. *Wis.* A.G., 1862–3, pp. 899–901; O.R., 107, 443, 215–17.

34. *History of the Sauk County Riflemen*, Philip Cheek and Mair Pointon, pp. 7–16; *The Sixth Wisconsin Volunteers*, R. R. Dawes, pp. 12–13. The departure of the Sauk County Riflemen for Madison is also described in *Wisconsin Newspaper Volumes*, Vol. I, pp. 231–2.

35. *A Memoir*, Rufus R. Dawes, pp. 11–12; *The Sixth Wisconsin Volunteers*, R. R. Dawes, pp. 5–6, 10.

36. *Capture and Escape*, John A. Kellogg, Wisconsin History Commission, pp. xi, xii.

37. *The Sixth Wisconsin Volunteers*, R. R. Dawes, pp. 6–7, 10–12.

38. *Ibid.*, p. 13; *History of the Sauk County Riflemen*, Philip Cheek and Mair Pointon, p. 16; *Wis.* A.G., 1861, pp. 25–6.

39. *Wisconsin in the War of the Rebellion*, William D. Love, p. 972; *History of Milwaukee, Wisconsin*, Frank A. Flower, pp. 789–92; *The Sixth Wisconsin Volunteers*, R. R. Dawes, p. 25.

40. *The Sixth Wisconsin Volunteers*, R. R. Dawes, pp. 26–7; *Wis.* A.G., 1861, pp. 26–7, states: "For some reason not known to this department, there has been more change in the Sixth Regiment among commissioned officers by resignation and otherwise than all other regiments combined." See also *Wisconsin Newspaper Volumes*, Vol. I, pp. 258–9, 261–2.

41. Biographical data about Atwood, including his reason for resignation, appears in *Wisconsin Historical Collections*, Vol. IX, edited by Lyman C. Draper, p. 454. Biographical data about Sweet appears in *Pioneer Courts and Lawyers of Manitowoc County, Wisconsin*, James S. Anderson, pp. 97–8; *History of the Bench and Bar of Wisconsin*, Vol. II, John Berryman, p. 110; *Wisconsin Necrology*, Vol. II, p. 68. For resignation and promotion dates, see *Wis.* A.G., 1865, p. 1339.

42. *Wis.* A.G., 1865, p. 1339; *Dictionary of American Biography*, Vol. II, pp. 587–8.

43. *The Battle of Gettysburg*, Frank A. Haskell, Wisconsin History Commission, 1908, pp. xi, xii; *Haskell MSS.*

44. *Wis.* A.G., 1861, p. 26; *The Sixth Wisconsin Volunteers*, R. R. Dawes, p. 18.

45. *History of the Sauk County Riflemen*, Philip Cheek and Mair Pointon, p. 17.

46. *Ibid.*, p. 17; *The Sixth Wisconsin Volunteers*, R. R. Dawes, pp. 19–21, 22–3; O.R., 107, 443.

47. Article by Harry T. Grube, *Military Collector and Historian*, Vol. V, No. 1, March, 1953, pp. 1–14.

48. O.R., 122, 70.

49. *An Autobiography*, Lew Wallace, p. 265; *Military Collector and Historian*, Vol. V, No. 1 March, 1953, pp. 1–4; *Camp Morton, 1861–1865*, Winslow and Moore, Indiana Historical Society, pp. 237, 239–44;

Terrell's Reports of the Adjutant General of the State of Indiana, 1861–5, Vol. II, p. 176. These reports are hereinafter identified as "*Ind. A.G.*"

50. *Indiana's Roll of Honor*, Vol. I, David Stevenson, pp. 347–8; *Indiana at Antietam*, report of the Indiana Antietam Monument Commission, pp. 107–8.

51. *Daily State Sentinel*, Nov. 4, 1861, p. 3; *ibid.*, Aug. 6, 1861, p. 2.

52. *The National Cyclopedia of Biography*, Vol. V, p. 56; *Life of Oliver P. Morton*, Vol. I, William Dudley Foulke, pp. 66–7. Meredith had three sons in the army, including Samuel H. Meredith, who began the war as a noncommissioned officer in the Nineteenth Indiana and was mustered out on Jan. 9, 1864, as first lieutenant of Company A of the Nineteenth, and died shortly thereafter.

53. *Daily State Sentinel*, June 28, 1861, p. 3; *Indiana True Republican*, June 20, 1861, p. 2; *Daily State Sentinel*, July 2, 1861, p. 3.

54. *Indiana at Antietam*, report of the Indiana Antietam Monument Commission, p. 107.

55. *Biographical Sketches of Members of the 41st General Assembly, State of Indiana*, James Sutherland, p. 91; *Ind. A.G.*, Vol. II, p. 20. *Indiana MSS* contain a letter of Dec. 2, 1862, from Meredith to Governor Morton, which refers to friction with Cameron prior to the latter's transfer. *Ind. A.G.*, Vol. II, p. 168.

56. *Indiana's Roll of Honor*, Vol. I, David Stevenson, pp. 381–2; p. 633; *Ind. A.G.*, Vol. II, p. 168.

57. *Ind. A.G.*, Vol. II, p. 176; *Daily State Sentinel*, Aug. 1, 1861, p. 3. The uniforms were made by Menderson and Frohman of Cincinnati, *Indianapolis Daily Journal*, Aug. 2, 1861, p. 3. *Daily State Sentinel*, July 26, 1861, p. 3.

58. *Indiana MSS*. See also *Indianapolis Daily Journal*, Aug. 5, 1861, p. 3. The band uniforms were made by the firm of "Messrs. Glasser & Bros.," according to *Indiana MSS*. The band instruments, estimated to cost $600, were purchased in Cincinnati according to the *Daily State Sentinel*, Aug. 4, 1861, p. 3.

59. *Indianapolis Daily Journal*, July 6, 1861, p. 2; *ibid.*, Aug. 20, 1861, p. 3.

60. *Indiana's Roll of Honor*, Vol. I, David Stevenson, pp. 348–9; O.R., 107, 443; *Daily State Sentinel*, Aug. 19, 1861, p. 2; *Indianapolis Daily Journal*, Sept. 26, 1861, p. 2.

61. O.R., 5, 168–184; *Daily State Sentinel*, Sept. 30, 1861, p. 3.

62. O.R., 5, 215–16; *Indiana's Roll of Honor*, Vol. I, David Stevenson, p. 349; *Indianapolis Daily Journal*, Sept. 26, 1861, p. 3; *ibid.*, Sept. 14, 1861, p. 2.

63. *Wisconsin Newspaper Volumes*, Vol. I, pp. 266–8; *Wis. A.G.*, 1861, pp. 28–9; *Wis. A.G.*, 1862–3, p. 901.

64. *Dictionary of American Biography*, Vol. X, pp. 382–3, 398–400; *Wis. A.G.*, 1862–3, p. 901. King's reporting for duty is recorded at O.R., 107, 438. His epilepsy is mentioned in *Dictionary of American Biography*, Vol. X, pp. 398–400.

65. *Wis.* A.G., 1861, pp. 28–9.
66. *Rollins MSS.*
67. *Camp Randall and Environs,* S. D. Forbes, pp. 1–6; *Wisconsin Newspaper Volumes,* Vol. I, p. 70. Prior to the war, the State Agricultural Society's Fairgrounds were described in this manner: "These grounds were already enclosed with a high board fence, with several buildings which might be fitted for use until more substantial ones could be built." *The Military History of Wisconsin,* E. B. Quiner, p. 60. See also *Young MSS.*
68. *Gallup MSS.*
69. *Young MSS.*
70. *Wis.* A.G., 1861, pp. 28–9; *Wisconsin Newspaper Volumes,* Vol. I, pp. 266–7; *ibid.,* Vol. III, pp. 280, 282; *Wis.* A.G., 1865, p. 1347.
71. *Wisconsin Newspaper Volumes,* Vol. III, pp. 281–2. See also Governor Randall to Secretary Cameron, O.R., 122, 763.
72. *Wis.* A.G., 1865, p. 1347; *Soldiers and Citizens Album of Biographical Record,* pp. 553–6.
73. *Wis.* A.G., 1865, p. 1347; *The Bench and Bar of Wisconsin,* Parker M. Reed, p. 104; *Report of the Annual Meeting of the Wisconsin State Bar Association,* held at Milwaukee, Feb. 17–18, 1903, p. 209; *Circular No. 2, Series 1902, Whole No. 349, Wisconsin Commandery, Military Order of the Loyal Legion; Wis.* A.G., 1862–3, pp. 901–2; *Wisconsin Newspaper Volumes,* Vol. I, p. 267.
74. *Wis.* A.G., 1861, p. 29; *Wisconsin Newspaper Volumes,* Vol. I, p. 272.
75. *Wis.* A.G., 1861, p. 29. "Special Orders No. 82, Headquarters Army of the Potomac, Washington, September 28, 1861 . . . The Seventh Wisconsin Volunteers is assigned to King's brigade in lieu of the Fifth Wisconsin Volunteers, hereby assigned to Hancock's brigade, and will report accordingly with as little delay as practicable. . . . By command of Major-General McClellan: S. Williams, Assistant Adjutant General." O.R., 107, 489.

1. A Winter in Camp (pages 31–42)

1. *The Sixth Wisconsin Volunteers,* R. R. Dawes, p. 25; *Wis.* A.G. 1862–3, p. 901; *Hughes MSS.*
2. *History of the Sauk County Riflemen,* Philip Cheek and Mair Pointon, p. 21; *Perry MSS; Indiana True Republican,* Dec. 19, 1861, p. 1.
3. O.R., 5, 16. Keyes' Brigade included the Fourteenth New York State Militia (Eighty-fourth Volunteers) and the Twenty-second, Twenty-fourth, and Thirtieth New York Volunteers. Wadsworth's Brigade included the Twelfth, Twenty-first, Twenty-third, and Thirty-fifth New York Volunteers.
4. O.R., 5, 15–17; *Young MSS; The Life of Billy Yank,* Bell Irwin Wiley, pp. 303–4, 321–4.

5. *Indiana True Republican*, Nov. 28, 1861, p. 1.

6. *Wis. A.G.*, 1861, p. 56. *History of Indiana*, Vol. II, Logan Esarey, pp. 629–31.

7. *The Life of Billy Yank*, Bell Irwin Wiley, pp. 41–4; *Indiana Politics During the Civil War*, Stampp, especially Chaps. 1 and 7. For an interesting discussion of abolition in the East and West, see *Lincoln Reconsidered*, David Donald, Chap. 2.

8. *Wisconsin Newspaper Volumes*, Vol. I, p. 89.

9. *Larke MSS*.

10. *Wisconsin Newspaper Volumes*, Vol. IV, p. 9. See also the letter from a soldier of the Seventh Wisconsin on Dec. 16, 1861, about the soldiers' sympathy for the escaped slaves, *Wisconsin Newspaper Volumes*, Vol. II, p. 5.

11. Available recruitment pledges appear in *Indiana MSS*; *The Sixth Wisconsin Volunteers*, R. R. Dawes, p. 6; and *History of the Sauk County Riflemen*, Philip Cheek and Mair Pointon, p. 9.

12. *The Sixth Wisconsin Volunteers*, R. R. Dawes, pp. 27–8; *History of the Sauk County Riflemen*, Philip Cheek and Mair Pointon, p. 18. The diary of Sergeant James M. Perry of the Seventh Wisconsin, *Perry MSS*, contains the following entry for Jan. 1, 1862, concerning the prices of the Wisconsin and Federal clothing issue:

Wisconsin		U.S.	
cap and cover	$1.00	cap	$ .63
woolen jacket and pants	9.50	coat	6.71
summer jacket and pants	4.63	overcoat	7.20
overcoat	7.50	pants	3.03
shoes	1.87	shirt	.88
stockings (two-pair)	.60	shoes	1.94
shirts (two)	2.75	stockings	.26
rubber blanket	1.00	drawers	.50
woolen blanket	3.50	blouse	2.15
		hat and trimmings	1.98
		blanket	2.95
		rubber blanket	1.00
		knapsack and straps	2.57
		haversack	.48
		canteen and strap	.48
		axe	.66
		[illegible]	.12
		spade	.56
		pick axe	.57
		[illegible]	.12
		camp kettle	.48
		mess pan	.17
		bugle	2.82
		fife B	.45
		fife C	.45
		drum	5.58

13. *O.R.*, 5, 708; *The Sixth Wisconsin Volunteers*, R. R. Dawes, p. 35.
14. *O.R.*, 5, 718.
15. *Wis. A.G.*, contradicts itself as to the dates of the new Company K, originally stating Dec., 1861 and later Dec., 1862. The former date, the first one used, is relied on here. A statement of the counties of origin of the men of the new Company K is not available. Dane and Milwaukee counties were the residences of the officers of the new company and the men were presumably from the same places, *Wis. A.G.*, 1865, pp. 1518 and 1589 ff.
16. *O.R.*, 5, 718, 713; *Daily State Sentinel*, Nov. 16, 1861, p. 3; *Indianapolis Daily Journal*, Oct. 16, 1861, p. 2. The Indiana newspapers carried conflicting accounts of the deaths in the Nineteenth. The highest number given was 150, *Indianapolis Daily Journal*, Nov. 15, 1861, p. 3. The number 60 was several times reported, and is accepted as reasonably accurate, *Daily State Sentinel*, Nov. 16, p. 3; *Indianapolis Daily Journal*, Nov. 27, p. 3. See also *Indianapolis Daily Journal*, Oct. 16, 1861, p. 2. *Wisconsin Newspaper Volumes*, Vol. III, p. 282, reported the deaths in the Seventh. *Chapman MSS* include the papers of Dr. Chandler B. Chapman, surgeon of the Sixth Wisconsin. These papers set forth in technical detail the medical history of the Sixth.
17. *Indianapolis Daily Journal*, Oct. 16, 1861, p. 2.
18. *Chapman MSS.*
19. *Indiana MSS.* That the Nineteenth had great difficulty in obtaining and keeping satisfactory medical officers is evidenced by the quantity of correspondence on the subject in *Indiana MSS.*
20. *O.R.*, 5, 708.
21. *The Sixth Wisconsin Volunteers*, R. R. Dawes, p. 27. *Indianapolis Daily Journal*, Oct. 10, 1861, p. 3; *Daily State Sentinel*, Oct. 10, 1861, p. 3; *Indianapolis Daily Journal*, Nov. 20, 1861, p. 2; *Wisconsin Newspaper Volumes*, Vol. I, p. 158.
22. The elopement took place on May 9, 1862. *Soldiers and Citizens Album of Biographical Record*, Vol. II, pp. 578–82; *Wisconsin Necrology*, Vol. XVI, pp. 13–14.
23. *Wisconsin Newspaper Volumes*, Vol. II, p. 211; *ibid.*, pp. 213–14; *Daily State Sentinel*, March 1, 1862, p. 3; *Indiana MSS.*
24. *Wisconsin Newspaper Volumes*, Vol. I, p. 91.
25. *The Sixth Wisconsin Volunteers*, R. R. Dawes, p. 30.
26. *O.R.*, 107, 64.
27. *Echoes of the Marches of the Famous Iron Brigade, 1861–1865*, Doc Aubery, pp. 13–15; *Wisconsin Newspaper Volumes*, Vol. II, p. 222.
28. *Indiana MSS; History of the Sauk County Riflemen*, Philip Cheek and Mair Pointon, pp. 21–2; *The Sixth Wisconsin Volunteers*, R. R. Dawes, pp. 32–3; *Wisconsin Newspaper Volumes*, Vol. IV, p. 30.
29. *Roberts MSS.*
30. *The Sixth Wisconsin Volunteers*, R. R. Dawes, p. 33.
31. *Personal Recollections of the Civil War*, John Gibbon, pp. iii, iv,

3–10, 6–9; *Register of Graduates and Former Cadets, United States Military Academy,* 1952 edition, pp. 184, 196; *The Sixth Wisconsin Volunteers,* R. R. Dawes, p. 43; *The Cannoneer,* Augustus Buell, pp. 23–4.

32. *The Cannoneer,* Augustus Buell, pp. 11–16, 17–20, 29; *Personal Recollections of the Civil War,* John Gibbon, pp. 10, 12–13. The personnel authorized for the battery was four commissioned officers, two staff sergeants (orderly and quartermaster), six line sergeants (chiefs of piece), twelve corporals (six gunners and six chiefs of caisson), five artificers, two buglers, one guidon, and 120 cannoneers and drivers (*The Cannoneer,* p. 17). During the period from Nov., 1861, until June, 1862, King's regiments contributed the following numbers of men to Battery B: Nineteenth Indiana, 22; Second Wisconsin, 13; Sixth Wisconsin, 15; Seventh Wisconsin, 13. From June, 1862, until Nov., 1862, the following additional: Nineteenth Indiana, 6; Second Wisconsin, 6; Sixth Wisconsin, 9; Seventh Wisconsin, 13 (*The Cannoneer,* pp. 19–20, 29).

33. *Personal Recollections of the Civil War,* John Gibbon, pp. 13–14; *The Cannoneer,* pp. 24–5, 57.

34. *The Sixth Wisconsin Volunteers,* R. R. Dawes, pp. 35–6. The statement of the field officers reflects the following resignations, transfers, and promotions, previously noted in the text: *Nineteenth Indiana,* Lt. Col. Cameron promoted and transferred; Maj. Bachman promoted to lieutenant colonelcy; Isaac May promoted from captain to major; *Second Wisconsin,* Col. Coon, Lt. Col. Peck and Maj. McDonald resigned; replaced by Col. O'Connor, Lt. Col. Fairchild, and Maj. Allen, the last named having been promoted from captain; *Sixth Wisconsin,* Lt. Col. Atwood resigned; Maj. Sweet promoted to lieutenant colonelcy and Edward S. Bragg promoted from captain to major; *Seventh Wisconsin,* Col. Vandor resigned; Lt. Col. Robinson promoted to colonel; Maj. Hamilton promoted to lieutenant colonel; Capt. Bill promoted to major—*Ind.* A.G., Vol. II, p. 168; *Wis.* A.G., 1865, pp. 1313, 1339, 1347.

2. Fredericksburg: A New Commander Orders Black Hats
(pages 43–60)

1. O.R., 107, 55; O.R., 5, 18–21.

2. *The Sixth Wisconsin Volunteers,* R. R. Dawes, p. 36; *Wisconsin Newspaper Volumes,* Vol. IV, p. 1; *Indianapolis Daily Journal,* March 20, 1862, p. 2; *Mead MSS; Indianapolis Daily Journal,* March 17, 1862, p. 2.

3. O.R., 5, 21; *The Sixth Wisconsin Volunteers,* R. R. Dawes, p. 37.

4. Frémont's numbers, approximately 35,000 men, appear in an "Abstract from Returns of the Mountain Department . . . for the month of May, 1862," O.R., 18, 308. Banks' 20,000 men are identified in an "Abstract from returns of the . . . Departments of the Rappahannock and of the Shenandoah . . . for the month of May, 1862," O.R., 18, 308. As of this return, Shields' Division was in McDowell's Department of the

Rappahannock. Accordingly, Banks' numbers appearing in O.R., 18, 308, must be adjusted to include Shields' Division. Shields' return for May is at O.R., 18, 309. McDowell's numbers are based on this same return.

Douglas Southall Freeman credits Johnson with 2,500 men, *Lee's Lieutenants*, Vol. I, p. 368. Jackson's numbers, excluding Johnson and Ewell, appear at O.R., 18, 879. Ewell's strength was 8,000, based on "Abstract from monthly report of Ewell's division, for July 31, 1862," O.R., 18, 964. The July 31 return has been reduced in stating an April return for Ewell because he apparently received reinforcements between April and July 31.

5. O.R., 18, 43; *The Sixth Wisconsin Volunteers*, R. R. Dawes, pp. 37–8.

6. *The Sixth Wisconsin Volunteers*, R. R. Dawes, pp. 38–9; *History of the Sauk County Riflemen*, Philip Cheek and Mair Pointon, pp. 24–5; O.R., 107, 576.

7. O.R., 15, 427–30, 432–7.

8. *The Sixth Wisconsin Volunteers*, R. R. Dawes, p. 40. The quotation is from *Young MSS*.

9. *Young MSS*. A good description of the countryside around Falmouth appears in a soldier's letter, *Wisconsin Newspaper Volumes*, Vol. IV, p. 1. *Roberts MSS* contain a description of the camp of Gibbon's Brigade.

10. O.R., 15, 279. *Young MSS* contain a good account of the bridge-building. See also *The Sixth Wisconsin Volunteers*, R. R. Dawes, pp. 42–3; *History of the Sauk County Riflemen*, Philip Cheek and Mair Pointon, pp. 28–9. These bridges were a matter of wonder and pride at the time. In the McDowell Court of Inquiry, General McDowell took occasion to discuss them in the face of the serious charges the court was considering, O.R., 15, 281, note.

11. O.R., 15, 280; O.R., 18, 126.

12. *Young MSS*.

13. *History of the Sauk County Riflemen*, Philip Cheek and Mair Pointon, pp. 29–30. The quotation appears in *Young MSS*.

14. *History of the Sauk County Riflemen*, Philip Cheek and Mair Pointon, pp. 29–30; *The Sixth Wisconsin Volunteers*, R. R. Dawes, p. 42. Church attendance is described in a soldier's letter in *Wisconsin Newspaper Volumes*, Vol. III, p. 256.

15. "Special Orders, No. 46. Hdqurs. Dept. of the Rappahannock, Opposite Fredericksburg, May 7, 1862. Brig. Gen. John Gibbon, U.S. Volunteers is assigned to the command of the Third Brigade, of King's division [Cutler's] and will report to Brigadier-General King for duty. By command of Major-General McDowell: Saml. Breck, Assistant Adjutant-General." O.R., 107, 605. *Personal Recollections of the Civil War*, John Gibbon, p. 36.

16. *Personal Recollections of the Civil War*, John Gibbon, pp. 26–7, 47.

17. *Bragg MSS*.

18. *Wisconsin Newspaper Volumes,* Vol. IV, p. 7.

19. *Personal Recollections of the Civil War,* John Gibbon, pp. 27, 31, 36–8; *Young MSS. Roberts MSS* comment on the strictness of affairs after Gibbon's appointment.

20. Article by Colonel J. A. Watrous in *Wisconsin Soldiers and Sailors Reunion Roster,* compiled by C. K. Pier, p. 259.

21. *Personal Recollections of the Civil War,* John Gibbon, p. 39.

22. *Bragg MSS; Personal Recollections of the Civil War,* John Gibbon, pp. 27–30, 36. On the question of Colonel Meredith's alleged conduct, Gibbon said this in his *Recollections:* "This feeling [i.e., the feeling against officers of the regular army], strong enough before, was somewhat increased by the action of one of the colonels, who, a politician and backed by strong political influence, openly protested against a Regular being placed in command of the brigade asserting that it should have been given to a volunteer and especially a western man, all the regiments being from that section of the country. His action in the matter might have produced more harm than it did but for the fact that not being anything of a soldier and too old to be made one, his influence in the command was not very great and he did not gain the support of the best military element in it." By a process of elimination, the colonel whom Gibbon was talking about must have been Meredith. Cutler of the Sixth Wisconsin was directly involved in the issue with Lieutenant Colonel Sweet. O'Connor of the Second and Robinson of the Seventh Wisconsin were neither old nor of a political background. The interesting question is whether Gibbon was correct in his allegation of Meredith's conduct. There is no collateral means of verifying Gibbon's belief. But to give Meredith his due, it is possible that Gibbon was in error about him. As will later appear in connection with Meredith's promotion to command of the brigade after Antietam, Gibbon strongly disapproved of Meredith and took pains to make this clear in his *Recollections.* Concerning Sweet's transfer, see *Wis.* A.G., 1865, pp. 1339, 1408. His colonel's commission was dated July 12, 1862.

23. *Personal Recollections of the Civil War,* John Gibbon, p. 93; *The Sixth Wisconsin Volunteers,* R. R. Dawes, pp. 43–4; *History of the Sauk County Riflemen,* Philip Cheek and Mair Pointon, p. 27. *Roberts MSS* are the source of the quote. Concerning the hat, Roberts wrote: "We have new hats; they are black with a feather in them, and they look gay." Another description appears in a soldier's letter in *Wisconsin Newspaper Volumes,* Vol. I, p. 148.

24. *The Sixth Wisconsin Volunteers,* R. R. Dawes, p. 53, contains an excerpt from Pope's consolidated morning report of July 31, 1862. The present-for-duty number of men was 2,664. To this were added 150 commissioned officers. *History of the Sauk County Riflemen,* Philip Cheek and Mair Pointon, p. 30, describes a typical situation in the brigade as of May 19: ". . . by reason of exposure and hard service, our company had only 68 what we call fighting men. Marshall Keyes died May 6th of typhoid fever, a good soldier."

25. O.R., 18, 196, 309; O.R., 15, 97, 281–2.
26. *The Sixth Wisconsin Volunteers*, R. R. Dawes, p. 45.
27. O.R., 15, 282; *The Sixth Wisconsin Volunteers*, R. R. Dawes, p. 45; *Personal Recollections of the Civil War*, John Gibbon, pp. 32–3.
28. *Personal Recollections of the Civil War*, John Gibbon, p. 33; *The Sixth Wisconsin Volunteers*, R. R. Dawes, p. 45.
29. *History of the Sauk County Riflemen*, Philip Cheek and Mair Pointon, p. 30; *Personal Recollections of the Civil War*, John Gibbon, pp. 33–4; O.R., 18, 233; O.R., 18, 284–5; *The Sixth Wisconsin Volunteers*, R. R. Dawes, p. 45.
30. Leaving McCall's Division at Fredericksburg, McDowell was moving his remaining forces toward Front Royal, Jackson's original point of contact with Banks' troops on May 23. Ord's Division was dispatched by water to Washington and Alexandria and from there to Front Royal. Shields' veterans were moving on Front Royal over the Blue Ridge. O.R., 18, 296, 303; O.R., 15, 282–3; O.R., 18, 295.
31. O.R., 18, 294.
32. *The Sixth Wisconsin Volunteers*, R. R. Dawes, pp. 46–7 The Wisconsin soldier's quotation appears in a letter in *Wisconsin Newspaper Volumes*, Vol. IV, p. 2.
33. O.R., 18, 300–01, 326–7.
34. O.R., 107, 650; O.R., 18, 318.
35. King had neither rail nor telegraphic communications with McDowell, Jackson's men having freely cut telegraph wires as they moved up the turnpike and toward their escape. After consulting with Patrick and Gibbon, King decided to concentrate his division at Haymarket. At noon on June 2, with Gibbon in the advance, the soldiers stepped off, but not before King had sent a dispatch to McDowell advising him of his concentration and his availability for orders at Thoroughfare by the night of June 2. At 6:00 P.M. on the 2nd, as King's column reached Haymarket, they met their colleagues from Patrick's and Augur's brigades returning from Front Royal. The division's artillery, cavalry, and trains also moved into Haymarket on the 2nd, having pulled back from Thoroughfare Gap. Thus King's Division was together again on the railroad at Haymarket. To establish communications with McDowell, King went on June 3 to Gainesville and wired the corps commander, suggesting a trip by the officers to see McDowell at Front Royal. Nothing came of the projected trip to Front Royal, but on June 5 McDowell finally directed King to move his division to Warrenton, cautioning him about 1,500 Confederate cavalry said to be there. On the following day, King did march to Warrenton, arriving there on the evening of June 6. He reported to McDowell that the town was quiet and had seen no Confederate troops. Then, as if begging for a little action, King dispatched scouting parties toward Strasburg, Gordonsville, and the Rappahannock. On June 8, King's men reconnoitered Sulphur Springs and the Gordonsville area again. But they found no Confederates. Also on the 8th, King was ordered by McDowell to prepare for a return to Fredericksburg, which was cor-

rectly interpreted by Gibbon's soldiers as the first step in a resumption of the long-projected move to Richmond. But on the following day, McDowell forwarded the news of Shields' repulse at Port Republic and instructed King to hold his division in readiness to move to Luray or Front Royal. King obediently halted his men and awaited further orders. But he was sensitive to the bewilderment of his soldiers and their apparently senseless marching and countermarching and advised McDowell that the "effect of another retrograde movement will be disheartening to the men." King's men were to be spared another "retrograde movement," at least for the time being. After the pause caused by the flare-up at Port Republic, Gibbon's Brigade and Battery B started again for Fredericksburg on June 10. The rest of the division was held at Catlett's briefly and proceeded to Fredericksburg later in the month. O.R., 18, 323, 326–7, 343, 351–2, 356, 361, 363, 365, 366; O.R., 107, 662; O.R., 15, 288.

36. O.R., 18, 432–3.

37. Wis. A.G., 1865, p. 1339. Dawes' commission was issued on June 30, 1862. The Sixth Wisconsin Volunteers, R. R. Dawes, pp. 48–50.

38. Indiana MSS.

39. Indiana MSS, Michigan MSS, and the manuscript collections at the State Historical Society of Wisconsin abound in correspondence, petitions, and documents concerning promotions.

40. The Sixth Wisconsin Volunteers, R. R. Dawes, p. 51. See also soldier's letter, Wisconsin Newspaper Volumes, Vol. IV, pp. 2–3, and Young MSS.

41. In his Personal Recollections of the Civil War, Gibbon demonstrates this philosophy in his discussions on pages 34, 47, 48–9. Lincoln and His Generals, T. Harry Williams, and The Army Under Pope, John Codman Ropes, p. 12, contain discussions of this general point of view and McClellan's manifestations of it.

3. John Pope's Army: An End to File Closing
(pages 61–79)

1. O.R., 15, 169. King's appointment appears at O.R., 18, 438: "It is ordered . . . That Brig. Gen. Rufus King be, and he is hereby, assigned to the command of the First Army Corps of the Army of Virginia in place of General Frémont, relieved. By order of the President: Edwin M. Stanton, Secretary of War." Authority for King's rejection of the assignment is found in Indiana True Republican, July 3, 1862, p. 3.

2. O.R., 18, 523. Shields' Division had been broken up; see Lincoln Finds a General, Kenneth P. Williams, Vol. I, p. 260. Concerning Ricketts' replacement by Ord, see O.R., 107, 675–6. Sigel and Banks were in the Shenandoah Valley, along the trail of Stonewall Jackson's escape route. Of McDowell's forces, King's Division was at Fredericksburg and Ricketts' was at Manassas Junction. Sigel was ordered to cross the Shen-

andoah Valley at Front Royal, pass through the Luray Gap, and take position at Sperryville. Banks was also ordered to come through Front Royal and take up his position near Little Washington, a few miles northeast of Sperryville. Ricketts' Division was ordered from Manassas to Waterloo Bridge on the Rappahannock. King remained at Fredericksburg, to maintain the line of communications on the north side of the Rappahannock and to preserve the railroad between Aquia Creek and Fredericksburg. *The Army Under Pope*, John Codman Ropes, p. 5.

3. O.R., 18, 450–52, 457, 463, 487, 499; O.R., 16, 102.

4. *The Sixth Wisconsin Volunteers*, R. R. Dawes, pp. 51–2. See also *Young MSS.*

5. *Personal Recollections of the Civil War*, John Gibbon, pp. 34–6.

6. O.R., 18, 503–04; O.R., 16, 105–06; *Personal Recollections of the Civil War*, John Gibbon, p. 41; *The Sixth Wisconsin Volunteers*, R. R. Dawes, p. 52. The Confederate movement is described in *The Army Under Pope*, John Codman Ropes, pp. 8–9. While Gibbon's advance party was proceeding to the outskirts of Orange Court House, the Sixth Wisconsin, in reserve, had an interesting experience with the war-provoked social revolution in the South. A slave had come into the Sixth Wisconsin's line in the middle of the night and had reported that a Confederate officer was in a house a mile away. Dawes was suspicious and questioned the Negro sharply. The slave told Dawes that "Fore God, Massa, we knows you uns is our friends. It's the Lord's will that the colored folks help you uns." Thus reassured, Dawes and an escort followed the Negro into the night and captured the officer. He was not in uniform and denied his identity, but the Negro disagreed, and Dawes relied on the slave in spite of the officer's insistence that the Federals not "take the word of a nigger." *The Sixth Wisconsin Volunteers*, R. R. Dawes, p. 52.

7. O.R., 18, 523.

8. *Ibid.*, 514.

9. O.R., 16, 121–5; *The Sixth Wisconsin Volunteers*, R. R. Dawes, pp. 53–5; *Personal Recollections of the Civil War*, John Gibbon, pp. 41–2; *Wisconsin Newspaper Volumes*, Vol. II, p. 281; *Noble MSS; Daily State Sentinel*, Aug. 9, 1862, p. 3.

10. On Aug. 7, Pope ordered Ricketts' Division from Waterloo Bridge on the Rappahannock to Culpeper, there to join elements of Banks' Corps. As Gibbon's Brigade marched back on the 8th from their raid on Frederick's Hall Station, the rest of Banks' Corps and all of Sigel's Corps were moved to Culpeper. Shortly thereafter, Banks' reunited corps was advanced eight miles beyond Culpeper to Cedar Mountain. *The Army Under Pope*, John Codman Ropes, pp. 16-17.

11. O.R., 18, 533. King did not receive this order until noon on Aug. 9, the delay having resulted from an interruption of the telegraph lines. There are numerous references to the undisputed fact of Rufus King's illness during Aug., 1862. The authority for the onset of the illness prior

to Aug. 9 is an article entitled "King's Division: Fredericksburg to Manassas" in *War Papers, Wisconsin Commandery, Military Order of the Loyal Legion*, Vol. II, pp. 345–56, by Theron Haight. Haight was an enlisted man in Hatch's Brigade, King's Division, and an eyewitness of the Aug., 1862, activities of King.

12. *O.R.*, 18, 533.

13. "King's Division: Fredericksburg to Manassas," Theron Haight, *War Papers, Wisconsin Commandery, Military Order of the Loyal Legion*, Vol. II, pp. 345–56; *The Sixth Wisconsin Volunteers*, R. R. Dawes, p. 55; *O.R.*, 18, 558.

14. *History of the Sauk County Riflemen*, Philip Cheek and Mair Pointon, pp. 30–31; *O.R.*, 18, 560.

15. *Young MSS; History of the Sauk County Riflemen*, Philip Cheek and Mair Pointon, p. 31.

16. *Personal Recollections of the Civil War*, John Gibbon, pp. 44–5; *The Sixth Wisconsin Volunteers*, R. R. Dawes, p. 56.

17. *O.R.*, 18, 580, 584.

18. In his *Personal Recollections of the Civil War*, Gibbon states at pp. 45–6 that an officer of one of his regiments was killed. This is in error. No casualty among the brigade's officers occurred at or about this time. *The Sixth Wisconsin Volunteers*, R. R. Dawes, pp. 56–7.

19. *History of the Sauk County Riflemen*, Philip Cheek and Mair Pointon, pp. 31–2; *The Sixth Wisconsin Volunteers*, R. R. Dawes, pp. 58–9.

20. *O.R.*, 18, 669, 670. The fact that King did give command to Reynolds is the statement of Gibbon in *Personal Recollections of the Civil War*, p. 46.

21. *O.R.*, 16, 70, 71–2; *O.R.*, 18, 685–6; *The Sixth Wisconsin Volunteers*, R. R. Dawes, pp. 58–9.

22. For an account of McDowell's activities on the night of the 27th, see *The Army Under Pope*, John Codman Ropes, pp. 66–7. Pope's acts are analyzed and discussed in *Lincoln Finds a General*, Kenneth P. Williams, Vol. I, pp. 299, 311–12, 315, and *The Army Under Pope*, John Codman Ropes, pp. 54–5.

23. *O.R.*, 15, 304. See also *The Army Under Pope*, John Codman Ropes, pp. 62, 65–6, 68.

24. "King's Division: Fredericksburg to Manassas," Theron Haight, *War Papers, Wisconsin Commandery, Military Order of the Loyal Legion*, Vol. II, pp. 355–6; *The Sixth Wisconsin Volunteers*, R. R. Dawes, p. 50.

25. The precise time of the firing on Reynolds is not specified in any of the records. The incident is described in the "Facts and Opinion of the McDowell Court of Inquiry," *O.R.*, 15, 329–30; Reynolds' report, *O.R.*, 16, 393; McDowell's report, *O.R.*, 16, 336–7. See also *The Army Under Pope*, John Codman Ropes, p. 70.

26. *The Sixth Wisconsin Volunteers*, R. R. Dawes, p. 59; *Personal Recollections of the Civil War*, John Gibbon, pp. 49–50.

27. *O.R.*, 15, 196; *The Army Under Pope*, John Codman Ropes, pp. 65–6, 71–2.

28. *O.R.*, 16, 337; *O.R.*, 15, 329, 316. It was McDowell's act of leaving his divisions to seek out Pope that the McDowell Court of Inquiry criticized, *O.R.*, 15, 316–17, 329–31.

29. *The Sixth Wisconsin Volunteers*, R. R. Dawes, p. 59; *Personal Recollections of the Civil War*, John Gibbon, p. 50.

30. *O.R.*, 16, 644; *The Army Under Pope*, John Codman Ropes, pp. 57–9.

31. *War Years With Jeb Stuart*, W. W. Blackford, pp. 116–18; *O.R.*, 16, 656.

32. King's present-for-duty strength on Aug. 16, 1862, was 10,345 officers and men, *O.R.*, 18, 580.

33. Gibbon's numbers are difficult to determine. In his book *Personal Recollections of the Civil War*, p. 55, Gibbon states that he took 1,800 men into the action. In his report of Sept. 3, 1862, *O.R.*, 16, 378, Gibbon states that his casualties of 751 on Aug. 28, 1862, amounted to "considerably over one-third of the command," which would place the command as between approximately 1,800 and 2,200. *Haskell MSS* contain two letters, one dated Aug. 31, 1862, and the other Sept. 19, 1862, both of which also state the 1,800 figure. But this is still difficult to accept in view of the July 31, 1862, present-for-duty statement of 2,664 men, *The Sixth Wisconsin Volunteers*, R. R. Dawes, p. 53, and an Aug. 16, 1862, return of 2,611 men present for duty, *O.R.*, 18, 580. Faced with this square conflict in the evidence, the figure of 2,100 officers and men has been adopted.

4. *The Battle at Brawner Farm* (pages 80–98)

1. This is a new name for this battle, which has been variously denominated by previous writers. Contemporary Federal writers, like Dawes, called it the "Battle of Gainesville," as do the *Official Records*. But this is not apt because the battle did not take place at Gainesville. Some modern authorities, like Kenneth P. Williams, have called it "Groveton," which is also perhaps inappropriate from a location standpoint and which tends to confuse it with the larger and foreshadowing engagements of the next two days. Other modern authorities, including Douglas Southall Freeman, have avoided the name problem by simply leaving the battle unnamed. Regardless of the general acceptability of this technique, in a history of the Iron Brigade the event on Aug. 28, 1862, must be named.

The writer has selected the name here used because it is distinctive, and thus confusion with other days' events may be avoided, and because it is geographically accurate. The battle did in fact take place on the farm of the Brawner family.

For identification of the Brawner ownership there are two widely different authorities. The first is Stonewall Jackson, whose report of the affair, written April 23, 1863, accurately sets forth the unlikely name of Brawner, O.R., 16, 645. The second is Joseph Mills Hanson, former superintendent of the Manassas National Battlefield Park. An unpublished manuscript in the park's files today contains an excerpt from a letter written under date of Dec. 21, 1946, by Hanson to the author of the manuscript, Fred W. Cross. Hanson said: "I believe . . . investigation would show the name of the place should be 'Brawner's.' . . . Brawner is a common name around Manassas; there are many here today." The only published Federal source which attempted to identify the property erred as to the name of the owner. In his *Personal Recollections of the Civil War*, John Gibbon includes a rough map at page 53 which sets forth the farmhouse, and calls it "Douglass House." On the following page, this name is spelled "Douglas." It may be that people by the name of Douglass or Douglas, another common name around Manassas, have at one time owned the ground. But the name applied by Stonewall Jackson at the time, and approved by Mr. Hanson, seems to the writer to be preferable. With final reference to the name, it will be seen that the only other Confederate participant who tried to name the farm owner was not so successful. Captain J. B. Evans' report for the Fourth Virginia in the Stonewall Brigade refers to the name as "Brown," incorrect but not unlikely. O.R., 16, 661.

2. *Personal Recollections of the Civil War*, John Gibbon, p. 51; Gibbon's report of Sept. 3, 1862, hereinafter referred to as "Gibbon's first report," O.R., 16, 377; Gibbon's report of Dec. 4, 1863, in the form of a letter to the adjutant-general, U.S. Army, hereinafter referred to as "Gibbon's second report," O.R., 16, 381.

3. *History of the Sauk County Riflemen*, Philip Cheek and Mair Pointon, p. 38, contains a reference to the Second's "air of superiority."

4. *B and L*, Vol. II, p. 510.

5. Map sources: (1) At the National Archives, Washington, D.C., "Map of the Battle-Grounds of August 28-29-30, In the Vicinity of Groveton, Prince William County, Va., Made by authority of the Hon. G. W. McCrary, Sec. of War, Surveyed in June 1878 by Bvt. Major General G. K. Warren, Major of Engineers, 1878, U.S.A." (2) O.R., 17, facing p. 1052. (3) Map 60, *Atlas to Accompany Steele's American Campaigns*, edited by Colonel Vincent J. Esposito, 1956 edition. (4) Gainesville Quadrangle, United States Department of the Interior Geological Survey, Mapped by Corps of Engineers, U.S. Army, revised 1953. (5) *The Sixth Wisconsin Volunteers*, R. R. Dawes, p. 66. (6) *Personal Recollections of the Civil War*, John Gibbon, p. 53.

An earlier description of the terrain by a member of Hatch's Brigade appears in an article entitled "Gainesville, Groveton and Bull Run" in *War Papers, Wisconsin Commandery, Military Order of the Loyal Legion*, Vol. II, pp. 357–72, by Theron Haight.

The only improvement on the ground which cannot be located on a map and the location of which is uncertain is the zigzag fence. O.R.,

16, 661, report of the Second Virginia in Baylor's Brigade, refers to the Federal line "stationed in the edge of a woods and behind a fence." Since Baylor's Brigade was on the Confederate right in the area of the farmhouse, the fence apparently extended to the west, at least to the north-west corner of the rectangular wood. William C. Oates of the 15th Alabama of Trimble's Brigade also mentions the fence in front of which he fought in the second brigade from the Confederate left, which would establish the fence as extending to the east and apparently as far as the northeast corner of the rectangular wood. *The War Between the Union and the Confederacy*, William C. Oates, pp. 138–43.

Close personal examination and measurement of the ground, which is outside the Manassas National Battlefield Park and in private hands, establishes that it is unchanged since 1862 with the exception of an additional barn and the size and shape of the rectangular wood, which would seem to be larger now, north and south, and to include a northern extension at the northeast corner which was not there in 1862. The farmhouse and barn are there, either the same ones as in 1862 or similarly located, and even the remnants of the orchard are plainly visible.

6. Gibbon's second report, *O.R.*, 16, 381; Gibbon's first report, *O.R.*, 16, 378; *Personal Recollections of the Civil War*, John Gibbon, p. 51; *The Sixth Wisconsin Volunteers*, R. R. Dawes, p. 60. "King's Division: Fredericksburg to Manassas," Theron Haight, *War Papers, Wisconsin Commandery, Military Order of the Loyal Legion*, Vol. II, pp. 345–56, is the authority for Hatch's discovery of mounted Confederates and their withdrawal. Haight was in Hatch's Brigade and is the only Federal authority available, since neither Hatch nor any of his regiments has a report in the *Official Records*. W. W. Blackford, Stuart's engineer officer, describes at length some of the Confederate cavalry probing, including exchanges of gunfire with Federals, at about the time of Hatch's reconnaissance, *War Years with Jeb Stuart*, pp. 118–20. Exactly where and when this firing was cannot be determined. Accordingly, it cannot be stated that Hatch's fire was answered.

7. See Note 2, above. That Hatch was out of sight is stated by Gibbon in *Personal Recollections of the Civil War*, John Gibbon, p. 51. That Gibbon was not closed up on Hatch is apparent from the latter's being out of Gibbon's sight. Gibbon said as much in his second report, *O.R.*, 16, 381, when he stated that the first Confederate artillery fire took place while Gibbon was closing up on Hatch. That Doubleday and Patrick were not closed up is an inference from the former's later arrival at the scene of action and the latter's absence from the scene of action entirely.

8. *The War Between the Union and the Confederacy*, William C. Oates, p. 137. Oates was in the Fifteenth Alabama of Trimble's Brigade, and an eyewitness. Gibbon's first report, *O.R.*, 16, 377–8; *History of the Sauk County Riflemen*, Philip Cheek and Mair Pointon, p. 37; *The Sixth Wisconsin Volunteers*, R. R. Dawes, p. 60.

9. Jackson's report, O.R., 16, 645; *The Sixth Wisconsin Volunteers*, R. R. Dawes, p. 61. The quotation is from George F. Noyes, of Doubleday's Brigade, in *The Bivouac and the Battlefield*, p. 115.

10. The problem of numbers is a difficult one. In the case of Ewell's Division, Aug. 20, 1862, returns are available, O.R., 18, 966, and have been used, including only present-for-duty infantry:

Lawton's Brigade:	officers	140
	men	1996
		2136
Early's Brigade:	officers	187
	men	1830
		2017
Trimble's Brigade:	officers	89
	men	1100
		1189
Hays' Brigade (Forno):	officers	120
	men	1738
		1858

Because of the absence of a current report, numbers in the Stonewall Division have been arrived at in a different manner. For Baylor's Stonewall Brigade, Douglas Southall Freeman's 635 rank and file, *Lee's Lieutenants*, Vol. II, p. 109, has been used. This figure Freeman developed from the regimental reports which exist for all the regiments in the brigade except the Fifth Virginia, O.R., 16, 660, 661, 662, 663. Freeman's 635 figure has been increased here to 700 to include officers. For the remaining brigades, a complicated process, based on *Numbers and Losses in the Civil War*, Thomas L. Livermore, has been resorted to. Livermore, p. 89, states the strength of Jackson's Division as of Aug. 10, 1862, as 5,365. This he would reduce to 93% of 5,365 for effective strength of 4,989, which figure must be further reduced to 4,286 by deducting, as Livermore does, the division's Cedar Mountain losses (I have used infantry only) of 703 (O.R., 16, 179-80). Assuming a relatively equal strength among the brigades other than Baylor's Stonewall Brigade, the final computation is:

4286—strength of division after Cedar Mountain
−700—Baylor's Stonewall Brigade

3586÷3 = 1195 in Starke's, Johnson's and Taliaferro's.

All of these figures, for narrative purposes, have been rounded to the nearest 100 men.

It is conceded that defects may exist in this method, especially as to the distribution of numbers among the brigades in the Stonewall Division. However, no substantial error is believed to exist and no alternative method presents itself. Previous writers, like John Codman Ropes, Freeman, and others have simply avoided the numbers problem. Others, like G. F. R. Henderson, who states Confederate numbers engaged as 4,500, do not identify the source of their computation. Henderson's figure is surely substantially low, and may result from a belief that only troops from the Stonewall Division were heavily engaged.

11. General Taliaferro's report locates Baylor's (First Brigade) on the right before the action commenced, O.R., 16, 656. The report for the Fourth Virginia of this brigade, O.R., 16, 661, states that the brigade formed "in line of battle in an open field on the farm of Mr. or Mrs. Brown, where we soon advanced. . . . The scene of action was near the dwelling of Mr. or Mrs. Brown, the right of the Fourth resting on some outbuildings." The reasonable inference is that in locating the brigade prior to the advance from behind the railroad embankment into the open field, its line extended toward Page Land Lane. As the action developed, the farmhouse, yard, and orchard to the east became the vortex, and the brigade converged in that direction from its original position slightly to the west thereof.

General Taliaferro also locates Starke's (Fourth Brigade) as next to Baylor's and to Baylor's left before the action commenced. This would have placed Starke's north of the farmhouse and extending to the east thereof, north of the orchard. Also according to General Taliaferro, Johnson's (Second Brigade) and Colonel A. G. Taliaferro's (Third Brigade) were not in the first Confederate line.

Early's report, O.R., 16, 710–11, is in error when it states that Trimble's and Lawton's went in on Starke's right. But his report makes it clear that Trimble's and Lawton's were in front of Early's and Hays' brigades, which is also apparent from the fact that the latter two brigades were never engaged.

The relationship between the two forward brigades, Trimble's and Lawton's, involves conflicting evidence. Rufus Dawes' map, *The Sixth Wisconsin Volunteers*, p. 66, places Trimble's next to Starke's and has Lawton's comprising the Confederate left. Since Dawes made a study of the battle and presumably talked after the war to Confederate participants, his view is entitled to some weight. In addition, William C. Oates, a member of Trimble's and a participant, states that Lawton's was on Trimble's left and refers to Trimble's advancing to prevent a breach in the Confederate line between General Taliaferro's left (Starke's) and Trimble's right. Against these authorities stands the report for the Second Virginia of Baylor's Stonewall Brigade, O.R., 16, 661, where it is stated that Lawton's was brought up "immediately on our left." The use of the word "our" is doubtless meant to denote the *division's* left, but since Starke's and not Baylor's was the division's left, the report could reasonably be in error as to which of Ewell's brigades actually was next to those of Taliaferro's Division. A note to General Taliaferro's article in *B and L*, Vol. II, p. 511, also states that Lawton's was next to Starke's and that Trimble's was on the Confederate left. The general, of course, was a participant, but is not entitled to as much credit with reference to the placing of Ewell's brigades as to the placing of his own. In addition, he had not apparently studied the battle fully, because he also states erroneously that the Federal artillery outnumbered the Confederate. The Dawes-Oates version is here adopted, largely because of Oates' evidence, the most qualified of the eyewitnesses as to his own brigade's location.

12. Reports for Archer's Brigade, Branch's Brigade (Lane), and Gregg's Brigade (McGowan), O.R., 16, 700, 675–6, 679. These refer to "the engagement was opened on our right," O.R., 16, 676, and locate Archer's with Field's Brigade on his right and Branch's behind Archer's, O.R., 16, 700. General Hill's report is of no value for Aug. 28, O.R., 16, 669.

13. General Taliaferro's report, O.R., 16, 656–7, and Jackson's report, O.R., 16, 645, place these three batteries in front of the Fourth (Starke's) Brigade, which brigade was located north of the farmhouse and extending to the east thereof, north of the orchard. See Note 11, above. Colonel Crutchfield's report, O.R., 16, 651–2, identifies Wooding's as a four-gun battery.

Despite the fact that both Taliaferro and Jackson flatly state that Poague and Carpenter, along with Wooding, actually fired, there is a reasonable theory to the contrary. Thus in *Gunner with Stonewall*, Poague states that he did not get up in time, and Crutchfield's report, O.R., 16, 652, is capable of the construction that only Wooding and Balthis were engaged. See Note 15, below.

14. General Taliaferro does not mention Balthis' battery as one of the three on the Confederate right, see Note 13, above. Colonel Crutchfield, Jackson's artillery chief, states that Wooding's and Balthis' "got up first," O.R., 16, 651–2. Since Taliaferro on the right did not mention Balthis', it is believed that he was not on the right. Crutchfield also identifies Balthis' as a four-gun battery, O.R., 16, 651.

15. Crutchfield states that at approximately 4:30 P.M., he received orders from Jackson "to move up the whole artillery force," O.R., 16, 651. Crutchfield also states that "the other batteries did not get up in time to participate," O.R., 16, 652, which would mean those batteries other than Wooding's, Carpenter's, Poague's and Balthis', per notes 13 and 14, above, or other than Wooding's and Balthis', if the participation of Poague and Carpenter is rejected.

Pelham has two reports dated, respectively, March 7, 1863, O.R., 16, 754, and June 10, 1863, O.R., 16, 753. Both refer to his order, just before nightfall, to bring up twenty pieces and to his arrival on the field after infantry fire had commenced. Both Stuart, O.R., 16, 735, and Rosser, O.R., 16, 750, locate the cavalry on Jackson's right.

16. *War Years with Jeb Stuart*, W. W. Blackford, p. 120, refers to Jackson's riding out to examine the approaching foe just as "the head of their column appeared coming down the turnpike." This was Hatch. Jackson was on the right, near the farm buildings, because that is where the battle began and where the Confederate troops came forward as described by Blackford. See Note 17, below.

17. *War Years with Jeb Stuart*, W. W. Blackford, pp. 120–21. Both William C. Oates, *The War Between the Union and the Confederacy*, and John Esten Cooke, *The Life of Stonewall Jackson*, identify a scene in which Jackson ordered Ewell to advance. This has been omitted here.

18. In his *Personal Recollections of the Civil War*, p. 51, Gibbon describes his emergence from behind the rectangular wood just prior to the first artillery fire. The Sixth Wisconsin, as the leading regiment, was just behind him as he emerged and was therefore enclosed by the wood. The locations of the remaining regiments and Battery B are based upon their positions in the column, see Note 8, above, as related to the geography and distances involved. That the Confederates were unseen behind the Brawner ridge is based upon the undisputed fact of the Federals' complete unawareness of their presence until the firing began, the existence of the depressed ground between the two ridge lines, and the fact that by this time the Confederates had moved out from behind the wooded railroad embankment.

19. *Personal Recollections of the Civil War*, John Gibbon, pp. 51-2; Gibbon's first report, O.R., 16, 378; Gibbon's second report, O.R., 16, 381. *The Sixth Wisconsin Volunteers*, R. R. Dawes, p. 60.

See Note 14, above, as to Balthis' being on the Confederate left. Colonel Crutchfield states that Wooding's and Balthis' "got up first and went into action," O.R., 16, 651-2. This supports the inference that the guns which fired first into the head of Gibbon's column were those of Balthis.

20. *Personal Recollections of the Civil War*, John Gibbon, pp. 51, 52; *History of the Sauk County Riflemen*, Philip Cheek and Mair Pointon, p. 38; *The Sixth Wisconsin Volunteers*, R. R. Dawes, p. 60.

In *The Bivouac and the Battlefield*, George F. Noyes states that Gibbon and Doubleday conferred just after the artillery firing began. The implication is that they jointly planned the Federal defense. This is rejected, as it is unmentioned in any of the reports and is inconsistent with the manner in which the battle later developed.

21. See Note 19, above, for identification of Wooding's and Balthis' as the first two batteries to fire. In *Personal Recollections of the Civil War*, p. 52, Gibbon identifies the second battery's location as to his left and near the Douglas (Brawner) house. See also Gibbon's first report, O.R., 16, 378, and his second report, O.R., 16, 381, for location of the second battery and the direction of its fire. The reports for the Fifty-sixth Pennsylvania, O.R., 16, 372, and the Ninety-fifth New York, O.R., 16,

371, both of Doubleday's Brigade, describe the fire of Wooding's battery into their ranks, as does *The Bivouac and the Battlefield*, George F. Noyes, p. 115.

22. *Personal Recollections of the Civil War*, John Gibbon, p. 52; Gibbon's first report, O.R., 16, 378; Gibbon's second report, O.R., 16, 381; *The Sixth Wisconsin Volunteers*, R. R. Dawes, p. 60. The road today still provides the slight embankment.

23. *Personal Recollections of the Civil War*, John Gibbon, p. 52; Gibbon's first report, O.R., 16, 378; Gibbon's second report, O.R., 16, 381.

24. In *Personal Recollections of the Civil War*, p. 52, Gibbon describes meeting the Second in the wood, conducting it through the wood "to the open ground beyond," and "outside of the wood" forming the regiment into line. From this position, the Second "moved up the gentle slope" in front. In his first report, O.R., 16, 378, consistent with his book, Gibbon states that the Second faced to the left and marched obliquely to the rear. This means that the Second moved to its left into the open field west of the wood, which field is in front of the Brawner farmhouse. This fact, in turn, buttresses the conclusion, see Note 21, above, as to Wooding's location.

In moving to their left, the Second had passed at least partially along the flank of the Seventh and Nineteenth, respectively. The Nineteenth was now the rear because Battery B had moved to the head of the brigade.

25. Gibbon's first report, O.R., 16, 378, identifies the right-flank fire as the Second "rose an intervening hill." In *Personal Recollections of the Civil War*, p. 52, Gibbon states essentially the same fact in different words: "As soon as it [the Second] reached the brow of the hill," it was fired upon. That the fire was directed from the farmhouse yard and orchard is a conclusion based upon the Second's route up the hill toward the house, see Note 24, above, and that the fire was from Starke's Brigade is a conclusion based upon its position in the Confederate line, see Note 11, above. The first fire may have been from Baylor's Brigade, but the report for the Second Virginia of that brigade, O.R., 16, 661, states that it was fired on by the Federals, "stationed in the edge of woods and behind a fence," before firing itself. Since the Second Wisconsin did not fire until fired on, Baylor's firing must not have opened the infantry engagement.

Gibbon's first report, O.R., 16, 378; *Personal Recollections of the Civil War*, John Gibbon, pp. 52, 54. Jackson's report, O.R., 16, 645, states that the Federal artillery fire forced Wooding's, Poague's, and Carpenter's batteries to withdraw.

26. It is apparent from both Gibbon's first report, O.R., 16, 378, his *Personal Recollections of the Civil War*, pp. 52, 54, and his second report, O.R., 16, 381, that the Second was heavily assailed immediately following the first exchange of fire. That Baylor's Brigade was now firing,

and into the Second's left flank, is an inference from Baylor's position, and its converging toward the farmhouse, see Note 11, above. The Second Virginia's report describes its returning the Federals' opening fire, O.R., 16, 661.

27. Gibbon's first report, O.R., 16, 378; *Personal Recollections of the Civil War*, John Gibbon, p. 54. That the Nineteenth fired into Baylor is an inference from Baylor's position (see notes 11 and 26, above) on the Confederate right and the Nineteenth's position left of the Second.

28. *The Sixth Wisconsin Volunteers*, R. R. Dawes, pp. 60–61; *Fairfield MSS; Haskell MSS*.

29. For the gap in the line and the Sixth's low ground, see *The Sixth Wisconsin Volunteers*, R. R. Dawes, pp. 61–2. *Haskell MSS* describes the artillery fire from behind the Sixth. Concerning Balthis' retreat, see Gibbon's first report, O.R., 16, 378. For Battery B's actions, see Note 31, below.

30. For overlapping on the left, see *Personal Recollections of the Civil War*, John Gibbon, p. 54. Although not directly stated, the physical facts and size of the Confederate force also establish that the Federal right was overlapped.

Taliaferro's words appear in *B and L*, Vol. II, p. 510. Colonel Crutchfield, O.R., 16, 651–2, describes the withdrawal of the three Confederate batteries, and General Taliaferro's report, O.R., 16, 557, locates them on Baylor's right. Pelham describes his own movements in both of his reports, O.R., 16, 753, 754–5, including his ability to get only two of his guns into action, and Stuart's report, O.R., 16, 735, locates Pelham as to the "extreme right of the battle-field." Crutchfield is the authority for the limitations resulting from the proximity of the infantry soldiers. O.R., 16, 652.

31. General Taliaferro's report, O.R., 16, 656, 658; Early's report, O.R., 16, 710–11. His casualties appear in O.R., 16, 811, and must have been from artillery fire, since his infantry did not participate in the infantry engagement. Hays' report (by Colonel Forno) O.R., 16, 718.

Battery B's advance is directly stated in *Haskell MSS* and implied by *The Bivouac and the Battlefield*, George F. Noyes. Haskell describes the battery's position as "near the crest of the hill below the woods." According to Noyes, Doubleday and his staff repaired to Battery B's position during the battle "on the bare crest of a hill adjoining the woods on the right." This position, according to Noyes, commanded a view of the rebel lines, and the Federals there saw "a mile of lightning leaping from rebel muskets."

32. Archer's report, O.R., 16, 700; Branch's report (Lane's), O.R., 16, 676; Gregg's report (McGowan), O.R., 16, 679.

33. Gibbon's first report, O.R., 16, 378; Gibbon's second report, O.R., 16, 381. A report for the Eightieth New York of Patrick's Brigade, O.R., 16, 376, states that that regiment was ordered forward and arrived on the field after the engagement ended. There is no evidence to indi-

cate that the movement forward began prior to the end of the battle. In his *Personal Recollections of the Civil War*, p. 56, John Gibbon indicates that Patrick's Brigade was not ordered up until the officers' council after the battle was over. Doubleday's report, O.R., 16, 369, states that he received no orders to advance. Gibbon's first report, O.R., 16, 378, and his second report, O.R., 16, 381, acknowledge Doubleday's assistance.

34. Doubleday's report, O.R., 16, 369. Lieutenant Colonel J. W. Hofmann of the Fifty-sixth Pennsylvania filed two reports, Sept. 5, 1862, O.R., 16, 373, and Sept. 10, 1862, O.R., 16, 372. In the latter he describes the artillery fire to which the regiment was subjected as it marched along the pike toward the battlefield. The artillery fire is also described in the report for the Ninety-fifth New York, O.R., 16, 371, which was the last of Doubleday's regiments to move along the pike to the battlefield. The identification of the Confederate batteries is based upon the position of Wooding, Poague, and Carpenter on the Confederate right. *The Sixth Wisconsin Volunteers*, R. R. Dawes, p. 62, tells how Doubleday's two regiments filled the gap in the Federal line. William C. Oates, in *The War Between the Union and the Confederacy*, pp. 138–43, speaks of "Yankees" penetrating the woods in front of the Fifteenth Alabama, Oates' regiment, presumably a reference to the arrival of these two regiments from Doubleday's Brigade. See also *History of the Seventy-sixth New York Volunteers*, A. P. Smith, pp. 117–18, which confirms the fact that Doubleday's leading regiments filled the gap between the Sixth and the Seventh Wisconsin.

Haskell MSS disagree with the foregoing as to the battle locations of Doubleday's regiments. In a letter dated Aug. 31, Haskell puts the Fifty-sixth Pennsylvania between the Nineteenth Indiana and the Second Wisconsin and locates the Seventy-sixth New York between the Sixth and the Seventh Wisconsin. *The Bivouac and the Battlefield*, George F. Noyes, would seem to rebut Haskell, although Noyes is not precise in his locations. Noyes was of Doubleday's staff, and was an eyewitness. His book was published in 1863 and is therefore a contemporaneous account.

35. The first report for the Fifty-sixth Pennsylvania, O.R., 16, 373, states that that regiment had "about 300 men in this fight." The second report, O.R., 16, 373, states that the "regiment took into action about 180 men; a large number had dropped out exhausted on the road." The larger number is used here. Absent a report or any other current source of numbers for the Seventy-sixth New York, the number 500 is used here, as the approximate average effective strength of Gibbon's regiments.

36. Doubleday's report, O.R., 16, 369; report for the Ninety-fifth New York, O.R., 16, 371.

37. There is considerable conflict as to the precise duration of the battle. This conflict is believed to result in part from differences among the witnesses as to what they were talking about. Some presumably

describe the time period between the first fire and the last, desultory fire. Others describe the time period between the first fire and the end of the heavy gunfire, which period was followed by a desultory fire until silence fell. In his *Personal Recollections of the Civil War*, Gibbon spoke of the duration as "over an hour," p. 54, and an "hour and a half," p. 55, which latter time he also used in his second report, O.R., 16, 381. General Taliaferro's report, O.R., 16, 657, identifies the duration of the battle as two and a half hours. *Haskell MSS* identify the duration as an hour and a half. *Mead MSS* put the opening artillery fire at 6:00 P.M. and the last infantry fire at 9:00 P.M. *Fairfield MSS* state an over-all time of one hour and fifteen minutes, and *Hughes MSS* give the three-hour duration. The "more than two hour" figure here is intended to cover the period from first fire until the last fire, and is probably a conservative estimate of the extent of this time period.

38. *Personal Recollections of the Civil War*, John Gibbon, p. 54; General Taliaferro's report, O.R., 16, 657; Gibbon's first report, O.R., 16, 378; *B and L*, Vol. II, p. 510.

The War Between the Union and the Confederacy, William C. Oates, pp. 138–43, refers to Trimble's advance, but the details of the movement are incomprehensible. *The Sixth Wisconsin Volunteers*, R. R. Dawes, pp. 62–3, tells of its advance. General Taliaferro's report states that "twice our lines were advanced until we had reached a farmhouse and orchard on the right of our line," O.R., 16, 657. This implies the existence of two movements forward, the first of which was driven back, and this was the place in the line at which Colonel Taliaferro's Brigade came in and the place of the fighting of the Nineteenth Indiana. General Taliaferro's report, O.R., 16, 657, states the physical objects held by the two sides and the static character of the lines.

39. General Taliaferro's report, O.R., 16, 657, and Gibbon's description in *Personal Recollections of the Civil War*, pp. 54–5, make it apparent that this was the climactic point of the battle. This is also the inference from *The Sixth Wisconsin Volunteers*, R. R. Dawes, pp. 61–3, which recites the Sixth's relatively low position and Dawes' observation of the furious work on his left. *History of the Sauk County Riflemen*, Philip Cheek and Mair Pointon, p. 39, refers to the yelling of both sides which, presumably, was not confined to any part of the line.

40. *Personal Recollections of the Civil War*, John Gibbon, p. 54. *Haskell MSS* called it "a roaring hell of fire." General Taliaferro's report, O.R., 16, 657; *The War Between the Union and the Confederacy*, William C. Oates, pp. 138–43.

41. Jackson's report, O.R., 16, 645; General Taliaferro's report, O.R., 16, 657.

42. *The War Between the Union and the Confederacy*, William C. Oates, pp. 138–43.

43. Gibbon's first report, O.R., 16, 378; King's dispatch to McDowell, 10:45 P.M., Aug. 28, 1862, O.R., 18, 717–18. See also Fairchild's letter

of Sept. 2, *Wisconsin Newspaper Volumes*, Vol. II, p. 295. O'Connor was originally buried in the field and later moved to Arlington. *Wisconsin Newspaper Volumes*, Vol. II, pp. 323–4. See also *Wisconsin Newspaper Volumes*, Vol. II, p. 293, identifying Allen's wounds as in the neck and the arm.

44. *The Sixth Wisconsin Volunteers*, R. R. Dawes, p. 62; Gibbon's first report, O.R., 16, 378.·

45. Gibbon's first report, O.R., 16, 378. See also Captain Callis' letter of Sept. 4 to the *Wisconsin State Journal*, *Wisconsin Newspaper Volumes*, Vol. IV, p. 14. Report for the Fifty-sixth Pennsylvania, O.R., 16, 373; *The Bivouac and the Battlefield*, George F. Noyes, p. 119.

46. Jackson's report, O.R., 16, 645; *Lee's Lieutenants*, Douglas Southall Freeman, Vol. II, p. 109, Footnote 61.

47. Stafford's report for Starke's Brigade, O.R., 16, 668; General Taliaferro's report, O.R., 16, 657.

48. Gibbon's first report, O.R., 16, 378; *Personal Recollections of the Civil War*, John Gibbon, p. 54. For the Sixth Wisconsin's movement, see *The Sixth Wisconsin Volunteers*, R. R. Dawes, pp. 63–4; report for the Sixth Wisconsin, O.R., 16, 382.

49. First report for the Fifty-sixth Pennsylvania, O.R., 16, 373; *War Years with Jeb Stuart*, W. W. Blackford, p. 122. In his report, O.R., 16, 657, General Taliaferro spoke of "driving" the Federals from the field. But in the same report he tells how "the enemy slowly and sullenly fell back." Jackson's report, O.R., 16, 645, also speaks of the Federals slowly falling back, and in his later article, *B and L*, Vol. II, p. 510, Taliaferro said nothing of the Federals' fleeing or being driven from the field.

50. Early's report, O.R., 16, 711; General Taliaferro's report, O.R., 16, 657. See Note 49, above. The quotation about the cheers is from *The Bivouac and the Battlefield*, George F. Noyes, p. 119.

51. Jackson's report, O.R., 16, 645, and *The Sixth Wisconsin Volunteers*, R. R. Dawes, p. 63, are responsible for the 9:00 P.M. time. Stafford's report for Starke's Brigade, O.R., 16, 668, uses the same time.

52. *Personal Recollections of the Civil War*, John Gibbon, pp. 55–6. In his article entitled "Gainesville, Groveton and Bull Run," *War Papers*, *Wisconsin Commandery, Military Order of the Loyal Legion*, Vol. II, pp. 357–72, Theron Haight, of Hatch's Brigade, states that Hatch did *not* turn back, for fear of visibly uncovering the division's flank. Hatch has no report. The quoted description is from *The Bivouac and the Battlefield*, George F. Noyes, p. 121.

53. *Personal Recollections of the Civil War*, John Gibbon, pp. 56–7; Gibbon's second report, O.R., 16, 381. In his *Personal Recollections of the Civil War*, p. 57, Gibbon states that the paper he prepared and circulated to the generals was used by King, "after adding something in his own handwriting," as King's dispatch to McDowell. Whether or not this is true, King's 10:45 P.M. dispatch to McDowell—undoubtedly the dispatch sent by King after the officers' council—appears at O.R., 18,

717–18. An able discussion of the significance of this decision appears in *The Army Under Pope,* John Codman Ropes, pp. 81–2. Pope's testimony before the McDowell Court of Inquiry and the Court's acceptance thereof appears in O.R., 15, 330–31. See Note 56, below.

54. A partial text of this letter appears in a note by Charles King, Rufus King's son, in *B and L,* Vol. II, p. 495. The full text has not been found in the *Official Records,* but appears in Charles King's article "Gainesville" in *War Papers, Wisconsin Commandery, Military Order of the Loyal Legion,* Vol. III, pp. 277–8.

55. Reynolds' report, O.R., 16, 393; testimony of Captain Haven, aide to McDowell, McDowell Court of Inquiry, O.R., 15, 208–9; *Personal Recollections of the Civil War,* John Gibbon, p. 57, which errs in one respect when it states that Reynolds actually moved his division to King's battlefield and found King gone. As Reynolds' report points out, he learned of King's abandonment of the field and their joint plan before he left King. King's dispatch to Ricketts has not been found in the *Official Records,* but it appears in "Gainesville," *War Papers, Wisconsin Commandery, Military Order of the Loyal Legion,* Vol. III, p. 276, by Charles King.

56. See Note 53, above; Ricketts' report, O.R., 16, 384; Pope's report, O.R., 16, 37–8. Omitted from the text is any reference to the controversial issue of whether or not Pope ordered—or sent orders to—King to hold his ground. Pope's report implies that this was done once by King's staff officer. The same statement appears in Pope's article in *B and L,* Vol. II, p. 470. But at 495 of *B and L,* Vol. II, appears a note by Rufus King's son, Charles, which meets Pope's claim that he sent a dispatch to King by King's staff officer. A much-enlarged version of this note, including a defense of King's activity on the night of Aug. 28, appears in Charles King's article "Gainesville," *War Papers, Wisconsin Commandery, Military Order of the Loyal Legion,* Vol. III, pp. 259–83.

57. O.R., 15, 330–31, concerns the Court of Inquiry. O.R., 16, 367, contains Hatch's report of Sept. 13, 1862, for Aug. 29 and 30. It is a report for the *division,* and states that it was "temporarily under my command" for parts of the 29th and 30th. O.R., 18, 816, contains a letter from King stating that he had turned command of the division over to Hatch, but not stating when. King was not formally relieved and replaced by Hatch until Sept. 14, 1862, O.R., 107, 831.

58. *Personal Recollections of the Civil War,* John Gibbon, pp. 54, 57; Gibbon's first report, O.R., 16, 378; *War Years with Jeb Stuart,* W. W. Blackford, pp. 122, 123–4; *The Sixth Wisconsin Volunteers,* R. R. Dawes, p. 64.

59. No reports are available for Battery B. In the battery's history, *The Cannoneer,* Augustus Buell, p. 30, it is stated that on the three days of Aug. 28, 29, and 30, the battery's casualties were one killed, one wounded mortally, and five wounded. That any of these casualties were suffered at Brawner's Farm is an inference, but a reasonable one.

60. Gibbon's first report, O.R., 16, 378. The official casualty returns are not by regiment. *Regimental Losses in the American Civil War*, William F. Fox, p. 117, states Gibbon's losses, perhaps for the 28th, 29th, and 30th, as "148 killed, 626 wounded, and 120 missing; total 894, out of about 2,000 engaged."

The Sixth Wisconsin Volunteers, R. R. Dawes, p. 64, states the Sixth's and Second's casualties. In a letter dated Sept. 2, to O'Connor's father, Fairchild states that the Second went into the battle with 430 of whom 56 were killed, 205 wounded, and 30 missing (*Wisconsin Newspaper Volumes*, Vol. II, p. 295). It is assumed that the Nineteenth and Seventh, both fighting on the left, suffered comparable losses, which, deducting from the total the known casualties in the Sixth and Second, would give the Nineteenth and Seventh 190 men apiece. Dawes' figures for the Sixth are adopted in preference to Bragg's, 75 of 504 men, O.R., 16, 382.

Doubleday's casualties are uncertain. The second report for the Fifty-sixth Pennsylvania, O.R., 16, 373, is the authority for 61 casualties. But, as stated in Note 35, above, this report and the second report for the same regiment are in conflict on other points. No report or casualty returns exist for the Seventy-sixth New York, and the figure of 100 is developed from applying the Fifty-sixth Pennsylvania's percentage loss to the Seventy-sixth's numbers.

Doubleday's report, O.R., 16, 369, states that "our loss in killed, wounded, and prisoners was nearly one-half of our force engaged." Although this language on its face applies to Aug. 28, his report also covers Aug. 29, and his statement of losses may apply to both days. In any event, the one-half cannot be accepted in the light of the report for the Fifty-sixth Pennsylvania and in the light of Doubleday's return of casualties for the period Aug. 16–Sept. 2, 1862, O.R., 16, 254. These show total losses for said period as follows: Fifty-sixth Pennsylvania, 187; Seventy-sixth New York, 147.

61. *The Sixth Wisconsin Volunteers*, R. R. Dawes, p. 70.

62. *Personal Recollections of the Civil War*, John Gibbon, p. 93.

63. *Lee's Lieutenants*, Douglas Southall Freeman, Vol. II, p. 109.

64. O.R., 16, 811.

65. These losses are constructed as follows:

Baylor's Brigade (*Lee's Lieutenants*, Freeman, Vol. II, p. 109, f.n. 57)	216 of 700 men—31%
Starke's Brigade (using same percentage as in Baylor's)	372 of 1200 men—31%
Taliaferro's Brigade (using same percentage as in Baylor's)	372 of 1200 men—31%
Lawton's Brigade (O.R., 16, 811)	414 of 2100 men—20%
Trimble's Brigade (O.R., 16, 812)	759 of 1200 men—63%

2133

The use of Baylor's percentage for Starke's and Taliaferro's seems justi-
fied by their fighting on the climactic Confederate right.

66. *Personal Recollections of the Civil War*, John Gibbon, p. 57; *The
Sixth Wisconsin Volunteers*, R. R. Dawes, p. 64. See Map 61, *Atlas to
Accompany Steele's American Campaigns*, edited by Colonel Vincent J.
Esposito, 1956 edition.

67. *War Years with Jeb Stuart*, W. W. Blackford, p. 124; O.R., 16,
280, 284, 289–90. See also Dr. William Frothingham's letter, *Wisconsin
Newspaper Volumes*, Vol. III, p. 265.

68. *The Sixth Wisconsin Volunteers*, R. R. Dawes, pp. 64–5; *Personal
Recollections of the Civil War*, John Gibbon, p. 58.

69. *B and L*, Vol. II, p. 510.

70. *Stonewall Jackson and the American Civil War*, G. F. R. Henderson, p. 451.

71. Concerning the "Black Hat Brigade," see *Personal Recollections
of the Civil War*, John Gibbon, p. 93. See also Frank Haskell's contemporaneous letter appearing in *Wisconsin Newspaper Volumes*, Vol. IV,
pp. 18–19. For Gibbon's quoted reference, see O.R., 16, 379.

5. Second Bull Run (pages 99–112)

1. *Personal Recollections of the Civil War*, John Gibbon, pp. 58–9.
Lincoln Finds a General, Kenneth P. Williams, Vol. I, p. 324, contains
a description of Pope's learning of the movements of King and Ricketts.

2. Map 61, *Atlas to Accompany Steele's American Campaigns*, edited
by Colonel Vincent J. Esposito, 1956 edition; O.R., 16, 367.

3. O.R., 17, 846; *Personal Recollections of the Civil War*, John Gibbon, p. 59.

4. *Personal Recollections of the Civil War*, John Gibbon, pp. 59–60;
O.R., 16, 76; *Lincoln Finds a General*, Kenneth P. Williams, Vol. I,
pp. 324–5.

5. *The Sixth Wisconsin Volunteers*, R. R. Dawes, pp. 68–9.

6. *Ibid.*, p. 69; *Personal Recollections of the Civil War*, John Gibbon,
p. 60. The report of numbers is an estimated figure, based on strength
just before Brawner Farm, and less casualties there. *Haskell MSS* state
that the brigade had 1,000 men at Second Bull Run.

7. This is an estimated figure based on strength just prior to Brawner
Farm, and less Brawner Farm casualties. Gibbon's report for Second Bull
Run, O.R., 16, 379, identifies the consolidation of the Second and
Seventh Wisconsin under Fairchild.

8. O.R., 17, 904.

9. The events in this paragraph are taken from *The Sixth Wisconsin
Volunteers*, R. R. Dawes, p. 70; *Personal Recollections of the Civil War*,
John Gibbon, pp. 60–61; O.R., 16, 339; Hatch's report, O.R., 16, 367.

10. *History of the Sauk County Riflemen*, Philip Cheek and Mair
Pointon, p. 42.

11. *The Sixth Wisconsin Volunteers*, R. R. Dawes, p. 70; Map 63, *Atlas to Accompany Steele's American Campaigns*, edited by Colonel Vincent J. Esposito, 1956 edition; "Personal Recollections of the War," D. H. Strother, *Harper's Monthly*, XXXV, 717 (Nov., 1867).

12. O.R., 16, 340; *Bull Run Remembers*, Joseph Mills Hanson, p. 117. Gibbon witnessed Pope's reaction to the reconnaissance, *Personal Recollections of the Civil War*, pp. 62–3. Porter's view and Pope's reaction thereto are described in the *The Army Under Pope*, John Codman Ropes, pp. 129–30. Pope's order appears in *The Army Under Pope*, John Codman Ropes, p. 131; O.R., 16, 340.

13. Jackson's report, O.R., 16, 646; *The Army Under Pope*, John Codman Ropes, p. 134.

14. *Bull Run Remembers*, Joseph Mills Hanson, pp. 120–22; Hatch's report, O.R., 16, 368.

15. O.R., 16, 472; Sykes' report, O.R., 16, 482; O.R., 16, 472.

16. Jackson's report, O.R., 16, 647; Longstreet's report, O.R., 16, 565.

17. Johnson's report, O.R., 16, 666.

18. Hatch's report, O.R., 16, 368; *The Sixth Wisconsin Volunteers*, R. R. Dawes, p. 70; Gibbon's report, O.R., 16, 379.

19. *Personal Recollections of the Civil War*, John Gibbon, p. 63; *The Sixth Wisconsin Volunteers*, R. R. Dawes, pp. 70–71.

20. "Gainesville, Groveton and Bull Run," *War Papers*, *Wisconsin Commandery, Military Order of the Loyal Legion*, Vol. II, pp. 357–72, Theron Haight. This is a stirring account by a participant in Hatch's assault of the railroad embankment. Hatch's report, O.R., 16, 368; Early's report, O.R., 16, 713.

21. *The Sixth Wisconsin Volunteers*, R. R. Dawes, p. 71.

22. Gibbon's report, O.R., 16, 379, describes the withdrawal, and Doubleday states, O.R., 16, 370, that Porter ordered the withdrawal. *Personal Recollections of the Civil War*, John Gibbon, p. 63; *The Sixth Wisconsin Volunteers*, R. R. Dawes, pp. 71–3.

23. *Personal Recollections of the Civil War*, John Gibbon, pp. 63–4; *The Sixth Wisconsin Volunteers*, R. R. Dawes, p. 73; *History of the Sauk County Riflemen*, Philip Cheek and Mair Pointon, pp. 42–3. This position is described in *Hughes MSS* as "in the northwest angle of the Warrenton and Sudley Roads."

24. *Bull Run Remembers*, Joseph Mills Hanson, p. 125; *The Army Under Pope*, John Codman Ropes, pp. 137–43; *The Sixth Wisconsin Volunteers*, R. R. Dawes, p. 73; *History of the Sauk County Riflemen*, Philip Cheek and Mair Pointon, p. 43. *The Army Under Pope*, John Codman Ropes, pp. 136–43, contains an excellent account of the Confederate attack and what it signified for the Federal army.

25. *The Sixth Wisconsin Volunteers*, R. R. Dawes, p. 73.

26. That Gibbon's immediate infantry opponents were of Jackson's Corps is an inference from the fact that Jackson joined in the Confederate

assault and from the direction of the troops which emerged from the wood in Gibbon's front.

27. *Personal Recollections of the Civil War*, John Gibbon, p. 64; *History of the Sauk County Riflemen*, Philip Cheek and Mair Pointon, pp. 43–4.

28. *Personal Recollections of the Civil War*, John Gibbon, p. 64. *Indianapolis Daily Journal*, Sept. 12, 1862, p. 2, contains Meredith's letter to Governor Morton, describing the battle of Aug. 30. See also *The Sixth Wisconsin Volunteers*, R. R. Dawes, p. 74.

29. *The Sixth Wisconsin Volunteers*, R. R. Dawes, p. 74; *Bull Run Remembers*, Joseph Mills Hanson, p. 126; *Personal Recollections of the Civil War*, John Gibbon, pp. 64–5.

30. *History of the Sauk County Riflemen*, Philip Cheek and Mair Pointon, p. 44.

31. *Personal Recollections of the Civil War*, John Gibbon, p. 65.

32. *Bull Run Remembers*, Joseph Mills Hanson, p. 125, is the source of the quotation. *The Army Under Pope*, John Codman Ropes, pp. 141–2 contains a balanced summary of the extent of the Federal defeat, the condition of the defeated army, and the character of the withdrawal.

33. *Personal Recollections of the Civil War*, John Gibbon, pp. 65–8.

34. There is a conflict here as to the precise time of withdrawal. In his *Personal Recollections of the Civil War*, John Gibbon says at p. 68 that he believes it was "scarcely" as late as 10:00 P.M. when he withdrew. In *The Sixth Wisconsin Volunteers*, R. R. Dawes at p. 75 puts the time as "after midnight." McDowell's report, O.R., 16, 344, relying on an unnamed colonel from Gibbon's Brigade, puts the time as "till some two hours after dark."

35. John Gibbon in *Personal Recollections of the Civil War*, p. 68, states that the brigade passed Cub Run. R. R. Dawes, *The Sixth Wisconsin Volunteers*, p. 75, says that it did not. Since Gibbon rode ahead to Centreville, Dawes is accepted as the more reliable witness.

36. *Personal Recollections of the Civil War*, John Gibbon, pp. 68–9. Gibbon's report dated Sept. 3, 1862, O.R., 16, 379, states his casualties as 16 killed, 68 wounded, and 36 missing. But this does not square with his Sept. 5 statement, O.R., 16, 380, of losses for the period Aug. 21 through Aug. 30, inclusive. The latter statement (148 killed, 626 wounded, and 120 missing), less losses at Brawner Farm on Aug. 28, has been used. *Haskell MSS* give a statement of 150 killed and wounded on Aug. 30.

37. *The Sixth Wisconsin Volunteers*, R. R. Dawes, p. 75, tells of the march to Centreville. The arrival of Franklin and Sumner is described in *Personal Recollections of the Civil War*, John Gibbon, p. 69. For McClellan's machinations delaying the arrival of these two corps, see *Lincoln Finds a General*, Kenneth P. Williams, Vol. I, Chaps. XI and XII. In the same book, at p. 338, Williams discusses the reorganization process at Centreville. *History of the Sauk County Riflemen*, Philip Cheek and Mair Pointon, p. 44, contains an eyewitness description of the confusion at

Centreville. For McDowell's camping place, see O.R., 16, 344; *Personal Recollections of the Civil War*, John Gibbon, p. 69.

38. *The Sixth Wisconsin Volunteers*, R. R. Dawes, p. 71; O.R., 18, 795.

39. *The Sixth Wisconsin Volunteers*, R. R. Dawes, p. 75; *Personal Recollections of the Civil War*, John Gibbon, p. 69; *History of the Sauk County Riflemen*, Philip Cheek and Mair Pointon, p. 45.

40. *Personal Recollections of the Civil War*, John Gibbon, p. 70; *The Sixth Wisconsin Volunteers*, R. R. Dawes, p. 75.

41. *The Sixth Wisconsin Volunteers*, R. R. Dawes, p. 76. Gibbon, at this time an admirer of McClellan, also describes the favorable reaction of the army in *Personal Recollections of the Civil War*, p. 70. See also *Young MSS*.

42. *History of the Sauk County Riflemen*, Philip Cheek and Mair Pointon, pp. 45–6.

43. *The Sixth Wisconsin Volunteers*, R. R. Dawes, pp. 76–7.

44. *History of the Sauk County Riflemen*, Philip Cheek and Mair Pointon, pp. 45–6.

45. The first quotation is from *Young MSS* and the second from a soldier's letter, dated Sept. 5, 1862, appearing in *Wisconsin Newspaper Volumes*, Vol. III, p. 261.

6. South Mountain: The Iron Brigade Is Named
(pages 113–130)

1. O.R., 27, 1, 169–80.

2. O.R., 27, 170; *History of the Republican Party of Indiana*, Russell M. Seeds, p. 356.

3. Wis. A.G., 1865, p. 1313; *Memoirs of Milwaukee County*, Jerome A. Watrous, Vol. II, pp. 753–4.

4. O.R., 27, 170; *Soldiers and Citizens Album of Biographical Records*, Vol. II, pp. 391–4.

5. *Personal Recollections of the Civil War*, John Gibbon, p. 71. The time of the march of Gibbon's Brigade is taken from the diary of Private W. N. Jackson of Muncie, Indiana, *Jackson MSS*. The Long Bridge route is an inference based upon the location of the brigade camp on Upton's Hill, the route past the White House and the location of the Seventh Street Road on which the march proceeded from Washington. The hot night and the Lincoln incident appear in *History of the Sauk County Riflemen*, Philip Cheek and Mair Pointon, p. 46.

6. *Personal Recollections of the Civil War*, John Gibbon, p. 71; *Jackson MSS*; O.R., 27, 40, and map in *Jackson MSS*.

7. Meredith's report, O.R., 27, 249.

8. *The Sixth Wisconsin Volunteers*, R. R. Dawes, pp. 78–9; *Personal Recollections of the Civil War*, John Gibbon, pp. 71–3.

9. The "lost order" is discussed in *Lincoln Finds a General*, Kenneth P. Williams, Vol. I, pp. 374–5; the organization of the Army of Northern Virginia appears in O.R., 27, 803–10.

10. Plate XXVII, *Atlas to the Official Records*. Both McClellan, O.R., 27, 27, and Hooker, O.R., 27, 214, provided descriptions of South Mountain.

11. *The Sixth Wisconsin Volunteers*, R. R. Dawes, pp. 78–9, describes weather and the bells. *Lincoln Finds a General*, Kenneth P. Williams, Vol. I, pp. 375–6, discusses McClellan's negligence and incredible delay; pp. 380–81 describe the ultimate Federal movements west.

12. *The Sixth Wisconsin Volunteers*, R. R. Dawes, p. 79; *Jackson MSS*; *Personal Recollections of the Civil War*, John Gibbon, pp. 73–5; *Perry MSS*.

13. *Personal Recollections of the Civil War*, John Gibbon, p. 75.

14. The skirmish is described in O.R., 27, 416–17; Dawes mentions the signs of the skirmish in *The Sixth Wisconsin Volunteers*, R. R. Dawes, p. 79; for Reno's morning action, O.R., 27, 417, and *B and L*, Vol. II, pp. 559ff.

15. *The Sixth Wisconsin Volunteers*, R. R. Dawes, pp. 79–80.

16. Burnside's report, O.R., 27, 417; Sturgis' report, O.R., 27, 443. Hooker's report places Meade's arrival at 2:00 P.M., O.R., 27, 214.

17. *The Sixth Wisconsin Volunteers*, R. R. Dawes, p. 80, describes the march to the right; *Personal Recollections of the Civil War*, John Gibbon, p. 76, identifies the direct order from Burnside; Burnside's report, O.R., 27, 417. See also *Fairfield MSS*.

18. Plate XXVII, *Atlas to the Official Records*, shows "McClellan's Headquarters." Burnside's report O.R., 27, 417, speaks of McClellan's having his headquarters with Burnside.

19. *B and L*, Vol. II, p. 580; D. H. Hill's report, O.R., 27, 1019–22; Longstreet's report, O.R., 27, 839.

20. *B and L*, Vol. II, p. 577, contains D. H. Hill's statement of Colquitt's numbers. *Ibid.*, pp. 561–2; Colquitt's report, O.R., 27, 1052–3. See also letter from Captain Aleck Gordon, Jr., dated Sept. 20, 1862, from Sharpsburg, and describing the South Mountain terrain and obstacles. *Wisconsin Newspaper Volumes*, Vol. IV, p. 21.

21. D. H. Hill tells of his placing of the regiments of Colquitt's Brigade, *B and L*, Vol. II, pp. 561–2; Colquitt's report, O.R., 27, 1053.

22. *The Sixth Wisconsin Volunteers*, R. R. Dawes, p. 80, is the source for the place of the brigade's wait and for both of the quotations.

23. *Loc. cit.* specifies the hour's wait; the same source and Burnside's report, O.R., 27, 417, describe the setting sun. *Hughes MSS* state that the assault began at 5:30. See also *Fairfield MSS*; *Personal Recollections of the Civil War*, John Gibbon, p. 76; Burnside's report, O.R., 27, 417. The fact of the rider is an inference based on the distance between headquarters and Gibbon's position.

24. Gibbon's report, O.R., 27, 247; the "by right of companies" forma-

tion appears in *Personal Recollections of the Civil War*, John Gibbon, p. 76. The distance and formation appear in Fairchild's report, O.R., 27, 252; *The Sixth Wisconsin Volunteers*, R. R. Dawes, p. 81, refers to the "seventh Wisconsin in front of us." *The Cannoneer*, Augustus Buell, p. 32; *History of the Sauk County Riflemen*, Philip Cheek and Mair Pointon, p. 48.

25. *The Sixth Wisconsin Volunteers*, R. R. Dawes, p. 81. The Confederate artillery location is an inference from the direction of the fire. It passed over the regiments to the right of the road into the regiments to the left. Fairchild's report, O.R., 27, 252, tells of the casualties.

26. Callis' report, O.R., 27, 256; *The Sixth Wisconsin Volunteers*, R. R. Dawes, pp. 81–2; Meredith's report, O.R., 27, 249–50.

27. Meredith's report, O.R., 27, 250; Gibbon's report, O.R., 27, 247.

28. Colquitt's report, O.R., 27, 1053, describes the thick growth of woods 400 yards (almost one quarter of a mile) in front of his line, from which wood the flank fire was delivered. Colquitt places this wood "upon the right of the road," apparently meaning the *Federal* right. In any event, the similarities of the situation as described by Colquitt and by the Federal reports, see Note 29 below, show that the same wood was described in all reports and that it was the anchor of the Confederate advance line, approximately a quarter of a mile in advance of the final Confederate line. The distances in Meredith's report, O.R., 27, 250, and Callis', O.R., 27, 256, notes 26 and 27, are consistent with the quarter-mile distance from Colquitt's main line.

29. Meredith's report, O.R., 27, 250; Callis' report, O.R., 27, 256; *The Sixth Wisconsin Volunteers*, R. R. Dawes, pp. 81–2; *History of the Sauk County Riflemen*, Philip Cheek and Mair Pointon, p. 48.

30. Fairchild's report, O.R., 27, 252; Bragg's report, O.R., 27, 253; Gibbon's report, O.R., 27, 247–8; *The Sixth Wisconsin Volunteers*, R. R. Dawes, p. 82.

31. Meredith's report, O.R., 27, 250, mentions 11 prisoners taken at the fence. That the flanking of the fence took place at the same time as the woods activity on the right is an estimate as to the sequence of events.

32. *History of the Sauk County Riflemen*, Philip Cheek and Mair Pointon, p. 48, describes the shouting and the exhausted and powder-burned condition of the attackers. See also *The Sixth Wisconsin Volunteers*, R. R. Dawes, pp. 82–3.

33. Colquitt's report, O.R., 27, 1053; *The Sixth Wisconsin Volunteers*, R. R. Dawes, p. 83; *B and L*, Vol. II, p. 576.

34. Fairchild's report, O.R., 27, 253; Meredith's report, O.R., 27, 250; Colquitt's report, O.R., 27, 1053. Battery B's arrival is described in Gibbon's report, O.R., 27, 248.

35. *The Sixth Wisconsin Volunteers*, R. R. Dawes, p. 83; *History of the Sauk County Riflemen*, Philip Cheek and Mair Pointon, p. 49; Bragg's report, O.R., 27, 253–4.

36. Callis' report, O.R., 27, 257; *The Sixth Wisconsin Volunteers*, R. R. Dawes, pp. 83–4.

37. Bragg's report, alone, describes this message from Gibbon, O.R., 27, 254.

38. Callis' report, O.R., 27, 257; Bragg's report, O.R., 27, 254; Colquitt's report, O.R., 27, 1053, refers to the Confederate ammunition shortage.

Authority on the time when firing ceased is hopelessly divided. 9:00 P.M. is simply a compromise. Burnside said 8:00 P.M., O.R., 27, 417; D. H. Hill said "an hour after night" in his report, O.R., 27, 1021, but in *B and L*, Vol. II, p. 576, he states that the Federals reached the stone wall at 9:00 P.M.; Meredith says 9:00 P.M., O.R., 27, 250; and Gibbon states that the fighting continued "until long after dark," O.R., 27, 248. See also *Hughes MSS.*

39. *B and L*, Vol. II, p. 571, contains D. H. Hill's mention of the Confederate meeting and his and Longstreet's advice. Lee's report, O.R., 27, 140, contains the essentials of Lee's knowledge of the situation and his decisions and instructions.

40. Meredith's report, O.R., 27, 250; *The Sixth Wisconsin Volunteers*, R. R. Dawes, p. 83; Bragg's report, O.R., 27, 254; Fairchild's report, O.R., 27, 252.

41. *History of the Sauk County Riflemen*, Philip Cheek and Mair Pointon, p. 49; Hill's report, O.R., 27, 1020.

42. O.R., 27, 184; Doubleday's report, O.R., 27, 222.

43. *The Sixth Wisconsin Volunteers*, R. R. Dawes, p. 84; Meredith's report, O.R., 27, 250; *Perry MSS; Fairfield MSS.*

44. Fairchild's report, O.R., 27, 253, and Meredith's, O.R., 27, 250, state the midnight arrival of Second Corps' relief. Callis' report, O.R., 27, 257, says that the Seventh Wisconsin was relieved at 10:30 P.M.

45. *The Sixth Wisconsin Volunteers*, R. R. Dawes, pp. 84–5; Bragg's report, O.R., 27, 254. In *Personal Recollections of the Civil War*, p. 78, John Gibbon erred in stating that Bragg believed it inadvisable to move the Sixth Wisconsin during the night.

46. Gibbon's report, O.R., 27, 248, and compilation, O.R., 27, 184. In *Personal Recollections of the Civil War*, p. 79, Gibbon neglected to note his missing, and therefore erred in the total given. The 25 per cent casualty figure is based on the *Recollections*, p. 79, and may or may not be correct. Except for the field return of Sept. 1, 1862, showing 1,427 officers and men available for duty, O.R., 18, 795, no statement of Gibbon's numbers is available. For the Sixth Wisconsin, Dawes gives a figure of "four hundred men" prior to the battle of Sept. 14, *The Sixth Wisconsin Volunteers*, p. 80.

47. *B and L*, Vol. II, p. 577.

48. O.R., 27, 184–8.

49. *Personal Recollections of the Civil War*, John Gibbon, p. 77, describes the view of the officers to the rear. His description is doubtless based on conversations with these officers as to their observation.

50. Burnside's report, O.R., 27, 417; McClellan's report, O.R., 27, 52. The McClellan and Hooker conversation, the only known story of the

naming of the brigade, is described by John B. Callis in a postwar letter. Callis' letter tells of what McClellan told him, after the war. The Callis letter is described in *Indiana at Antietam*, Indiana Antietam Monument Commission, p. 111. According to McClellan, he and Hooker had spoken during the action of Gibbon's Brigade and the following conversation took place:

"McClellan: What men are those fighting on the pike?
"Hooker: General Gibbon's Brigade of Western men.
"McClellan: They must be made of iron.
"Hooker: By the Eternal, they are iron! If you had seen them at Bull Run as I did, you would know them to be iron.
"McClellan: Why, General Hooker, they fight equal to the best troops in the world."

McClellan also said that after the battle, at a place near where the brigade fought, Hooker called out, "General McClellan, what do you think now of my Iron Brigade?"

This story, told years after the war, is a little too pat to be accepted as literally true. At the same time, there is no sound basis for rejecting the incident entirely, especially since a contemporaneous letter from Captain Aleck Gordon, Jr., of the Seventh, states that "Gen. McClellan has given us the name of the Iron Brigade." See *Wisconsin Newspaper Volumes*, Vol. IV, pp. 21–2. The letter was dated Sept. 21, 1862. O. B. Curtis' *History of the Twenty-fourth Michigan*, except for Dawes' book the only regimental history for an Iron Brigade regiment, also states (p. 463) that the name was acquired at South Mountain. Curtis was himself a member of the Twenty-fourth, and presumably had acquired his knowledge of the fact from members of the original regiments. The South Mountain origin of the name is also supported by an article in *The National Tribune*, Washington, D.C., Sept. 22, 1904, by W. H. Adkins, a Wisconsin veteran of the brigade. Dawes, another possible source, never identifies the origin of the name.

In *Personal Recollections of the Civil War*, Gibbon states at p. 93: "How or where the name of the 'Iron Brigade' was first given I do not know, but soon after the battle of Antietam the name was started and ever after was applied to the brigade." This statement is not entirely reconcilable with the South Mountain origin of the name, even though Antietam was fought only two days later. In any event, granting this contrary evidence, the weight of the evidence supports the South Mountain theory.

According to William F. Fox, *Regimental Losses in the American Civil War*, p. 117, the name "Iron Brigade" did not originate with *the* Iron Brigade, Gibbon's organization from the West. Thus Fox states that prior to the fall of 1862, Hatch's Brigade, composed of the Second United States Sharpshooters, the Twenty-second, Twenty-fourth, Thirtieth, and Eighty-fourth New York (Fourteenth Brooklyn), was called the Iron

Brigade. Hatch's Brigade was then in the First Division of the First Corps, the same division that included Gibbon's Brigade. Fox notes that Hatch's organization was broken up in 1863 by the muster out of the Twenty-second, Twenty-fourth, and Thirtieth New York, which were two-year organizations, and that the name Iron Brigade, having been applied to Gibbon's men, stayed with them. The same story of the naming of Hatch's Brigade appears in *The History of the Fighting Fourteenth*, the regimental history of the Fourteenth Brooklyn, published in 1911.

Neither Fox nor the regimental of the Fourteenth cites any authority for the account of the name of Hatch's Brigade. The writer of this book has searched for some contemporaneous evidence that the name Iron Brigade was, in fact, applied to Hatch's outfit. No such authority has been found. On the other hand, immediately after South Mountain and Antietam, the name was generally applied to the Western organization, both in the contemporaneous letters of the soldiers and in the *Official Records*.

It may also be noted that the name has been applied to General Joseph O. Shelby's brigade of Confederate raiders in the Arkansas-Missouri area. This was an organization that acquired a reputation for harsh, guerrilla-type warfare in the turbulent and divided Border States area. The word "iron" applied to Shelby's men apparently implied cruelty and "no-quarter" tactics.

51. See, for example, the Second Corps incident described at the outset of the next chapter. A good description of the South Mountain battle appears in Colonel Meredith's letter to the *Indianapolis Daily Journal*, Sept. 29, 1862, p. 2.

7. Antietam (pages 131–148)

1. Meredith's absence from command and the reason therefor appears in Dudley's report, O.R., 27, 251. *Jackson MSS* are the authority for Meredith's remaining in the field, although not in command. Jackson tells of Meredith's leaving for Washington on Sept. 21. *Daily State Sentinel*, Oct. 7, 1862, p. 3, contains a letter from a soldier of the Nineteenth which states that Meredith had two broken ribs.

Fairchild's absence is something of a mystery. Gibbon's report, O.R., 27, 249, states that Allen commanded the regiment at Antietam. It is also established that Fairchild was shortly thereafter in command again. Because of Allen's wound at Antietam, there is no report for the Second Wisconsin. That Fairchild was simply temporarily indisposed is an inference.

2. Hooker's report, O.R., 27, 216, states that this was the first food since the previous morning. *The Sixth Wisconsin Volunteers*, R. R. Dawes, p. 85, tells of the interruption of breakfast.

3. *Personal Recollections of the Civil War*, John Gibbon, pp. 79–80.

4. *The Sixth Wisconsin Volunteers*, R. R. Dawes, pp. 85–6; *Hughes*

MSS; *Haskell MSS; Mead MSS. Jackson MSS* describe similar exhaustion and sickness in the Nineteenth Indiana. The condition was presumably common to all four regiments.

The strength figure is based on a letter from Frank A. Haskell, Sixth Wisconsin Volunteers, printed in *The Portage Republican* and appearing in Vol. IV, pp. 18–19, *Wisconsin Newspaper Volumes*. Haskell's letter, although erroneously stating the Antietam casualties at 380 killed and wounded, identifies this number as 47.5 per cent of the brigade. Hence the strength of 800.

5. McClellan's report, O.R., 27, 29, places his corps at the Antietam after sunrise on Sept. 16. His strength appears in *Numbers and Losses in the American Civil War*, Thomas L. Livermore, p. 92, and in *Lincoln Finds a General*, Kenneth P. Williams, Vol. II, p. 446. *Lee's Lieutenants*, Douglas Southall Freeman, Vol. II, pp. 201, 204, describes the movements of Lee's detached commands. McLaws' report, O.R., 27, 856, states his arrival time. Lee's strength is also taken from Livermore.

6. McClellan's report, O.R., 27, 29, 30, 55; Plate XXIX, *Atlas to the Official Records*; Hooker's report, O.R., 27, 217; *The Sixth Wisconsin Volunteers*, R. R. Dawes, p. 87.

7. Plate XXIX, *Atlas to the Official Records*, is the authority for the distance stated. Hooker's report, O.R., 27, 217, puts Meade's Division in front. *The Sixth Wisconsin Volunteers*, R. R. Dawes, p. 87. Hooker's report, O.R., 27, 217–18, states "Doubleday's Division was posted on the right, Ricketts' on the left, and Meade's in reserve."

8. Hooker's report, O.R., 27, 218. Early's report, O.R., 27, 970, contains Early's analysis of Hooker's purpose, with reference to the topography. General Cox's article in *B and L*, Vol. II, pp. 636–7, contains a valuable map and description of the ground and Hooker's plan.

The distances stated are approximate. Plate XXIX, *Atlas to the Official Records*, and the map in *B and L*, Vol. II, p. 636, are the principal map sources for the terrain. A simple but good map also appears in *Lee's Lieutenants*, Douglas Southall Freeman, Vol. II, p. 205. Description of the improvements, vegetation, and woods appear in *Personal Recollections of the Civil War*, John Gibbon, p. 82; *The Sixth Wisconsin Volunteers*, R. R. Dawes, pp. 88–90; *The Cannoneer*, Augustus Buell, pp. 33, 40 (the map on page 40 errs in extending the cornfield to the west side of the pike); *B and L*, Vol. II, pp. 637–8. The fact that the post-and-rail fences were on both sides of the pike is stated by Dawes in *The Sixth Wisconsin Volunteers*, p. 95; report for Starke's Brigade, O.R., 27, 1017. The well-known Brady photographs of the field in the Dunker Church area do not show these fences on both sides of the pike. It is assumed that there were openings in the fence at the church, and at the entrance to the Miller yard and barnyard. These openings may account for the appearances of Brady's pictures and for the absence in the reports, Dudley's and Callis', for example, of any reference to climbing the fences when moving laterally in the area.

9. Stuart's report, *O.R.*, 27, 819–20; Early's report, *O.R.*, 27, 967; Jones' report, *O.R.*, 27, 1007.

10. For the relationship of the three brigades of Ewell's Division, one to another, see report for Trimble's Brigade, *O.R.*, 27, 976, which states that Lawton's Brigade was on its left, and Hays' report, *O.R.*, 27, 978, which places him behind Lawton's. As to the location of these three brigades, the report for Trimble's Brigade, *O.R.*, 27, 976, states that its right met D. H. Hill's left in a right angle. In addition, it was the brigades of Hood and E. M. Law which later replaced the three brigades of Ewell's Division, after the latter had been badly beaten. The reports for Hood's and Law's brigades, *O.R.*, 27, 928 and 937, clearly have them moving out from behind the church, crossing to the east side of the pike and advancing toward the cornfield. Thus the three brigades from Ewell's Division were similarly located before being relieved.

11. Hood's report, *O.R.*, 27, 923; Law's report, *O.R.*, 27, 937; report for Hood's Brigade, *O.R.*, 27, 927–8.

The question of numbers is, as usual, a difficult one. Using the Confederates' figures, insofar as any are available, the following calculation appears:

Ewell's Division	3500 men	(Early, *O.R.*, 27, 973)
Jackson's Division	1600 men	(Jones, *O.R.*, 27, 1008)
Hood's Brigade	854 men	(Wofford, *O.R.*, 27, 929)
Law's Brigade	?	
D. H. Hill's Division	3000 men	(Hill, *O.R.*, 27, 1022)

8954, plus Law's Brigade

D. H. Hill, *O.R.*, 27, 1022, states that Colquitt's, Ripley's, and Garland's brigades went to Hood's support, and indicates that this was early in the action on the left.

12. "Earliest dawn" are Gibbon's words in *Personal Recollections of the Civil War*, John Gibbon, p. 81. He also describes the firing. *The Sixth Wisconsin Volunteers*, R. R. Dawes, p. 87.

13. Doubleday's report, *O.R.*, 27, 223–4; Hooker's report, *O.R.*, 27, 218; Gibbon's report, *O.R.*, 27, 248; Meade's report, *O.R.*, 27, 269; Ricketts' report, *O.R.*, 27, 259.

14. *The Sixth Wisconsin Volunteers*, R. R. Dawes, p. 87; *Personal Recollections of the Civil War*, John Gibbon, p. 81.

15. *The Sixth Wisconsin Volunteers*, R. R. Dawes, pp. 87–8; Gibbon's report, *O.R.*, 27, 248.

16. *Personal Recollections of the Civil War*, John Gibbon, p. 82; *The Sixth Wisconsin Volunteers*, R. R. Dawes, p. 88; Bragg's report, *O.R.*, 27, 254–5.

17. Hooker's report, *O.R.*, 27, 218; Gibbon's report, *O.R.*, 27, 248.

18. Gibbon's report, *O.R.*, 27, 248; Dudley's report, *O.R.*, 27, 251; Callis' report, *O.R.*, 27, 257; Stewart's report, *O.R.*, 27, 229; *The Can-*

noneer, Augustus Buell, p. 33. The reports of Callis and Dudley indicate that they were to the right of Stewart's section. Indeed, they would have to have been, else Stewart would have been firing into them.

19. Ricketts' report, O.R., 27, 259; *The Sixth Wisconsin Volunteers*, R. R. Dawes, pp. 88–9; Dudley's report, O.R., 27, 251; Callis' report, O.R., 27, 257; Stewart's report, O.R., 27, 229. Because of the undulating ground, Stewart states that he fired spherical case.

20. Early's report, O.R., 27, 968.

21. Callis' report, O.R., 27, 257; Stewart's report, O.R., 27, 229; report for the Fifth Virginia, O.R., 27, 1012, describes the backward movement of the Stonewall Brigade.

22. Stewart's report, O.R., 27, 229; *The Cannoneer*, Augustus Buell, pp. 33, 40.

23. Hooker's report, O.R., 27, 218.

24. *The Sixth Wisconsin Volunteers*, R. R. Dawes, p. 89; Bragg's report, O.R., 27, 254–5; *Personal Recollections of the Civil War*, John Gibbon, pp. 84–5.

25. Jackson's report, O.R., 27, 956; *The Sixth Wisconsin Volunteers*, R. R. Dawes, p. 90; Doubleday's report, O.R., 27, 224; Meade's report, O.R., 27, 269–70.

26. Distances in this paragraph are estimated, based on descriptions of the movement of the troops.

27. Doubleday's report, O.R., 27, 224; *The Sixth Wisconsin Volunteers*, R. R. Dawes, pp. 90–91.

28. Jackson's report identifies the wounding of Jones and Lawton and the killing of Starke, Jones' successor, O.R., 27, 956. Early's report, O.R., 27, 968.

29. *The Sixth Wisconsin Volunteers*, R. R. Dawes, p. 91; Law's report, O.R., 27, 937; report for Hood's Brigade, O.R., 27, 928.

30. *The Sixth Wisconsin Volunteers*, R. R. Dawes, p. 91. The data about the Sixth's color party appears in Bragg's report, O.R., 27, 255. *The Cannoneer*, Augustus Buell, p. 34.

31. Dudley's report, O.R., 27, 251; Callis' report, O.R., 27, 257–8; Gibbon's report, O.R., 27, 248.

32. Hood's report, O.R., 27, 923; Frank A. Haskell to his brother in *Haskell MSS.*

33. *Personal Recollections of the Civil War*, John Gibbon, p. 83; *The Cannoneer*, Augustus Buell, p. 39.

34. Early's report, O.R., 27, 970; Dudley's report, O.R., 27, 251–2; Callis' report, O.R., 27, 258. For the action at the cornfield, see Stewart's report, O.R., 27, 229, and *Personal Recollections of the Civil War*, John Gibbon, pp. 83–4.

35. O.R., 27, 189–91.

36. Stewart's report, O.R., 27, 229; *The Cannoneer*, Augustus Buell, p. 34; *Personal Recollections of the Civil War*, John Gibbon, pp. 83–4.

37. Doubleday's report, O.R., 225; *Jackson MSS* and *Young MSS* also contain good descriptions of the battle.

38. *The Sixth Wisconsin Volunteers,* R. R. Dawes, p. 92; Dudley's report, O.R., 27, 252; Callis' report, O.R., 27, 258. The time of the withdrawal is uncertain, ranging from Dudley's 2:00 P.M., which is surely too late, to General Cox's indication of 7:00 A.M., *B and L,* Vol. II, pp. 638–9, surely too early. Midmorning is simply a general estimate. Cox's account is otherwise not entirely accurate, and overlooks the action of the Seventh Wisconsin and Nineteenth Indiana west of the pike. For Battery B's later action, see Stewart's report, O.R., 27, 230.

39. *The Sixth Wisconsin Volunteers,* R. R. Dawes, p. 94, *Personal Recollections of the Civil War,* John Gibbon, pp. 88–9.

40. *Personal Recollections of the Civil War,* John Gibbon, p. 89.

41. Stewart's report, O.R., 27, 229; *The Cannoneer,* Augustus Buell, pp. 34, 35, 24–5, 53.

42. *History of the Sauk County Riflemen,* Philip Cheek and Mair Pointon, p. 52; *Personal Recollections of the Civil War,* John Gibbon, p. 89.

43. *The Sixth Wisconsin Volunteers,* R. R. Dawes, pp. 94–5; *History of the Sauk County Riflemen,* Philip Cheek and Mair Pointon, p. 51; Hooker's report, O.R., 27, 218. A letter from Bragg to his wife, contained in *Bragg MSS,* also describes the field, as does *Jackson MSS.*

44. *Young MSS.*

45. *Ibid.*

46. *The Sixth Wisconsin Volunteers,* R. R. Dawes, p. 100.

47. *Jackson MSS.*

48. Bragg's return to camp was on Sept. 28, according to *Bragg MSS.* This name is applied by Dawes in *The Sixth Wisconsin Volunteers.*

49. *The Sixth Wisconsin Volunteers,* R. R. Dawes, pp. 99–100.

50. *Bragg MSS.*

51. *The Sixth Wisconsin Volunteers,* R. R. Dawes, p. 99.

52. *Bragg MSS.* Gibbon's letter also stated, "It ought to be an understood thing throughout the army and the country that any newspaper or telegraph agent falsely reporting an officer killed should be shot on sight by the subject of the notice."

53. *Personal Recollections of the Civil War,* John Gibbon, p. 90.

54. *History of the Sauk County Riflemen,* Philip Cheek and Mair Pointon, p. 53, describes the dress parade and Gibbon's order of Oct. 7, 1862, quoting McClellan's letter to the governor of Wisconsin. That McClellan's letter to Indiana's governor was also the object of an order by Gibbon is an inference arising from the fact that the Indiana letter was written by McClellan at the same time and the unlikelihood that Gibbon would have discriminated against the Indiana regiment. McClellan's words to Governor Morton appear as an indorsement on a letter from Gibbon to Morton seeking reinforcements, *Indiana MSS.* McClellan's letter was printed in the *Indianapolis Daily Journal,* Oct. 13, 1862, p. 2.

55. *Fairfield MSS.* The dates of the quoted entries identify South Mountain as the place where Fairfield and Whaley were wounded.

8. Reorganization (pages 149–167)

1. Except as otherwise noted, facts concerning the raising of the Twenty-fourth Michigan, its officers and men, are taken from *History of the Twenty-fourth Michigan*, by O. B. Curtis.

2. *Michigan in the War*, John Robertson, p. 30, states the Detroit gratuities, by ward, as follows: First, $30; Second, $10; Third, $20; Fourth, $10; Fifth, $15; Sixth, $10; Seventh, $20; Eight, $25; Ninth, $20; Tenth, $10. O. B. Curtis in *B and L*, Vol. III, p. 142, tells of the $100 Federal bounties for all volunteers.

3. *Michigan in the War*, John Robertson, pp. 174, 188, 206, 234.

4. This is an inference from the fact that by this time in the war the uniform described had become standard government issue.

5. O.R., 28, 368. For Morrow's politics, see *History of the Twenty-fourth Michigan*, O. B. Curtis, p. 115. *Michigan MSS* contain Morrow's letter of Sept. 4, 1862, to Michigan's adjutant general, describing Fort Lyon.

6. O.R., 28, 197.

7. O.R., 28, 373.

8. O.R., 107, 877.

9. *The Sixth Wisconsin Volunteers*, R. R. Dawes, p. 104. That the regular army coats were in the process of wearing out—and were later replaced, if at all, only on an occasional basis—is an inference from the following facts: photographs showing Iron Brigade soldiers without regular army coats; the short coat worn by the Twenty-fourth Michigan soldier on the Gettysburg Monument of that regiment; and the absence of any mention in the unit histories and manuscript data of the acquisition of the regular army coat after the date of its original issue to the brigade. It is also believed that the leggings mentioned in the text as being virtually worn out immediately after Antietam were not replaced thereafter. In any event, there is no mention anywhere of their having been replaced. Accordingly, it is believed that after the late fall of 1862, the Iron Brigade was distinguished from a uniform standpoint only by the black hat. As will be noted later in the text, the black hats were supplied to the Twenty-fourth Michigan in 1863, and all photographs and other data support the fact that this distinctive mark of the brigade was maintained throughout the war.

10. Private George E. Smith's note in *B and L*, Vol. III, p. 142. Smith was of the Second Wisconsin.

11. *Personal Recollections of the Civil War*, John Gibbon, p. 92. Gibbon dates the review of the Twenty-fourth as occurring on Oct. 16. Since all other evidence points to the 9th, this date is used.

12. *The Sixth Wisconsin Volunteers*, R. R. Dawes, p. 101.

13. *Young MSS*.

14. *The Cannoneer*, Augustus Buell, p. 43; *History of the Twenty-fourth Michigan*, O. B. Curtis, p. 68.

15. *Ind. A.G.*, Vol. IV, p. 390; *The Life of Billy Yank*, Bell Irwin Wiley, p. 157 and Note 24, Chap. VII, p. 395. The 80-man figure is an estimate based on the usual size of regimental bands. Curiously enough, some of the officers of the Nineteenth Indiana sought to retain at least one of the bandsmen by recommending him to the governor for appointment as an officer in the regiment. *Indiana MSS.* "Gibbon's Brigade Band" is officially noted in *Wis. A.G.* 1862–3, p. 121. It is also mentioned, as of Sept. 16, 1863, in *The Sixth Wisconsin Volunteers*, R. R. Dawes, p. 204. *Jackson MSS* also mention the brigade band as late as April 4, 1864. The elimination of regimental bands did not apply to new regiments. Thus the Twenty-fourth Michigan had a band until May 19, 1864, at which time it was disbanded and the musicians were assigned as regular soldiers to the various companies. *History of the Twenty-fourth Michigan*, O. B. Curtis, p. 247.

16. See Chap. 1, Note 15.

17. *The Sixth Wisconsin Volunteers*, R. R. Dawes, pp. 103, 100.

18. *The Life of Billy Yank*, Bell Irwin Wiley, p. 342, generally describes the invalid and Veteran Reserve Corps. *Indiana MSS* contain numerous original documents covering the transfer of Nineteenth Indiana soldiers from the Veteran Reserve Corps to the regiment, reciting that the soldier had again "become fit for active service in the field."

19. See Note 25, below.

20. *Ind. A.G.*, Vol. IV, pp. 390–408.

21. *Indiana MSS.*

22. *Daily State Sentinel*, Indianapolis, Jan. 27, 1862, p. 3; *Daily State Sentinel*, Indianapolis, March 26, 1862, p. 3; *Wisconsin Newspaper Volumes*, Vol. IV, p. 24; *Indianapolis Daily Journal*, Nov. 15, 1861, p. 3; *Michigan MSS.*

23. *Indiana MSS.* The Yorktown citizen's letter is dated Aug. 30, 1862.

24. For example, on Oct. 7, 1862, Gibbon wrote to the adjutant general of Indiana, stating, "I earnestly request that Gov. Morton may be asked to call for volunteers from those Regt's [new regiments which are now forming] for the 19th and forward at once to the 19th such men not exceeding five hundred who offer their services." McClellan endorsed Gibbon's letter. *Indiana MSS.* See also Secretary Stanton's report for 1862, *O.R.*, 123, 904. For an interesting discussion of this problem, see Appendix I of Vol. II, *Lincoln Finds a General*, Kenneth P. Williams.

25. *Ind. A.G.*, Vol. I, Document No. 1, p. 3, of "Statistics and Documents." The total given excludes "unassigned recruits," 229 men who were credited to the Nineteenth but who did not serve with it in the field and who had no practical connection with it. Also excluded are the numbers of the re-enlisted veterans, 213 men who re-enlisted when their original term expired. Were these latter numbers included, men who enlisted originally and then re-enlisted would be counted twice. Minor

discrepancies of total numbers are also rationalized in the statistics given in the text.

War Department records differ slightly from the state records, and credit the Nineteenth with a total enrollment of 1,250 men. *History of the Twenty-fourth Michigan*, O. B. Curtis, p. 464.

See also *The Military History of Wisconsin*, E. B. Quiner, pp. 472, 482. See above for the exclusions from the statistics given for the Wisconsin regiments. The numbers used for the later-acquired Company K are estimated at 100 officers and men. No other figure is available. War Department reports credit the Wisconsin regiments with total numbers as follows: Second, 1,200; Sixth, 1,940; Seventh, 1,630. *History of the Twenty-fourth Michigan*, O. B. Curtis, p. 464.

History of the Twenty-fourth Michigan, O. B. Curtis, pp. 346–51. Not counted here are unassigned recruits and recruits of Jan., Feb., and March, 1865, who reached the regiment after it was sent from the front to Springfield, Illinois. The War Department lists 1,240 men from the Twenty-fourth (*ibid.*, p. 464).

26. *The Sixth Wisconsin Volunteers*, R. R. Dawes, p. 101. The presence at this precise time of the three field officers is an inference from the fact that Stevens was not wounded at Antietam and that both Fairchild and Allen were with the regiment at the battle of Fredericksburg, O.R., 31, 479; *Soldiers and Citizens Album of Biographical Record*, Vol. I, pp. 695–7. The latter authority states that Allen did not leave the regiment even when wounded at Antietam.

27. *The Sixth Wisconsin Volunteers*, R. R. Dawes, pp. 102–4. The absence of Robinson and Hamilton at this precise time is an inference from the command situation at the time of Gibbon's promotion on Nov. 4. Robinson, at least, was surely still away from the regiment at that time. Both men did return prior to Fredericksburg, O.R., 31, 477; *The Bench and Bar of Wisconsin*, Parker M. Reed, pp. 104–5. *Wis. A.G.*, 1865, p. 1347.

28. *Jackson MSS* state that Meredith left the field on Sunday, Sept. 21, and went to Washington for medical treatment.

29. *A Portrait and Biographical Record of Delaware County, Indiana*, pp. 604–5.

30. *Indianapolis City Directory*, 1860–61, p. 131.

31. *Indiana MSS*; *Bragg MSS*; *Ind. A.G.*, Vol. II, p. 168; *Daily State Sentinel*, Indianapolis, Sept. 27, 1862.

32. *The Sixth Wisconsin Volunteers*, R. R. Dawes, pp. 101–04.

33. *History of the Twenty-fourth Michigan*, O. B. Curtis, pp. 71–5.

34. *Personal Recollections of the Civil War*, John Gibbon, p. 95; O.R., 107, 922.

35. *The Sixth Wisconsin Volunteers*, R. R. Dawes, p. 50.

36. O.R., 27, 460; O.R., 17, 821; *Indianapolis Daily Gazette*, Feb. 7, 1863, p. 3; *Dictionary of American Biography*, Vol. X, p. 400.

37. All of these subsequent events in Gibbon's career appear in his *Personal Recollections of the Civil War*.

38. *Ibid.*, pp. 95–6.

39. The soldier, calling himself "Vindex," wrote his letter to the *Wisconsin Daily Patriot*, and it appears in *Wisconsin Newspaper Volumes*, Vol. IV, p. 25.

40. *Young MSS*.

41. The first quote is from *Jackson MSS*. The second is from an article by Colonel J. A. Watrous in *Wisconsin Soldiers and Sailors Reunion Roster*, compiled by C. K. Pier, p. 259. The third is from *Haskell MSS*.

42. *The Sixth Wisconsin Volunteers*, R. R. Dawes, pp. 43, 105.

43. *Wisconsin Soldiers and Sailors Reunion Roster*, compiled by C. K. Pier, p. 259.

9. Return to Fredericksburg: The Twenty-fourth Michigan Earns the Black Hat (pages 168–188)

1. *History of the Twenty-fourth Michigan*, O. B. Curtis, pp. 75–6; *The Sixth Wisconsin Volunteers*, R. R. Dawes, p. 105.

2. *History of the Twenty-fourth Michigan*, O. B. Curtis, pp. 68, 77; *The Sixth Wisconsin Volunteers*, R. R. Dawes, p. 105.

3. *Young MSS*.

4. *Jackson MSS*.

5. *History of the Sauk County Riflemen*, Philip Cheek and Mair Pointon, pp. 54–5, 215–16.

6. *History of the Twenty-fourth Michigan*, O. B. Curtis, pp. 77, 80, 79.

7. *The Sixth Wisconsin Volunteers*, R. R. Dawes, p. 105.

8. *Young MSS*.

9. *O.R.*, 31, 48–61.

10. *Indiana MSS* contain several letters to Indiana's adjutant general mentioning Meredith's efforts to obtain a general officer's commission. The Indiana newspapers of 1861 and 1862, both those friendly and unfriendly to Governor Morton and to Meredith, contain frequent similar reports. For example, see the *Indianapolis Daily Journal*, Oct. 16, 1861, p. 2. Meredith's commission was dated as of Oct. 6, 1862, *Ind. A.G.*, Vol. II, p. 168, and apparently issued at about the same time, *Indianapolis Daily Journal*, Oct. 10, 1862, p. 3. For the plan for the Indiana brigade, see *Jackson MSS*; *Indianapolis Daily Journal*, Nov. 5, 1862, p. 2; Nov. 7, 1862, p. 3.

11. *Personal Recollections of the Civil War*, John Gibbon, p. 108.

12. *Indiana MSS*. Meredith's assignment is at *O.R.*, 107, 951, dated Nov. 25, 1862.

13. *Bragg MSS*.

14. *Personal Recollections of the Civil War*, John Gibbon, pp. 107–09.

15. *Young MSS*.

16. *Jackson MSS.*

17. *Indiana MSS. Ind.* A.G., Vol. II, p. 168, dates these commissions as of Oct. 7, 1862, but the correspondence described in the preceding paragraph of the text and contained in *Indiana MSS* makes it clear that the commissions were not actually issued until Jan., 1863, at the earliest.

18. *A Portrait and Biographical Record of Delaware County, Indiana,* pp. 602–3; *Ind.* A.G., Vol. II, p. 168.

19. *The Sixth Wisconsin Volunteers,* R. R. Dawes, p. 106; *History of the Twenty-fourth Michigan,* O. B. Curtis, p. 80. Burnside's quote appears at O.R., 31, 99.

20. *The Sixth Wisconsin Volunteers,* R. R. Dawes, p. 107; *History of the Twenty-fourth Michigan,* O. B. Curtis, p. 83. *Jackson MSS* are the source of the quotation.

21. *The Sixth Wisconsin Volunteers,* R. R. Dawes, p. 107.

22. *History of the Twenty-fourth Michigan,* O. B. Curtis, pp. 83-4.

23. *Ibid.,* p. 85; *Jackson MSS.*

24. Burnside's report, O.R., 31, 88; Map 72, *Atlas to Accompany Steele's American Campaigns,* edited by Colonel Vincent J. Esposito, 1956 edition.

25. Reynolds' report, O.R., 31, 452–3; *History of the Twenty-fourth Michigan,* O. B. Curtis, pp. 86–7; *Jackson MSS; The Sixth Wisconsin Volunteers,* R. R. Dawes, p. 108.

26. Reynolds' report, O.R., 31, 453; *Jackson MSS; History of the Twenty-fourth Michigan,* O. B. Curtis, p. 88; *The Sixth Wisconsin Volunteers,* R. R. Dawes, p. 109.

27. *History of the Twenty-fourth Michigan,* O. B. Curtis, p. 88.

28. Doubleday's report, O.R., 31, 461. In *The Sixth Wisconsin Volunteers,* p. 109, R. R. Dawes states that the Iron Brigade did not cross until after 4:00 P.M., but Doubleday's officially reported time is used here. Reynolds' report, O.R., 31, 453; *History of the Twenty-fourth Michigan,* O. B. Curtis, p. 90; Meredith's report, O.R., 31, 475–6.

29. *The Sixth Wisconsin Volunteers,* R. R. Dawes, p. 109.

30. Meredith's report, O.R., 31, 476.

31. Reynolds' report, O.R., 31, 453; Lee's report, O.R., 31, 547; Map 72, *Atlas to Accompany Steele's American Campaigns,* edited by Colonel Vincent J. Esposito, 1956 edition.

32. *The Sixth Wisconsin Volunteers,* R. R. Dawes, p. 110; Reynolds' report, O.R., 31, 453–5; Doubleday's report, O.R., 31, 461.

33. Doubleday's report, O.R. 31, 462; Meredith's report, O.R., 31, 476.

34. *The Sixth Wisconsin Volunteers,* R. R. Dawes, p. 112.

35. Meredith's report, O.R. 31, 476; *History of the Twenty-fourth Michigan,* O. B. Curtis, p. 93.

36. Doubleday's report, O.R., 31, 462.

37. Meredith's report, O.R., 31, 476; Reynolds' report, O.R., 31, 455.

38. Doubleday's report, O.R., 31, 462.

39. Stewart's report, O.R., 31, 468.

40. *History of the Twenty-fourth Michigan*, O. B. Curtis, pp. 93–4.
41. Doubleday's report, *O.R.*, 31, 462–3.
42. *The Sixth Wisconsin Volunteers*, R. R. Dawes, p. 111; *Young MSS* also contain a description of this cannonade. See also *Hughes MSS*.
43. *Young MSS*; Doubleday's report, *O.R.*, 31, 463. See also Stewart's report, *O.R.*, 31, 468.
44. Doubleday's report, *O.R.*, 31, 463. The *Indianapolis Daily Journal*, Dec. 20, 1862, p. 2, originally reported that Meredith had been "arrested."
45. *History of the Twenty-fourth Michigan*, O. B. Curtis, p. 97; *Daily State Sentinel*, Dec. 20, 1862, p. 3. No order has been found officially reinstating Meredith, but all references make it perfectly clear that he was again in command as soon as the brigade recrossed the river. The Indiana newspapers reported his reinstatement on Dec. 25, 1862, *Daily State Sentinel*, Dec. 25, 1862, p. 3.
46. Cutler's report, *O.R.*, 31, 478. Just before this location was accomplished by Cutler, Doubleday had withdrawn the Sixth and Seventh Wisconsin from the left and moved them to the center of the division's line, Doubleday's report, *O.R.*, 31, 464.
47. *Young MSS*.
48. *The Sixth Wisconsin Volunteers*, R. R. Dawes, pp. 111–12.
49. Reynolds' report, *O.R.*, 31, 456; *The Cannoneer*, Augustus Buell, p. 46. Private George E. Smith's note in *B and L*, Vol. III, p. 142, tells of the fight. Smith was of the Second Wisconsin.
50. Doubleday's report, *O.R.*, 31, 464.
51. Doubleday's report, *O.R.*, 31, 464; Reynolds' report, *O.R.*, 31, 456.
52. *The Cannoneer*, Augustus Buell, pp. 46–7. Colonel C. S. Wainwright, Chief of Artillery for the First Corps, cited Battery B's withdrawal as deserving of "special praise," *O.R.*, 31, 460.
53. Doubleday's report, *O.R.*, 31, 464, spoke of the fact that the "pickets and their supports were necessarily left out all night," another way of saying that the pickets were not included in the plan of withdrawal. Cutler's report, *O.R.*, 31, 478, was more direct in alluding to the abandonment of the pickets: "I was also instructed to give no intimation to the pickets of our march, for fear of betraying our movement to the enemy. Being unwilling to leave any men to be captured, I finally obtained permission of General Reynolds to make the effort to save our pickets after the troops were safely withdrawn."
54. *Jackson MSS*. Cutler's report, *O.R.*, 31, 478–9, specifies the three miles.
55. Reynolds' report, *O.R.*, 31, 456, tells of the withdrawal of all of the pickets by Doubleday's aide, Lieutenant Rogers of the Sixth Wisconsin, without any particular mention of the Nineteenth or Cutler's arrangements for them. Doubleday, *O.R.*, 31, 464, separately describes Rogers' work of withdrawing the pickets and the saving of the Nineteenth, "the last to cross the river." Cutler's report, *O.R.*, 31, 478–9, is

the authority for the fact that the arrangements to save the Nineteenth were separate and apart from the withdrawal of the other pickets of the First Corps. A description of the Nineteenth's escape may also be found in *Indianapolis Daily Journal*, Dec. 24, 1862, p. 2.

56. Cutler's report, *O.R.*, 31, 479; Doubleday's report, *O.R.*, 31, 464, *Jackson MSS.*

57. *The Sixth Wisconsin Volunteers*, R. R. Dawes, p. 114.

58. *O.R.*, 31, 138.

59. Stewart's report, *O.R.*, 31, 468; Wainwright's report, *O.R.*, 31, 460; Doubleday's report, *O.R.*, 31, 462, 463.

60. *Young MSS.*

61. *The Cannoneer*, Augustus Buell, p. 44.

62. Meredith's report, *O.R.*, 31, 476; *The Sixth Wisconsin Volunteers*, R. R. Dawes, p. 112.

63. *Echoes of the Marches of the Famous Iron Brigade, 1861–1865*, Doc Aubery, p. 51; Private George E. Smith's note in *B and L*, Vol. III, p. 142.

64. *History of the Sauk County Riflemen*, Philip Cheek and Mair Pointon, pp. 61–2.

65. *History of the Twenty-fourth Michigan*, O. B. Curtis, p. 102. Another tribute to the conduct of the Twenty-fourth appeared in a letter of Dec. 17, 1862, from Stephen Durkee of the Seventh, contained in *Wisconsin Newspaper Volumes*, Vol. IV, pp. 28–9.

The historian of the Twenty-fourth, O. B. Curtis, a corporal, was hospitalized at Brooks Station on the eve of the battle. When the battle opened, he obtained his release and hastened to the front, joining the Third Brigade of the Second Division of the Second Corps. Fighting with this brigade, he lost his left arm and was, of course, permanently disabled. *History of the Twenty-fourth Michigan*, O. B. Curtis, p. 99.

10. Belle Plain: Winter Quarters and Hopefulness
(pages 189–208)

1. *History of the Twenty-fourth Michigan*, O. B. Curtis, pp. 102, 106; *History of the Sauk County Riflemen*, Philip Cheek and Mair Pointon, p. 57; *Young MSS* state that "our camp is two miles below Belle Plain on the bank of the Potomac River. . . ."

2. *Young MSS.*

3. *Jackson MSS*; *Young MSS*; *History of the Twenty-fourth Michigan*, O. B. Curtis, p. 106; *The Sixth Wisconsin Volunteers*, R. R. Dawes, p. 115.

4. *History of the Twenty-fourth Michigan*, O. B. Curtis, p. 105; *Jackson MSS.*

5. *History of the Twenty-fourth Michigan*, O. B. Curtis, p. 106. Another good description appears in *Young MSS.*

6. *Jackson MSS; The Sixth Wisconsin Volunteers*, R. R. Dawes, p. 116.

7. *Young MSS.*

8. *History of the Twenty-fourth Michigan*, O. B. Curtis, pp. 114, 116. *Roberts MSS* provide the quotation.

9. This description, appearing at pages 150–51 of *The Sixth Wisconsin Volunteers*, concerns camp life at White Oak Church in May and early June of 1863. Since it doubtless also accurately describes the Belle Plain routine, it is used here. A similar description, applying expressly to Belle Plain, appears in *Jackson MSS*.

10. *Bird MSS*, appearing in *History of the Twenty-fourth Michigan*, O. B. Curtis, p. 119. *Currier MSS* are the diary quoted.

11. *The Sixth Wisconsin Volunteers*, R. R. Dawes, pp. 142–6; *Jackson MSS*.

12. *The Sixth Wisconsin Volunteers*, R. R. Dawes, pp. 116–17; *History of the Twenty-fourth Michigan*, O. B. Curtis, pp. 110–12.

13. *The Sixth Wisconsin Volunteers*, R. R. Dawes, p. 117. *Jackson MSS* also contain a vivid description of the Mud March.

14. *History of the Twenty-fourth Michigan*, O. B. Curtis, p. 112; *Jackson MSS; Currier MSS*. Two of the quotations are from *History of the Sauk County Riflemen*, Philip Cheek and Mair Pointon, p. 58. The middle quotation appears in *The Sixth Wisconsin Volunteers*, R. R. Dawes, pp. 117–18.

15. *The Sixth Wisconsin Volunteers*, R. R. Dawes, p. 118.

16. *Ibid.*, p. 117; *Young MSS*.

17. *Jackson MSS*.

18. The quotations appear, respectively, in *The Sixth Wisconsin Volunteers*, R. R. Dawes p. 132; *The Cannoneer*, Augustus Buell, p. 49; and a soldier's letter printed in *Indianapolis Daily Journal*, Jan. 8, 1863, p. 2.

19. *The Sixth Wisconsin Volunteers*, R. R. Dawes, pp. 115, 119.

20. *The Cannoneer*, Augustus Buell, p. 49.

21. *The Sixth Wisconsin Volunteers*, R. R. Dawes, p. 132.

22. *O.R.*, 40, 11–12; *The Sixth Wisconsin Volunteers*, R. R. Dawes, pp. 125, 133.

23. *The Sixth Wisconsin Volunteers*, R. R. Dawes, p. 132. See also *History of the Twenty-fourth Michigan*, O. B. Curtis, p. 117.

24. *History of the Twenty-fourth Michigan*, O. B. Curtis, pp. 115–16.

25. *Young MSS* tell of the Christmas dinner. The new diet is mentioned in *The Sixth Wisconsin Volunteers*, R. R. Dawes, p. 125; *History of the Twenty-fourth Michigan*, O. B. Curtis, p. 114. *Jackson MSS* are the quoted diary.

26. *History of the Twenty-fourth Michigan*, O. B. Curtis, p. 107; *The Sixth Wisconsin Volunteers*, R. R. Dawes, pp. 115–16.

27. *Young MSS; The Cannoneer*, Augustus Buell, p. 49.

28. See table of organization, May 1–6, 1863, *O.R.*, 39, 157–8. For Doubleday's assignments, see *O.R.*, 31, 876; *O.R.*, 107, 974. The assignment of Wadsworth was dated Dec. 22, 1862.

29. *Young MSS; The Sixth Wisconsin Volunteers*, R. R. Dawes, p. 129.

30. Compare tables of organization, Dec. 31, 1862, *O.R.*, 31, 932–3; Jan. 31, 1863, *O.R.*, 40, 23; May 1–6, 1863, *O.R.*, 39, 157. Cutler's commission was apparently issued on or about March 25, 1863, *O.R.*, 107, 995, and was dated back to Nov. 29, 1862, *The Military History of Wisconsin*, E. B. Quiner, p. 986. Despite an indication that he at one time commanded the First Brigade, *O.R.*, 107, 1057, Cutler was initially assigned to the Second Brigade. *The Sixth Wisconsin Volunteers*, R. R. Dawes, p. 129, tells of Kellogg's selection.

31. *The Sixth Wisconsin Volunteers*, R. R. Dawes, pp. 129, 131; *Wis.* A.G., 1865, pp. 35–42.

32. *Indiana MSS* contain a number of letters from such officers as May and Bachman seeking higher commands in other regiments. *Wis.* A.G., 1865, p. 1313, sets forth the promotions.

After the war, Allen became a resident of Oshkosh and published the *Northwestern*, a daily and weekly newspaper. He then sold the *Northwestern* and purchased the *Wisconsin Telegraph*. In 1866 he was elected, as a Republican, to the office of Secretary of State, completing his term in 1870. He was also a delegate to the Republican National Convention in 1872 and Commander of the Wisconsin Department of the Grand Army. *History of Winnebago County, Wisconsin*, Publius V. Lawson, Vol. II, pp. 850–53; *Biographical Dictionary of Representative Men of Chicago, Wisconsin and the Columbian Exposition*, pp. 411–12; *Wisconsin Necrology*, Vol. VIII, p. 140; *Soldiers and Citizens Album of Biographical Record*, Vol. I, pp. 695–7.

33. *Wis.* A.G., 1865, p. 1347; *Circular No. 2, Series 1902, Whole No. 349, Wisconsin Commandery, Military Order of the Loyal Legion*. Hamilton at first returned to Milwaukee and the law. Apparently late in the 1860s he went to New York because of his father's ill health, and remained there managing his father's affairs until 1875. Returning then to Milwaukee, Hamilton was elected to the legislature, and in 1880 he was elected judge of the Milwaukee Judicial District. Following this office, he returned to the East in 1886 and died there. He also served as Commander of the Wisconsin Commandery of the Military Order of the Loyal Legion. *Bench and Bar of Wisconsin*, Parker M. Reed, pp. 104–5; *Report of the Annual Meeting of the Wisconsin State Bar Association*, held at Milwaukee, Feb. 17–18, 1903, pp. 209–11; *Circular No. 2, Series 1902, Whole No. 349, Wisconsin Commandery, Military Order of the Loyal Legion*.

34. *Young MSS.*

35. *Wis.* A.G., 1865, pp. 43–9. Richardson's wounds are stated in *Soldiers and Citizens Album of Biographical Record*, Vol. II, p. 579. *History of the Twenty-fourth Michigan*, O. B. Curtis, p. 358.

36. *The Cannoneer*, Augustus Buell, p. 49.

37. *Young MSS* contain the 1862 returns. The 1863 figure is developed from Dawes' statement that "the regiment gave one hundred and

eighty-four Republican majority." Dawes also stated that the Republican majority in the three Wisconsin regiments was "something over six hundred." See *The Sixth Wisconsin Volunteers*, R. R. Dawes, p. 132. See also *History of the Sauk County Riflemen*, Philip Cheek and Mair Pointon, p. 60. In the 1864 presidential election, the recorded vote was Seventh Wisconsin—147 Rep. to 30 Dem.; Sixth Wisconsin—126 Rep. to 36 Dem., *O.R.*, 89, 577.

38. *The Sixth Wisconsin Volunteers*, R. R. Dawes, pp. 105, 126, 123, 127–8.

39. *History of the Twenty-fourth Michigan*, O. B. Curtis, p. 113.

40. *Jackson MSS*.

41. *History of the Twenty-fourth Michigan*, O. B. Curtis, p. 110.

42. *Jackson MSS*. The incident was also described in *History of the Twenty-fourth Michigan*, O. B. Curtis, p. 114.

43. *Currier MSS*.

44. *History of the Twenty-fourth Michigan*, O. B. Curtis, pp. 119–20.

45. *Ibid.*, p. 144; *The Sixth Wisconsin Volunteers*, R. R. Dawes, p. 150; *History of the Sauk County Riflemen*, Philip Cheek and Mair Pointon, pp. 68–9.

46. *History of the Twenty-fourth Michigan*, O. B. Curtis, p. 109, states that all but two men, who had died of typhoid, were exchanged. Since the regiment's captured was listed as nine men, *O.R.*, 31, 138, seven must have been the number of men exchanged.

The number of prisoners to date is an estimate based on the "captured and missing" casualties previously reported in the text. The prisoners to be taken after the winter of 1862–3 is also an estimate, based on casualty figures later appearing in the text.

47. *History of the Twenty-fourth Michigan*, O. B. Curtis, pp. 376–8; *Indiana MSS*, which contain many letters from Nineteenth Indiana prisoners; *Capture and Escape*, John A. Kellogg, Wisconsin History Commission, p. xiii; *Report of the Unveiling and Dedication of Indiana Monument at Andersonville, Georgia*, p. 76.

48. *History of the Twenty-fourth Michigan*, O. B. Curtis, pp. 376–8. The number given includes nine men who died immediately following imprisonment and as a result thereof. *Currier MSS* set forth a typical sequence of events for a prisoner, capture, movement to prison in crowded cars, illness, and death.

49. *Capture and Escape*, John A. Kellogg, Wisconsin History Commission, is Kellogg's narrative of his experience. *Indiana MSS* contain the letters.

50. From letters of Iron Brigade soldiers contained in *Fairfield MSS* and *Indiana MSS*. In *Fairfield MSS* is the quoted letter.

51. *Indiana MSS* contain a number of these letters, some of them very pitiful. Thus on Aug. 10, 1863, Sergeant Will Wilson of Company F, Nineteenth Indiana, wrote the Indiana Sanitary Commission from Gettysburg, requesting transfer to an Indiana hospital: "I am getting

well very fast having had my left leg amputated below the knee and feeling a great desire to go home as soon as I can is my reason for troubling you." *Fairfield MSS* tell of the hospital escape.

52. *Perry MSS.*

53. *History of the Twenty-fourth Michigan*, O. B. Curtis, pp. 109, 138. *Jackson MSS* also contain frequent references to Sunday "meetings" and the sermons of the chaplains.

54. *History of the Twenty-fourth Michigan*, O. B. Curtis, p. 360.

55. *Indiana MSS; Ind. A.G.*, Vol. II, p. 169.

56. *Wis. A.G.*, 1865, pp. 1348, 1314, 1340.

57. *Chapman MSS.*

58. *Wis. A.G.*, 1865, p. 1340; *The Sixth Wisconsin Volunteers*, R. R. Dawes, p. 245.

59. *Jackson MSS.*

60. *The Sixth Wisconsin Volunteers*, R. R. Dawes, pp. 120–23; *History of the Sauk County Riflemen*, Philip Cheek and Mair Pointon, pp. 58–9; *Hughes MSS*; Fairchild's report, O.R., 39, 16-17.

61. *History of the Sauk County Riflemen*, Philip Cheek and Mair Pointon, p. 59; *Hughes MSS*; O.R., 39, 73-4.

62. *The Sixth Wisconsin Volunteers*, R. R. Dawes, p. 135.

63. *History of the Twenty-fourth Michigan*, O. B. Curtis, pp. 121-4.

64. *Ibid.*, pp. 117–18; *Currier MSS.*

65. *Young MSS.*

66. *History of the Twenty-fourth Michigan*, O. B. Curtis, pp. 118–19. See also *The Sixth Wisconsin Volunteers*, R. R. Dawes, p. 131; *History of the Sauk County Riflemen*, Philip Cheek and Mair Pointon, p. 61; *Jackson MSS; Currier MSS.*

67. *The Sixth Wisconsin Volunteers*, R. R. Dawes, pp. 131–2. The history of the horse appears in *The Cannoneer*, Augustus Buell, pp. 30–31.

68. *History of the Twenty-fourth Michigan*, O. B. Curtis, p. 116, reports the April 1 strength as 619 officers and men present for duty and 55 "present sick." The number appearing in the text is simply a fair estimate of the regiment's average strength.

This is an estimated figure for the brigade. Regimental numbers at this time are available as follows: 24th Michigan, 625; 6th Wisconsin, 400, see Dawes, p. 130; 2nd Wisconsin, 267, see *O.R.*, 39, 73. No return is available for the other two regiments, but in *Regimental Losses in the American Civil War*, William F. Fox states that 1,883 was the number of the brigade engaged at Gettysburg. The figure of 2,000 given in the text is based on these authorities and, in relation to Fox's figure, allows for losses at Chancellorsville and en route to Pennsylvania.

69. *The Cannoneer*, Augustus Buell, pp. 47–8. *History of the Twenty-fourth Michigan*. O. B. Curtis, p. 114, places at forty the number of Michigan men detached to the battery in February. This is believed to be in error.

70. *The Sixth Wisconsin Volunteers*, R. R. Dawes, pp. 130–31. Even

the enlisted men, looking about, conceded that the soldiers seemed well and hardy, *Young MSS.*

71. *Young MSS.*

11. *Chancellorsville and the March to Pennsylvania* (*pages 209–232*)

1. O.R., 39, 156 ff.

2. Hooker's order, O.R., 40, 268. See Plates XXXIX and XLI, *Atlas to the Official Records.*

3. *History of the Twenty-fourth Michigan,* O. B. Curtis, pp. 125, 137. Colonel Robinson's report, O.R., 39, 273; Phelps' report, O.R., 39, 262.

4. *The Sixth Wisconsin Volunteers,* R. R. Dawes, pp. 135–6; *History of the Twenty-fourth Michigan,* O. B. Curtis, p. 125.

5. Bragg's report, O.R., 39, 271; Colonel Robinson's report, O.R., 39, 273.

6. *History of the Twenty-fourth Michigan,* O. B. Curtis, p. 125; Reynolds' report, O.R., 39, 253; Meredith's report, O.R., 39, 266–7; Bragg's report, O.R., 39, 271–2.

7. *History of the Twenty-fourth Michigan,* O. B. Curtis, p. 125; *The Sixth Wisconsin Volunteers,* R. R. Dawes, pp. 135–6; Meredith's report, O.R., 39, 267; Bragg's report, O.R., 39, 272; *History of the Sauk County Riflemen,* Philip Cheek and Mair Pointon, pp. 62–3.

Verification of the presence of the enemy regiments is unavailable in Confederate reports. The identification appears in Reynolds' report, O.R., 39, 253, and *History of the Twenty-fourth Michigan,* O. B. Curtis, p. 125.

8. *History of the Twenty-fourth Michigan,* O. B. Curtis, p. 125. Bragg's report, O.R., 39, 272, states that the firing across the river continued for two hours, but it is believed that he exaggerated.

9. Reynolds' report, O.R., 39, 253.

10. *The Sixth Wisconsin Volunteers,* R. R. Dawes, p. 136.

11. *Ibid.,* p. 136.

12. *The Sixth Wisconsin Volunteers,* R. R. Dawes, pp. 136–7; *History of the Twenty-fourth Michigan,* O. B. Curtis, pp. 125–6; Meredith's report, O.R., 39, 267; Fairchild's report, O.R., 39, 270; Reynolds' report, O.R., 39, 253. Additional material, including the two quotations, appears in *History of the Sauk County Riflemen,* Philip Cheek and Mair Pointon, pp. 63–4.

13. *The Sixth Wisconsin Volunteers,* R. R. Dawes, p. 137.

14. *History of the Sauk County Riflemen,* Philip Cheek and Mair Pointon, pp. 64–5.

15. *History of the Twenty-fourth Michigan,* O. B. Curtis, p. 126.

16. *History of the Sauk County Riflemen,* Philip Cheek and Mair Pointon, p. 65.

17. *Ibid.,* p. 65.

18. *The Sixth Wisconsin Volunteers*, R. R. Dawes, p. 137, contains both quotations.

19. Meredith's report, O.R., 39, 267; Bragg's report, O.R., 39, 272; Williams' report, O.R., 39, 269; Fairchild's report, O.R., 39, 270; Colonel Robinson's report, O.R., 39, 273. Reynolds' report O.R., 39, 253, states when the pontoons were down.

20. Bragg's report, O.R., 39, 272.

21. *History of the Twenty-fourth Michigan*, O. B. Curtis, p. 126. Wadsworth's congratulatory order, his only report of the affair, carefully avoided the question of which regiment was first, O.R., 39, 262.

22. *History of the Sauk County Riflemen*, Philip Cheek and Mair Pointon, p. 65.

23. *History of the Twenty-fourth Michigan*, O. B. Curtis, pp. 128, 131, reported five killed and twenty wounded on April 29 and 30. Since four of these were casualties on the latter day, according to *History of the Twenty-fourth Michigan*, O. B. Curtis, p. 127, the crossing on April 29 resulted in twenty-one casualties. Curtis' figure is preferred to that of O.R., 39, 173, which gives the regiment twenty-four casualties from April 29 through May 2. See also Reynolds' report, O.R., 39, 253. Reynolds' figure for prisoners is preferred to others which are larger. See, for example, Meredith's report, O.R., 39, 267. For other accounts of the crossing, see *Young MSS, Currier MSS*, and *Converse MSS*.

24. Reynolds' report, O.R., 39, 254; *History of the Twenty-fourth Michigan*, O. B. Curtis, p. 127.

25. *The Cannoneer*, Augustus Buell, p. 51.

26. Reynolds' report, O.R., 39, 254. Meredith's report, O.R., 39, 267–8, also describes the events from April 29 through May 1.

27. Reynolds' report, O.R., 39, 254–5; Meredith's report, O. R., 268. *The Sixth Wisconsin Volunteers*, R. R. Dawes, p. 138, is clearly wrong in its reference to the First Corps' crossing at Bank's Ford. See also *History of the Twenty-fourth Michigan*, O. B. Curtis, p. 134.

28. *Lincoln Finds a General*, Kenneth P. Williams, Vol. II, p. 591.

29. Meredith's report, O.R., 39, 268; Reynolds' report, O.R., 39, 255. *History of the Twenty-fourth Michigan*, O. B. Curtis, p. 134, is the authority for the route of march, although the references are obscure.

30. On the 3rd, Fairchild was assigned temporarily to Wadsworth's staff, leaving Lieutenant Colonel Stevens in command of the regiment, Fairchild's report, O.R., 39, 270; Stevens' report, O.R., 39, 271. See also *History of the Twenty-fourth Michigan*, O. B. Curtis, p. 134; *Jackson MSS; The Sixth Wisconsin Volunteers*, R. R. Dawes, p. 138.

31. *The Sixth Wisconsin Volunteers*, R. R. Dawes, p. 138; *History of the Sauk County Riflemen*, Philip Cheek and Mair Pointon, p. 66.

32. *History of the Twenty-fourth Michigan*, O. B. Curtis, p. 134; Meredith's report, O.R., 39, 268.

33. *The Sixth Wisconsin Volunteers*, R. R. Dawes, p. 139.

34. *Loc. cit.; History of the Twenty-fourth Michigan*, O. B. Curtis, p. 135; Meredith's report, *O.R.*, 39, 268.

35. Meredith's report, *O.R.*, 39, 268. For good descriptions of the withdrawal, see *Young MSS, Currier MSS, Daily State Sentinel*, May 14, 1863, p. 2.

36. *The Sixth Wisconsin Volunteers*, R. R. Dawes, p. 139.

37. *Berdan's United States Sharpshooters*, Captain C. A. Stevens, pp. 277–8.

38. *History of the Twenty-fourth Michigan*, O. B. Curtis, p. 135. The route to this camp is vague because of the use in the reports of local and obscure names for the roads, Meredith's report, *O. R.*, 39, 268; Reynolds' report, *O.R.*, 39, 256.

39. *The Sixth Wisconsin Volunteers*, R. R. Dawes, p. 145.

40. *Jackson MSS*.

41. *History of the Twenty-fourth Michigan*, O. B. Curtis, p. 137; *Jackson MSS*.

42. *The Sixth Wisconsin Volunteers*, R. R. Dawes, p. 142; *History of the Sauk County Riflemen*, Philip Cheek and Mair Pointon, p. 68.

43. *Currier MSS*. See also *History of the Twenty-fourth Michigan*, O. B. Curtis, p. 139, concerning swimming back and forth. *Converse MSS* describe another technique, involving a board with twine attached. The twine was tied around a rock and the rock was thrown across the river, permitting the board to be pulled over.

44. *The Sixth Wisconsin Volunteers*, R. R. Dawes, pp. 145, 149.

45. *History of the Twenty-fourth Michigan*, O. B. Curtis, p. 140. Reynolds' order is in *O.R.*, 40, 507.

46. *O.R.*, 40, 511.

47. *Jackson MSS*.

48. *The Sixth Wisconsin Volunteers*, R. R. Dawes, p. 143.

49. *Jackson MSS*.

50. Morrow's report, *O.R.*, 39, 1112–15. See also *History of the Twenty-fourth Michigan*, O. B. Curtis, pp. 140–41.

51. *History of the Twenty-fourth Michigan*, O. B. Curtis, p. 142.

52. Compare returns of May 10, 1863, *O.R.*, 40, 464, and June 30, 1863, *O.R.*, 43, 151.

53. Compare tables of organization for May 1–6, 1863, *O.R.*, 39, 157, and for July 1–3, 1863, *O.R.*, 43, 155. Stannard's Vermont Brigade did not join Doubleday's Division until the night of July 1, *O.R.*, 43, 348. Regarding Battery B, although no precise information is available, only a few New York "detached volunteers" remained as a result of the 1863 mustering out of approximately forty of the New Yorkers, whose places had been taken by Wisconsin and Michigan men and six New York three-year men. *The Cannoneer*, Augustus Buell, pp. 47-8. In the light of the previous transfers from the Iron Brigade regiments, as previously described in the text, and the mustering out in 1862 of approximately thirty of the regulars (Buell, p. 29), it is safe to assume that

the Iron Brigade accounted for well in excess of one-half of the strength of the battery as of the spring of 1863.

54. *History of the Twenty-fourth Michigan*, O. B. Curtis, p. 142.

55. *The Sixth Wisconsin Volunteers*, R. R. Dawes, p. 146.

56. *History of the Twenty-fourth Michigan*, O. B. Curtis, p. 142.

57. *The Sixth Wisconsin Volunteers*, R. R. Dawes, p. 147.

58. *Ibid.*, pp. 147–8; *Jackson MSS.*

59. *The Sixth Wisconsin Volunteers*, R. R. Dawes, p. 151; *History of the Twenty-fourth Michigan*, O. B. Curtis, p. 144; O.R., 43, 141.

60. *The Sixth Wisconsin Volunteers*, R. R. Dawes, pp. 151, 146, 149.

61. O.R., 43, 141. The quotations are from *The Sixth Wisconsin Volunteers*, R. R. Dawes, pp. 151–2. See also *History of the Twenty-fourth Michigan*, O. B. Curtis, pp. 144–9.

62. *The Sixth Wisconsin Volunteers*, R. R. Dawes, p. 152.

63. The quotations are from *The Sixth Wisconsin Volunteers*, R. R. Dawes, pp. 152–3. See also O.R., 43, 142.

64. The quotation is from *The Sixth Wisconsin Volunteers*, R. R. Dawes, p. 153. *History of the Twenty-fourth Michigan*, O. B. Curtis, pp. 149–50; O.R., 43, 142.

65. O.R., 43, 142. *History of the Twenty-fourth Michigan*, O. B. Curtis, pp. 149–50; *The Sixth Wisconsin Volunteers*, R. R. Dawes, p. 154.

66. The quotation is from *The Sixth Wisconsin Volunteers*, R. R. Dawes, pp. 156, 158. See also *History of the Twenty-fourth Michigan*, O. B. Curtis, p. 150; *Currier MSS*; O.R., 43, 143.

67. *History of the Twenty-fourth Michigan*, O. B. Curtis, p. 150.

68. *The Sixth Wisconsin Volunteers*, R. R. Dawes, p. 158.

69. *History of the Twenty-fourth Michigan*, O. B. Curtis, p. 150.

70. O.R., 43, 143; *The Sixth Wisconsin Volunteers*, R. R. Dawes, p. 156; *History of the Twenty-fourth Michigan*, O. B. Curtis, p. 150.

71. *The Sixth Wisconsin Volunteers*, R. R. Dawes, p. 157.

72. *History of the Twenty-fourth Michigan*, O. B. Curtis, p. 152.

73. O.R., 43, 143–4; *History of the Twenty-fourth Michigan*, O. B. Curtis, p. 152; *The Sixth Wisconsin Volunteers*, R. R. Dawes, pp. 157–8.

74. O.R., 43, 151. Meade's numbers are taken from *Numbers and Losses in the Civil War*, Thomas L. Livermore, p. 102. The number given is "effectives." Confederate strength appears in *Numbers and Losses*, p. 103. The number given is "total engaged."

75. *The Cannoneer*, Augustus Buell, pp. 61–2.

76. The only available statement of numbers for the brigade is that of *Regimental Losses in the American Civil War*, William F. Fox, p. 117. Two of the regiments reported their numbers at Gettysburg, as follows: Second Wisconsin, 302 officers and men, O.R., 43, 274; Twenty-fourth Michigan, 496 officers and men, O.R., 43, 269. These reports, from the largest and the smallest of the five regiments, generally support Fox's total for the brigade. See Note 68, Chap. 12.

77. *The Cannoneer*, Augustus Buell, p. 62.

12. Gettysburg: *The Last Stand* (pages 233–259)

1. *History of the Twenty-fourth Michigan*, O. B. Curtis, p. 155, tells of breakfast and the distribution of ammunition. See also *Klein MSS*.

The precise times of day of the events on July 1 are impossible to settle. *The Cannoneer*, Augustus Buell, p. 64, is the source of the 8:00 A.M. time. Dudley's 1878 report for the Iron Brigade identifies the time as "about 9 o'clock," and 9:00 A.M. is the time set forth in Morrow's report for the brigade's arrival at Gettysburg, O.R., 43, 267. Perhaps the most specific and reliable statement of time is that of Buford, O.R., 43, 924, who at 10:10 A.M. reported from Gettysburg that the First Division was "within 3 miles" of the town. This time has been selected as the base from which to calculate and verify other statements of time during the morning.

The Cannoneer, Augustus Buell, p. 64, describes the custom of alternating brigades and the fact that Cutler's Brigade was first. Cutler's report, O.R., 43, 281, describes the detachment of the Seventh Indiana, which rejoined Cutler on the night of July 1. Wadsworth's report, O.R., 43, 265–6, also tells of the organization of his column. Dudley's 1878 report for the Iron Brigade and *The Sixth Wisconsin Volunteers*, R. R. Dawes, p. 164, describe the brigade guard and its place in the column.

Authority for Reynolds' presence with the First Division is Wadsworth's report, O.R., 43, 265. Reynolds' command is described in Doubleday's report, O.R., 43, 244, which also describes Reynolds' orders to Doubleday and the fact that the scattered locations of the other divisions delayed Doubleday for "an hour and a half to two hours." Technically, Doubleday took the First Corps as of Reynolds' assumption of "wing" command, at which time a corresponding adjustment in division leadership was also effective. In the text, this has been disregarded for purposes of clarity in identifying units and organizations. Meade's report, O.R., 43, 114, describes his order to Reynolds, a copy of which appears at O.R., 45, 416. Howard's report, O.R., 43, 701, refers to his order from Reynolds.

2. *The Sixth Wisconsin Volunteers*, R. R. Dawes, p. 164; *History of the Sauk County Riflemen*, Philip Cheek and Mair Pointon, p. 71. The route step is identified in *History of the Twenty-fourth Michigan*, O. B. Curtis, p. 156. Contrary to some popular accounts, the music was not *band* music and could not have been because the Sixth's band was mustered out in August of 1862.

3. *The Cannoneer*, Augustus Buell, pp. 63–4.

4. *The Sixth Wisconsin Volunteers*, R. R. Dawes, p. 164; Morrow's report, O.R., 43, 267.

5. Heth's report, O.R., 44, 637–8; Hill's report, O.R., 44, 606–7. For Pegram's batteries, see O.R., 44, 28, 290. For the time of the beginning of the engagement between Heth and the cavalry Buford states between 8:00 and 9:00 A.M., O.R., 43, 927. Calef's report, O.R., 43, 1030–31.

6. *Chancellorsville and Gettysburg*, Abner Doubleday, p. 126.

7. For the Confederate table of organization, including the artillery reserve, see O.R., 44, 287–90. Confederate numbers are estimated. Of all of the Confederate divisions at Gettysburg, Rodes' alone has an available and timely strength report, that of June 30, 1863, O.R., 44, 564, listing 8,125 effectives. That this number may be reasonably attributed to the other divisions is determined from the fact that the total Confederate effective strength of 75,000 is generally accepted, and the fact that the recently reorganized army of three corps was composed of nine divisions. Although Rodes' Division was admittedly composed of five brigades, while the other divisions included four brigades each, it is still fair to infer that the divisions were relatively equal in strength (75,000 ÷ 9). The 8,000 number for Heth also finds support in a letter appearing in the records, from a captain of the Twenty-sixth North Carolina to North Carolina's Governor Vance, O.R., 44, 645. For the location of the Confederate forces, see Hill's report, O.R., 44, 607, and Ewell's, O.R., 44, 444. That Buford knew of the Confederates' whereabouts is apparent from his messages of June 30 and July 1, O.R., 43, 923–924.

The June 30 effective strength of the First Corps, appearing at O.R., 43, 151, was 8,716 men and 687 officers. The numbers of the Iron Brigade, 1,883 officers and men, are also available, as reported in the previous chapter. But the strength of the divisions within the corps are estimated, as follows: 1st, 4,000; 2nd, 4,000; 3rd, 1,500; based on the number of regiments in each division as set forth on the table of organization, O.R., 43, 155–7, which also identifies the First Corps batteries. The strength of the Eleventh Corps appears at O.R., 43, 151, and its organization is set forth at O.R., 43, 164–5.

8. *War Diaries and Letters of Stephen Mott Weld, 1861–1865.* A good discussion of Reynolds' decision and actions appears in *Toward Gettysburg*, Edward J. Nichols, Chap. XII.

9. Morrow's report, O.R., 43, 267, describes the column's haste. For Heth's deployment, see his report, O.R., 44, 637. For the regimental identification, see O.R., 44, 289. The strength of each brigade is estimated at one-fourth of the strength of the division. This estimate is consistent with Davis' strength report of 2,577 for his four regiments as of May 31, 1863, O.R., 26, 1086. At Gettysburg only three of the regiments were available according to Davis' report, O.R., 44, 649, which permits the 2,000 estimate.

10. This time is variously stated, and the choice of 10:30 is based on Buford's message at 10:10 A.M., O. R., 43, 924. Other official statements are Morrow's—9:00 A.M., O.R., 43, 267; Colonel Robinson's—10:00 A.M., O.R., 43, 278; and Mansfield's—10:00 A.M., O.R., 43, 273.

11. *History of the Twenty-fourth Michigan,* O. B. Curtis, p. 156. Wadsworth's report, O.R., 43, 265, states that the column left the road approximately a mile from the town. *Gettysburg*, R. K. Beecham, p. 62, tells of the artillery fire.

12. The dismounting of the officers is described in Mansfield's report,

O.R., 43, 273. Dudley's 1878 report for the Iron Brigade describes the column's organizing for battle. Dawes' report, O.R., 43, 275, and his *The Sixth Wisconsin Volunteers*, pp. 164–5, describes the treatment of the brigade guard. Although there is no direct authority on the point, it is assumed that the guard remained in Dawes' regiment throughout the action of the day.

13. Morrow's report, O.R., 43, 267; Colonel Robinson's report, O.R., 43, 279; Dawes' report, O.R., 43, 275; Dudley's 1878 report for the Iron Brigade. *Gettysburg*, R. K. Beecham, pp. 62–3, also contains a good description of the advance. For the units north of the pike, see Cutler's report, O.R., 43, 281–2; Hall's report for the Second Maine Battery, O.R., 43, 359; Wadsworth's report, O.R., 43, 266. For Dawes' detachment, see Dawes' report, O.R., 43, 275.

14. *Gettysburg*, R. K. Beecham, pp. 64–5. Wadsworth's report, O.R., 43, 266, and Dudley's 1878 report for the Iron Brigade state that Cutler's advance had become engaged before the Iron Brigade's charge. Dudley and *The Sixth Wisconsin Volunteers*, R. R. Dawes, pp. 164–5, describe the *en echelon* formation.

15. Mansfield's report, O.R., 43, 273. *Gettysburg*, R. K. Beecham, p. 65, is the source of the quotation.

16. Report for Archer's Brigade, O.R., 44, 646.

17. Mansfield's report, O.R., 43, 273–4; Colonel Robinson's report, O.R., 43, 279; Morrow's report, O.R., 43, 267.

The number of captured men of Archer's Brigade varies widely from report to report. Since no positive verification is available, the report for Archer's Brigade, O.R., 44, 646, is accepted. It is, of course, one of the lower figures reported. Mansfield's report, O.R., 43, 274, tells of Maloney's capture of Archer, the first Confederate general officer captured under Lee's command of the Army of Northern Virginia.

18. Colonel Robinson's report, O.R., 43, 279; Morrow's report, O.R., 43, 267; Dudley's 1878 report for the Iron Brigade. See also Heth's report, O.R., 44, 638, and the report for Archer's Brigade, O.R., 44, 646.

19. Cutler's report, O.R., 43, 281–2; Wadsworth's report, O.R., 43, 266.

20. Hall's report for the Second Maine Battery, O.R., 43, 359–60; Dawes' report, O.R., 43, 275–6. *The Sixth Wisconsin Volunteers*, R. R. Dawes, p. 164, credits the Sixth with 342 officers and men, to which number the text adds the brigade guard.

21. The epithet applied to the enemy in the cut is taken from *Klein MSS*. The remainder of the account of the Sixth's action is found in Dawes' report, O.R., 43, 275–8, and in his *The Sixth Wisconsin Volunteers*, pp. 165–71. The losses of the Sixth and the Confederates are taken from the report. See also Dudley's 1878 report for the Iron Brigade; Wadsworth's report, O.R., 43, 266, which erroneously states that two entire regiments and their flags were captured; Davis' report, O.R., 44, 649; Heth's report, O.R., 44, 637; *History of the Sauk County Riflemen*,

Philip Cheek and Mair Pointon, pp. 71–5; and Doubleday's report, O.R., 43, 246. Both the Fourteenth Brooklyn (its report is at O.R., 43, 286–7) and the 95th New York (reported at O.R., 43, 287–8) claim the leadership in the railroad-cut action, but Doubleday's report and Wadsworth accept the Sixth as the spearhead. The victory at the railroad cut also rescued the 147th New York, previously trapped by Davis' Brigade; see Cutler's report, O.R., 43, 282. *History of the Twenty-fourth Michigan*, O. B. Curtis, p. 157, erroneously places Archer's Brigade in the cut.

22. Buford's report, O.R., 43, 927. Dudley's 1878 report for the Iron Brigade; Mansfield's report, O.R., 43, 274–5; Colonel Robinson's report, O.R., 43, 279, which erroneously puts the Seventh on the right flank; and Morrow's report, O.R., 43, 267–8. *History of the Twenty-fourth Michigan*, O. B. Curtis, p. 159, describes the angle of the brigade's line, which was recessed along the northern face of the woods, so as to protect against an advance down the pike. See also *Gettysburg*, R. K. Beecham, pp. 68–9, and Wadsworth's report, O.R., 43, 266.

23. Calef's report, O.R., 43, 1031; Wadsworth's report, O.R., 43, 266; and Cutler's report, O.R., 43, 282.

24. The only report of the Second's casualties appears in *Gettysburg*, R. K. Beecham, p. 69. Heth's report, O.R., 44, 637–8. See also Davis' report, O.R., 44, 649.

25. All reports for the Iron Brigade regiments describe the heavy skirmish and artillery fire. This time is again difficult to specify. Heth stated that the lull was for more than an hour, O.R., 44, 638; Mansfield's report states "two hours or more," O.R., 43, 274, and Dudley's 1878 report for the Iron Brigade specifies three hours. But 3:00 P.M. is the generally accepted time for the renewal of the Confederate attack.

26. Doubleday's report, O.R., 43, 246. See also Howard's report, O.R., 43, 701–2.

27. Howard's report, O.R., 43, 702; Hall's report for the Second Maine Battery, O.R., 43, 359–60. For the First Corps line, see Doubleday's report, O.R., 43, 247–8; Stone's report, O.R., 43, 329; Rowley's report, O.R., 43, 313; and General Robinson's report, O.R., 43, 289. The battery locations are described in the battery reports, O.R., 43, 362 (Reynolds'); O.R., 43, 364 (First Pennsylvania); and O.R., 43, 360 (Fifth Maine). See also Wainwright's report, O.R., 43, 356–7. Battery B has no official report for Gettysburg, but *The Cannoneer*, Augustus Buell, pp. 65ff., is a careful and accurate account of its action.

28. This well-known event is chronicled in a number of places, but few accounts are either firsthand or contemporaneous. Not surprisingly, the stories differ in detail and some—purporting years later to quote conversations with Burns—are plainly unreliable. See, for example, the following probably colored accounts: John B. Callis', quoted in *History of the Sauk County Riflemen*, Philip Cheek and Mair Pointon, pp. 77–9; *History of the Twenty-fourth Michigan*, O. B. Curtis, p. 182; the account by George Eustice of the Seventh Wisconsin, *B and L*, Vol. III, p. 276; and *History*

of the 150th Regiment, Pennsylvania Volunteers, Thomas Chamberlin, pp. 113–14. Regardless of details, the John Burns story did happen at Gettysburg and he did fight with the Iron Brigade, Doubleday's report, O.R., 43, 255. Although the event was plainly a sideshow, and probably not worth all of the attention it has received, a recent book seems to go overboard in attacking Burns. In *High Tide at Gettysburg,* Glenn Tucker calls Burns a "bushwhacker," surely an inappropriate term to apply to a man who was fighting in the battle line. Tucker also is critical of Burns, and accuses him of cowardice and untruthfulness, because he would not, when found by the Confederates, admit that he had been a combatant. But Tucker, who writes from a Confederate point of view, forgets that Burns was for the Union. He was under no obligation to tell the *enemy* anything, and acted with perfect propriety in the circumstances. In addition to these considerations, perhaps a writer should be more restrained in characterizing the actions of an old man, a citizen of the United States who had been wounded three times and who was lying on the ground surrounded by the troops which he had fought and which were in armed rebellion against the United States. The quotations appear in *The Battle of Gettysburg,* Frank A. Haskell, Wisconsin History Commission, 1908, p. 11, and *History of the 150th Regiment, Pennsylvania Volunteers,* Thomas Chamberlin, p. 113.

29. Ewell's report, O.R., 44, 444; Heth's report, O.R., 44, 638. For regiments comprising these brigades, see O.R., 44, 289. Pender's report, O.R., 44, 656. Lane's Brigade originally deployed north of the pike, between Thomas and Scales, but was then sent to the right of the division.

30. Morrow's report, O.R., 43, 268; Mansfield's report, O.R., 43, 274.

31. Morrow's report, O.R., 43, 268; Dudley's 1878 report for the Iron Brigade.

32. Dudley's 1878 report for the Iron Brigade describes the opening fire. Doubleday's report, O.R., 43, 254, identifies the wounds of Meredith, Dudley, and Lindley. See also *Indianapolis Daily Journal,* Aug. 1, 1863, p. 2; July 4, 1863, p. 4. The latter report of Meredith's injuries states that he was also bruised on the top of the head by a shell fragment.

33. Mansfield's report, O.R., 43, 274; Colonel Robinson's report, O.R., 43, 279.

34. The quotation is from *History of the Twenty-fourth Michigan,* O. B. Curtis, p. 188. The account of the overlapping of the Nineteenth appears in Morrow's report, O.R., 43, 268, and Colonel Robinson's, O.R., 43, 279. The precise time of Callis' wounding is uncertain. Colonel Robinson simply marks it as "late in the day," O.R., 43, 281. Doubleday's report, O.R., 43, 255.

35. Dudley's 1878 report for the Iron Brigade; Morrow's report, O.R., 43, 268. The quotation is from *Gettysburg,* R. K. Beecham, pp. 72–3. Report for Pettigrew's Brigade, O.R., 44, 643; Heth's report, O.R., 44, 639.

36. The quotation is Morrow's, O.R., 43, 269. That it was accurate appears from the report for Pettigrew's Brigade, O.R., 44, 643, which states that the Iron Brigade made another stand in the woods. For the position in the ravine see Morrow's report, O. R., 43, 268, which refers to "a slight ravine," and Gettysburg, R. K. Beecham, p. 77. The changing of fronts between rounds is repeated in the division and regimental reports.

37. This color was the regiment's original one, Michigan in the War, John Robertson, pp. 266–7. The account is taken from Morrow's report, O.R., 43, 268–9, and also appears in History of the Twenty-fourth Michigan, O. B. Curtis, pp. 163–4. Curtis' account identifies six different battle lines for the Iron Brigade, an analysis which is not used here because the withdrawal probably was not so specifically systematic. A dramatic incident involving the Second Wisconsin's color is described in Mansfield's report, O.R., 43, 275. The flag of the Nineteenth Indiana was also a center of death on July 1 and is the subject of a memoir by Henry C. Marsh, a hospital steward in the Nineteenth, Indiana State Library MSS.

38. Doubleday's report, O.R., 43, 250–51; Rowley's report, O.R., 43, 313–14; General Robinson's report, O.R., 43, 289–90; Cutler's report, O.R., 43, 282–3; Ewell's report, O.R., 44, 444–5. Although Howard did not acknowledge it, it is generally accepted that the Eleventh was beaten and withdrew, uncovering the First Corps. There was ill feeling about this among the First Corps veterans. An Iron Brigade soldier referred to the Eleventh Corps as the "flying half moons," an allusion to the organization's corps badge, and also wrote of the corps as the "collapsible Eleventh," Klein MSS. For the fact of Wadsworth's order, see his report, O.R., 43, 266.

39. Colonel Robinson's report, O.R., 43, 280. See also Mansfield's report, O.R., 43, 274; Morrow's report, O.R., 43, 269.

40. For the location and description of this barricade, see Gettysburg, R. K. Beecham, pp. 79–80; Dudley's 1878 report for the Iron Brigade; Colonel Robinson's report, O.R., 43, 280; and Doubleday's report, O.R., 43, 250. Contrary to Beecham's account in Gettysburg, pp. 79–80, the Second Maine Battery was at this time on Cemetery Hill, not Seminary Ridge, O.R., 43, 360. In addition to the battery reports, and Doubleday's report, O.R., 43, 250, Maine at Gettysburg, pp. 83–6, contains a good description of the massed artillery on Seminary Ridge, written by Greenlief T. Stevens, commander of the Fifth Maine. On page 84, the following appears: "In all twelve guns were massed at this point so closely that they were hardly five yards apart; four guns of Cooper's battery B, First Penn., six guns of Stevens' Fifth Maine battery and two guns of Reynolds' battery L, 1st N.Y., under command of Lt. Wilber. The other four guns of Reynolds' battery, under Lt. Breck, at this hour were on the same ridge south of the Seminary." Stewart's Battery B was, of course, north of the Seminary.

41. Wadsworth's report, *O.R.*, 43, 266, states the order to the brigade. Doubleday's report, *O.R.*, 43, 250.

42. Colonel Robinson's report, *O.R.*, 43, 280. *Gettysburg*, R. K. Beecham, p. 80, contains the quotation.

43. A *Colonel at Gettysburg and Spottsylvania*, Varina D. Brown, p. 79. The quotation is that of Colonel Joseph Newton Brown of the Fourteenth South Carolina, Perrin's Brigade, whose personal account is printed in the book published by Varina Brown. Colonel Robinson's report, *O.R.*, 43, 280.

44. *Histories of the Several Regiments and Battalions from North Carolina*, Vol. III, pp. 89–90. The account quoted is by John H. Thorp of the Forty-seventh North Carolina, Pettigrew's Brigade. Scales' report, *O.R.*, 44, 670.

45. Colonel Robinson's report, *O.R.*, 43, 280; Mansfield's report, *O.R.*, 43, 274.

46. Morrow's report, *O.R.*, 43, 269, 272.

47. Doubleday's report, *O.R.*, 43, 250; *The Sixth Wisconsin Volunteers*, R. R. Dawes, p. 174.

48. Doubleday's report, *O.R.*, 43, 250; Perrin's report, *O.R.*, 44, 661–2.

49. Doubleday's report, *O.R.*, 43, 251; Wadsworth's report, *O.R.*, 43, 266. Wainwright's report, *O.R.*, 43, 357, concerns the gun lost by the First Corps.

50. Colonel Robinson's report, *O.R.*, 43, 280–81. The quotation about the men falling and taken is from *Young MSS.* Sergeant Jefferson Coates of the Seventh was awarded a Congressional Medal of Honor as a result of this action, *O.R.*, 43, 281.

51. *The Cannoneer*, Augustus Buell, pp. 65–6; *The Sixth Wisconsin Volunteers*, R. R. Dawes, p. 174.

52. *The Cannoneer*, Augustus Buell, pp. 67–70, 100.

53. *The Sixth Wisconsin Volunteers*, R. R. Dawes, pp. 175–6; *The Cannoneer*, Augustus Buell, p. 73.

54. *The Sixth Wisconsin Volunteers*, R. R. Dawes, p. 176. The soldier who stepped into the battery is mentioned in *The Cannoneer*, Augustus Buell, p. 99.

55. *The Cannoneer*, Augustus Buell, pp. 73–6.

56. *Ibid.*, pp. 73–4, 76, 100–03, 99, 78, 77, 75.

57. Colonel Robinson's report, *O.R.*, 43, 280; Dudley's 1878 report for the Iron Brigade. Contrary to the statements of some writers, Morrow at no time commanded the brigade at Gettysburg.

58. *The Sixth Wisconsin Volunteers*, R. R. Dawes, 178, contains the quotation. The state of organization is described in Doubleday's report, *O.R.*, 43, 252–3, and in *The Cannoneer*, Augustus Buell, p. 74. *Gettysburg*, R. K. Beecham, p. 95, describes the wounding and imprisonment.

59. The route appears in Colonel Robinson's report, *O.R.*, 43, 280. For prompt reforming, see Doubleday's report, *O.R.*, 43, 253. The brigade's original position on Cemetery Hill is indistinctly described in

History of the Twenty-fourth Michigan, O. B. Curtis, p. 163; Colonel Robinson's report, O.R., 43, 280; and Doubleday's report, O.R., 43, 252. The move to Culp's Hill is also noted in these descriptions.

60. Dawes' movement appears in *The Sixth Wisconsin Volunteers*, R. R. Dawes, pp. 176, 179. For good personal accounts of the entire action and withdrawal, see *Noble MSS, Fairfield MSS*, and *Hughes MSS*. See also *Indianapolis Daily Journal*, July 9, 1863, and Dudley's 1878 report for the Iron Brigade.

61. For Heth's wounding, see O.R., 44, 650. Brockenbrough's Brigade is without a report. For Pettigrew's losses, see O.R., 44, 643. The fate of the Twenty-sixth North Carolina is described in a letter to Governor Vance, O.R., 44, 645. The report for Perrin's Brigade is at O.R., 44, 663, and for Scales', O.R., 44, 670 and 44, 671. These losses are again described in the report for Pender's Division, O.R., 44, 657–8.

62. For Callis' story, see his letter in *History of the Sauk County Riflemen*, Philip Cheek and Mair Pointon, p. 79. Morrow's experiences appear in his report, O.R., 43, 272–3, and in his Detroit speech, reported at pp. 188–9 of the *History of the Twenty-fourth Michigan*, O. B. Curtis. See also letters from a soldier of the Twenty-fourth appearing at p. 184 of Curtis' book.

63. *The Sixth Wisconsin Volunteers*, R. R. Dawes, p. 171. For the predatory farmer, see *Perry MSS. The Cannoneer*, Augustus Buell, p. 76, contains the Ackerman story.

64. The Michigan prisoners are named in *History of the Twenty-fourth Michigan*, O. B. Curtis, p. 179. Thirty-nine additional prisoners were paroled on the field or march. For the prisoners of the Nineteenth, see *Indianapolis Daily Journal*, July 22, 1863, p. 3. The exploit of the Sixth's drum major is described in *The Sixth Wisconsin Volunteers*, R. R. Dawes, p. 207. *Currier MSS* contain the personal experience of a prisoner taken to the South. Facilities for the wounded, and their agonies, are described in *The Cannoneer*, Augustus Buell, pp. 120–21, and *History of the Twenty-fourth Michigan*, O. B. Curtis, pp. 185–6; the burying of the dead is also described by Curtis at p. 185.

65. *The Sixth Wisconsin Volunteers*, R. R. Dawes, pp. 181–2; Wadsworth's report, O.R., 43, 266–7; *The Cannoneer*, Augustus Buell, pp. 81–91. Buell's account is valuable as that of a witness at long range of the action to the left on the second and third days. In *War Papers, Wisconsin Commandery, Military Order of the Loyal Legion*, Vol. II, Cornelius Wheeler of the Second Wisconsin gives a good description of the first day's fight and also states that the brigade was moved to Hancock's front on July 3, just as Pickett was repulsed. This latter allegation is without support by other authorities.

66. The "stout hearts" quotation is from *Regimental Losses in the American Civil War*, William F. Fox, p. 66. Federal losses appear at O.R., 43, 173–87. In the comparative figures given in the text, the three-day totals are used.

67. Mansfield's report, O.R., 43, 275; Morrow's report, O.R., 43, 269.

68. The strength figure, previously used, is from *Regimental Losses in the American Civil War,* William F. Fox, p. 117, and is corroborated by the detailed table appearing in Dudley's 1878 report for the Iron Brigade. Also as previously noted, only two of the five regiments officially reported their strength: Second Wisconsin, 302 officers and men, O.R., 43, 274; Twenty-fourth Michigan, 496 officers and men, O.R., 43, 269. To these reports may be added Dawes' unofficial but probably reliable report for the Sixth, appearing at p. 164 of his book, 340 officers and men. Doubleday's report, O.R., 43, 253, credits the Nineteenth Indiana with 288 officers and men.

According to Dudley, the following was the strength:

Second Wisconsin	302
Sixth Wisconsin	344
Seventh Wisconsin	343
Nineteenth Indiana	288
Twenty-fourth Michigan	496
Brig. General and Staff	8
Brigade Guard	102
Total	1883

This, of course, indicates that the regimental reports did not take credit for the brigade guard. Dudley had carefully studied the official reports, which his conclusions reflect, and his conclusions are probably reliable.

Again there are several sources of losses: the official table, O.R., 43, 173, which reports for each regiment and does not separately list the losses of the brigade guard; *Regimental Losses in the American Civil War,* William F. Fox, p. 117, which does not show a regimental breakdown; and Dudley's 1878 report for the Iron Brigade, which separately lists the brigade guard. In addition to these, Morrow (O.R., 43, 269) and Mansfield (O.R., 43, 274) reported their losses, and Doubleday (O.R., 43, 253) reported for the Nineteenth Indiana. *History of the Twenty-fourth Michigan,* O. B. Curtis, p. 180, also reports in detail for the Twenty-fourth, as does a note in *B and L,* Vol. III, p. 142, and these reports differ from all others. The comparison of the *Official Records* table, Fox, and Dudley shows the following:

1. OFFICIAL RECORDS	Killed	Wounded	Captured or Missing	Total
Staff		1		1
Nineteenth	27	133	50	210
Twenty-fourth	67	210	86	363
Second	26	155	52	233
Sixth	30	116	22	168
Seventh	21	105	52	178
Total	171	720	262	1153

2. Fox	Killed	Wounded	Missing	Total
	162	724	267	1153

3. DUDLEY	Killed	Wounded	Missing	Total
Brig. General and Staff		3		3
Nineteenth	27	133	50	210
Twenty-fourth	79	237	83	399
Second	27	153	53	233
Sixth	30	117	20	167
Seventh	26	109	43	178
Brigade Guard		22		22
Total	189	774	249	1212

Dudley's record, which takes the brigade guard into account and was prepared with an effort of rationalizing all of the data, is accepted here. The percentage losses in the text are based on Dudley's figures of strength and losses.

The conclusion that the Iron Brigade led all brigades in losses is correct, regardless of which total figures are accepted. And although the First Minnesota had the highest percentage losses at Gettysburg, the Twenty-fourth Michigan had the highest total loss, both by the authority of the *Official Records* table and William F. Fox (see Fox, p. 439). For congratulatory messages to and about the Twenty-fourth, see Curtis' book, pp. 168, 186.

69. Morrow's report, O.R., 43, 270; *History of the Twenty-fourth Michigan*, O. B. Curtis, p. 181.

70. According to Dudley's 1878 report for the Iron Brigade, the effective strength of each regiment and the brigade guard, after the battle, was Second, 69; Sixth, 177; Seventh, 165; Nineteenth, 78; Twenty-fourth, 97; brigade guard, 80. For the minimum companies, see *History of the Twenty-fourth Michigan*, O. B. Curtis, p. 181. Mansfield's quote is from his report, O.R., 43, 275.

71. *The Cannoneer*, Augustus Buell, pp. 79–80. There has been a good deal of careless writing about an alleged "routing" of the First Corps. A recent account of the battle by Glenn Tucker states that the Iron Brigade was "swept away." But, as the instant text shows, there was no rout or sweeping away. Among those who knew this were Ewell and Lee, who did not attack Cemetery Hill.

72. *The Cannoneer*, Augustus Buell, pp. 80–81.

73. *History of the Twenty-fourth Michigan*, O. B. Curtis, pp. 191–2.

74. *The Sixth Wisconsin Volunteers*, R. R. Dawes, p. 180.

75. Doubleday's report, O.R., 43, 250; Meade's report, O.R., 43, 115.

Epilogue (pages 263–282)

1. The quotation is from Rufus Dawes' letter of July 9, 1863, appearing in *The Sixth Wisconsin Volunteers*, R. R. Dawes, p. 185. Lee's report describes the river crossing, O.R., 44, 323.

The details of the maneuvers, omitted from the text, are available in a variety of authorities, including Cutler's report for the First Division (covers the Mine Run campaign), O.R., 48, 689; *The Sixth Wisconsin Volunteers*, R. R. Dawes, Chaps. IX, X, and XI; *Jackson MSS; Roberts MSS;* and *History of the Sauk County Riflemen*, Philip Cheek and Mair Pointon, pp. 79–89. On Oct. 25, 1863, the Seventh Wisconsin lost forty men, and the Sixth lost one man, in skirmishing near Haymarket, Virginia, *The Sixth Wisconsin Volunteers*, R. R. Dawes, p. 214. At Mine Run, Nov. 26 to Dec. 2, the Sixth and Twenty-fourth lost one man each, O.R., 48, 678. An emotional high light of the period was a visit to Brawner Farm, where the dead of the brigade were reburied. See *The Sixth Wisconsin Volunteers*, R. R. Dawes, pp. 219–20, and *History of the Sauk County Riflemen*, Philip Cheek and Mair Pointon, p. 82.

2. The order out of which this event developed was dated July 13, 1863, from Adjutant General Williams to Colonel E. Schriver, commanding at Frederick, and provided as follows: "The commanding general directs . . . the One hundred and sixty-seventh . . . Pennsylvania Volunteers . . . to the First Corps. . . ," O.R., 45, 674–5. The Pennsylvanians joined the brigade on July 16, by which time the brigade had reached the north bank of the Potomac, *History of the Twenty-fourth Michigan*, O. B. Curtis, pp. 200, 196. The 167th appears as a part of the brigade in the table of organization for July 31, 1863, O.R., 45, 795. The strength of the new regiment appears in *The Sixth Wisconsin Volunteers*, R. R. Dawes, p. 194, as "about eight hundred men."

3. O.R., 45, 451; *The Compendium*, F. H. Dyer, p. 1620; *The Sixth Wisconsin Volunteers*, R. R. Dawes, p. 194.

4. *The Sixth Wisconsin Volunteers*, R. R. Dawes, pp. 194, 202; *History of the Twenty-fourth Michigan*, O. B. Curtis, p. 200; *The Compendium*, F. H. Dyer, p. 1620. Concerning the New Yorkers, see O.R., 45, 451. The New York battalion included only four companies, O.R., 45, 692. For history of the battalion, see *The Compendium*, F. H. Dyer, p. 1405. The New Yorkers first appear as part of the brigade in the table for Aug. 31, 1864, O.R., 49, 119.

5. In order to determine the organizational status of the Iron Brigade regiments after Gettysburg, the following tables of organization have been consulted, all of them appearing in the *Official Records:*

Date	Citation	Regiments Brigaded with Iron Brigade Regiments
July 31, 1863	45,795	167th Pennsylvania
August 31, 1863	49,119	1st Battalion New York Sharpshooters
October 10, 1863	48,217	1st Battalion New York Sharpshooters
November 20, 1863	48,667	1st Battalion New York Sharpshooters
December 31, 1863	49,599	1st Battalion New York Sharpshooters
January 31, 1864	60,463	1st Battalion New York Sharpshooters 76th New York
April 30, 1864	60,1041	1st Battalion New York Sharpshooters 7th Indiana
May 5, 1864	67,110	1st Battalion New York Sharpshooters 7th Indiana
May 31, 1864	67,203	1st Battalion New York Sharpshooters 7th Indiana
June 30, 1864	81,546	1st Battalion New York Sharpshooters 7th Indiana
July 31, 1864	82,733	1st Battalion New York Sharpshooters 7th Indiana
August 31, 1864	88,616	1st Battalion New York Sharpshooters 7th Indiana
October 31, 1864	89,461	1st Battalion New York Sharpshooters 7th Indiana 143rd Pennsylvania 149th Pennsylvania 150th Pennsylvania
December 31, 1864	89,1118	143rd Pennsylvania 149th Pennsylvania 150th Pennsylvania
January 31, 1865	96,328	143rd Pennsylvania 149th Pennsylvania 150th Pennsylvania
February 28, 1865	96,742	none
March 29, 1865	95,570	91st New York
April 30, 1865	97,1030	91st New York

For the organizational status of the Nineteenth Indiana, following its merger with the Twentieth on Oct. 18, 1863, the above-reported tables, beginning with that of Oct. 31, 1864, must be examined with reference to the Second Corps. For a consecutive statement of the brigade, division, and corps status of the Iron Brigade and the remnants thereof, see *The Compendium,* F. H. Dyer, p. 1675, for the Sixth Wisconsin.

6. For the Nineteenth Indiana, see *Ind. A.G.,* Vol. I, Document No. 1, p. 3 of "Statistics and Documents." For the Wisconsin regiments, see *The Military History of Wisconsin,* E. B. Quiner, pp. 472, 482. For the Twenty-fourth Michigan, see *History of the Twenty-fourth Michigan,* O. B. Curtis, pp. 346–51.

The epithets appear in *The Sixth Wisconsin Volunteers,* R. R. Dawes,

p. 202. The grudging acknowledgment is in *History of the Sauk County Riflemen*, Philip Cheek and Mair Pointon, p. 161. The quotations about the Indians appear in *The Sixth Wisconsin Volunteers*, R. R. Dawes, pp. 248, 265. The war whoop is mentioned by Dawes and in *History of the Twenty-fourth Michigan*, O. B. Curtis, p. 279, where the sound was identified as "Baw-baw-baw." The final quotation is from *The Sixth Wisconsin Volunteers*, R. R. Dawes, p. 202.

7. *The Sixth Wisconsin Volunteers*, R. R. Dawes, p. 199. A copy of the music, in the possession of the writer, contains the "con spirito." The author of the march was H. N. Hempsted and it was "Entered according to Act of Congress A.D. 1863 by H. N. Hempsted in the Clerk's office of the District Court of Wisconsin."

8. The quotations appear in *History of the Twenty-fourth Michigan*, O. B. Curtis, pp. 202–04, which also contains a good description of the flag. The flag now resides in the War Museum at the Capitol in Madison, Wisconsin, where it is on public view. Other descriptions of the flag and the ceremony appear in *The Sixth Wisconsin Volunteers*, R. R. Dawes, pp. 203, 205; *Jackson MSS*; *History of the Sauk County Riflemen*, Philip Cheek and Mair Pointon, p. 80, which is the source of the quote about the enlisted men's "swiping"; *Michigan MSS*.

The brigade flag was not the only new color that concerned the survivors of the Iron Brigade. Colonel Morrow received a new color for the Twenty-fourth Michigan, in April of 1864, in public ceremonies in Detroit. The original regimental color was then cut into pieces and distributed among the survivors of the regiment. *History of the Twenty-fourth Michigan*, O. B. Curtis, pp. 225–7. For the Sixth Wisconsin, a new color was provided by the state in August of 1863, at which time its predecessor was returned to Madison. *The Sixth Wisconsin Volunteers*, R. R. Dawes, p. 187. The other Wisconsin regiments were doubtless also the recipients of new colors at the same time as the Sixth. *Indiana MSS* contain a moving letter from Major William Orr, commanding the Nineteenth Indiana on Sept. 8, 1864, and addressed to Indiana's adjutant general. According to Orr's letter, a new National color was needed to replace the one received "in the winter of 1862 and carried . . . at Fitzhugh Crossing, Chancellorsville, Gettysburg, Mine Run, and in all the Battles of this campaign." On March 7, 1865, General Orders No. 10 prescribed the names of the battles and campaigns which each regiment then existing could inscribe on its colors. O.R., 96, 856ff. The Sixth and Seventh Wisconsin were allowed these battles: Cedar Mountain, Gainesville, Second Bull Run, South Mountain, Antietam, Fredericksburg, Chancellorsville, Gettysburg, Mine Run, Wilderness, Spottsylvania, North Anna, Totopotomoy, Bethesda Church, Petersburg, Weldon Railroad, and Hatcher's Run. The Second Wisconsin was allowed all of these and also First Bull Run. The Twenty-fourth Michigan was credited with the same list, but beginning at Fredericksburg. The Nineteenth Indiana, by then merged with the Twentieth, was not included in the order, although the

Second Wisconsin, by then officially part of the Sixth, was provided for.

9. Newton remained as the commander until the corps lapsed. See tables of organization set forth in Note 5 above. The order granting Wadsworth's leave appears at O.R., 45, 717. He does not reappear in the records until appointed to command the Fourth Division of the Fifth Corps on March 25, 1864, O.R., 60, 738. He first reappears on a table of organization on April 30, 1864, O.R., 60, 1041. Cutler's leadership of the division is signified by the tables of July 31, 1863, O.R., 45, 795; Oct. 10, 1863, O.R., 48, 217; and Dec. 31, 1863, O.R., 49, 599. Briggs was the commander from Aug. 5 until Aug. 23, O.R., 49, 119. Rice replaced Briggs on Aug. 23, O.R., 49, 119, and also appears on the tables of organization for Aug. 31, and Jan. 31, 1864, O.R., 60, 463. The command of the brigade was Cutler's when he was not serving as division commander. When Cutler was so employed, Colonel Robinson had the brigade.

10. *Jackson MSS; Indiana True Republican*, Aug. 6, 1863, p. 2; *Indianapolis Daily Journal*, Aug. 20, 1863, p. 2. The *Daily State Sentinel*, July 29, 1863, p. 1, contains a story about Meredith's being ordered to Fortress Monroe, but this is nowhere confirmed. Meredith's assignment to command the division was dated Nov. 12, 1863, at which time Cutler took the brigade. O.R., 107, 1121–2. The two-week tenure is an estimate, based on Meredith's appearance on the table of organization of Nov. 20, O.R., 48, 667, and his disappearance by the time of the report of the Mine Run casualties, Nov. 26–Dec. 2, O.R., 48, 678. The Cairo and Paducah commands are described in *The National Cyclopedia of Biography*, Vol. V. The 1864 political campaign is discussed in *Indiana Politics During the Civil War*, Kenneth M. Stampp, pp. 226–7. Although Meredith lost to the incumbent George W. Julian, he received the overwhelming vote of the Nineteenth Indiana, *Jackson MSS*. Meredith's formal relieving from the Army of the Potomac did not occur until March 23, 1864, O.R., 60, 717–18. After the war, Meredith operated his farm, "Oakland," near Cambridge City, Indiana, and acted as financial agent for the Indiana Central Railroad. During the years 1868–71, he was, by presidential appointment, Surveyor-General of the Montana Territory, and was in residence there. *National Cyclopedia of Biography*, Vol. V, p. 56.

11. *Ind. A.G.*, Vol. II, p. 168. Dudley's discharge was effective April 9, 1864. In Richmond, Indiana, Dudley was admitted to the bar and engaged in the active practice. He was also elected Clerk of Wayne County, served as cashier of the Richmond Savings Bank and, in 1879, was appointed United States Marshal. Under President Garfield he was Commissioner of Pensions. *History of the Republican Party of Indiana*, Russell M. Seeds, p. 356. Dudley's administration of the Pension Bureau was allegedly corrupt and his public reputation was severely damaged. *History of the Civil War Military Pensions 1861–1865*, John William Oliver.

12. *History of the Twenty-fourth Michigan*, O. B. Curtis, pp. 194, 200.

See also table of organization for Aug. 31, 1863, *O.R.*, 49, 119. Flanigan was brevetted as colonel and as brigadier under date of March 13, 1865. His discharge was dated Nov. 21, 1863. Edwin Wight's discharge was dated Nov. 17, 1863. William W. Wight was commissioned as lieutenant colonel on Feb. 1, 1864, to rank from Nov. 22, 1863. Edwards' majority was also issued on Feb. 1 and dated as of Nov. 22, 1863. *History of the Twenty-fourth Michigan*, O. B. Curtis, pp. 357–8.

13. Fairchild's resignation was dated Oct. 20, 1863, *Wis. A.G.*, 1865, p. 1313; his brigadier general's commission was dated Oct. 20, 1863, *The Military History of Wisconsin*, E. B. Quiner, p. 994. Fairchild was also later National Commander of the Grand Army. See *The Military History of Wisconsin*, E. B. Quiner, pp. 993–4. Mansfield appears as returned to duty by the table of organization of Oct. 10, 1863, *O.R.*, 48, 217.

14. *Bragg MSS* contain Bragg's letter to his wife, dated July 12, 1863, announcing his arrival at the camp of the brigade, one mile from Hagerstown. Although announcing that he was "ailing and not very well," Bragg wrote that "could you have heard the cheers of the men when I rode down the street and overtook them you would not wonder that I am determined I shall share their fortune in this battle, sick or well." In *The Sixth Wisconsin Volunteers*, R. R. Dawes, p. 189, Dawes wrote that Bragg had "gone home sick" by July 18. At p. 201, he wrote of his return to duty on Aug. 28. *Wis. A.G.*, 1865, p. 1339, dates Hauser's resignation at March 18, 1864, and Plummer's majority at April 12, 1864. Hauser's consulship is mentioned by Dawes in *The Sixth Wisconsin Volunteers*, pp. 238, 242.

15. *Wis. A.G.*, 1865, p. 1347. Following his discharge, Callis purchased a flour mill at Annaton, Wisconsin. He left this in 1864 when appointed as a major in the Veteran Reserve Corps, serving in an administrative capacity in the War Department in Washington. It was said that during Early's 1864 raid he had gone to Fort Sumner to participate in the fighting. Following the war, he entered the regular army with the rank of colonel and was assigned to the 45th U.S. Infantry, stationed in Huntsville, Alabama. In February of 1868, he resigned from the army and was elected to Congress from Alabama's Fifth District. There he authored the original legislation directed against the Ku Klux Klan, which was passed by a subsequent Congress. He was also a leader in the congressional group which sought to remove political disabilities from the South. He resigned from Congress after the session and returned to Lancaster, Wisconsin. There he operated a real-estate and insurance business and was elected to the legislature. His political career ran a course from prewar Whig to the Republicans after the war and, after 1872, to independent "reform." *Soldiers and Citizens Album of Biographical Record*, Vol. II, pp. 391–4.

16. The basic veteranizing order was General Order No. 191, issued by the War Department, June 25, 1863, *O.R.*, 124, 414–16. General Order No. 376, Nov. 21, 1863, provided for the furlough and the

three-fourths quota, *O.R.*, 124, 1084. The procedure of re-enlistment is described in detail in General Order No. 359, Nov. 6, 1863, *O.R.*, 124, 997ff. The order permitting the consolidation of reduced regiments apparently predated the re-enlistment order. It was mentioned in a letter from Rufus Dawes, dated April 13, 1863, and appearing in *The Sixth Wisconsin Volunteers*, R. R. Dawes, p. 133.

17. *History of the Sauk County Riflemen*, Philip Cheek and Mair Pointon, p. 84.

18. *The Sixth Wisconsin Volunteers*, R. R. Dawes, pp. 232–3. See also *Roberts MSS*, the letter from an enlisted man of the Seventh reporting that "Some of our boys reenlisted this morning. They are very anxious to have me go, but I don't know yet."

19. *Jackson MSS*.

20. *The Sixth Wisconsin Volunteers*, R. R. Dawes, pp. 235, 232–3, 235–6. *Wis. A.G.*, 1865, p. 742, is the authority for the number of 227 men. Dawes' figure is 233, but he apparently included new recruits in this total, see pp. 235–6 of his book. *The Military History of Wisconsin*, E. B. Quiner, p. 482, gives the number as 237. See also *History of the Sauk County Riflemen*, Philip Cheek and Mair Pointon, pp. 84–5, which agrees with the adjutant general's figure of 227.

21. *Jackson MSS*.

22. The Seventh Wisconsin figures are the adjutant general's, *Wis. A.G.*, 1865, p. 742. The Second's report, which the adjutant general's does not contain, is taken from *The Military History of Wisconsin*, E. B. Quiner, p. 472, which authority, at p. 482, reports 218 re-enlisted men in the Seventh regiment. The Indiana report is from *Ind. A.G.*, Vol. I, Document No. 1, p. 3, of "Statistics and Documents." No current strength is available for the Second or the Nineteenth. Thus the precise extent by which they missed the quota is unknown.

23. *Wis. A.G.*, 1865, p. 742, notes that the nonveterans remained in camp. On Jan. 5, 226 men from the Sixth and 201 from the Seventh were scheduled to be sent home, *O.R.*, 60, 358, but they apparently in fact left on Jan. 7 and Jan. 3, respectively, *O.R.*, 60, 460. The Nineteenth left on Jan. 11, *O.R.*, 60, 460. See also *Jackson MSS* and *Wisconsin Newspaper Volumes*, Vol. X, p. 123. It is assumed that the veterans of the Second left at about this same time. The quotation is from *The Sixth Wisconsin Volunteers*, R. R. Dawes, p. 236. An account of the train trip appears in *History of the Sauk County Riflemen*, Philip Cheek and Mair Pointon, pp. 86–7.

24. *The Sixth Wisconsin Volunteers*, R. R. Dawes, pp. 236–7.

25. *History of the Sauk County Riflemen*, Philip Cheek and Mair Pointon, p. 87.

26. *The Sixth Wisconsin Volunteers*, R. R. Dawes, pp. 237–8. The dates of the return of the Wisconsin regiments appear in *O.R.*, 60, 623. *Wisconsin Newspaper Volumes*, Vol. X, p. 123, states that the Seventh took 100 recruits with it, for total numbers of 330 officers and men.

27. *History of the Twenty-fourth Michigan*, O. B. Curtis, p. 221.

28. *The Sixth Wisconsin Volunteers*, R. R. Dawes, pp. 241–2.

29. O.R., 60, 717, 722–3. Compare tables of organization for Jan. 31, 1864, O.R., 60, 463, and April 30, 1864, O.R., 60, 1041. The Wisconsin quote is Dawes', *The Sixth Wisconsin Volunteers*, p. 239. The Michigan quote is from *History of the Twenty-fourth Michigan*, O. B. Curtis, p. 222. See also *The Cannoneer*, Augustus Buell, p. 152. For Newton's farewell, see O.R., 60, 735.

30. O.R., 60, 723. For assignments to command, dated March 25, see O.R., 60, 737–8. Tables of organization of April 30, 1864, O.R., 60, 1041; May 5, 1864, O.R., 67, 110. The reference to "Bloody B" appears in *The Cannoneer*, Augustus Buell, p. 130.

31. *The Cannoneer*, Augustus Buell, pp. 150–52.

32. The quotations appear, respectively, in *History of the Twenty-fourth Michigan*, O. B. Curtis, p. 229; *The Cannoneer*, Augustus Buell, p. 155; *History of the Twenty-fourth Michigan*, O. B. Curtis, p. 247.

33. For the action of the Westerners' Brigade, see Cutler's reports for the division, O.R., 67, 610 (covering May 3 to June 13), and O.R., 80, 473 (covering June 13 to June 18). In the latter report, the following statement appears: "The changes in the command have been so frequent, and the losing of nearly every original brigade, regimental, and company commander, render it impossible to make anything like an accurate report as to details." See also Dawes' reports for the Sixth Wisconsin, O.R., 67, 618, 621. No other regimental reports are available, nor are there reports for the brigade. See *The Sixth Wisconsin Volunteers*, R. R. Dawes, pp. 259–91; *History of the Sauk County Riflemen*, Philip Cheek and Mair Pointon, pp. 89–114; *The Cannoneer*, Augustus Buell, Chaps. VII and VIII; *History of the Twenty-fourth Michigan*, O. B. Curtis, pp. 229–262; and *Jackson MSS*.

34. *The Sixth Wisconsin Volunteers*, R. R. Dawes, p. 291, provides the quotation. The casualties, from the *Official Records*, are reported as follows:

1. O.R., 67,125—*for May 5–7*

19th Indiana	103
24th Michigan	104
2nd Wisconsin	40
6th Wisconsin	63
7th Wisconsin	217

Total   527

2. O.R., 67,143—*for May 8–21*

19th Indiana	36
24th Michigan	60
2nd Wisconsin	6
6th Wisconsin	83
7th Wisconsin	80

Total   265

3. *O.R.*, *67,158—for May 22–June 1*

19th Indiana	16
24th Michigan	24
6th Wisconsin	12
7th Wisconsin	28

Total   80

4. *O.R.*, *67,171—for June 2–15*

19th Indiana	7
24th Michigan	10
6th Wisconsin	8
7th Wisconsin	5

Total   30

Grand Total   902

35. See return of casualties, *O.R.*, 67, 124; table of organization for May 31, 1864, *O.R.*, 67, 203.

36. *Indiana MSS.*

37. *Wis. A.G.*, 1865, p. 1346. The circumstances of Plummer's death were described by Bragg in *Wisconsin Soldiers and Sailors Reunion Roster*, compiled by C. K. Pier, p. 261.

38. *History of the Twenty-fourth Michigan*, O. B. Curtis, pp. 357–8. Morrow's wound was a leg wound, and took place on May 5. Wight left the field at Bethesda Church and resigned on June 9, 1864. Mansfield was wounded on May 5 and was temporarily a prisoner. *Wis. A.G.*, 1865, p. 1320, and letter of Major Otis in *Wisconsin Newspaper Volumes*, Vol. X, p. 115. He was mustered out on Aug. 14, 1864, *Wis. A.G.*, 1865, p. 1313. His Veteran Reserve Corps commission, dated Dec. 3, 1864, is noted in *Roster of Wisconsin Volunteers*, Vol. I. Parsons' wounding is noted in *Roster of Wisconsin Volunteers*, Vol. I. He had previously been wounded at South Mountain and Gettysburg. Having been promoted to lieutenant colonel on May 25, 1864, he was mustered out on Dec. 19, 1864, *Wis. A.G.*, 1865, p. 1313. See also *Racine County Militant*, E. W. Leach, p. 267.

39. *Roster of Wisconsin Volunteers*, Vol. I. His return to duty by May 31 is apparent from the table of organization of that date, *O.R.*, 67, 203.

40. The detachment from the brigade occurred on May 11. Otis' commission as major was dated May 25 and his muster-out was as of June 29, 1864. See *Wis. A.G.*, 1865, pp. 728–9, 1313; *O.R.*, 80, 191. The Second last appeared on the table of organization of May 5, 1864, *O.R.*, 67, 110. *Echoes of the Marches of the Famous Iron Brigade, 1861–1865*, Doc Aubery, p. 45, describes the withdrawal of the regiment from the field on June 11. The men marched twenty-five miles to White House, then went by steamer to Baltimore and by train to Madison, arriving on June 18. Aubery's pamphlet also contains many interesting anecdotes

and statistics, based in part on contemporaneous diaries and accounts. Among the statistics are quartermaster reports and an estimate of miles marched by the Second; 1861–175; 1862–895; 1863–605; 1864–205.

41. *Regimental Losses in the American Civil War*, William F. Fox, p. 393.

42. For details of the brigade's action in these engagements, see the following: (1) *Globe Tavern*, Aug. 18–21 (sometimes called "Yellow House Station"), Bragg's reports for the brigade, O.R., 87, 534–6, 538–9; Crawford's report for the division, O.R., 87, 491; *History of the Sauk County Riflemen*, Philip Cheek and Mair Pointon, pp. 129–32; and *Jackson MSS*. (2) *Boydton Plank Road*, Oct. 27–8 (sometimes called "Burgess Mill" or "First Hatcher's Run"), Crawford's report for the division, O.R., 87, 495, and *History of the Sauk County Riflemen*, Philip Cheek and Mair Pointon, pp. 141–4. (3) *Weldon Railroad*, Dec. 6–12, Crawford's report for the division, O.R., 87, 497, and *History of the Sauk County Riflemen*, Philip Cheek and Mair Pointon, pp. 144–8. (4) *Hatcher's Run*, Feb. 5–10, *History of the Sauk County Riflemen*, Philip Cheek and Mair Pointon, pp. 151–5.

43. O.R., 67, 171; *The Military History of Wisconsin*, E. B. Quiner, pp. 995–6. Beginning on May 7, and until June 7, Bragg had commanded Roy Stone's Pennsylvania Brigade. See his report therefor, O.R., 67, 636ff.

44. The casualties, probably incomplete, are reported in the *Official Records*, as follows:

1. O.R., 87,125—*for August 18–21*

Independent Wisconsin Battalion	6	
19th Indiana	9	
24th Michigan	26	
6th Wisconsin	45	
7th Wisconsin	3	
Total		89

2. O.R., 87,157—*October 27–28*

Independent Wisconsin Battalion	4	
24th Michigan	1	
6th Wisconsin	1	
7th Wisconsin	1	
Total		7

3. O.R., 95,66—*February 5–7*

24th Michigan	22	
6th Wisconsin	103	
7th Wisconsin	26	
Total		151
Grand Total		247

45. *O.R.*, 87, 125. Cutler's career after he left the field appears in *History of Milwaukee, Wisconsin*, Frank A. Flower, pp. 791–2, and *The Military History of Wisconsin*, E. B. Quiner, p. 986. Cutler died at Milwaukee on July 30, 1866.

46. *History of the Twenty-fourth Michigan*, O. B. Curtis, p. 288. Morrow's Brigade was the Third Brigade of the Third Division of the Fifth Corps. His assignment to this command took place on Jan. 25, 1865, after the lapsing of Cutler's Fourth Division, as later described in the text. According to the table of organization of Jan. 31, 1865, *O.R.*, 96, 328, this was a temporary assignment for Morrow. The division commander was General Samuel Crawford, and the quotation is from his report, *O.R.*, 97, 977.

47. Robinson resigned on July 9, 1864, *Wis. A.G.*, 1865, p. 1347. Robinson returned to Wisconsin, to Sparta, where he was engaged in farming until 1873. In 1873 he moved to Chippewa Falls and was appointed to the consulship in 1875. In 1886, he returned to Chippewa Falls and went into the coal business with his son. *Soldiers and Citizens Album of Biographical Record*, pp. 553–6. Finnicum's discharge was dated Aug. 3, 1864. His final rank was that of lieutenant colonel. Dawes' colonelcy was dated July 5, 1864, and his discharge was effected on Aug. 10. *Wis. A.G.*, 1865, p. 1339.

48. *Fairfield MSS*. The Dawes quotations are from *The Sixth Wisconsin Volunteers*, R. R. Dawes, pp. 277, 275, 305. The "murder" remark was applied to a soldier whose discharge date had arrived. Other remarks by Dawes, concerning his preoccupation with death and his escape from being wounded, appear at pages 188, 217–18, and 225 of his book.

Following his discharge, Dawes was brevetted a brigadier. He returned to Marietta, Ohio, and went into business. In 1880 he was elected to Congress as a Republican and he was defeated for re-election in 1882. In 1889 he was a strong but unsuccessful contender for the Republican nomination for governor. President McKinley appointed Dawes as Minister to Persia, an appointment that was declined for reasons of health. Veterans' affairs, the temperance movement, and education also interested him, and he was a trustee of Marietta College and the Ohio Institution for the Deaf and Dumb. He died in 1899 after an illness of several years, having spent the last years of his life in a wheel chair. *A Memoir*, Rufus R. Dawes, pp. 21–31.

49. Warren had proposed the elimination of the Fourth Division as early as July 26, 1864, at which time the First Brigade was reduced to 886 officers and men. *O.R.*, 82, 469–70. Cutler bitterly opposed Warren, and on July 26 wrote a strong letter to corps headquarters which included the following statements about his division: "I cannot help remembering that it is the oldest division and about all there is left of the First Corps. I believe its history will show that its losses are greater in killed and wounded and less in prisoners than any body of men of its

size in the army. It has, I think, a larger proportion of veterans than most divisions. . . . I am the only general officer left in what was the First Corps, and I believe about the only one who entered the service with rank above captain." *O.R.*, 82, 470–71. Significantly, the division was not eliminated until after Cutler's wounding on Aug. 21. *History of the Twenty-fourth Michigan*, O. B. Curtis, p. 275, dates the merger as of Aug. 25. It was done in two steps: at first, the brigade was assigned as the Third Brigade of Crawford's Third Division (see table of organization of Aug. 31, *O.R.*, 88, 616); then it became the First Brigade of that division (see table of organization of Oct. 31, *O.R.*, 89, 461). See also *O.R.*, 87, 64.

50. *Ind.* A.G., Vol. II, p. 177. See table of organization of Oct. 31, 1864, *O.R.*, 89, 461. See also *OR.*, 87, 64; *Wis.* A.G., 1865, p. 730; and *History of the Sauk County Riflemen*, Philip Cheek and Mair Pointon, p. 143.

51. According to *Ind.* A.G., Vol. II, p. 122, the Fourteenth was merged with the Twentieth on Aug. 31. The same authority dates the merger of the Seventh with the Nineteenth as of Sept. 23, p. 177, although *O.R.*, 87, 64, gives the date as Sept. 6. The merger of the Nineteenth and the Twentieth appears in *Ind.* A.G., Vol. II, p. 177; *O.R.*, 89, 181.

52. See table of organization of Oct. 31, 1864, *O.R.*, 89, 459. Orr's colonelcy appears in *Ind.* A.G., Vol. II, p. 186, dated Nov. 1, 1864. The same authority, at page 168, dates Lindley's muster out as of Oct. 24, 1864. After the war, Orr, who was honorably discharged on May 15, 1865, settled in Muncie and practiced law there. *A Portrait and Biographical Record of Delaware County, Indiana*, pp. 602–3.

53. *Jackson MSS; History of the Sauk County Riflemen*, Philip Cheek and Mair Pointon, p. 139.

54. Grant's order is at *O.R.*, 96, 513. Meade's appears at *O.R.*, 96, 519–20. At the time, the brigade had 78 officers and 1,261 men, *O.R.*, 96, 519.

55. For the absence of the Sharpshooters, see tables of organization of Dec. 31, Jan. 31, Feb. 28, March 29, and April 30, Note 5, above. Crawford's correspondence appears at *O.R.*, 96, 532, 533.

56. *O.R.*, 96, 533. Bragg's career in Baltimore is mentioned in *The Military History of Wisconsin*, E. B. Quiner, p. 996. After the war, Edward S. Bragg was probably the best known national figure from the Iron Brigade. He returned to Fond du Lac and resumed the practice of law and his political career. The latter included his being a delegate to the Union National Convention in 1866; election to the Wisconsin Senate in 1867, as a Democrat; election as a delegate to the Democratic National Convention which nominated Greeley in 1872; four terms in Congress as a Democrat (1877–1883, and 1885–87); and election as a delegate in 1884 and 1896 to the Democratic National Convention. At the national conventions of 1884 and 1896, he was the chairman of the

Wisconsin delegation, and in 1884, in seconding Cleveland's nomination, he coined the famous epigram "We love him for the enemies he has made," which was a response by Bragg to the jeering of the Tammany representatives at that convention. In 1896 Bragg was a "Gold Democrat," and he refused to support Bryan. This led to his supporting McKinley in 1900. He was appointed Minister to Mexico in 1889 but did not fulfill this appointment. In 1902 Roosevelt appointed him consul general at Hong Kong. He was in residence there for four years. Returning to the country in 1906, he supported Taft in 1908. He died at Fond du Lac on June 20, 1912. *Dictionary of American Biography*, Vol. II, pp. 587–8.

The Twenty-fourth Michigan remained at Camp Butler in Springfield until the end of the war. There it added several hundred drafted recruits. Until Morrow's arrival at Springfield (see text), commander of the regiment was Albert M. Edwards and second-in-command was William Hutchinson, who had been promoted to the lieutenant colonelcy and the majority, respectively, on July 17, 1864. Hutchinson had been wounded on July 19, at Petersburg. The regiment returned to Detroit after Appomattox and was discharged on June 30, 1865. *History of the Twenty-fourth Michigan*, O. B. Curtis, pp. 296–8; 351–6, 358, 317; *Mich. A.G.*, 1866, p. 151; *O.R. 104, 548.*

57. The brigade was identified as "provisional," O.R., 95, 96. See table of organization, Feb. 28, 1865, O.R., 96, 742.

58. *The Sixth Wisconsin Volunteers*, R. R. Dawes, pp. 310–11. *Wis. A.G.*, 1865, p. 1339, dates Kellogg's majority as of Sept. 1, 1864, his lieutenant colonelcy as of Oct. 19, 1864, and his colonelcy as of Dec. 10, 1864. In *The Sixth Wisconsin Volunteers*, R. R. Dawes, p. 305, it is stated that the Sixth had only eighty men as of Sept. 1, 1864.

Kerr was commissioned major on Oct. 19, 1864, and advanced to lieutenant colonel on Dec. 10, 1864. Dailey's commission in the Sixth was dated Dec. 21, 1864. *Wis. A.G.*, 1865, p. 1339. See also *The Sixth Wisconsin Volunteers*, R. R. Dawes, p. 311. The command arrangements in the Seventh are obscure because of the status of Martin C. Hobart, who, according to the Wisconsin adjutant general, was commissioned major on Sept. 2 and lieutenant colonel on Dec. 29. If these commissions were issued, the Seventh would have had *two* lieutenant colonels at the same time, since Richardson was awarded this commission on Aug. 3, 1864, and held it until mustered out in July of 1865. In addition, Hobart's majority would have conflicted with Hoyt's, the latter having been commissioned major on Dec. 29. *Wis. A.G.*, 1865, p. 1347. This confusion is apparently explained by the fact that Hobart, a native of New York and resident of Fall River, Wisconsin, was wounded and captured in the Wilderness and apparently remained a prisoner until the war's end. Thus, Hobart was awarded the two commissions, but was never mustered as either major or lieutenant colonel. *Wis. A.G.*, 1865, pp. 1349, 1353; *Roster of Wisconsin Volunteers*, Vol. I; *Wisconsin*

Necrology, Vol. XVII, p. 193. This made the way for Richardson and Hoyt, the latter a resident of Allen's Grove, Wisconsin, who were commissioned and mustered.

Biographical data about Kerr are available in *History of Milwaukee, From Its First Settlement to the Year 1895*, Vol. I, p. 114; *Milwaukee City Directory*, for the years 1858, 1859–60, 1860–61, 1865, 1867–8, 1868–9, 1869–70, 1872–3, and 1879. In addition to his carpenter's trade, Kerr had also been a fireman, assistant city engineer, and a candidate for constable, all before the war. After the war, he returned to his trade in Milwaukee, became a contractor and builder and continued his activities in local politics. In the last-named respect, the *Milwaukee Daily Sentinel*, Oct. 30, 1866, p. 1, lists him as a nominee for county treasurer.

Dennis B. Dailey is a source of mystery. He entered the army as a member of Company B of the Second Wisconsin, the La Crosse Light Guards. But he is listed in *Roster of Wisconsin Volunteers*, Vol. I, as a native of Lebanon, Ohio. Diligent search there and in Wisconsin has failed to disclose any further facts.

59. The 91st was added to the brigade on March 3, and the "provisional" title of the brigade was officially dropped on March 15, 1865, O.R., 95, 96. See also table of organization of March 29, 1865, O.R., 95, 570. The strength of the brigade is noted in *The Sixth Wisconsin Volunteers*, R. R. Dawes, p. 311. Dawes gives the number as "about three thousand five hundred men." *History of the Sauk County Riflemen*, Philip Cheek and Mair Pointon, p. 157, states that the 91st numbered 1,800 men and that the strength of the brigade was "about 3,000." The 91st New York had a varied history, on virtually all fronts of the war. Organized at Albany in 1861, it had served at Pensacola, New Orleans, Port Hudson, and around Vicksburg, *The Compendium*, F. H. Dyer, pp. 1440–41.

60. Casualties for the period March 29 to April 9 appear at O.R., 95, 585. The Sixth accounted for 119 and the Seventh 81. The wounding of Kerr, Richardson, and Dailey—and Dailey's command of the 147th New York in Coulter's Third Brigade of Crawford's Division—are noted on the table of organization for March 29, O.R., 95, 570. Kerr and Dailey were hit on March 31 and Richardson on April 1. For Dailey's assignment to the 147th New York, see also O.R., 97, 977. The action of the brigade is described in Kellogg's reports, O.R., 95, 882, 883, and 885; Crawford's report of the action on April 1, O.R., 95, 879; and *History of the Sauk County Riflemen*, Philip Cheek and Mair Pointon, 159–70. See also Kellogg's account in *Wisconsin Soldiers and Sailors Reunion Roster*, compiled by C. K. Pier, p. 263.

61. For the route of the brigade and the quotation from Kellogg, see his reports, O.R., 95, 883. The remaining data, and the description of the soldiers' receipt of the news, appear in *History of the Sauk County Riflemen*, Philip Cheek and Mair Pointon, p. 170.

After the surrender, the brigade moved to Black and White Station on the Southside Railroad, approximately sixty miles from Petersburg, *History of the Twenty-fourth Michigan*, O. B. Curtis, p. 307 (letter from Henry A. Morrow, dated May 19, 1865). The march to Washington, through Petersburg, Richmond, and Fredericksburg, is also described in Morrow's letter. See also *History of the Sauk County Riflemen*, Philip Cheek and Mair Pointon, pp. 177–8. The brigade arrived at Washington and went into camp near its 1861–2 camp, on May 12.

Kellogg returned to Mauston after the war, but in 1866 he was appointed U.S. Pension Agent, at La Crosse, and he moved to that city. He resided in La Crosse until 1875, when he resigned as Pension Agent and moved to Wausau. There he resumed the practice of law and in 1879–80 he was elected to represent his district in the Wisconsin Senate. He died at Wausau in 1883, at the age of 55. *Capture and Escape*, John A. Kellogg, Wisconsin History Commission, pp. xiv–xv.

62. Preparations for the review, including the obtaining of white gloves, are described in *History of the Sauk County Riflemen*, Philip Cheek and Mair Pointon, p. 179. The quotation is from the same source, pp. 179–80. The order governing the parade of the Fifth Corps appears at O.R., 97, 1186–7.

63. That the battery paraded, led by Stewart, is evidenced by O.R., 97, 1187. Stewart had left the battery in October of 1864, an enforced disability leave, and had been temporarily attached to Battery A of the Fourth U.S., which had just been filled up with recruits and was training at Camp Barry. In Stewart's absence, Orderly Sergeant John Mitchell, advanced to lieutenant, had commanded the battery. *The Cannoneer*, Augustus Buell, pp. 315–16. According to Buell, as of Nov. 4, one detached volunteer from the brigade, Fred Detloff, remained, but he apparently left the battery during the same month. The battery had been filled up with "new regulars," and volunteer artillerymen from the Sixth and Fifteenth New York Heavy Artillery and other volunteer batteries. *The Cannoneer*, Augustus Buell, pp. 314–16. Battery B's casualty record is the conclusion of William F. Fox, quoted in *History of the Twenty-fourth Michigan*, O. B. Curtis, p. 471. See also *Regimental Losses in the American Civil War*, William F. Fox.

64. *History of the Twenty-fourth Michigan*, O. B. Curtis, p. 307; O.R., 97, 1186. There is no record of Kellogg's whereabouts after Morrow's return. After the war, Morrow was mustered out and appointed Collector of the Port of Detroit. As the result of a factional political dispute over Morrow's appointment, he resigned and in February, 1867, re-entered the army as a regular, commissioned lieutenant colonel of the Thirty-sixth Regiment, United States Infantry. He was stationed in Louisiana during Reconstruction, and in Utah during the Mormon disturbances of 1872–3. In 1877, during the Pennsylvania railroad riots, his conduct merited special commendation from General Hancock. In all of these affairs he showed, as he had shown during the war, the characteristics of charity, discretion, and understanding. He died in 1891 and was buried in

Niles, Michigan, his wife's native city. *History of the Twenty-fourth Michigan*, O. B. Curtis, pp. 477–8.

65. *O.R.*, 97, 1187. After his muster-out, Richardson settled in Baltimore and resumed the practice of law. He was a delegate to the Republican Convention which nominated Grant the first time. In 1870 Richardson returned to Chippewa Falls, continuing his professional career. In 1900 he moved to Seattle, Washington, and acquired a ranch there, near Keyport. During the Spanish War he was a civilian employee of the Quartermaster Department and traveled several times to the Philippine Islands. *Wisconsin Necrology*, Vol. XVI, pp. 13–14; *Soldiers and Citizens Album of Biographical Record*, Vol. II, pp. 578–82.

66. *Regimental Losses in the American Civil War*, William F. Fox, pp. 116–17. The First Vermont Brigade (2nd, 3rd, 4th, 5th, 6th, and 11th) had the highest absolute loss, 1,172 as compared to 1,131 for the Iron Brigade. Fox's analysis shows that *three* of the Iron Brigade regiments were among the highest *fifteen* regiments in total (not percentage) losses, killed in action and died of wounds. These regiments, their numerical position on Fox's list of fifteen, and their losses were:

Regiment	Position on List	Numbers
Seventh Wisconsin	third	281
Sixth Wisconsin	tenth	244
Second Wisconsin	thirteenth	238

Although not appearing on Fox's table, he shows the Nineteenth Indiana with a total of 199 and the Twenty-fourth Michigan with 189, killed and died of wounds. This would put these two regiments in the top fifty regiments in total numbers killed and wounded.

From a percentage standpoint, Fox's honor roll of maximum losses, killed and died of wounds, after correction as described below, shows the following:

Regiment	Position on List	Percentage
Second Wisconsin	first	19.7
Seventh Wisconsin	sixth	17.2
Nineteenth Indiana	eleventh	15.9
Twenty-fourth Michigan	twentieth	15.2

Fox omitted the Nineteenth Indiana from his table (p. 8), but he later acknowledges that the Nineteenth had percentage losses of 15.9 (p. 343), which would place that regiment eleventh on his list and would move the Twenty-fourth Michigan to the rank of twentieth, instead of nineteenth, as shown on the table. The Sixth Wisconsin, listing 12.5 per cent, would rank approximately thirtieth on the percentage list. *

All of the foregoing data, together with statistics on total enrollment and deaths by disease, accident, and in prison, appear in Fox's monumental book, at pp. 3, 8, 343, 390, 393, 396, and 397. These show the following:

Correction: Fox correctly lists the Nineteenth Indiana as eleventh and correctly omits the Twenty- fourth Michigan from the highest regiments' category. He states its losses at ll.4%.

	Total Enrollment	Died of Disease, Accident, in Prison, etc.
Nineteenth Indiana	1246	117
Twenty-fourth Michigan	1654	139
Second Wisconsin	1203	77
Sixth Wisconsin	1940	113
Seventh Wisconsin	1630	143

Additional statistics, those from the War Department records, appear in *History of the Twenty-fourth Michigan*, O. B. Curtis, p. 464.

These are as follows:

	Total Strength	Battle Deaths	Disease Deaths	Total Deaths	Percent of Deaths
Nineteenth Indiana	1200	238	80	318	26.5
Twenty-fourth Michigan	1240	176	142	318	25.6
Second Wisconsin	1200	238	80	318	26.5
Sixth Wisconsin	1940	244	116	360	18.6
Seventh Wisconsin	1630	281	146	427	26.2

See Note 25, Chap. Eight.

67. The official story of the muster-out of the Iron Brigade regiments shows that the Twentieth Indiana and Sixth and Seventh Wisconsin, on June 5, 1865, under Morrow, were ordered to Louisville, Kentucky, to report to General John A. Logan, then commanding the Army of the Tennessee. O.R., 97, 1255–6. In Louisville, under date of June 20, the three regiments, and others from Michigan and Ohio, became parts of two brigades of a newly organized Provisional Division of the Army of the Tennessee. Morrow was assigned as commander of the division, and Kellogg reappeared, as the Second Brigade commander. The Seventh Wisconsin remained under Richardson's leadership, and the command of the Sixth was listed as vacant. O.R., 104, 1037, 1066.

The Twentieth Indiana was mustered out at Louisville on July 12, 1865, at which time there were 390 men and 23 officers present for duty. Returning to Indianapolis on the same day, it received the usual official welcome and was then discharged. *Ind.* A.G., Vol. II, p. 193. The Seventh Wisconsin was mustered out at Louisville on July 3 and arrived in Madison on July 5. The Sixth was mustered out on July 14 and reached Madison on the 16th. These regiments, too, were publicly welcomed before they were dismissed. The last such ceremony, on the Capitol grounds, was that conducted for the Sixth. At the conclusion of the ceremonies, "the words of command were given; the bronzed veterans wheeled to the right; drums and fifes struck up their stormy music, and with guns at 'right shoulder shift,' and bayonets gleaming in the slant sunbeams, under the green arches of the summer trees, the last organized fragments of the old Iron Brigade of the army of the Potomac, bearing the rent and shot torn banners, on which are inscribed the names of such historic battles as South Mountain, Antietam, Chancellorsville, Gettysburg, The Wilderness, Cold Harbor, Petersburg, Weldon Railroad, Hatcher's Run and Five Forks, passed on; to dissolve and disappear from men's eyes forever, but to live immortal in history and in the memory of a grateful people." *Wis. A.G.*, 1865, pp. 752–3.

The Twenty-fourth Michigan, at Springfield, had a final role to play in connection with the end of the era. That regiment served as the escort for Lincoln's funeral in Springfield. The regiment was then sent to Detroit, arriving there on June 20, and mustering out on June 30. *History of the Twenty-fourth Michigan*, O. B. Curtis, pp. 305, 296 ff.; *Mich. A.G.*, 1865–66, pp. 151, 171.

A final and appealing note about the Iron Brigade concerns its postwar veterans' organization. *Perry MSS* contain an undated newspaper clipping setting forth the Rules and Regulations of The Iron Brigade Association. Among these are the following:

"2nd— That all soldiers and officers who have been honorably discharged, are entitled to full membership, by reporting their names and sending 25¢ to the secretary.

"5th— The organization is intended to be civil in nature, and the humblest private is just as eligible to the highest office, as the many gallant officers who commanded corps, divisions, brigades and companies."

According to a report in the *Fond du Lac Reporter*, September 11, 1916, the association was organized in 1880.

SELECTED BIBLIOGRAPHY

In the case of works for which an author's name is not the key, the work is given alphabetically with its full title.

1. OFFICIAL PUBLICATIONS AND REPORTS

Alphabetical General Index to Michigan Soldiers and Sailors Individual Records. Lansing, 1915.

Annual Report of the Adjutant General of the State of Michigan. Lansing, 1861, 1862, 1863, 1864, 1865–6.

Annual Report of the Adjutant General, State of Wisconsin. Madison, 1861, 1862–3, 1864, and 1865.

Dudley, William W., *The Iron Brigade at Gettysburg,* 1878. Official Report of the Part Borne by the 1st Brigade, 1st Division, 1st Army Corps. Cincinnati, 1879.

Eastabrook, Charles E., *Wisconsin Losses in the Civil War.* Madison, Commission on Civil War Records, 1915.

———, ed., *Wisconsin Records and Sketches of Military Organizations.* Madison, Commisson on Civil War Records, 1914.

Hastrieter, Robert, *Troops Furnished by Wisconsin During the Civil War, 1861–65.* Madison, 1898.

The Official Atlas of the Civil War. New York, Thomas Yoseloff, 1958.

Record of Service of Michigan Volunteers in the Civil War, 1861–1865 (Vol. 24). Kalamazoo.

Report of the Adjutant General of the State of Indiana (8 vols.), W. H. H. Terrell. Indianapolis, 1869.

Roster of Wisconsin Volunteers, War of the Rebellion, 1861–1865 (2 vols.). Madison, 1886.

War of the Rebellion, Official Records of the Union and Confederate Armies. Washington, Government Printing Office, 1882–1900.

References are by serial number and page, following the abbreviation

385

O.R.: e.g., O.R., 17, 250. A key transferring serial numbers into series, volumes, and parts is given in the index of the complete work.

2. MANUSCRIPTS

Bachman MSS.   Prewar and war letters of Alois O. Bachman of the Nineteenth Indiana. Privately owned.

Bragg MSS.   War letters of Edward S. Bragg to his wife. Also includes war letters to Bragg from Gibbon and other officers. State Historical Society of Wisconsin.

Chapman MSS.   War papers and letters of Chandler B. Chapman, Surgeon of the Sixth Wisconsin. State Historical Society of Wisconsin.

Converse MSS.   War letters of Rollin P. Converse, an officer of the Sixth Wisconsin. Privately owned.

Cook MSS.   War papers of John H. Cook, an enlisted man of the Sixth Wisconsin. State Historical Society of Wisconsin.

Currier MSS.   War diary of Horace Currier, an enlisted man of the Seventh Wisconsin. State Historical Society of Wisconsin.

Fairfield MSS.   War diary of George Fairfield, an enlisted man of the Sixth Wisconsin. Also war letters to him from comrades. State Historical Society of Wisconsin.

Gallup MSS.   War records and clothing and equipment returns of Andrew Gallup, an officer of the Sixth Wisconsin. State Historical Society of Wisconsin.

Gordon MSS.   War letters of John M. Gordon, an officer of the Twenty-fourth Michigan. Privately owned.

Haskell MSS.   War letters of Frank A. Haskell, an officer of the Sixth Wisconsin. State Historical Society of Wisconsin.

Hughes MSS.   War diary of Robert H. Hughes, an officer of the Second Wisconsin. Also includes postwar letters of reminiscence. State Historical Society of Wisconsin.

Indiana MSS.   War correspondence from the field to the executive offices of the State of Indiana concerning the Nineteenth Indiana. Includes letters of Gibbon, McClellan, Meredith, Cameron, Bachman, Lindley, Williams, and Orr. Archives, Indiana State Library.

Indiana State Library MSS.   An account by Color Sergeant Cunningham of the Nineteenth Indiana of the initial action at Gettysburg. Indiana Room, Indiana State Library.

Jackson MSS.   War diary of W. N. Jackson, an enlisted man of the Nineteenth Indiana. Privately owned.

Klein MSS.   War letter of Augustus Klein, an enlisted man of the Sixth Wisconsin. Privately owned.

Larke MSS.   War letters of Alured Larke, an officer of the Second Wisconsin. State Historical Society of Wisconsin.

Larsen MSS.   War letters of Peter Larsen, an enlisted man of the Seventh Wisconsin. State Historical Society of Wisconsin.

Mead MSS.   Journal of Sydney B. Mead, an enlisted man of the Second Wisconsin. State Historical Society of Wisconsin.

Michigan MSS. A collection of field returns, muster rolls, soldiers' war letters, and executive correspondence concerning the Twenty-fourth Michigan. Michigan Historical Commission.

Neff MSS. War letters of George F. Neff (sometimes spelled "Neef"), an enlisted man of the Twenty-fourth Michigan. Privately owned.

Noble MSS. War diary of William Noble, an officer of the Second Wisconsin. State Historical Society of Wisconsin.

Perry MSS. War diaries of James M. Perry, an enlisted man of the Seventh Wisconsin. State Historical Society of Wisconsin.

Roberts MSS. War letters of William Roberts, an enlisted man of the Seventh Wisconsin. State Historical Society of Wisconsin.

Rollins MSS. War diary of Nathaniel Rollins, an officer of the Second Wisconsin. State Historical Society of Wisconsin.

Young MSS. War letters of Henry F. Young, an officer of the Seventh Wisconsin. A part of *Warner MSS.*, State Historical Society of Wisconsin.

3. Unit Histories and Personal Accounts

Aubery, Doc (Cullen B.), *Echoes of the Marches of the Famous Iron Brigade, 1861–1865.* Milwaukee, 1900.

Beecham, R. K., *Gettysburg.* Chicago, A. C. McClurg & Co., 1911.

Birdsong, James C. *Brief Sketches of North Carolina Troops in the War Between the States.* Raleigh, 1894.

Blackford, W. W., *War Years with Jeb Stuart.* New York, Charles Scribner's Sons, 1945.

Brown, Varina D., *A Colonel at Gettysburg and Spottsylvania.* Columbia, S.C., The State Company, 1931.

Buell, Augustus, *The Cannoneer.* Washington, The National Tribune, 1897.

Caldwell, J. F. J., *History of a Brigade of South Carolinians Known First as Gregg's and Subsequently as McGowan's Brigade.* Philadelphia, 1866.

Casler, John O., *Four Years in the Stonewall Brigade.* Marietta, Ga., 1951.

Chamberlin, Thomas, *History of the 150th Regiment, Pennsylvania Volunteers.* Philadelphia, J. B. Lippincott & Co., 1895.

Cheek, Philip, and Mair Pointon, *History of the Sauk County Riflemen.* 1909.

Clark, Walter, ed., *Histories of the Several Regiments and Battalions from North Carolina* (5 Vols.). Raleigh, 1901.

Cooke, John Esten, *Stonewall Jackson and the Old Stonewall Brigade.* Charlottesville, University of Virginia Press, 1954.

Curtis, O. B., *History of the Twenty-fourth Michigan.* Detroit, Winn & Hammond, 1891.

Dawes, R. R., *The Sixth Wisconsin Volunteers.* Marietta, E. R. Alderman & Sons, 1890.

Fitch, Michael H., *Echoes of the Civil War As I Hear Them.*   New York, R. F. Fenno & Co., 1905.

Gates, Theodore B., *The Ulster Guard* (20th N.Y.S.M.).   New York, 1879.

Gibbon, John, *Personal Recollections of the Civil War.* New York, G. P. Putnam's Sons, 1928.

History of the Fighting Fourteenth (14th Brooklyn). New York, 1911.

Hussey, George A., and William Todd, *History of the Ninth Regiment* (83rd N.Y.S.V.).   New York, 1889.

Locke, William Henry, *The Story of the Regiment* (11th Pa. V.).   Philadelphia, J. B. Lippincott & Co., 1868.

Noyes, George F., *The Bivouac and the Battlefield.*   New York, Harper & Brothers, 1863.

Oates, William C., *The War Between the Union and the Confederacy.* New York, The Neale Publishing Company, 1905.

Osbourn, Francis A., *The Twentieth Indiana Infantry.*

Poague, William Thomas, *Gunner with Stonewall,* ed. Monroe F. Cockrell. Jackson, Tennessee, McCowat-Mercer Press, Inc., 1957.

Smith, A. P., *History of the Seventy-sixth New York Volunteers.* New York, Cortland, 1867.

Stevens, C. A., *Berdan's United States Sharpshooters.* St. Paul, 1892.

Thomson, O., *Narrative of the Service of the Seventh Indiana Infantry.*

4. NEWSPAPERS

Beloit Free Press
Chicago Tribune
Daily State Sentinel, Indianapolis
Delaware County Free Press, Muncie, Indiana
Detroit Advertiser and Tribune
Detroit Free Press
Goshen Democrat, Goshen, Indiana
Home Intelligencer, Mineral Point, Wisconsin
Indiana True Republican, Centerville, Indiana
Indianapolis Daily Gazette
Indianapolis Daily Journal
Janesville Daily Gazette, Janesville, Wisconsin
La Crosse Tribune and Leader
Mauston Star, Mauston, Wisconsin
Milwaukee Daily News
Milwaukee Sentinel
Muncie Times, Muncie, Indiana
National Tribune, Washington, D.C.
New York Herald
New York Tribune
Oshkosh Northwestern
Plymouth Republican, Plymouth, Indiana

Portage Republican, Portage, Wisconsin
Richmond Palladium, Richmond, Indiana
Valparaiso Republic, Valparaiso, Indiana
Wisconsin Daily Patriot, Madison, Wisconsin
Wisconsin Newspaper Volumes (10 vols.), Contemporaneous newspaper clippings, organized by regiment, and containing letters of Wisconsin soldiers, from *Milwaukee Daily News; Milwaukee Sentinel; Wisconsin State Journal*, Madison; *Beloit Free Press; Janesville Daily Gazette; Mauston Star; Home Intelligencer*, Mineral Point; and others. Available at the State Historical Society of Wisconsin.
Wisconsin State Journal, Madison, Wisconsin
Wood County Reporter, Grand Rapids, Wisconsin

5. ARTICLES, PAMPHLETS, AND PERIODICALS

Adkins, W. H., *The Iron Brigade*. Washington, The National Tribune, 1904.
Beecham, R. K., *Adventures of an Iron Brigade Man*. Washington, The National Tribune, 1902.
Burgwyn, William S., *Unparalleled Loss of Company E, 26th North Carolina, Pettigrew's Brigade, at Gettysburg*. Southern Historical Society Papers, XXVIII.
Bushnell, A. R., *The Iron Brigade*. Madison, Madison Democrat, 1906.
Forbes, S. D., *Camp Randall and Environs*. Madison, 1862.
Haight, Theron, *Gainesville, Groveton, and Bull Run*, War Papers, Wisconsin Commandery, Military Order of the Loyal Legion, Vol. II. Milwaukee, 1896.
———, *King's Division: Fredericksburg to Manassas*, War Papers, Wisconsin Commandery, Military Order of the Loyal Legion, Vol. II. Milwaukee, 1896.
Heth, Harry, *Gettysburg*. Southern Historical Society Papers, IV.
Kilmer, G. L., a series of undated pamphlets: *In the Iron Brigade—The Heroic Deeds of the 24th Michigan; Sol Meredith's Men—Battles of the 19th Indiana; Wisconsin's Pride—Story of Her Heroic Second Regiment in Battle; Written in Blood—The Battle Record of the Second Wisconsin Infantry; The Badger Tigers—War Stories of the Seventh Wisconsin Volunteers*.
King, Charles, *Gainesville*, War Papers, Wisconsin Commandery, Military Order of the Loyal Legion, Vol. III. Milwaukee, 1903.
Military Collector and Historian, Vol. V, No. 1, March, 1953; Vol. VIII, No. 1, Spring, 1956.
Pier, C. K., comp., *Wisconsin Soldiers and Sailors Reunion Roster*. Fond du Lac, Wisconsin Soldiers and Sailors Reunion Association, 1880.
Program of the Iron Brigade Association's Meeting. Des Moines, 1926.
Reader, W. A., *The Iron Brigade*. Fond du Lac, Fond du Lac Bulletin, 1906.
Reunion Proceedings, Nineteenth Indiana Volunteers, for 1871–4, 1889.

Strother, D. H., *Personal Recollections of the War*, Harper's Monthly, XXXV, 717 (Nov., 1867).

Watrous, J. A., *Time's Legacy to the Officers and Privates of the Iron Brigade*. Milwaukee, *Milwaukee Sentinel*, 1905.

Wheeler, Cornelius, *Reminiscences of the Battle of Gettysburg*, War Papers, Wisconsin Commandery, Military Order of the Loyal Legion, Vol. II. Milwaukee, 1896.

Winslow, Hattie Lou, and Joseph R. H. Moore, *Camp Morton, 1861–1865*. Indianapolis, Indiana Historical Society, 1940.

6. LOCAL HISTORIES AND BIOGRAPHICAL MATERIALS

Alphabetical List of the Soldiers and Sailors of the Late War Residing in the State of Wisconsin, June 20, 1885. Madison, The Secretary of State, 1886.

Anderson, James S., *Pioneer Courts and Lawyers of Manitowoc County, Wisconsin*. Manitowoc, Manitowoc Pilot, 1922.

Berryman, John, *History of the Bench and Bar of Wisconsin* (2 vols.). Chicago, H. C. Cooper, Jr. & Co., 1898.

Biographical Dictionary of Representative Men of Chicago, Wisconsin and the Columbian Exposition. Chicago, American Biographical Publishing Co., 1895.

Burton, Clarence M., ed., *History of the City of Detroit, 1701–1922* (4 vols.). Detroit. L. J. Clarke Publishing Co., 1922.

Conrad, Howard L., *History of Milwaukee, From Its First Settlement to the Year 1895* (3 vols.). Chicago, American Biographical Publishing Company, 1895.

Dictionary of American Biography. New York. Charles Scribner's Sons, 1928.

Esarey, Logan, *History of Indiana* (3 vols.). Dayton, Dayton Historical Publishing Company, 1922.

Farmer, Silas, *History of Detroit and Michigan* (2 vols.). Detroit, Silas Farmer & Co., 1884.

Flower, Frank A., *History of Milwaukee, Wisconsin*. Chicago, Western Historical Company, 1881.

Foulke, William Dudley, *Life of Oliver P. Morton* (2 vols.). Indianapolis, Bowen-Merrill Company, 1899.

Haskell, Frank A., *The Battle of Gettysburg*. Madison, Wisconsin History Commission, 1908.

Indianapolis City Directory, 1860. Indianapolis, Sutherland and McEvoy, 1860.

———, 1861. Indianapolis, Bowen, Stewart & Co., 1861.

Lawson, Publius V., *History of Winnebago County, Wisconsin* (2 vols.). Chicago, 1908.

Leach, E. W., *Racine County Militant*. Racine, 1915.

A Memoir, Rufus R. Dawes. New York, 1900.

Michigan Biographies (2 vols.). Lansing, Michigan Historical Commission, 1924.
Michigan State Gazetteer & Business Directory, 1860. Detroit, George W. Hawes, 1859.
———, 1863–4. Detroit, Charles F. Clarke, 1863.
Military Order of the Loyal Legion of the United States, Commandery of Wisconsin, Circular No. 2, Series 1902, Whole No. 349. Milwaukee, January 15, 1902.
Milwaukee City Directory, 1857–58. Milwaukee, Erning, Burdick & Co., 1858.
———, 1858. Milwaukee, Smith Du Moulin & Co., 1858.
———, 1859–60. Milwaukee, Franklin E. Town, 1860.
———, 1860–61. Milwaukee, Starr & Sons, 1861.
———, 1866. Milwaukee, Richard Edwards, 1866.
———, 1874–75. Milwaukee, John Wickens, 1875.
The National Cyclopedia of Biography. New York, James T. White & Company, 1898.
Oliver, John William, *History of the Civil War Military Pensions.* A thesis submitted for a doctorate at the University of Wisconsin, 1915.
A Portrait and Biographical Record of Delaware County, Indiana. Chicago, A. W. Bower & Co., 1894.
Reed, Parker M., *The Bench and Bar of Wisconsin.* Milwaukee, P. M. Reed, 1882.
Register of Graduates and Former Cadets, United States Military Academy, 1952 ed. West Point, 1952.
Report of the Annual Meeting of the Wisconsin State Bar Association, Milwaukee, February 17-18, 1903. Madison, Taylor, Gleason Book & Job Printers, 1903.
Robertson, John, Adjutant General, *The Flags of Michigan.* Lansing, 1877.
Seeds, Russell M., *History of the Republican Party of Indiana.* Indianapolis, The Indiana History Company, 1899.
Soldiers and Citizens Album of Biographical Record (2 vols.). Chicago, Grand Army Publishing Company, 1888.
Sutherland, James, *Biographical Sketches of Members of the 41st General Assembly, State of Indiana.* Indianapolis, 1861.
Tucker, E., *History of Randolph County, Indiana.* Chicago, A. L. Kingman, 1882.
Wallace, Lew, *An Autobiography* (2 vols.). New York, Harper & Brothers, 1906.
Watrous, Jerome A., ed., *Memoirs of Milwaukee County* (2 vols.). Madison, 1909.
Wisconsin Necrology. Fifty-one volumes, composed of newspaper and similar obituaries, 1846-1944, collected at the State Historical Society of Wisconsin.

7. ORDNANCE, REGULATIONS, AND TACTICS

Butterfield, Daniel, *Camp and Outpost Duty for Infantry*. New York, Harper & Brothers, 1863.

Casey, Silas, *Infantry Tactics* (3 vols.). New York, D. Van Nostrand, 1862.

Coppée, Henry, *The Field Manual for Battalion Drill*. Philadelphia, J. B. Lippincott & Co., 1863.

Fuller, Claude E., *Springfield Muzzle-Loading Shoulder Arms*. New York City, Francis Bannerman Sons, 1930.

Gibbon, John, *The Artillerist's Manual*. New York, D. Van Nostrand, 1860.

Hicks, James E., *Notes on United States Ordnance* (2 vols). Mount Vernon, N. Y., 1946.

Instruction for Field Artillery (Board of Artillery Officers). Philadelphia, J. B. Lippincott & Co., 1860.

Peterson, Harold L., *Notes on Ordnance of the American Civil War, 1861–1865*. Washington, The American Ordnance Association, 1959.

Revised Regulations for the Army of the United States, 1861. Philadelphia, George W. Childs, 1862.

8. GENERAL

Annals of the War. Philadelphia, The Times Publishing Co., 1879.

Atkinson, C. F., *Grant's Campaigns of 1864 and 1865*. London, Hugh Rees, Ltd., 1908.

Basler, Roy P., ed., *The Collected Works of Abraham Lincoln* (8 vols. and index). New Brunswick, Rutgers University Press, 1953.

Cooke, John Esten, *The Life of Stonewall Jackson*. New York, Charles B. Richardson, 1863.

————, *Stonewall Jackson*. New York, D. Appleton and Co., 1876.

Dietz, J. Stanley, comp., *The Battle Flags and Wisconsin Troops in the Civil War and War with Spain*. Madison, 1943.

Donald, David, *Lincoln Reconsidered*. New York, Alfred A. Knopf, Inc., 1956.

Doubleday, Abner, *Chancellorsville and Gettysburg*. New York, Charles Scribner's Sons, 1886.

Draper, Lyman C., ed., *Wisconsin Historical Collections*, Vol. IX. Madison, Wisconsin History Commission, 1909.

Dyer, F. H., *A Compendium of the War of the Rebellion*. New York, Thomas Yoseloff, 1959.

Esposito, Vincent J., *Atlas to Accompany Steele's American Campaigns*. West Point, United States Military Academy, 1956.

Fox, William F., *Regimental Losses in the American Civil War*. Albany, Albany Publishing Company, 1889.

Freeman, Douglas S., *Lee's Lieutenants* (3 vols.). New York, Charles Scribner's Sons, 1942–44.

Freeman, Douglas S., *R. E. Lee: A Biography* (4 Vols.). New York, Charles Scribner's Sons, 1935.

Hanson, Joseph Mills, *Bull Run Remembers.* Manassas, National Capitol Publishers, Inc., 1953.

Henderson, G. F. R., *Stonewall Jackson and the American Civil War.* New York, Grosset, 1936.

Humphreys, Andrew A., *The Virginia Campaign of '64 and '65.* New York, Charles Scribner's Sons, 1883.

Indiana at Antietam. Indianapolis, Indiana Antietam Monument Commission, 1911.

Indiana at Gettysburg, Report of the Fiftieth Anniversary Commission. Indianapolis, 1913.

Johnson, Robert V. and C. C. Buel, eds., *Battles and Leaders of the Civil War* (4 vols.). New York, The Century Company, 1884–1887.

Kellogg, John A., *Capture and Escape.* Madison, Wisconsin History Commission, 1908.

Livermore, Thomas L., *Numbers and Losses in the Civil War.* Bloomington, Indiana University Press, 1957.

Love, William D., *Wisconsin in the War of the Rebellion.* Chicago, Church & Goodman, 1866.

Maine at Gettysburg, Report of the Maine Commissioners. Portland, The Lakeside Press, 1898.

Michigan at Gettysburg. Detroit, Michigan Monument Commission, 1889.

Nichols, Edward J., *Toward Gettysburg.* The Pennsylvania State University Press, 1958.

Nicolay, John G., *The Outbreak of Rebellion.* New York, Charles Scribner's Sons, 1881.

Palfrey, F. W., *The Antietam and Fredericksburg.* New York, Charles Scribner's Sons, 1882.

Pennsylvania at Gettysburg (2 vols.). Harrisburg, 1904.

Phisterer, Frederick, *Statistical Record of the Armies of the United States.* New York, Charles Scribner's Sons, 1897.

Quiner, E. B., *The Military History of Wisconsin.* Chicago, Clarke & Co., 1866.

Randall, James Garfield, *Lincoln the President* (4 vols.). New York, Dodd, Mead & Company, 1945–55.

Report of the Unveiling and Dedication of the Indiana Monument at Andersonville, Georgia. Indianapolis, Wm. B. Burford, 1909.

Robertson, John, *Michigan in the War.* Lansing, 1880.

Ropes, John Codman, *The Army Under Pope.* New York, Charles Scribner's Sons, 1882.

Sandburg, Carl, *Abraham Lincoln, The War Years* (4 vols.). New York, Harcourt, Brace and Co., 1939.

Scribner, Theodore T., *Indiana's Roll of Honor,* Vol. II. Indianapolis, A. D. Streight, 1866.

Sherman, William T., *Memoirs* (2 vols.). New York, D. Appleton and
Company, 1875.

The Soldier of Indiana in the War for the Union (2 vols.).   Indianapolis, Merrill and Company, 1866.

Stampp, Kenneth M., *Indiana Politics During the Civil War*.   Indianapolis, Indiana Historical Bureau, 1949.

Stevenson, David, *Indiana's Roll of Honor*, Vol. I.   Indianapolis, 1864.

Wiley, Bell Irwin, *The Life of Billy Yank*.   Indianapolis, The Bobbs-
Merrill Company, 1951.

Williams, Kenneth P., *Lincoln Finds a General* (5 vols.).   New York,
The Macmillan Company, 1950–59.

Williams, T. Harry, *Lincoln and His Generals*.   New York, Alfred A.
Knopf, Inc., 1952.

INDEX

Ranks shown for officers are the highest held in either Federal or Confederate service at any time during the war except that brevet ranks are not used. Enlisted men are not identified by rank, but are identified by regiment or unit.

Where text references are not related directly to material in the notes, material in the notes is directly referred to.

Federal strength and casualty references are generally confined to the Iron Brigade, its regiments, and Battery B. Where the Iron Brigade's action was merged with that of a larger unit, strength and casualty references are given for that larger unit. Confederate strength and casualty references are confined to Confederate units directly engaged with the Iron Brigade or directly engaged with the larger Federal unit of which the Iron Brigade was a part.

In order to refer to the division of which the Iron Brigade was a part during the period of its formal life, *see* McDowell's Division, King's Division, Hatch's Division, Doubleday's Division, and Wadsworth's Division.

-----

* Designates Third Division of First Corps, to which command Doubleday was assigned after Fredericksburg.

mand, 114; wounded and leaves division command, 128

Hatcher's Run, Battle of, 275, 276

Hatch's Brigade, 65, 71, 80, 83, 86, 100, 102, 105, 106

Hatch's Division, 114, 121; South Mountain, 120-129

Hauser, Maj. John F., 232, 257, background and pre-war career, 16, 197; career after resignation, 267; commissioned major, 197; resignation, 267

Haymarket, Va., 57, 74

Hays' Brigade, 84, 89, 135, 139, 140

Heathsville, Va., 203, 220

Heintzelman, Maj. Gen. S. P., 100, 103, 104, 107

Heintzelman's Corps. See Third Corps, Army of the Potomac

Henry County, Ind., 202

Herndon Station, Va., 227

Heth, Maj. Gen. Harry, 234, 241, 243, 245, 253

Heth's Division, 234, 235, 243, 247, 252, 253

Hill, Lieut. Gen. A. P., 227, 228

Hill, Lieut. Gen. D. H., 121, 122, 127, 128, 129

Hill's Corps (A. P. Hill), 225, 227, 234, 235

Hill's Division (A. P. Hill), 84, 89, 107, 133, 137, 143

Hill's Division (D. H. Hill), 118, 122

Hofmann, Lieut. Col. J. William, 137

Hood, Lieut. Gen. John B., 141

Hood's Brigade, 137, 140

Hood's Division, 121, 137

Hooker, Maj. Gen. Joseph, 77, 78, 114, 117, 121, 124, 127, 130, 134, 137, 138, 139, 163, 171, 172, 194, 195, 206, 207, 208, 209, 214, 215, 216, 217, 218, 220, 223, 225, 228, 229, 230

Hooker's Corps. See First Corps, Army of the Potomac

Hooker's Division, 71, 75

Hooker's Grand Division, 171, 175, 178, 180

Hospitals. See Disease and wounds

Howard, Sen. Jacob M., 152, 155

Howard, Maj. Gen. Oliver O., 218, 242

Hoyt, Capt. Charles A., 256

Hoyt, Maj. George S., commissioned major, 280

Humphreville, Lieut. Reuben H., 256

Huron Township, Mich., 153

Hutchinson, Maj. William, 155; background and pre-war career, 155; wounded, 256, 378 (n. 56, Epilogue)

Illinois, Cavalry: 8th, 220, 221, 222

Independent Battalion Wisconsin Volunteers, 275, 277; casualties, see Casualties; consolidated with Sixth Wisconsin, 277

Indiana, Cavalry: 3rd, 65; Infantry: 6th, 21; 7th, 114, 171, 197, 224, 233, 273, 277; 9th, 21; 14th, 277; 20th, 277, 278, 282, mustered out, 382 (n. 67, Epilogue); 34th, 21

Indianapolis, Ind., 3, 19, 20, 28, 95, 164

Indianapolis Law School, 175

Iron Brigade, arms, 35; assigned to McDowell's Division, 31; brigade guard, at Gettysburg, 233, 239; casualties, see Casualties; command: Gibbon assigned, 50, King assigned, 28, 31, Meredith assigned, 171-172; corps badges, 194, 273; destruction of organizational integrity, 264, 265; detachments to Battery B, 40, 160, 207; flag, 265; named, 130; organized, 28; original Federal uniforms, 34; return of men from Battery B, 273, 281, 380 (n. 63, Epilogue); soldiers' motives, 32-33; strength, see Strength; survivors after Gettysburg, 263-282; training, 51-52, 63; uniform, 53, 54, 159-160; veterans' organization, 383 (n. 67, Epilogue); STATIONS AND EVENTS: Antietam, 133-145; Brawner Farm, 80-98; Chancellorsville, 215-218; Fitzhugh's Crossing (Chancellorsville), 209-215; Frederick's Hall Raid, 64-67; Fredericksburg, 177-188; Gettysburg, 233-259; march to Fort Tillinghast, 31; march to Gettysburg, 226-232; Mud March, 191-193; pursuit of

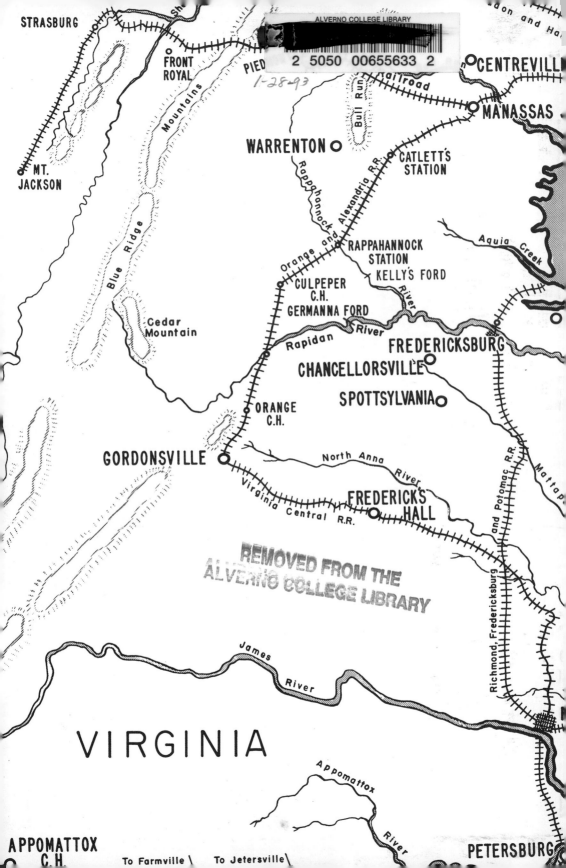

STRASBURG

FRONT
ROYAL

MT.
JACKSON

Blue Ridge

Shenandoah Mountains

Cedar
Mountain

PIED

Bull Run

Railroad

CENTREVILL

MANASSAS

WARRENTON

CATLETT'S
STATION

Rappahannock

Orange and Alexandria R.R.

Aquia Creek

RAPPAHANNOCK
STATION
KELLY'S FORD

CULPEPER
C.H.

GERMANNA FORD

River

Rapidan River

FREDERICKSBURG

CHANCELLORSVILLE

SPOTTSYLVANIA

ORANGE
C.H.

GORDONSVILLE

North Anna River

Virginia Central R.R.

FREDERICK'S
HALL

Richmond, Fredericksburg and Potomac R.R.

Mattap

James River

VIRGINIA

Appomattox

APPOMATTOX
C.H.

PETERSBURG

To Farmville \   To Jetersville \   Appomattox River